Lecture Notes in Business Information Processing 412

More information about this series at http://www.springer.com/series/7911

Gert Janssenswillen

Unearthing the Real Process Behind the Event Data

The Case for Increased Process Realism

Springer

Author
Gert Janssenswillen
Research Group Business Informatics
Hasselt University
Diepenbeek, Belgium

ISSN 1865-1348 ISSN 1865-1356 (electronic)
Lecture Notes in Business Information Processing
ISBN 978-3-030-70732-3 ISBN 978-3-030-70733-0 (eBook)
https://doi.org/10.1007/978-3-030-70733-0

This book is a revised version of the PhD dissertation written by the author at Hasselt University in Belgium. The original PhD dissertation is accessible at: http://hdl.handle.net/1942/28268.

This Springer imprint is published by the registered company Springer Nature Switzerland AG
The registered company address is: Gewerbestrasse 11, 6330 Cham, Switzerland

In loving remembrance of Joannis JANSSEN († 1695)
and Adriana SWILDEN († 1712)

In appreciation of their legacy,
and for a lifetime of spelling, correcting,
and explaining my surname.

Preface

Companies in the 21st century possess a large amount of data about their products, customers and transactions. The prominent role of business processes in the modern organisation in recent decades has led to a remarkable increase in the amount of event data that is available. Event logs are *logbooks* that contain information about everything that happens in a company on a daily basis. A customer who places an order, an employee who logs in to the customer management system to handle the order, a supplier who delivers a quotation for the products, a production line that is started, etc. The digitisation of all these events enables us to analyse business processes at a level that was previously unthinkable.

The increase in available event data gave rise to process mining, a discipline that focuses on extracting insights about processes from event logs. However, correctly displaying business processes is not a trivial task. Due to the high complexity of most processes, event logs contain only a limited sample of all the possible ways and combinations in which business processes can be performed. Errors and inconsistencies in the available data create additional difficulties. In response to these challenges, process discovery algorithms were developed - algorithms that discover process models based on event logs. However, the crucial question is: how good are these discovered models? Are they able to correctly represent business operations?

The concept of process realism is introduced in this dissertation. To optimise processes, evidence-based decision making is needed. Consequently, it is essential to map these processes in a realistic way. Blindly relying on both partial and/or inconsistent data and on algorithms can lead to wrong actions being taken.

Process realism is approached from two perspectives in this dissertation. First, quality dimensions and measures for process discovery are analysed on a large scale and compared with each other on the basis of empirical experiments. Which measures are best suited to assess the quality of a discovered process model? What are their weaknesses and strengths? And what challenges still need to be overcome in order for it to evolve into a reliable quality measurement?

The experiments in this thesis show that there are important differences between the different quality measures in terms of feasibility, validity and sensitivity. Moreover, the role and meaning of the generalisation dimension is unclear. Existing generalisation measures do not succeed in adequately assessing the fit between process models and the underlying process. Fitness and precision measures also do not constitute unbiased estimators of the quality of the model as a representation of the underlying process. Furthermore, with regard to experimental set-up, various challenges have been identified that are necessary for measures to evolve towards a correct quality measurement.

In addition to the focus on process models, process realism is also approached from a data point of view. By developing a transparent and extensible toolset, a framework is offered to analyse process data from different perspectives. Exploratory and descriptive analysis of process data and testing of hypotheses again leads to increased process realism.

The developed framework is applied in this dissertation to two case studies. First, how can we use process data to better understand students' study trajectories and to better guide students? Secondly, how can applying process analysis in a railway context map out the use of the rail infrastructure and analyse deviations between the timetable and implementation in order to achieve a smoother service for passengers?

Both case studies show that the framework has clear added value, and that the answers to the questions asked can help to improve the processes under consideration. At the same time, however, unresolved challenges within process mining are also emphasised, such as the analysis of processes at the right level of granularity, and the assumption that process instances are independent of each other.

From both perspectives, process model and process data, recommendations are made for future research, and a call is made to give the *process realism* mindset a central place within process mining analyses.

Acknowledgements

Many great actions are committed in small struggles.

Victor Hugo

There are so many who have—each in their own way—left their fingerprints on this dissertation, and thereby also on my heart. Like so many projects, this has not been a solitary journey, and I am indebted to all those who have travelled with me along the way. All those who have shared their expertise, passion, support, and laughter. Growing as a person is an incremental process influenced by a near-infinite sequence of experiences and influences. It would be impossible to mention all those who have contributed to this growth, but allow me to spend some words on those whose influence was paramount.

First and foremost, my genuine gratitude goes to my supervisor, Benoît Depaire. Over the years, you have not only been my supervisor, but also have become a true mentor and friend. You have been my strength when I felt weak. My guiding light when I felt lost. You have continually challenged the limits of what I thought I could do. Teaching together with you has taught me to take all details into account, and to never assume that things are happening by themselves. You have given me the freedom and encouragement to explore other topics and take roads less travelled, which made this dissertation what it is now, and me the person I am today.

On the first day of my PhD, your advice to me was to learn R programming. Honestly, I was sceptical at first—I could already program in Python, why would I need R? But you also set me a goal: *try to recreate this graph in Disco using R*. About six months later, there was a first R package for process analysis which started to look like something useful. Another eight months later, the first version of `edeaR` was published on CRAN. Today, I can confidently say `bupaR` can do everything which Disco can, and much more. Thank you for giving me that initial spark which has ignited a fiRe within me. And thank you for the opportunity to pass along that spark to my students each year—I hope that one day they will appreciate its true value.

A sincere thank you also goes to Mieke Jans. Through your diverse experience from both industry and academia, you have always provided my with an alternative perspective on my work and valuable feedback that few others would be able to give. Your distinctive angle on things has influenced and improved my dissertation in more ways than you would guess. Teaching together with you has shown me how an effective, well-oiled process should run. On a personal level, you have taught me to be proud of my achievements and challenged me to leave my comfort zone—which in my case is not at all straightforward.

Furthermore, my appreciation also goes to Koen Vanhoof. Thank you for all the things you do for our research group. Together with Mieke and Benoît, you have made the business informatics group into what it is today—an excellent place to work (and study). An achievement you should all three be genuinely proud of.

I would like to profoundly thank Benoît, Mieke, Koen and all the members of the jury for reading my thesis and for providing me with useful remarks and suggestions, which have markedly improved the quality of my dissertation.

In particular, I would like to thank Sabine Verboven. While you have not followed my PhD from up-close from the very start, you were there before it started. At Infrabel, you have guided me in my very first process mining adventures, an experience and opportunity I am grateful for and will never forget. Together we also learned the importance of a welcoming culture and executive-level support for process mining and data science in general. I am hopeful we will continue to be partners in this never-ending endeavour.

Moreover, I would like to especially thank Jorge Munoz-Gama and his colleagues, particularly Marcos Sepúlveda, Wai Lam Jonathan Lee, and Juan Pablo Salazar. Not only have you all influenced or improved my dissertation in several ways, you have also provided me with a warm welcome in your group during my visit, of which I hope many more will follow.

You can never go wrong when you have a great team to work with. I am grateful for every member of our research group, for creating the extraordinary atmosphere in which we work. Especially, I would like to thank my office mates Frank Vanhoenshoven, Mathijs Creemers and Mehrnush Hosseinpour, for welcoming me in their office during the last months of my PhD. Thank you for allowing me to occasionally disturb your work with weird facts, anecdotes, and frustrations.

Particular heartfelt thanks goes to the best colleagues one can possibly imagine, my *breakfast besties*, Hanne Pollaris and Marijke Swennen. Thank you both for being my personal stylists. Hanne, even on the saddest and gloomiest days, you are that one person who can put a smile on my face, just by entering the room. Your positivity in life is an inspiration for us all. Thank you for always believing in me and supporting me.

Marijke, I would honestly not know where I would be without you. Whenever anything happens, the first thing I think of is telling you, and asking your advice. You have stayed with me through so many ups and downs. I am forever in your debt, and count myself as one of the luckiest persons on earth to have you as a friend.

Together with you, Jeroen Corstjens, Niels Martin and Stef Moons, we have been on countless trips, enjoyed innumerable meals and, most of all, shared an everlasting amount of laughter, happiness, and joy. But despite having spent all these moments together, I think I may have often forgot to thank you all for being terrific friends!

Finally, and most importantly, I would like to deeply thank my family for their ongoing support.

I am grateful for my siblings, for providing me with endless distractions from my, at times tedious, work. Thank you also for occasionally reminding me what a *real* job looks like. Thank you for reminding me not to be too hard on my students, because *they are all doing their best.* But most of all, thank you for being the best siblings one can imagine! Words will never be enough to show my appreciation for you.

But the two persons who deserve the most praise are my parents. Dear mom and dad, I have let so many years pass without thanking you both. But you haven't let a single second pass without loving me unconditionally. Thank you for who I am, and thank you for all the things I'm not. Forgive me for the words unsaid. Thank you for the wings you have given me, for having taught me how to soar up into the sky and expand my horizons. It may take a lifetime, but I'll do everything to repay for what you have done for me. Thank you for being there, even when I'm stupid enough to think I'd rather be alone.

So much of me,
is made of what I learned from you.
You'll be with me forever,
like a handprint on my heart.

December 2020 Gert Janssenswillen

Contents

Part I
Introduction

Chapter 1
Process Realism

> Any truth is better than indefinite doubt.
>
> Arthur Conan Doyle

---

realism[1]
(ree-uh-liz-uh m)
noun

1. interest in or concern for the actual or real, as distinguished from the abstract, speculative, etc.
2. the tendency to view or represent things as they really are.

In current times, organisations possess a tremendous amount of data concerning their customers, products and processes. Many activities which are taking place in their operational processes are being recorded in event logs [10]. Techniques from the process mining field, which has grown steadily over the last decades, can be applied to gain insights into these event data [9]. Over the past decade, a lot of attention has been given to the discovery of process models from event logs [57, 97, 138, 139], and subsequently the quality measurement of these models [6, 11, 12, 99, 123].

The results of process mining analyses, if acted upon, can have important ramifications for business operations in two ways. First are improvements to the performance of processes. Performance—or a lack thereof—can be expressed in many different

[1] https://www.dictionary.com/browse/realism.

G. Janssenswillen: Unearthing the Real Process Behind the Event Data, LNBIP 412
https://doi.org/10.1007/978-3-030-70733-0_1

manners, such as the time spent on the process or the incurred operational costs. Performance issues, such as the execution of superfluous activities which constitute wasted resources, or the presence of bottlenecks in the process, can be laid bare by adequate analysis of process data.

Secondly—and of equal importance—are improvements in compliance. Compliance with rules and regulations, whether imposed internally in organisations or by (inter)national laws, is important to prevent fraud and other types of risk. Checking compliance of a process can occur in many different ways, depending on the precise nature of the rule or regulation to check, such as the order between activities, the (co-)occurrence of activities or the link between activity executions and the person(s) who executed them.

Both of these aspects—performance and compliance—strongly rely on the ability to accurately delineate the process and all its relevant characteristics based on the process data that has been extracted from the organisation's information systems. This thesis aims to contribute on several facets related to this accurate representation. In the next section, a further introduction to process mining is given, including a discussion of its relevance in the broader field of business process management, and the available tool-support. Subsequently, Sect. 1.2 will discuss the need for process realism and the specific research objectives of this thesis. Section 1.3 will describe the methodology and outline of the thesis.

1.1 Introduction to Process Mining

Companies traditionally have a functional layout in which tasks are assigned to departments. Departments typically consist of employees who have a similar set of knowledge and skills. Purchasing, marketing, production, human resources, finance, IT, etc. All these departments are largely responsible for the internal organisation and planning.

Visually presented, this boils down to Fig. 1.1, where each department is responsible for a set of tasks. Each of these tasks forms part of the value creation of the company.

In 1993, in their book *Re-engineering the Corporation: A manifesto for business revolution*, Hammer and Campy [66] shifted the focus from more *task-oriented* thinking in Smith's Division of Labor (1776) and Taylor's Scientific Management (1911) to *process-oriented* thinking.

> It is no longer necessary or desirable for companies to organise their work around Adam Smith's division of labour. Task-oriented jobs in today's world of customers, competition, and change are obsolete. Instead, companies must organise work around processes (Hammer and Campy [66])

The Theory of Constraints (Goldratt, 1990 [61]) teaches that improvements to a component do not necessarily lead to an improvement of the whole. If, for example, a baker wants to increase his production, it is essential that he can identify the weak-

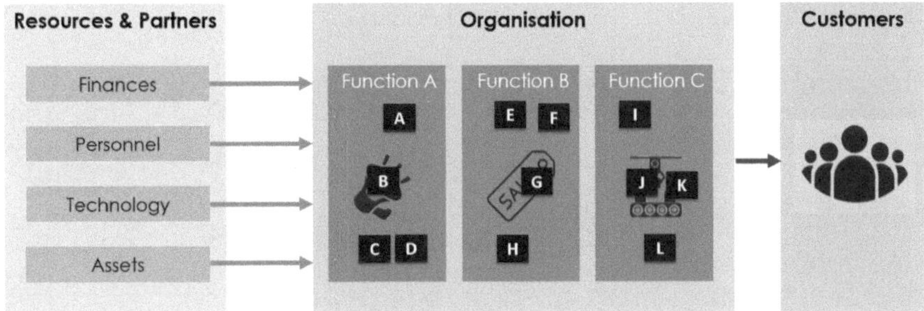

Fig. 1.1 Functional-oriented company view. Adapted from [119].

est link in his process, the so-called bottleneck. If his oven can bake 200 loaves per hour, but he can only knead 100 loaves per hour, then improving the oven should not be the priority in a process improvement. This insight is self-evident in relatively simple processes, but the Theory of Constraints applies equally to long and complex processes. You can make incremental progress by continuously improving the bottlenecks of your process. For example, a cashier can scan faster if a scanner is built into the counter. Perhaps you could also consider making the shopping trolley and the counter more ergonomic so that overloading is smoother. However, if you expect revolutionary improvements, then this is only possible when you look at the process as a whole and dare to thoroughly rethink it.

Process-oriented thinking means that we approach the organisation as a set of business processes that ultimately convert inputs—personnel, assets, technology—into output—a product or service for their customers, as depicted in Fig. 1.2. A *business process* is a set of activities that are performed in a coordinated manner with a specific business purpose in mind:

> A set of logically related tasks performed to achieve a defined business outcome. (Davenport (1990) [41])

Typical business processes are order-to-cash, procure-to-pay, application-to-approval, or fault-to-resolution. However, this rather traditional classification is insufficient for the diversity of processes in today's organisations. When you think of recent, disruptive enterprises (Uber, Spotify, Netflix, AirBnb, and others), you must indeed conclude that they haven't invented a new product at all. We've known taxis, songs, series, and hotels for many years. These companies are not innovative in the way they offer new products, they are innovative in the way they offer existing products. The focus of innovation has shifted from product to process. Process innovation is used to gain a decisive competitive advantage. To this end, there is a need for Business Process Management.

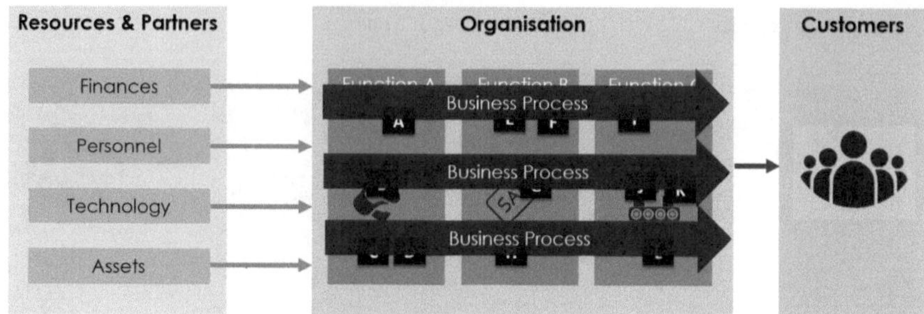

Fig. 1.2 Process-oriented company view. Adapted from [119].

1.1.1 Business Process Management

When is a process well managed? Two different aspects are key. On the one hand, we want the value for the customer to be as high as possible. Concretely, this means that the process

1. runs as quickly as possible;
2. delivers a product or service which meets the quality requirements; and
3. is as inexpensive as possible.

On the other hand, good process management also means that risks are managed correctly. Processes must therefore comply with all relevant rules and procedures - both those defined within the company and those arising from the legal framework in which the company operates.

Both these aspects are the objectives of Business Process Management. Business Process Management (BPM) can be approached as a cyclical process in itself, using the BPM life-cycle (Fig. 1.3). This life-cycle consists of an initialisation phase followed by a cycle of 5 successive phases. In the following paragraphs, each of the phases is briefly described.

1.1.1.1 Process Identification

Which processes are relevant to the goods or services offered by the company? The result of this step is a process architecture that gives an overall picture of the processes in the company, and how they are related to each other. This architecture can then be used to decide which process(es) will be selected for detailed analysis throughout the next 5 phases of the life-cycle.

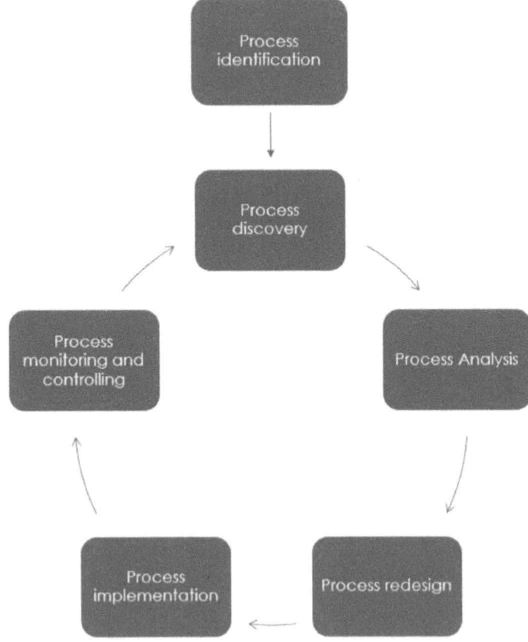

Fig. 1.3 BPM Lifecycle [51].

1.1.1.2 Process Discovery

In the process discovery phase, or as-is process modelling phase, the selected processes are mapped in their current form. The result of this phase is thus a (set of) as-is process model(s).

1.1.1.3 Process Analysis

After mapping the *as-is* situation, problems are identified, documented, and if possible quantified according to performance measures. The goal of this phase is to make a structured overview of the bottlenecks in the process. These can also be prioritised according to potential *impact* and *effort* to solve them.

1.1.1.4 Process Redesign

In the redesign phase, the bottlenecks with the highest impact and/or lowest effort are further examined, and possible changes to the process are examined. Each change is evaluated according to the performance measures, which means that process analysis and process redesign are often performed hand in hand - alternating - each possible change must be analysed and compared with the alternatives. Ultimately, the retained changes are combined in a reworked version of the as-is process.

1.1.1.5 Process Implementation

In this phase, the changes identified in the previous phase are implemented. Both process automation - adapting the IT systems that support the process - and operational change management - adapting the way the actors in the process work - are important tasks within the implementation phase.

1.1.1.6 Process Monitoring and Controlling

Once the reworked process is in production, relevant data must be collected to evaluate whether the changes have the desired effects on the performance measures. Limited side effects or unforeseen consequences can be solved with corrective measures. If new problems are identified, the BPM life-cycle can be re-initiated by mapping the new as-is process.

1.1.2 The Emergence of Process Mining

Traditionally, in the process discovery phase, process documentation and interviews were mainly used to map as-is processes. The increasing complexity of business processes in recent decades, partly due to the emergence of more and more information technology, caused this method to come under pressure. The processes that were discovered using the traditional tools were too often not a correct representation of reality. Several underlying problems caused these discrepancies.

First of all, every actor in a process sees only his part. Often no one has a complete end-to-end overview of the business processes. Secondly, processes are constantly changing. Process documentation, such as memos, procedures or outlined processes are therefore becoming obsolete more and more quickly. Finally, there are also more and more exceptions that further blur the image of processes.

However, the arrival of more and more information technology also had an additional effect: more and more data was stored, also about business processes. This gave rise to the domain *process mining* in which process management is no longer done (exclusively) with traditional methods, but also by getting insights from large amounts of data [3].

In process mining—as schematically depicted in Fig. 1.4—data recorded by all kinds of IT systems about processes is used to map these processes (*process discovery*) and compare them with normative or descriptive process models (*conformance checking*). Data that is recorded about processes is called event data, or event logs.

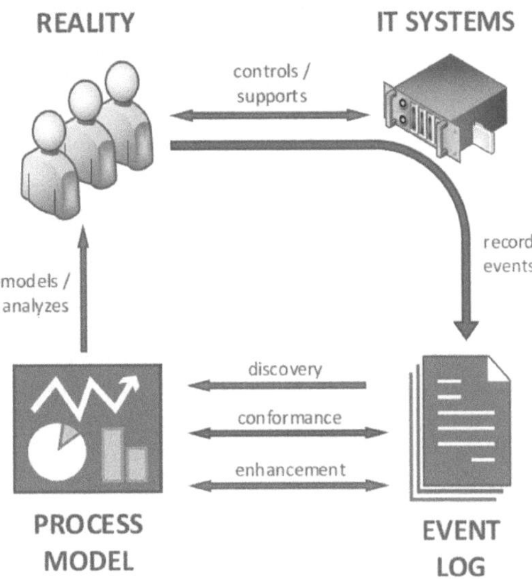

Fig. 1.4 Process mining overview. [109]

Generally speaking, we can distinguish two different goals, or types, of analyses within domain process mining: process discovery and conformance checking. In other words, *understanding the process* and *controlling the process*.[2]

Process discovery refers to learning processes from data. The goal is to map processes from event logs. This type of process mining is therefore linked to the phase of the same name in the BPM life-cycle (Fig. 1.3), but we should not simply equate the two. Within the BPM life-cycle, process discovery is a much broader concept, where other types of information, such as documents, interviews, observations, etc., are also included.

Conformance checking refers to comparing process data with normative or descriptive process models. Normative process models are models that *enforce* a certain way of working, whereas descriptive process models rather *describe* a certain way of working. If we look at whether the process corresponds with the normative process model, this means that we are examining whether work is done as it should be. Normative models often impose constraints that are relevant in the context of risk management. This type of conformance checking is thus strongly related to *process compliance*.

---

[2] As Fig. 1.4 shows, there often is a third type of process mining, called *process enhancement*. While it is defined as techniques to *improve or extend existing process models using information about the actual process recorded in some event log* [3], the term is often used as a catch-all category for everything that is not discovery or conformance. In process mining literature, discovery and conformance are much more established as separate, unified research tracks. In reality, enhancing, or improving, the process (model) under consideration is always the end goal of process discovery or process conformance analysis, and defining it as a separate category is somewhat confusing. As such, we will limit the discussion to these two categories.

Fig. 1.5 Elephant path.

If we check the process data with respect to a descriptive model, we want to know whether our view of the process is correct, without necessarily concluding that the process execution is faulty when it differs from our model. It is often the case that processes in reality are carried out differently than we think. Employees active in a process often have a better idea of what is a correct, fast, or qualitative way of working. Conformance checking in this context means that you want to check whether the *desire lines* of the process corresponds with the way we think about the process. Desire lines can best be compared with the concept of "elephant paths", as shown in Fig. 1.5.

Naturally, both aspects of conformance checking—normative and descriptive—are important. Desire lines can be an important source for process innovation and redesign, as long as they do not entail any unauthorised risks by, for example, bypassing certain procedures.

Process discovery and conformance checking go hand in hand. After all, you need a good understanding of the process (discovery) before you can check it with a normative or descriptive model (conformance). Understanding and checking the process will eventually lead to the proposition of process improvements, as outlined in the BPM Life-cycle (Fig. 1.3).

1.1.3 Perspectives

While so far we have talked about process models, process mining goes beyond the flow-chart-like diagrams that this concept conjures up. Mapping a process does not just mean "what activities happen and in what order?" It also means that we get a view on which activities are carried out by which actors, what are the lead times of different parts of the process, the costs associated with certain activities, and so on. We therefore speak of different *perspectives* or *dimensions* within process mining. The most common perspectives are control-flow, organisation and time.

1.1.3.1 Control-Flow

Control-flow refers to everything that has to do with the *flow* of the process, i.e. the traditional process model notion. Typical research questions to start from are:

- What activities does the process consist of?
- How structured is the process? Is there a lot of variance, or little?
- What is the *happy path*, i.e. the most common end-to-end course of the process.
- Does each case end with one of the allowed "outcome" activities?

Control-flow will be the main focus in this thesis, especially in Part II. An introduction to different control-flow modelling notations will be given in Chap. 2.

1.1.3.2 Organisation

In addition to control-flow, we can also look at the actors, or resources, in the process. We call this the organisational perspective. Initial research questions here can be:

- Which actors are active in the process?
- What is the workload of the actors?
- Which actors are specialised in certain tasks?

1.1.3.3 Time

A third common dimension is the time dimension. This includes both the investigation of patterns through time, and everything related to performance of the process. Starting points for analysis can be:

- What is the arrival rhythm of new cases in the process?
- How is the throughput time of the process distributed?
- What seasonal effects exist in the process?

In addition to these three common dimensions, other dimensions are possible depending on the exact context or available data, such as, for example, a cost dimension.

1.1.3.4 Multi-perspective Analyses

While the above example research questions are always about one specific perspective, there are also *multi-perspective* research questions. These are research questions that cross the boundaries of a specific perspective. Examples are

- Can differences in throughput time be explained by the flow of the case?
- How does the workload of actors vary over time?
- Is there a difference in flow between invoices for different departments?

Finally, it should be noted that the perspectives and types of process mining (discovery vs. conformance) are independent of each other. For example, the question "Does each case end with one of the allowed 'outcome' activities?" is a clear conformance checking question, while the question "Which actors are specialised in certain tasks?" is clearly focused on process discovery.

1.1.4 Tools

Over the past couple of decades, a broad set of software tools has been developed to support process mining techniques. A full list can be found in Table 1.1. Among the available tools are a broad range of commercial tools, as well as some open-source tools.[3] The open-source tool `bupaR` will be introduced and illustrated in Part III.

One of the most extensive and open-source process mining framework to date is ProM [133]. It contains most of the state-of-the-art techniques which are developed in related literature. RapidProM [8] and PM4Py can be seen as variants of ProM that have been developed in the RapidMiner framework and python programming language, respectively.

The main difference between most commercial tools and most open-source tools, is that the commercial tooling scores higher on interactiveness, especially due to the use of interactive graphical visualisations. Another major differences relates to the provided functionalities. While ProM is a repository of leading-edge academic techniques that has been continually evolving, most commercial tools do not contain many of these academic algorithms. Most tools use the more simple directly-follows graphs to discovery processes—possibly combined with (intelligent) filtering approaches—instead of the state-of-the-art process discovery algorithms that have been developed to learn Petri Nets or BPMN models, such as the Inductive Miner [98] or Split Miner [14]. Conformance checking techniques have been incorporated in some commercial tools, such as Celonis, only relatively recently. Conversely, commercial tools have a much larger focus on interactivity, user experience, but also the multi-perspective nature of process analysis. In Part III, a more comprehensive comparison of the tool landscape will be provided. Furthermore, some drawbacks of current solutions that gave rise to the development of `bupaR` as a new alternative tool will be outlined.

[3]Note that Apromore both provides commercial solutions as well as open-source variants.

Table 1.1 Overview of process mining software.

Tool	Vendor	Type	Website
Apromore	Apromore	Open source, Commercial	apromore.org
bupaR	—	Open source	bupar.net
PM4Py	—	Open source	pm4py.org
ProM	—	Open source	promtools.org
RapidProm	—	Open source	rapidprom.org
Aris	Software AG	Commercial	ariscommunity.com
Celonis	Celonis	Commercial	celonis.com
Disco	Fluxicon	Commercial	fluxicon.com/disco
EverFlow	Icaro Tech	Commercial	icarotech.com
Kofax Insight	Kofax	Commercial	kofax.com
Lana Process Mining	Lana Labs	Commercial	lana-labs.com
Minit	Minit	Commercial	minit.io
myInvenio	Cognitive Technology	Commercial	my-invenio.com
PAFnow	Process Analytics Factory	Commercial	pafnow.com
ProcessGold	ProcessGold	Commercial	processgold.com
ProDiscovery	Puzzle Data	Commercial	puzzledata.com
QPR ProcessAnalyzer	QPR Software	Commercial	qpr.com
Signavio Process Intelligence	Signavio	Commercial	signavio.com
StereoLogic Process Analytics	StereoLOGIC	Commercial	stereologic.com

1.1.5 Towards Evidence-Based Business Process Management

The emergence of process mining as a new approach for analysing business processes does not mean that established Business Process Management principles and procedures have become obsolete. Process mining should be seen as a tool that can support Business Process Management. In particular, it will move the focus from a confidence-based BPM to evidence-based, data-driven BPM. Process mining can help to understand AS IS processes in more accurate ways, support hypotheses with evidence, and quantify the impact of process redesigns.

However, for process mining to be truly valuable, it is essential that the results of process mining techniques are reliable to act upon. We therefore introduce and motivate the concept of process realism in the following section, which will act as the common thread in this thesis.

1.2 The Case for Process Realism

1.2.1 Motivation

In order to obtain improvements in the performance or compliance of business processes, insights need to be gathered from event data, upon which appropriate actions have to be taken. For these actions to lead to the expected result, it is imperative that the insights gathered are correct and trustworthy—a real characteristic of the process, and not just a peculiarity that surfaced as an artefact in the data or a byproduct of a certain used algorithm.

In order to measure the quality of process models discovered from event data, quality dimensions has been defined, and several measures for each dimension have been developed. However, the use of these measures in practice poses several challenges. First of all, different measures for the same dimension will give different values, while it is unclear how these differences should be interpreted or where they stem from.

Secondly, there are trade-offs between the quality dimensions, a balance on which little guidance exist. For instance, how can one decide which of the dimensions are important in a certain situation based on the particular context, such as the goal of the analysis?

A better understanding of the measures and the significance of the current dimensional framework is necessary to deal with these challenges, a notion to which this thesis will contribute. Since quality measures are never an end in itself, the direct need for this understanding principally derives from an academic motivation—being able to reliably measure the quality of discovered process models in order to assess and compare different process discovery algorithms; a higher level motivation which certainly has important consequences for practitioners. While a point estimate of a process model's quality in itself will not directly lead to actionable insights, a high-quality process model will.

Nevertheless, a secondary necessity can be derived from the viewpoint of practitioners. A process model, notwithstanding how superior in quality it might be, will always make abstraction of certain information—such as information on resources, time, or other attributes—thereby partly sacrificing the realism one has about the process. While a model can indicate certain surprising or interesting patterns with regards to the process, the practitioner will want to have a means to further investigate these patterns, to understand why and how it came about, before he can decide whether corrective actions are required to improve the performance or compliance of the process.

As such, this thesis is also motivated by the necessity for such a means, a toolset to analyse process data in a flexible and powerful way, able to focus on very specific segments or perspectives of the projects. Important in this respect is the capability to use proven data analytics techniques—from statistics to contemporary data mining tools—in order to truly unravel these patterns and confirm their reality. While many developments with respect to process analysis tools have been already

Fig. 1.6 Napoleon crossing the Alps. Romanticism versus realism. **Left**: Jacques-Lous David. Napoleon crossing the alps. 1800. Oil on canvas. Chateau de Malmaison, Rueil-Malmaison. **Right**: Paul Delaroch. Napoleon crossing the alps. 1850. Oil on canvas. Walker Art Gallery London.

made, important limitations can still be found which prevent these type of flexible and transparent inquiries.

In the next section, these motivations with respect to both process model quality and process data analytics will be further formalised, and the explicit contributions of this thesis will be put forward.

1.2.2 Research Objective

As the title of this thesis signals, its overall aim is to highlight the need for more process realism. As shown at the start of this introduction, the term realism is defined as *the interest in or concern for the actual and real, as distinguished from the abstract, speculative; the tendency to view or represent things as they really are.* Achieving a state of process realism, thus representing processes as they really are, lies at the hart of reliable, evidence-based decision making. The objective of this thesis is to contribute to evidence-based decision making in two separate ways—in the area of process model quality as well as the area of process data analytics. Both contributions are detailed below.[4]

[4]For the interested reader who is inquisitive about the origin of the term *process realism*, Fig. 1.6 shows the crossing of Napoleon through the Alps as depicted by a realist painter (right) versus by a romanticist painter (left)—an art movement characterised by an emphasis on individualism and glorification, not a desire to present events or objects in an actual, truthful way.

1.2.2.1 Process Model Quality

When looking at the results of a process discovery algorithm, the outcome is often too easily (mis)taken for absolute truth about the underlying process. However, the fact that it was discovered from a sample of event data, which probably also contains measurement errors, tells us that this is not necessarily the case. Simultaneously, it is not a reliable representation of the original event data either, because of the filters and other choices and assumptions imposed by the discovery algorithm used. As such, awareness about whether you are describing the event data, making assertions about the underlying process, or an ambiguous mix of both is currently missing.

Being able to accurately quantify the quality of discovered process models, which is an important component of conformance checking, is critical for process discovery. Only through accurate quality measurement can the trustworthiness of discovered process models be assessed, to see whether the insights they deliver are reliable. It is crucial to know whether a discovered process model is a precise and fitting representation of the event data or the underlying process. Many quality measures—fitness, precision and generalization—have been developed over the past years, but they have so far only been evaluated narrowly on how they compare to each other. Moreover, it is not clear how to interpret or combine different dimensions such as precision and generalization. The research objective related to process model quality is therefore twofold:

- analyse quality measures to examine their usefulness in terms of validity, sensitivity and feasibility, and
- analyse the ability of the measures to quantify the quality of the model as a representation of the underlying process.

As a result, the contribution of this thesis will be a clearer understanding of the quality dimensions, the implemented measures, and their limitations. Based on the results of the analyses, recommendations will be given in order to proceed towards a more mature conformance checking discipline, and important challenges which will need to be tackled to advance to that state will be identified.

1.2.2.2 Process Analytics

With regard to process analytics, it was described above that a tool-set which facilitates flexible and transparent examination of process data, and which enables the use of existing techniques, is currently missing. The contribution of the second part of this thesis will therefore be the development of such a tool-set, answering to the specific requirements which will be identified based on the inventory of state-of-the-art tools, both of open-source and commercial nature.

Of vital importance in the definition of the requirements will be the ability to obtain a more realistic view of the process under consideration. Particular attention will be given to the following characteristics.

- **Flexibility**—where we refer to the ability of the tool to analyse multiple perspectives of the process besides the omnipresent focus on control-flow. Also non-standard case and event attributes should receive their place in the analysis of the process.
- **Connectivity**—where we refer to the ability to use existing tools and techniques. Existing techniques can be useful for exploring and describing process data, e.g. visualisations, clustering analysis, etc.; as well as when testing hypotheses or conducting predictive analyses. Being connected with these existing functionalities will prevent that process analysis will end up as a specialised discipline, isolated from the advances in the broader data science field.
- **Transparency**—where we refer to abolishing the often obscuring characteristics of process analytics tools, such as hidden assumptions and ambiguous, behind-the-scenes pre- or postprocessing steps. In order to bring about process realism, the tool should clearly document the workings of all the functionalities and allow for reproducible work-flows.

As a result, the second contribution of this thesis will be a flexible, transparent and connected tool-set to view and analyse process data as they really are.

1.3 Methodology and Outline

In this section, the methodology used in both parts of this thesis is described, together with a comprehensive outline of subsequent chapters. An overview of the structure of the thesis is given in Fig. 1.7.

1.3.1 Process Model Quality

In Chap. 2 a further introduction to process mining—and conformance checking in particular—will be given. The chapter will introduce the different quality dimensions used for measuring the quality of discovered process models, and lists the developed measures for each of them.

Chapters 4 and 5 will be central to the contribution of creating a better understanding of the quality dimensions and their metrics through the execution of experiments. A first empirical analysis will be conducted in Chap. 4, where the state-of-the-art quality measures will be compared on three different topics: feasibility, validity and sensitivity. In order to achieve this, a large and diverse collection of models and logs will be created on which the quality measures will be applied.

In Chap. 5, a second empirical study will be performed which will focus on the different dimensions and there meaning. In this chapter, the aim is to investigate to which extent the existing measures can tell us something about the quality of a process model as a representation of the underlying process. The setup of both

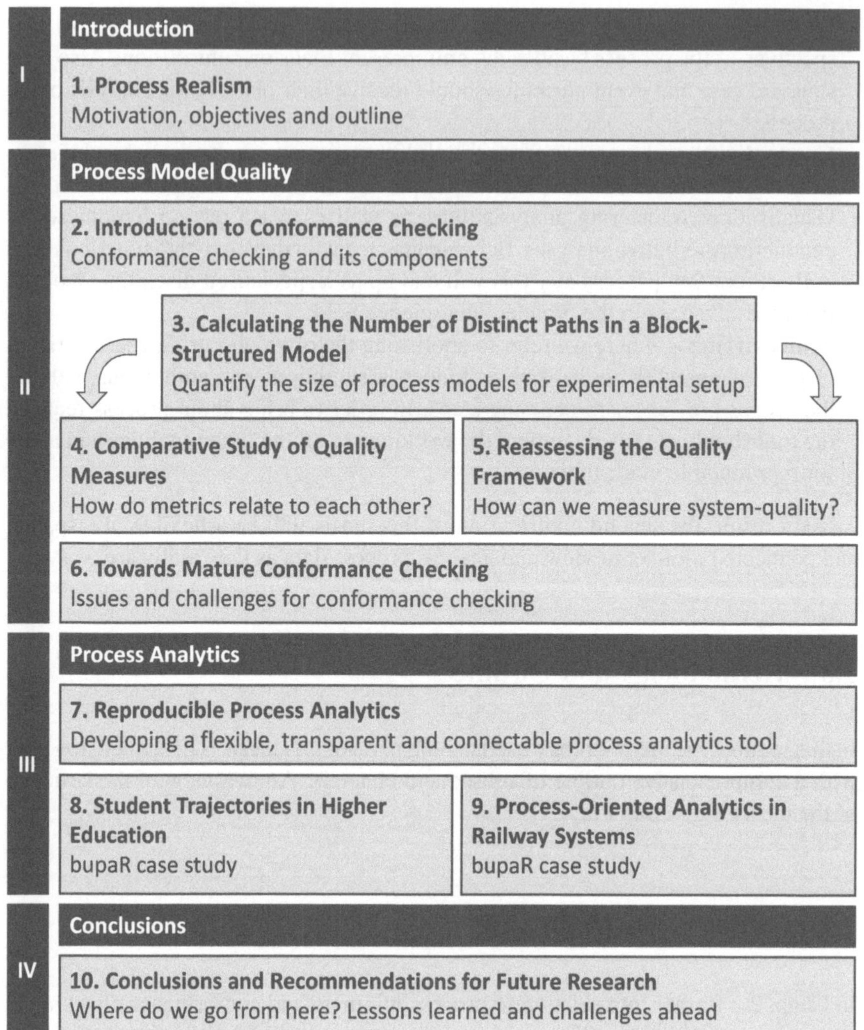

Fig. 1.7 Outline of the thesis.

experiments will be based on the methodology described in [135] for comparing process discovery algorithms. From a practical point, the framework for generating process models and simulating logs described in [91] will be used to set up the experiment.

Before proceeding to the empirical analysis, Chap. 3 introduces an algorithm to calculate the number of distinct execution paths in finite-behaviour, block-structured process models. The calculation will be used in subsequent chapters to calculate the behavioural size of process models, and enabling us to measure the completeness of event logs. Chapter 6 will conclude the first part by giving an overall summary of the assessment of quality measures, formulating recommendations as to their usage, and indicating relevant challenges for future research.

1.3.2 Process Analytics

The design and development of the second contribution—a new tool-set for process analytics—will be largely based on the Design Science methodology [88]. Chapter 7 describes the motivation for the tool-set, starting from the specific problem statement. It further defines its requirements and discusses its development. Furthermore a demonstration of its main functionalities will be given.

Chapter 8 and Chap. 9 will provide two real-life case study to evaluate the design requirements of the tools, and to illustrate how it can contribute to finding relevant insights based on process data. Chapter 8 describes an application to learning analytics while Chap. 9 shows an application in the context of railway infrastructure management. Both chapters serve a dual objective: one the one hand they will provide a realistic evaluation of the usefulness of the tool, and on the other hand they will indicate the added value of a process-oriented analysis for both applications.

Chapter 10 will provide the overall conclusion of the thesis and revisit the contributions put forward in the previous section. The peer-reviewed journal publications and conference proceedings on which the work in this thesis is based are listed below.

Part II
Process Model Quality

Chapter 2
Introduction to Conformance Checking

> Quality is everyone's responsibility.
>
> W. Edwards Deming

In this chapter, a further introduction to the domain of process mining and some essential notations are provided in Sect. 2.1. In subsequent sections, the field of conformance checking will be discussed in more detail, including the different quality dimensions (Sect. 2.2) and implemented measures (Sect. 2.3). Section 2.4 concludes this chapter and initiates the subsequent chapters on conformance checking.

2.1 Introduction to Process Mining

Traditionally, three main types of process mining are distinguished: process discovery, conformance checking, and process enhancement [7]. Each of these aim at closing the gap between recorded process data on the one hand, and process models on the other hand. Figure 2.1 situates the three types into the bigger process mining context [109]. Process models are used to model and analyse the reality, i.e. the way in which work gets done in business processes. Information about the enactment of these process gets recorded by myriad IT systems into event logs. Event logs, e.g. *log books* of the events which have happened in the context of a process, contain the raw data one has about a process. On the other hand, the process models typically show the belief one has about the process—*descriptive* models—or how they should be running—*prescriptive* models. These models might or might not be in agreement with the data, a discrepancy which process mining aims to resolve. The following paragraphs will elaborate on the three main process mining types [3].

Process discovery concerns the learning of process models from recorded event data, and can be seen as the origin of process mining. It is the primary connection between process data and process models, and is often needed because a clear under-

G. Janssenswillen: Unearthing the Real Process Behind the Event Data, LNBIP 412
https://doi.org/10.1007/978-3-030-70733-0_2

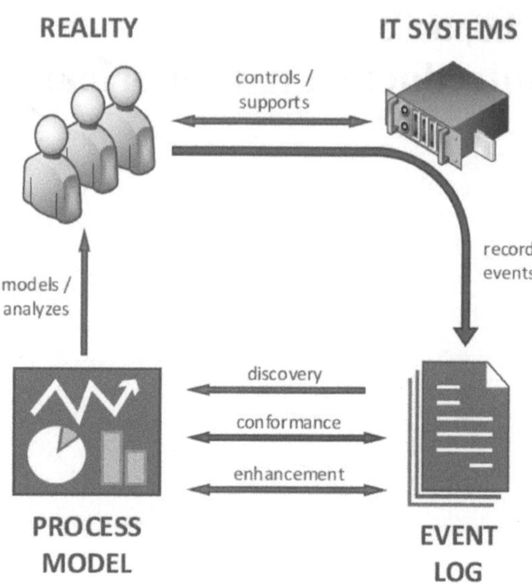

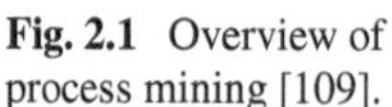
Fig. 2.1 Overview of process mining [109].

standing of the process at hand is missing. The pioneering algorithms to discover models from event data were created at the end of the 20th century. While these initial attempts mainly returned directed graphs connecting transitions or states [13, 35, 40], later approaches were able to discover Petri Nets [10], which were better suited at representing more complex process constructs, such as parallelism. Whereas these earlier algorithms tended to result in spaghetti-like models, the focus of more recent and advanced algorithms was to tackle issues such as long-term dependencies, noise, and duplicate tasks, among others [14, 98, 139]. An overview and comparison of state-of-the-art discovery algorithms can be found in [15].

Conformance checking is the next main task in process mining and has received considerable attention in the literature. The goal in conformance checking is to compare a process model with event data in order to highlight inconsistencies between the two. In this comparison, there rarely is a single correct representation of the process: both the process model and the event data can contain inaccuracies [116], which is important to take into account during any conformance checking task.

Conformance checking can be performed in several ways. On the one hand, an overall impression of the ability of the model to adequately represent the log can be expressed by computing quality measures along several dimensions. The dimensions mostly used are fitness, precision, generalization and simplicity [27], which will be introduced in more detail in Sect. 2.2 and analysed in the following chapters. For each of the dimensions, different measures have been implemented [85], of which we will provide an overview in Sect. 2.3.

On the other hand, the discrepancies between model and log can also be visualised in more detail. Such *diagnostics* will clearly show *where* log and model are in conflict with each other, allowing the analyst to have a more detailed understanding of the

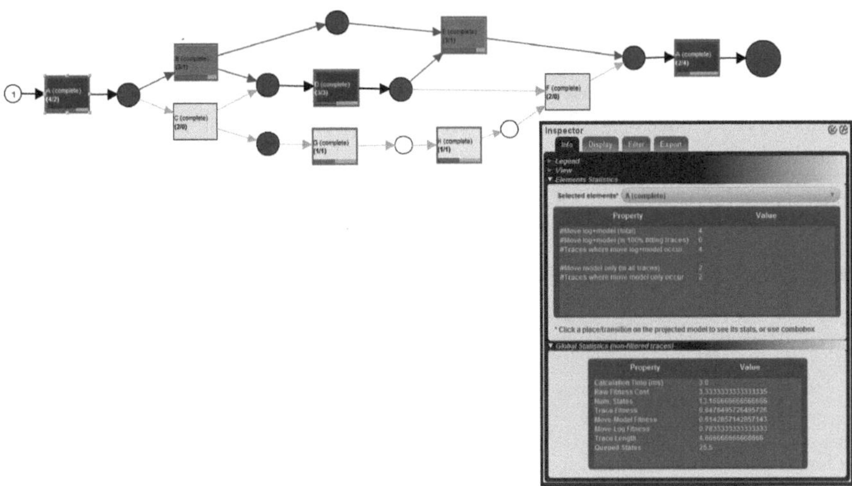

Fig. 2.2 Screenshot of the *Replay for Conformance Analysis* plug-in in ProM [6, 133].

disagreement, i.e. is it an inaccuracy in the model or in the data? Fig. 2.2 shows an example screenshot of the *Replay a Log on Petri Net for Conformance Analysis* plugin in ProM [6, 133]. It can be seen that both places and transitions of the Petri Net have been annotated with colours to highlight to which extent they involve discrepancies between log and model. The pop-up window further describes the details of these divergences. This more detailed understanding of the conformance issues enables practitioners to decide on the appropriate action that should be taken. In this part, the focus will however be only on the quality measures, and not on the diagnostics. Examples of conformance checking diagnostics can be found in Chap. 9 of Part III.

Process enhancement aims to *improve* the process model used to analyse and describe the process, based on the recorded process behaviour. It is a logical continuation of conformance checking, where the discrepancies between the a priori process model and the data can be assessed and used to improve the process model representation of the process.

In the remainder of this section, we will introduce some required notation on processes, event logs and models. Section 2.2 will introduce the different quality dimensions used in conformance checking, and Sect. 2.3 will introduce the implemented metrics for each dimension.

2.1.1 Preliminaries

Before introducing processes, event logs and models, some preliminary notations are required. Below we define activity sequences, and prefixes of activity sequences.

Definition 2.1 (Activity sequences). Let $\mathscr{A}$ be the activity alphabet, i.e. the collection of all activities which can be executed in a particular process. $\mathscr{T} = \mathscr{A}^*$ is the set of all finite sequences over $\mathscr{A}$, representing the universe of activity sequences. An activity sequence $\sigma \in \mathscr{T}$, also called trace or process variant, is a finite sequence of activities $\langle a_1, \ldots, a_n \rangle$, where

- $\forall a_i \mid a_i \in \mathscr{A}$,
- $|\sigma| = n$ refers to the number of activities in the sequence.

Definition 2.2 (Prefixes of activity sequences). $\lhd(\sigma, k)$ refers to the prefix of length k of activity sequence σ. $\lhd(\sigma, 0)$ refers to the empty trace $\langle\rangle$. Let $\lhd(\sigma)$ refer to the set of all prefixes of σ, i.e. $\lhd(\sigma) = \{\lhd(\sigma, k) \mid 0 \leq k \leq |\sigma|\}$.

2.1.2 *Process*

The terms *Process* and *System* are used interchangeably to refer to the *real process* in the upper left corner of Fig. 2.1. It is used to refer to the real way in which work is done, which is generally unknown. The term *System* should not be confused with the *information system* that might support the process. In fact the process or system can differ from any prescriptive model used or implemented by an information system, as process participants can use additional unwritten rules or customs in doing their work, or even abuse loopholes and workarounds to perform the work in ways which are different than those anticipated by the information systems or process documentations. The term *System* should instead be understood as the prevailing set of principles and procedures according to which the process is performed.

Formally, we can define the Process or System S as a set of possible activity sequences.[1]

Definition 2.3 (System). We define System S as a subset of the universe of activity sequences, i.e. $S \subseteq \mathscr{T}$, such that:

- $|S|$ indicates the number of distinct activity sequences of the system.
- $\mathbf{S} = \mathbb{P}(\mathscr{T})$ represent the domain of all possible systems given the set of activity sequences $\mathscr{T}$, where $\mathbb{P}(\mathscr{T})$ is the power set of $\mathscr{T}$.

2.1.3 *Event Log*

The event log is the recorded data of the process and can have a lot of detailed information on different aspects of the process. An example is shown in Table 2.1. Minimally, an event log contains events which 1) have an activity label, 2) are part

[1]Note that we use the symbol S to refer to the underlying process or system instead of the symbol P to avoid confusion with the symbol used for precision, which will be introduced further.

Table 2.1 Example event log.

Case	Date	Activity type	Resource
Claim01	06/08/2018 16:20	File Claim	Carla
Claim01	07/08/2018 15:04	Check Contract	Elliot
Claim01	08/08/2018 14:31	Check Franchise	Joy
Claim01	08/08/2018 16:00	Investigate	Manuel
Claim01	08/08/2018 23:16	Pay Claim	Giovanni
Claim02	06/08/2018 21:33	File Claim	Joe
Claim02	07/08/2018 00:54	Check Franchise	Carla
Claim02	07/08/2018 18:38	Check Contract	Joy
Claim02	08/08/2018 07:23	Reject	Manuel
Claim03	06/08/2018 22:14	File Claim	Carla
Claim03	07/08/2018 03:18	Check Franchise	Carla
Claim03	07/08/2018 23:21	Check Contract	Joy
Claim03	08/08/2018 08:19	Investigate	Manuel
Claim03	08/08/2018 16:20	No Refund	Joe
Claim04	01/08/2018 06:22	File Claim	Giovanni
Claim04	01/08/2018 21:07	Check Franchise	Joy
Claim04	02/08/2018 01:20	Check Contract	Manuel
Claim04	02/08/2018 21:31	Reject	Elliot

of a case, and 3) have a timestamp. On top of that, additional information can be added, such as information about resources, transactional life cycle, but also any other custom data attributes.

For a more detailed discussion on event data, we refer to Part III. For now, we will use a *simplified* event log notation [3], which abstracts from case identifiers and timestamps. Instead, we represent an event log as a multiset of activity sequences. The event log in Table 2.1 can be represented in this simplified notation as follows:

$$\{\langle FileClaim, CheckContract, CheckFranchise, Investigate, PayClaim\rangle^1,$$
$$\langle FileClaim, CheckFranchise, CheckContract, Reject\rangle^2,$$
$$\langle FileClaim, CheckFranchise, CheckContract, Investigate, NoRefund\rangle^1\}$$

Indeed, the four different claims in the event log can be described by three different activity sequences, or variants, of which the second one occurs two times. Formally, we define an Event log L thus as follows.

Definition 2.4 (Event log). An event log L is a multiset [18] of activity sequences, such that:

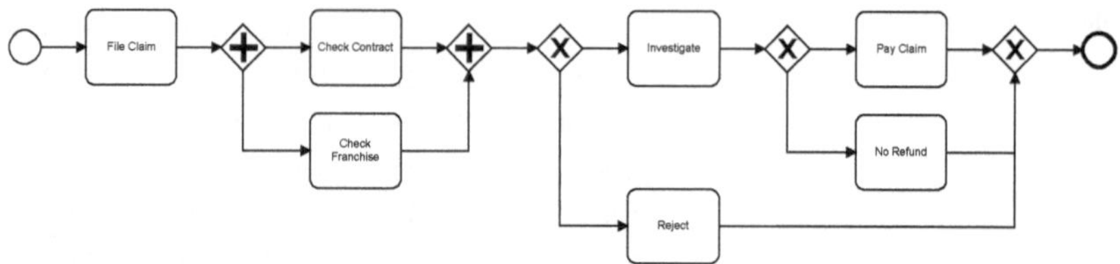

Fig. 2.3 Example BPMN model.

- the support set[2] of L, as defined in set theory [124], denoted by $supp\ L$, is the set of unique activity sequences in L. Note that $supp\ L = \{\sigma \mid \sigma \in L\}$.
- for an activity sequence $\sigma \in supp\ L$, the frequency of σ is defined as $L(\sigma)$.
- the number of distinct activity sequences in an event log, i.e. the size of the support set of the log, is defined as $|supp\ L|$.
- the size of an event log, i.e. the amount of cases, is defined as $|L| = \sum_{\sigma \in supp\ L} L(\sigma)$
- the domain of all possible logs is defined as $\mathbf{L} = \mathbb{B}(\mathscr{T})$, where $\mathbb{B}(\mathscr{T})$ is the set of all possible multisets of $\mathscr{T}$.

2.1.4 Model

Finally, we introduce the notation of a Model M. Here, it is important to distinguish between the conceptual notation of a model, introduced below, and the practical representation of a model, which can make use of any process modelling notation available, such as Petri Nets, BPMN models, process trees, etc. With the conceptual notation of a model, we refer to what is typically called the *language* of a particular process model: the set of execution paths it allows for. For example, consider the BPMN model in Fig. 2.3. We can draw a Petri Net which allows for the same behaviour as this model (Fig. 2.4), as well as a Process tree (Fig. 2.5).[3] Each of the models is thus a different practical representation of the same *language*.

In the following sections, we will abstract from these specific process modelling notations, and use only a conceptual representation of a model M, defined as follows.

Definition 2.5 (Model). A model M is a subset of the universe of activity sequences, and can be defined as $M \subseteq \mathscr{T}$.

- $|M|$ indicates the number of distinct activity sequences part of the model.

---

[2]Note that the concept of support set from set theory should not be confused with the concept of support in association rule mining. In set theory, the support (set) of a multiset is a *set* with the unique elements of that set, also called the *indistinguishables* of a multiset [18, 124]. As such, the support (set) of a multiset is an actual set. In order to avoid confusion we will always use the term support set, and not just support, while the two are used interchangeably in literature. In the context of association rule mining, support of a set is the number of times that set occurs. In the latter case it is thus a number, and not a set.

[3]A formal introduction to process trees will be given in Chap. 3.

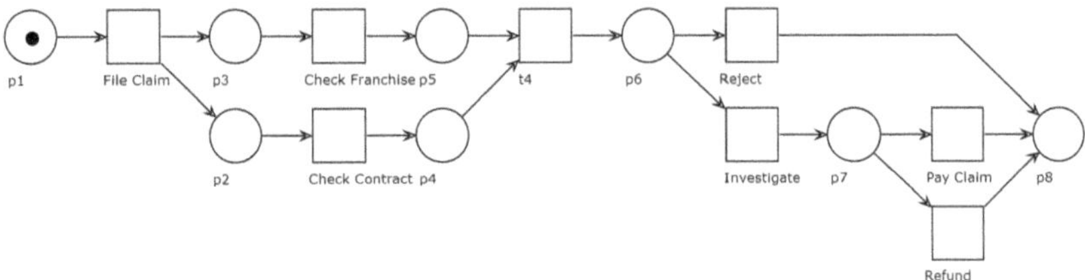

Fig. 2.4 Example Petri Net.

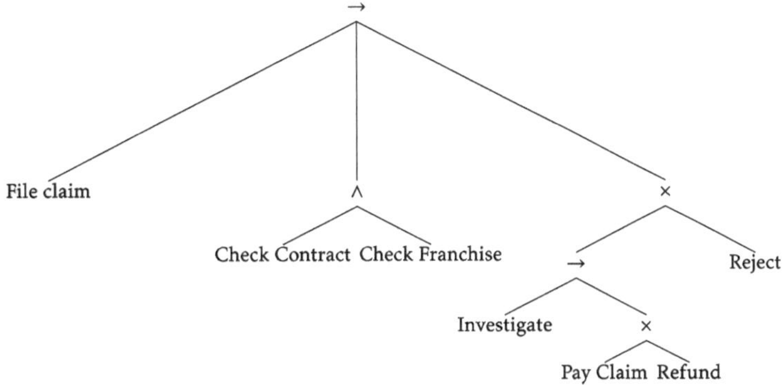

Fig. 2.5 Example process tree.

- **M** $= \mathbb{P}(\mathscr{T})$ represents the domain of all possible models, where $\mathbb{P}(\mathscr{T})$ is the power set of $\mathscr{T}$.

Following this definition, each of the process models in Figs. 2.3, 2.4 and 2.5—which can replay exactly the same traces—can be represented as the following set:

$$\{\langle FileClaim, CheckContract, CheckFranchise, Investigate, PayClaim\rangle,$$
$$\langle FileClaim, CheckContract, CheckFranchise, Investigate, NoRefund\rangle,$$
$$\langle FileClaim, CheckContract, CheckFranchise, Reject\rangle,$$
$$\langle FileClaim, CheckFranchise, CheckContract, Investigate, PayClaim\rangle,$$
$$\langle FileClaim, CheckFranchise, CheckContract, Investigate, NoRefund\rangle,$$
$$\langle FileClaim, CheckFranchise, CheckContract, Reject\rangle\}$$

In the next section, we will use these concepts—process, model and event log — to introduce and discuss the different quality dimensions used in conformance checking.

2.2 Quality Dimensions

The event log, model and system can each be seen as a set of process behaviour. As a result, they can be depicted visually as a Venn-diagram, displayed in Fig. 2.6,

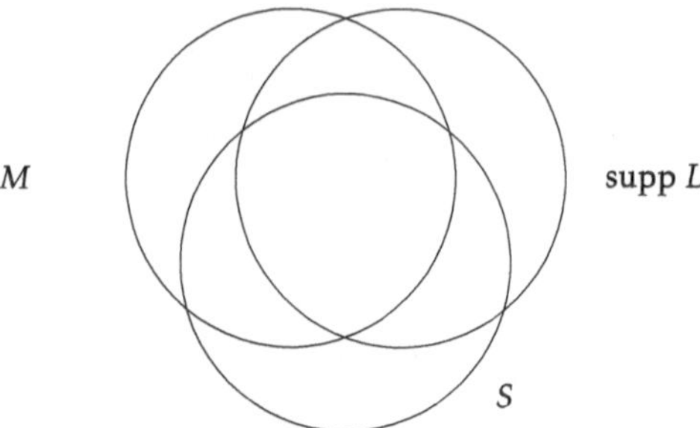

Fig. 2.6 Venn diagram representing the behaviour in the Model M, System S and support of event log L, supp L [26].

which constitutes a useful framework to discuss the different quality dimensions in conformance checking, as shown in [26].

In the following paragraphs, we assume that the amount of behaviour in S, M and supp L, and intersections thereof, is countable.[4] For the sake of clarity, this is reflected by the use of a hypothetical count function $\#(\ldots)$. We use this hypothetical function as a means to formalise the different quality dimensions on a conceptual level. In reality there are different ways to count and compare the behaviour in M, S, or supp L. One of them is by counting unique activity sequences (as denoted with $|\ldots|$ in the preceding definitions). An alternative approach can be to look at the amount of possible directly-follows relation in each of them. The number of different approaches is one of the main reasons that different implementations exist, as we will see further.

Furthermore, we do not claim that all quality measures should be implemented along the formulas introduced below. There can be other ways to quantify how *precise* or how *fitting* a model is. Nonetheless, the goal of these formulas is to provide a common, conceptual understanding about the aspect that each dimension tries to quantify, and to do this with a clarity that a verbal description or definition alone cannot offer.

Note that in Fig. 2.6, the support of the event log, i.e. the recorded behaviour, is not a subset of the system behaviour. While this might seem counter-intuitive, it is in fact possible to recorded behaviour which does not belong to the system. Indeed, the recorded behaviour is influenced by data inconsistencies and inaccuracies, and subsequently might contains fragments of behaviour which do not confirm with the way work is done. As defined above, the system refers to the prevailing set of principles and procedures by which the process is implicitly executed. However, these are not necessarily well captured in the data.

Moreover, also note that the model is not a subset, nor a pure superset of the recorded behaviour or the system. The process model can be any model drawn by hand or discovered from event data using discovery algorithms. In the first case, it is logical that there might not be an explicit relationship between the two sets of behaviour, modelled or recorded, as it will depend purely on how familiar the process

[4]In these and subsequent paragraphs we use the set supp L and not the multiset L because the latter cannot straightforwardly be compared with sets M and S.

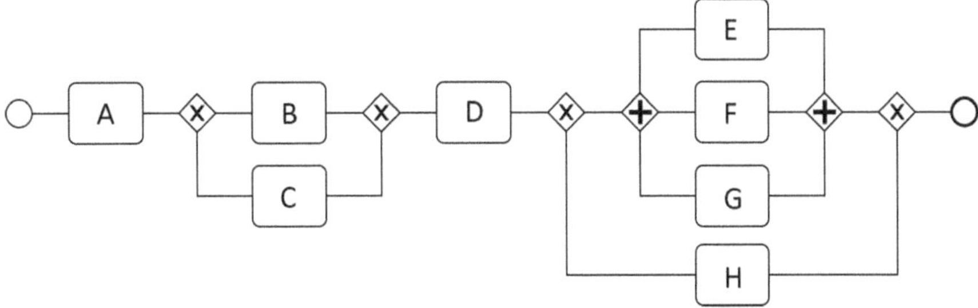

Fig. 2.7 Running example - Model 1

modeller is with the process at hand. But even when, in the second case, the model is discovered from the data, it will happen that some behaviour is discarded (because it is deemed to infrequent) while other behaviour is added (in order to make the model more general than the sample of event data). This lies exactly at the heart of this thesis, and is the reason why adequate quality measures are needed.

2.2.1 *Fitness*

The fitness dimensions indicates how much of the behaviour in the log is part of the model. As such it measures whether the event log *fits* the model or not. It is similar to the concept of *recall* used in information retrieval and binary classification [67]. In the context of Fig. 2.6, fitness can be defined as follows.

$$fitness(L, M) = \frac{\#(\text{supp } L \cap M)}{\#(\text{supp } L)} \tag{2.1}$$

For instance, consider the following example event log L_1 below, and Model 1 and 2 in Fig. 2.7 and 2.8, respectively. Model 1 is able to replay all six sequences in the event log L_1, and as such it has a perfect fitness. On the other hand, Model 2 does not allow for the traces σ_3 and σ_4, and as a result has a lower fitness.

$$\begin{aligned} L_1 = \{\sigma_1 &= \langle A, B, D, E, F, G\rangle, \\ \sigma_2 &= \langle A, B, D, F, E, G\rangle, \\ \sigma_3 &= \langle A, B, D, G, E, F\rangle, \\ \sigma_4 &= \langle A, B, D, G, F, E\rangle, \\ \sigma_5 &= \langle A, B, D, H\rangle, \\ \sigma_6 &= \langle A, C, D, H\rangle\} \end{aligned} \tag{2.2}$$

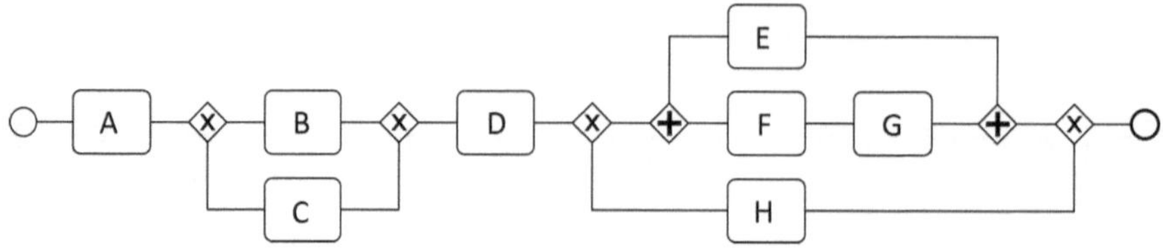

Fig. 2.8 Running example - Model 2

2.2.2 Precision

Just as in data mining, fitness (or recall) goes hand in hand with precision. In process mining, the precision dimension indicates how precise the model fits *only* the recorded behaviour, and not behaviour that was not seen. Using Fig. 2.6, precision can be defined as follows.

$$precision(L, M) = \frac{\#(\text{supp } L \cap M)}{\#(M)} \tag{2.3}$$

More specifically, it is the ratio of all behaviour in the model which is also part of the event log. If we reconsider the event log and models from before, we can see that Model 1 (Fig. 2.7) contains 8 sequences which are not present in the event log, i.e.

$$\begin{aligned} \{&\langle A, B, D, E, G, F\rangle, \\ &\langle A, B, D, F, G, E\rangle, \\ &\langle A, C, D, E, F, G\rangle, \\ &\langle A, C, D, F, E, G\rangle, \\ &\langle A, C, D, G, E, F\rangle, \\ &\langle A, C, D, G, F, E\rangle, \\ &\langle A, C, D, E, G, F\rangle, \\ &\langle A, C, D, F, G, E\rangle\} \end{aligned} \tag{2.4}$$

On the other hand, Model 2 (Fig. 2.8) only allows for 4 sequences which were not observed in the data, i.e.

$$\begin{aligned} \{&\langle A, B, D, F, G, E\rangle, \\ &\langle A, C, D, E, F, G\rangle, \\ &\langle A, C, D, F, E, G\rangle, \\ &\langle A, C, D, F, G, E\rangle\} \end{aligned} \tag{2.5}$$

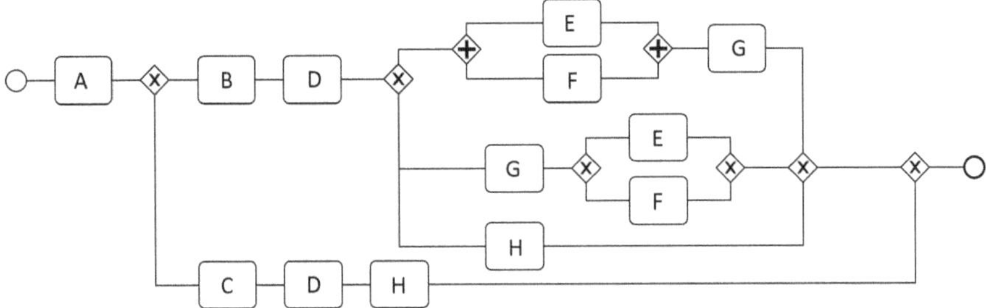

Fig. 2.9 Running example - Model 3

Based on these counts we can say that Model 1 is less precise than Model 2. However, it is important to note that the way in which behaviour is counted here might impact these rankings. For example, you could count in terms of extra allowed *events* rather than extra allowed sequences. In certain situations, these subtle differences might have an important impact on the measurements.

Model 3 (Fig. 2.9) is perfectly precise with respect to the event log, i.e. it does not allow for any other sequences than those observed in the event log. Note that this model is also perfectly fitting with this log. As a result, it is an exact representation of the event log: it contains all the behaviour recorded and nothing more. At the same time, it shows that such a model is not evident to construct, for instance requiring the duplication of tasks. This reduces the simplicity of the model, which will be discussed later. Also, a perfect representation might not be desirable because it could overfit the data and might not fit well with new observations. This is discussed next.

2.2.3 Generalization

In order to avoid *overfitting*—a model that perfectly allows for recorded behaviour but not unrecorded behaviour, which is therefore targeting too much at the sample data—the dimension of generalization was introduced. In contrast with fitness and precision, for which there are clear agreed-upon definitions, there are several slightly different definitions of generalization, among which:

- *Generalization indicates the models ability to avoid overfitting* [21].
- *Generalization quantifies the likelihood of previously unseen but allowed behaviour being supported by the process model* [26].
- *Generalization can be defined as the probability that the next, not yet observed, case can be replayed by the process model* [4].
- *The discovered model should generalize the example behaviour seen in the event log* [3].

- *Generalization assesses the extent to which the resulting model will be able to reproduce future behaviour of the process. In that sense, generalization can also be seen as a measure for the confidence on the precision* [27].

In sharp contrast to the abundance of different definitions, only a few generalization metrics have been implemented. In the context of Fig. 2.6, the following formalisation matches best with the definitions above. It measures the proportion of the system behaviour which can be replayed by the model.

$$generalization = \frac{\#(M \cap S)}{\#(S)} \tag{2.6}$$

When looking at Model 1 (Fig. 2.7) and 2 (Fig. 2.8), it is not immediately clear which one scores better on generalization, starting from the definitions above. Both allow for unobserved behaviour, Model 1 more so than Model 2. However, it is difficult to judge what the *appropriate* amount of additional behaviour, hence generalization, exactly is. How can we know which behaviour should be allowed? The only thing we can say at first sight is that these models generalise better than Model 3 (Fig. 2.9), which does not generalize at all.

2.2.4 Simplicity

The fourth quality dimension is *simplicity*. This dimension is inherently different from the ones discussed above, as it does not compare observed and modelled behaviour. Instead, it only takes into account the model. According to this dimension, simple models are preferred over more complex ones. There are different interpretations of the term *simple*. On the one hand, simple can refer to the *complexity* of the model: how many activities, how many edges, etc. On the other hand, simple can refer to the *understandability* of the model: how easy can it be comprehended and interpreted by a human being? Looking at the models above, it is quite clear that Model 3 (Fig. 2.9) is more complex in terms of the number of nodes and flows, as well as harder to understand—e.g. because the presence of duplicate activities.

In this and the following chapters, we will exclusively examine the quality of models with respect to recorded behaviour. The simplicity dimension will therefore not be considered further.

2.3 Quality Measures

In this section, the existing quality measures for dimensions fitness, precision and generalization are inventoried. For each dimension, all measures are discussed chronologically, i.e. in the order in which they were published. For the sake of

Table 2.2 Overview of Existing Quality Metrics for Fitness (F), Precision (P) and Generalization (G). Based on [85].

	Metric	Author	Date	Range	Model[a]
F	Parsing measure	Weijters et al. [138]	2006	[0, 1]	HN
	Continuous Parsing Method	Weijters et al. [138]	2006	[0, 1]	HN
	Completeness	Greco et al. [63]	2006	[0, 1]	WS
	Partial Fitness - Complete	Alves de Medeiros [105]	2007	$[-\infty, 1]$	HN
	Token-Based Fitness	Rozinat et al. [117]	2008	[0, 1]	PN
	Proper Completion	Rozinat et al. [117]	2008	[0, 1]	PN
	Behavioural Recall	vanden Broucke et al. [22]	2009	[0, 1]	PN
	Behavioural Profile Conformance	Weidlich et al. [137]	2011	[0, 1]	PN
	Alignment-Based Fitness	van der Aalst et al. [6]	2012	[0, 1]	PN
P	Soundness	Greco et al. [63]	2006	[0, 1]	WS
	(Advanced) Behavioral Appropriateness	Rozinat et al. [117]	2008	[0, 1]	PN
	Behavioural Specificity	Goedertier et al. [60]	2009	[0, 1]	PN
	ETC-Precision	Munoz-Gama et al. [110]	2010	[0, 1]	PN
	Alignment-Based Precision	van der Aalst et al. [6]	2012	[0, 1]	PN
	Behavioural Precision	vanden Broucke et al. [22]	2014	[0, 1]	PN
	One Align Precision	Adriansyah et al. [12]	2015	[0, 1]	PN
	Best Align Precision	Adriansyah et al. [12]	2015	[0, 1]	PN
	Anti-Alignment Precision	van Dongen et al. [50]	2016	[0, 1]	PN
G	Alignment-Based Generalization	van der Aalst et al. [6]	2012	[0, 1]	PN
	Frequency of Use	Buijs et al. [26]	2014	[0, 1]	PT
	Behavioural Generalization	vanden Broucke et al. [22]	2014	[0, 1]	PN
	Anti-Alignment Generalization	van Dongen et al. [50]	2016	[0, 1]	PN

[a]HN = Heuristics Net, WS = Workflow Schema, PN = Petri Net, PT = Process Tree

comparison, the state-of-the-art measures have been expressed formally in terms of the earlier introduced notations for event logs L and models M as far as possible. An overview of all the measures can be found in Table 2.2.

2.3.1 *Fitness*

Fitness is often regarded as the primary quality dimension to assess process models, before considering precision and generalization. This, and the fact that fitness is conceptually the easiest quality to quantify,[5] has led to a large number of implemented fitness measures. While initial measures were relatively straightforward, later mea-

[5]Fitness can be considered the easiest concept to quantify because it measures a proportion of the event log, which is finite. In contrast, precision has to deal with models containing an infinite amount of behaviour while generalization moreover deals with unobservable characteristics (i.e. is the behaviour real or not).

sures, such as those based on negative events or alignments are more sophisticated. The latter of these have become the *de facto* standard for measuring fitness. Over the years, there is a clear evolution from more narrow and specific process model notations used by the measures towards the use of the more generic Petri Nets (See Table 2.2), which became one of the most common notations for process models, next to BPMN and Process trees.

In the remainder of this section, we will introduce the different fitness measures which have been implemented. We will focus more extensively on the metrics which are still regularly used in literature and can thus be considered as state-of-the-art.

2.3.1.1 Parsing Measure

Parsing Measure is defined as the percentage of correctly parsed traces in the event log, and is therefore a quite coarse-grained measure [138]. It was defined in the context of the heuristics miner, and therefore exclusively works for heuristics nets. Similar measures have been defined for other model notations, such as *Completeness* for workflow schema's and *Proper Completion* for Petri Nets (see further).

2.3.1.2 Continuous Parsing Method

The Continuous Parsing Method is a more fine-grained variant of the *Parsing Measure*, as it records errors and then continues parsing [138]. As such, it is defined as the percentage of successfully parsed *events*. As well as the Parsing Measure, it expects a heuristics net as input.

2.3.1.3 Completeness

Completeness [63] is defined in the same way as the Parsing Measure, with the only difference that it expects a workflow schema, as described in [63], as input. Consequently, Completeness is also a coarse-grained, naive measure.

2.3.1.4 Partial Fitness - Complete

Partial Fitness - Complete was originally defined in [105], and is similar to the *Continuous Parsing Method*, to the extent that it expects a heuristics net and it is a fine-grained measure. However, it does not only count activities which can be parsed but also punishes for tokens which are left behind. Whereas the measures above have output values between 0 and 1, the range of possible values for this measure extends from $-\infty$ to 1.

2.3.1.5 Token-Based Fitness

Token-Based Fitness [117] (from here on also referred to as F_{tb}) is one of the first fitness measures that was defined to be used with Petri Nets. As the name suggest, it is highly dependent on the Petri Net representation of the model under consideration. The metric penalizes both when tokens are missing, i.e. an observed activity cannot be replayed, and when tokens are remaining in the model after replay. While the first penalty takes into account whether an activity sequence from the log is part of the model, the latter penalty makes sure that the requirement of proper completion is taken into account. Formally, Token-Based Fitness is computed as follows:

$$\begin{aligned} F_{tb} = & \frac{1}{2}\left(1 - \frac{\sum_{\sigma \in \text{supp } L} L(\sigma) \times m_M(\sigma)}{\sum_{\sigma \in \text{supp } L} L(\sigma) \times c_M(\sigma)}\right) \\ & + \frac{1}{2}\left(1 - \frac{\sum_{\sigma \in \text{supp } L} L(\sigma) \times r_M(\sigma)}{\sum_{\sigma \in \text{supp } L} L(\sigma) \times p_M(\sigma)}\right) \end{aligned} \tag{2.7}$$

where $m_M(\sigma)$ refers to the number of missing tokens when replaying trace σ on model M. c, r, and p refer to consumed, remaining and produced tokens, respectively.[6]

Given the fact that the Token-Based Fitness measure relies on the tokens flowing through the Petri Net, it is highly dependent on the representation of the model. As a result, two different Petri Nets which are equivalent in terms of behaviour can have a very different Token-Based Fitness. Subsequent measures therefore focussed more on the behaviour allowed by the Petri Nets instead of specific characteristics of the used notation, such as token flow.

2.3.1.6 Proper Completion

Proper Completion is the Petri Net based alternative to the Parsing Measure and Completeness metric [117]. It can be regarded as the course-grained, naive counterpart to *Token-Based Fitness*. In particular, it is defined as the percentage of traces without any missing of remaining tokens after trace replay.

2.3.1.7 Behavioural Recall

Behavioural Recall (from here on also referred to as F_{ne}), also known as *Negative Event Recall* uses the notions of precision and recall known from the field of information retrieval and binary classification [60]. If we define True Positives (TP) as the number of events in the log that can be correctly replayed, and False Negatives

---

[6]While extensive familiarity with the Petri Net notation and its execution semantics is not essential for understanding this and the next chapters, we kindly direct the interested reader to [46] for an elaborate introduction of Petri Net notation and its execution semantics.

(FN) as the number of events in the log for which a transition was forced to fire, Behavioural Recall can be defined as follows:

$$F_{ne} = \frac{TP}{TP + FN} \tag{2.8}$$

Note that this formula is the same as the well-known formula for recall in binary classification. In this case, the log is regarded as the *true condition* while the model is regarded as the *predicted condition*. Behavioural Recall is thus the proportion of the behaviour in the event log which can be replayed without forcing transitions to fire.

The negative event conformance metrics are based on the induction of artificial negative events. While these negative events are not of importance for the above formula for negative event recall, they do impact the Behavioural Precision and Generalization measures which will be addressed further on.

2.3.1.8 Behavioural Profile Conformance Measures

Behavioural Profile Conformance Measures, defined in [137], are a set of measures which relate to different constraints imposed by a model, such as precedence relations and co-occurrence of activities. It is therefore fundamentally different as the other measures quantify fitness with a single value. In particular, six different types of compliance are discussed

- Constraint-relative Behavioural Compliance (CBC)
- Model-relative Behavioural Compliance (MBC)
- Constraint-relative Co-occurrence Compliance (CCC)
- Model-relative Co-occurrence Compliance (MCC)
- Constraint-relative Case Compliance (CC)
- Model-relative Case Compliance (MC)

Whether the compliance is model-relative or constraint-relative defines how it is normalized, taking into account exclusiveness constraints in the model or not. While Behavioural Compliance focuses on behavioural relations (e.g. the order between activites), the Co-occurrences measures look at whether the case contains the correct activities (regardless of their order). Finally, the Case Compliance measures provide an aggregation of the Co-occurence and Behavioral Compliance measures. Compared with the other, single value measures, the Behavioral Profile Conformance are thus able to give a more detailed image about the fitness of a model and lean more towards the diagnositics side of conformance checking. This makes it difficult to compare these measures.

2.3.1.9 Alignment-Based Fitness

Alignment-Based Fitness (from here on also referred to as F_{ab}) is a fitness measure which differs from Token-Based Fitness in that it does not rely on the notion of tokens flowing through a Petri Net [6]. Instead, it *aligns* log and model in terms of activities. This means that for non-fitting traces, i.e. $\{\sigma | \sigma \in supp(L) \wedge \sigma \notin M\}$, the algorithm looks for the execution path in the model which is *most alike*, as measured by a cost function. The result is an alignment between the log trace and the model trace, which by default has a cost of 1 for each insertion and 1 for each deletion.[7] Formally, the total cost of aligning a log and a model is defined as

$$f_{cost} = \sum_{\sigma \in \text{supp } L} \delta(\sigma, M) \times L(\sigma) \tag{2.9}$$

where $\delta(\sigma, M)$ is the cost of the optimal alignment of activity sequence σ with model M. Given this cost, the Alignment-Based Fitness is defined as follows:

$$F_{ab} = 1 - \frac{f_{cost}}{\sum_{\sigma \in \text{supp } L} L(\sigma) \times \left(|\sigma| + \min_{\tau \in M} |\tau|\right)} \tag{2.10}$$

Note that the denominator of F_{ab} is equal to the maximum possible cost: the number of events in the case and the number of activities in the shortest path of the model times the number of cases in the event log.

Alignment-Based Fitness is very similar to Token-Based Fitness, except for the fact that it counts inserted and deleted activity instances, instead of missing and remaining tokens. These are also called *deviation moves*, or *model-only* or *log-only moves*, for deleted and inserted activities, respectively.

2.3.2 *Precision*

In contrast to fitness, quantifying precision is (even) more challenging. While fitness is defined as the *proportion* of the event log which can be replayed—in whatever way that proportion is measured—precision relates to the possibly infinite amount of behaviour in the model, which is much less fathomable. Because of the existence of loops and parallel constructs, it makes little sense to require that there is absolutely no behaviour in the model that was not recorded. Taking this into account properly is a non trivial task. Below, an overview of the evolution of precision measures is laid out.

---

[7] In practice, these costs can be configured for each activity type individually, to reflect that certain deviations should be penalized more than others.

2.3.2.1 Soundness

Soundness is a measure which can be regarded as the precision counterpart of the Completeness fitness measure[8] [63]. It is defined as the proportion of cases in a model which is also part of the log. As for Completeness, a workflow schema is expected as input. Because the workflow schemas defined in [63] did not allow for loops, such proportion can be computed.

2.3.2.2 (Advanced) Behavioural Appropriateness

(Advanced) Behavioural Appropriateness is a footprint-based measure which compares *follows* and *precedes* relationships between model and log [117]. By looking at these more local concepts, one avoids quantifying the total behaviour in the model. In contrast with the previous metric, this metric takes a Petri Net as input. However, it is rather coarse-grained and computationally expensive, as it requires a state space exploration of the Petri Net.

2.3.2.3 Behavioural Specificity

Behavioural Specificity uses the induction of negative events [60], just as the Behavioural Recall introduced earlier. It is defined as the percentage of negative events that are correctly classified, i.e. events that should not be able to happen because they were regarded as negative, and which are indeed not allowed in the model. Formally, this can be stated as follows, where the True Negatives (TN) and False Positives (FP) form all the truly negative events.

$$\frac{TN}{TN + FP} \tag{2.11}$$

Note that the interpretation of Behavioural Specificity deviates slightly from other precision metrics. Instead of measuring the proportion of the model that has been observed, it measures how many of the events that should not be allowed (i.e. negative events) are indeed not allowed by the model. While both proportions clearly lead to the same state when optimised, i.e. a model where all the behaviour is observed, they will quantify differently *how far* we are from such a state.

Because of the slight deviations from the mainstream precision definition and somewhat counter-intuitive interpretation, Behavioural Specificity has not been widely used. Instead, Behavioural Precision, or Negative Event Precision was introduced [22].

[8] The Soundness measure as defined in [63] should not be confused with the soundness criteria for work-flow nets as defined in [2].

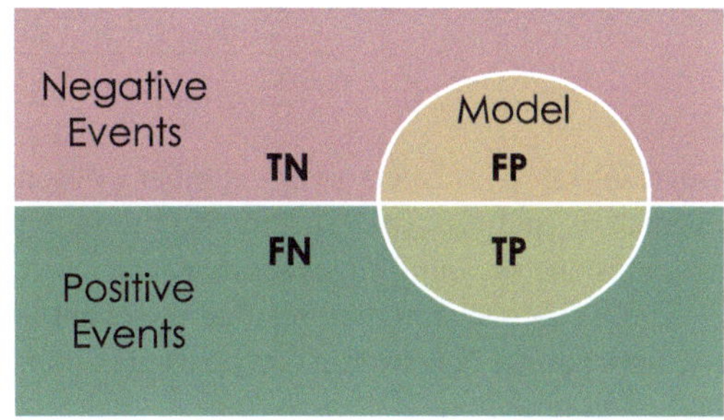

Fig. 2.10 Illustration of TN, FN, TP and FP in the context of negative events.

2.3.2.4 Behavioural Precision

Behavioural Precision (from here on referred to as P_{ne}), also called Negative Event Precision, is an alternative measure to measure precision using negative events. Just like Behavioural Recall, its formula equals the well known precision formula from the field of binary classification.

$$P_{ne} = \frac{TP}{TP + FP} \tag{2.12}$$

In this case, False Positives (FP) are events which are allowed by the model but should not be, as they are considered negative. True Positives (TP) are events that are allowed by the model and are not negative. As such, TP + FP are all events allowed by the model, and P_{ne} is the proportion of *positive* events allowed by the model.

The difference between Behavioural Specificity and Behavioural Precision can be illustrated using Fig. 2.10. Both can be optimised by making sure there are no false positives (FP), i.e. no behaviour in the model which is considered negative. However, both will measure the deviation from this ideal situation differently. Behavioural Specificity uses the size of TN as a reference point, while Behavioural Precision uses the size of TP as a reference point. The latter definition is more intuitive and in line with the concept of precision in process mining.

Since negative events are not available in process mining, they have to be induced artificially. The creation of artificial negative events is discussed in [60]. During the induction of negative events, a confidence for each negative event is also calculated, which makes it possible to also compute a weighted Behavioural Precision.

2.3.2.5 ETC Precision

ETC Precision (from here on also referred to as P_{etc}), or precision based on *escaping edges*, is a precision measure which constructs an automaton of the behaviour in the log [110]. Subsequently, it looks for *escaping edges*, which essentially are events which are allowed by the model in a certain state, but which were never observed. The precision is then defined as follows,

$$P_{etc} = 1 - \frac{\sum_{\sigma \in \text{supp } L} L(\sigma) \sum_{j=1}^{|\sigma|+1} |E(\lhd(\sigma, j))|}{\sum_{\sigma \in \text{supp } L} L(\sigma) \sum_{j=1}^{|\sigma|+1} |A(\lhd(\sigma, j))|} \tag{2.13}$$

where $E(\lhd(\sigma, j))$ refers to the number of escaping edges after the $j - th$ activity of trace σ, and $A(\lhd(\sigma, j))$ refers to the number of allowed tasks (both observed activities and escaping edges) at that state.

The ETC-precision requires that the event log has a perfect fitness which limits its applicability. However, it can be used in combination with alignments, as will be discussed further.

2.3.2.6 Alignment-Based Precision

Alignment-Based Precision (from here on also referred to as P_{ab}) computes the precision of a model based on the same concept of alignments such as Alignment-Based Fitness [6]. It starts from an *aligned* log, in which all the non-fitting traces are replaced with (one of) their optimal alignment(s). Based on this event log, it considers the activity prefix $\lhd(\sigma, k)$ of each event, and counts which activities are *enabled* in the model after this activity prefix $(en_M(\lhd(\sigma, k)))$, and which did occur in the log after this activity prefix $(en_L(\lhd(\sigma, k)))$. It follows that precision is defined as:

$$P_{ab} = \frac{\sum_{\sigma \in \text{supp } L} L(\sigma) \sum_{j=0}^{|\sigma|-1} \frac{en_L(\lhd(\sigma,j))}{en_M(\lhd(\sigma,j))}}{\sum_{\sigma \in \text{supp } L} |\sigma| \cdot L(\sigma)} \tag{2.14}$$

The precision measured by this formula will decrease when for one or more activity prefixes, more activities are enabled in the model than did occur in the log.

2.3.2.7 One Align Precision

One Align Precision [12] is a combination of ETC-precision [110] and alignments [6]. One Align Precision refers to the application of $P_{etc}(L_a, M)$ where L_a is an aligned log using *one* optimal alignment for each non-fitting trace. Note that more than one optimal alignment can be available for a certain trace. In order to take into account different optimal alignments, Best Align precision can be used.

2.3.2.8 Best Align Precision

Best Align Precision [12] is similar to One Align Precision, with the only difference that it does not use one alignment but aggregates over all the optimal alignments for each trace.

2.3.2.9 Anti-alignment Precision

is a more recent, novel way to calculate precision [50]. An (n, δ)-anti-alignment is an activity sequence of the model of length n which is separated from the log by a distance δ, as measured with a given distance function d. The rationale to use precision with anti-alignments is to compute the anti-alignment distance between each trace in the log, and the complement of the log. If the model is precise—i.e. it contains the same behaviour as the log, and nothing else—the anti-alignment will be the trace itself for each trace. As such, the overall distance will be zero, leading to a perfect precision. On the other hand, if the distance between each trace and its anti-alignment is maximal, precision will be zero. In [50], Anti-Alignment Precision is defined as a weighed average between a trace-based precision measure and a log-based precision measure. Each of those is given a weight of 0.5. Since the measure assumes perfect fitness, it depends upon a preliminary alignment of log and model, similar to Best Align Precision and One Align Precision.

2.3.3 *Generalization*

Generalization has been the dimension most difficult to quantify properly, which is reflected by the few implementations that exist. Below, we introduce Alignment-Based Generalization [6], Behavioural Generalization [22], Frequency of Use [26] and Anti-Alignment Generalization [50].

2.3.3.1 Alignment-Based Generalization

Alignment-Based Generalization

(from here on also referred to as G_{ab}) was the first generalization measure to be implemented, and uses trace alignments just like the related fitness and precision measures [6]. It starts from an aligned log, and for each event calculates the probability that the next time this state is visited, a new path will be observed. Given N the number of unique activities enabled in this state, and F the number of times the state was visited, the probability is defined as

$$pnew(N, F) = \begin{cases} \frac{N(N+1)}{F(F-1)}, & \text{if } F - N \geq 2 \\ 1, & \text{otherwise} \end{cases} \tag{2.15}$$

For example, in a state with 2 unique activities and 2 visits, pnew = 1, as is also the case with 3 visits. If F = 4, pnew = $\frac{2\times3}{4\times3} = 0.5$. If F = 5, $\frac{2\times3}{5\times4} = 0.3$. The larger the difference between the number of visits and the number of unique activities, the lower the probability. If the average probability over the log is low, then generalization is assumed to be high. As such,

$$G_{ab} = 1 - \frac{\sum_{\sigma \in \text{supp } L} \sum_{j=0}^{|\sigma|-1} p_{new}(en_L(h(\sigma, j)), f(h(\sigma, j))}{\sum_{\sigma \in \text{supp } L} |\sigma| \cdot L(\sigma)} \tag{2.16}$$

where $en_M(h(\sigma, j))$ is the number of activities that are *enabled* in the model after this activity prefix and $f(h(\sigma, j))$ is the frequency with which this state is visited in the log.

2.3.3.2 Behavioural Generalization

Behavioural Generalization (from here on also referred to as G_{ne}), also called Negative Event Generalization, is related to Behavioural Recall and Precision and relies on the induction of artificial negative events [22]. Behavioural Generalization is defined as

$$G_{ne} = \frac{AG}{AG + DG} \tag{2.17}$$

where AG denotes to the number of *allowed generalised events* and DG denotes to the number of *disallowed generalised events*. Generalised events are events which were not observed but at the same time not considered as negative. In other words, they are supposed to reflect real behaviour and thus belong to the system S. The more of those generalised events are allowed by the model, the better the generalization score.

2.3.3.3 Frequency of Use

Frequency of use is a generalization measure defined for process trees which estimates the generalization by looking at the frequencies of executions in the process tree [26]. When certain parts of the process tree are infrequent, the tree is regarded as overfitting, and thus has a lower generalization. Formally, it can be defined as follows.

$$G_{fr} = 1 - \frac{\sum_{nodes} \sqrt{\#executions}^{-1}}{\#nodes\ in\ model} \tag{2.18}$$

In other words, it iterates over all nodes, and computes the inverse of the square root of the number of executions. The higher the number of executions, the lower this value. If there is only one execution for an activity, this number will equal one. If all activities are only executed once, it thus means that the generalization measure will be zero.

2.3.3.4 Anti-alignment Generalization

Anti-Alignment Generalization [50] is a generalization measure using anti-alignments introduced earlier. It introduces the concept of *recovery distance* which can be seen as a proxy for how different an anti-alignment is from the log in terms of visited states. Subsequently it will give models a good generalization score if the anti-alignment distance is high but the recovery distance is low. In other words, the model generalises to other traces, but without introducing additional states—which is claimed to characterise unobserved but realistic behaviour. Again, it is defined as a weighed average between a trace-based and log-based measure. Since perfect fitness is assumed, the measure depends on a preliminary alignment between log and model.

2.3.3.5 Other Approaches for Generalization

Next to the use of a measure to compute generalization, other approaches have been proposed. In [14], generalization is measured using k-fold cross validation for both fitness and precision. The log is divided in k parts, and the model is discovered from $k - 1$ parts. Fitness is then measured using the remaining part, while precision is measured against the complete log. This procedure is repeated, taking out each of the k parts in turn, after which the obtained values are averaged. While the focus in subsequent chapters is only on the measures introduces, we will return to this other approach in Chap. 6.

2.4 Conclusion

This chapter provided an introduction to conformance checking as one of the three main types of process mining, next to process discovery and process enhancement. After introducing some necessary notations, conformance checking was further discussed, by introducing the four generally used quality dimensions as well as an overview of implemented measures for fitness, precision and generalization. These quality dimension each concern the relationship between observed and modelled behaviour.

There are clear evolutions to be noticed when looking at the different measures that exist. Firstly, there is a move from specific process model notations to the more general and formal Petri Net notation. Secondly, measures are clearly becoming more sophisticated, especially when comparing alignment-based measures or negative event measures with the earlier naive, course-grained measures. The fact that precision can be measured regardless of the fitness level, by way of using aligned event logs, increases the applicability of said measures.

Nonetheless, also some questions can be raised. The fact that fitness has received clearly more attention than precision, and precision more than generalization, seems to be indicating the overall difficulties of the community in quantifying these latter dimensions. Especially in the case of generalization, the different implementations are each using a very different approach towards measuring generalization. How do these approaches compare with each other? Are we measuring the same aspect, or are we using the same name to measure different things? And if we are measuring the same thing, what are the differences between various implementations in terms of sensitivity and feasibility, for example.

In Chap. 4 a comparative study of the state-of-the-art measures will be introduced to see how they relate to each other both within and among the dimensions. In this chapter, the validity, feasibility and sensitivity of the implemented measures will be examined. These results will be used as input for Chap. 5, where the dimensions itself will be evaluated and reassessed. Before proceeding to these experiments, we will introduce a method to calculate the number of execution paths in a process model in the next chapter. This calculation is necessary to appropriately configure aspects such as log completeness in subsequent experiments.

2.5 Further Reading

1. Janssenswillen, G., Donders, N., Jouck, T., Depaire, B.: A comparative study of existing quality measures for process discovery. Information Systems **71**, 1–15 (2017)
2. Adriansyah, A., Muñoz-Gama, J., Carmona, J., van Dongen, B.F., van der Aalst, W.M.P.: Alignment based precision checking. In: Business Process Management Workshops, pp. 137–149. Springer (2012)
3. vanden Broucke, S.K.L.M., De Weerdt, J., Vanthienen Jan, B., Baesens, B.: Determining process model precision and generalization with weighted artificial negative events. Knowledge and Data Engineering, IEEE Transactions on **26**(8), 1877–1889 (2014)
4. Buijs, J.C.A.M.: Flexible Evolutionary Algorithms for Mining Structured Process Models. Ph.D. thesis, Technische Universiteit Eindhoven, Eindhoven (2014)
5. van Dongen, B.F., Carmona, J., Chatain, T.: A unified approach for measuring precision and generalization based on anti-alignments. In: International Conference on Business Process Management, pp. 39–56. Springer (2016)
6. Goedertier, S., Martens, D., Vanthienen, J., Baesens, B.: Robust process discovery with artificial negative events. The Journal of Machine Learning Research **10**, 1305–1340 (2009)
7. Greco, G., Guzzo, A., Ponieri, L., Sacca, D.: Discovering expressive process models by clustering log traces. Knowledge and Data Engineering, IEEE Transactions on **18**(8), 1010–1027 (2006)
8. de Medeiros, A.K.A.: Genetic process mining. Ph.D. thesis, Technische Universiteit Eindhoven, Eindhoven (2006)
9. Muñoz-Gama, J., Carmona, J.: A fresh look at precision in process conformance. In: Business Process Management, vol. 6336, pp. 211–226. Hoboken, NJ, USA (2010)

10. Rozinat, A., van der Aalst, W.M.P.: Conformance checking of processes based on monitoring real behavior. Information Systems **33**(1), 64–95 (2008)
11. Weidlich, M., Polyvyanyy, A., Desai, N., Mendling, J., Weske, M.: Process compliance analysis based on behavioural profiles. Information Systems **36**(7), 1009–1025 (2011)
12. Weijters, A.J.M.M., van Der Aalst,W.M.P., De Medeiros, A.K.A.: Process mining with the heuristics miner-algorithm. Tech. rep., Technische Universiteit Eindhoven (2006)

Chapter 3
Calculating the Number of Distinct Paths in a Block-Structured Model

Some infinities are bigger than other infinities.

John Green

3.1 Introduction

When formalising the quality dimensions in the previous chapter, we already slightly touched upon the difficulties that exist in quantifying process behaviour. Not only are there various ways to *count* process behaviour—e.g. count in terms of distinct end-to-end sequences of in terms of more local flows—constructs such as parallel gateways or loops make counting behaviour inconceivable. Nonetheless, there are often situations where it is desirable to quantify the amount of behaviour of a process model. The *precision* dimension expresses to what extent the behaviour in the model does not exceed the behaviour in the log [27], which to a certain extent requires that we can quantify the behaviour in the model. Similarly, the implicit realism measure [45] uses the number of unique paths in a model to calculate the probability that a certain amount of behaviour from the model did not show up in the log. The amount of behaviour in a model can moreover be used as a proxy for model complexity and for the variance of the behaviour. As it can be computationally hard to compute the amount of behaviour, several measures to calculate model complexity use proxies instead [106].

Determining the amount of behaviour in a process model—which we quantify in this chapter as the number of unique execution paths—is a challenging task. One could naively traverse the process model recursively and count the number of unique paths, but this quickly becomes computationally unfeasible due to a combinatorial explosion of different (parallel) paths.

G. Janssenswillen: Unearthing the Real Process Behind the Event Data, LNBIP 412
https://doi.org/10.1007/978-3-030-70733-0_3

In this chapter, an algorithm is proposed to compute the number of unique paths in a block-structured finite-behaviour process model in a computationally efficient way. As we will show, this is possible by exploiting the block-structuredness of the model. In particular, the following topics are discussed in the chapter:

- A *block function*, which calculates the number of unique paths in a block, is defined for each of the following process constructs: *sequence* ($\rightarrow$), *exclusive choice* ($\times$), *parallelism* ($\wedge$) and *structured finite loops* ($\circlearrowleft^k$).
- A generic approach to determine the total amount of behaviour in a block-structured finite-behaviour process model is described.
- An implementation of the approach for process trees is given.

Section 3.2 describes the general approach used by the algorithm, while in Sect. 3.3 the implementation is elaborated upon.[1] The performance of the technique in terms of run-time is discussed in Sect. 3.4.

3.2 Formal Algorithm

In this section, the formal approach of the calculation will be described. First, some assumptions will be made regarding the type of models taken into account. In the subsequent paragraphs, the different block functions for each of the specific operator types will be defined. Finally, some limitations to the formal approach will be pointed out, together with workarounds to solve them.

3.2.1 Assumptions and Used Notations

It is important to keep in mind that we impose two restrictions on the process models. Firstly, we assume finite-behaviour models, since it would otherwise make no sense to determine the number of unique traces. As a result, loops in our models are only allowed a maximum number of iterations. While this appears very restrictive, this can be justified by accepting a so-called *fairness assumption*, which states that a task of a process cannot be postponed indefinitely. This assumption therefore rules out infinite behaviours that are considered unrealistic [17]. Secondly, we assume that models are block-structured, i.e. they can be decomposed in properly nested sub-processes [97].

For the development and discussion of our approach, we will use the process tree notation, since process trees are block-structured by definition. However, the ideas in this paper are applicable to other notation languages as long as the models are block-structured and finite in behaviour. We formally define a Finite-behaviour Process Tree, which is largely based on the definition in [26], as follows:

[1] While the algorithm introduced in this chapter is used in the experiments of subsequent chapters, non-technical readers can skip this chapter without any harm to the continuity.

Definition 3.1 (Finite-behaviour Process Tree). Let $\mathscr{A}$ be the activity alphabet and $A \subseteq \mathscr{A}$ be a finite set of activities, then $PT = (N, r, m, c)$ is a process tree such that:

- N is a non-empty finite set of nodes consisting of operator (N_O) and leaf nodes (N_L) such that: $N_O \cap N_L = \emptyset$
- $r \in N_O$ is the root node of the tree
- $O = \{\rightarrow, \times, \wedge, \circlearrowleft^k, \vee\}$, the set of operator types.
- $m : N \rightarrow A \cup O$ is a function mapping each node to an operator or activity:

$$m(n) = \begin{cases} a \in A \cup \{\tau\}, & \text{if } n \in N_L. \\ o \in O, & \text{if } n \in N_O. \end{cases}$$

  where τ represents a silent activity.
- $c : N \rightarrow N^*$ is the direct-child-relation function:
  $c(n) = \langle\rangle$ if $n \in N_L$
  $c(n) \subset N$ if $n \in N_O$, such that

  - each node except the root node has exactly one parent:
    $\forall n \in N \backslash \{r\} : \exists p \in N_O : n \in c(p) \wedge \nexists q \in N_O : p \neq q \wedge n \in c(q)$;
  - the root node has no parent:
    $\nexists n \in N : r \in c(n)$;
  - each node appears only once in the list of children of its parent:
    $\forall n \in N : \forall_{1 \leq i < j \leq |c(n)|} : c(n)_i \neq c(n)_j$;
  - a node with a loop operator type has exactly three children such that the first child is always executed first, the second child is executed maximum k times, each time followed by the first child, and finally the third child is executed once:
    $\forall n \in N : (m(n) = \circlearrowleft^k) \Rightarrow |c(n)| = 3$.

A process tree can have five different types of operators: sequence ($\rightarrow$), parallelism ($\wedge$), exclusive-choice ($\times$), non-exclusive choice ($\vee$) and a finite loop ($\circlearrowleft^k$). Figure 3.1 shows a process tree and illustrates how it can be decomposed into blocks. A block always consists of a root node which determines the block type. We distinguish between an activity block, a sequence block, an exclusive choice block, a parallelism block, a structured finite-behaviour loop block and a non-exclusive choice block. The example in Fig. 3.1 consists of 8 blocks: 5 activity blocks, 1 sequence block, 1 exclusive choice block and 1 parallelism block. Note that the entire tree is also considered as a separate block.

3.2.2 Generic Approach

The generic approach to determine the number of unique paths in a block-structured finite-behaviour process model is a two-step approach. First, we define for each block type a function which calculates the number of unique paths in a block. The input for these block functions are the number of unique traces x_i in each of its child-blocks. Next we can calculate the total number of unique paths through recursive composition of the appropriate block functions.

In order to illustrate this approach, consider the process tree in Fig. 3.1 and assume the block functions $F_{\rightarrow}(x_1, \ldots, x_u)$, $F_{\times}(x_1, \ldots, x_u)$ and $F_{\wedge}(x_1, \ldots, x_u)$ which calculate the number of paths in a sequence, choice and parallel construct, respectively, based on the number of paths their u children have. The total number of unique paths in this process tree can then be determined by applying the sequence block function for the outer block: $F_{\rightarrow}(c_1, c_2, c_3)$, where c_1, c_2, and c_3 refer to the children of the root node. The first block is an activity block, which implies $c_1 = 1$ as it contains only a single path. To determine the number of paths in the second and third block, we must apply the appropriate block functions on their children. This results in $F_{\rightarrow}(c_1, F_{\times}(c_4, c_5), F_{\wedge}(c_6, c_7))$—where c_4 until c_7 refer to the children of the exclusive choice and parallel blocks—which can be calculated once we have defined the block functions in the next paragraphs. Nodes c_4 until c_7 in this formula are each activity blocks.

3.2.3 *Block Functions*

3.2.3.1 Activity

There is always only one way to execute a single activity. Therefore the activity block function is a constant value:

$$F_a = 1 \tag{3.1}$$

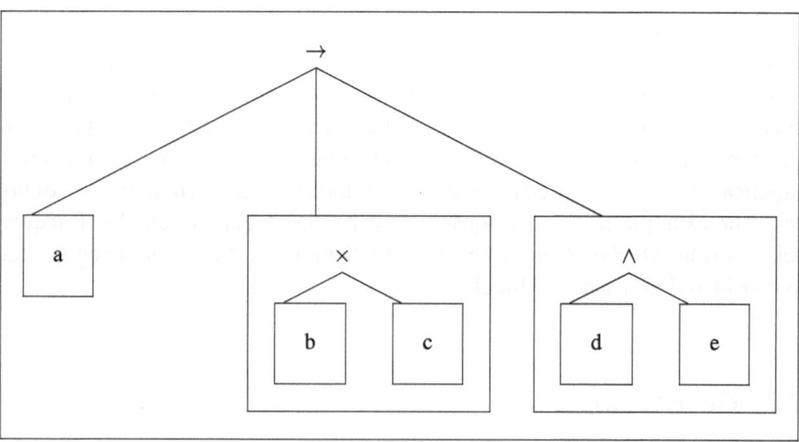

Fig. 3.1 Process tree with indicated blocks.

Note that silent activities, shown as τ, also have $F_a = 1$ since there is in fact exactly one way to execute a silent activity.

3.2.3.2 Sequence

Consider a sequence block consisting of u child-blocks such that each child-block i contains x_i unique paths. As the blocks are executed in sequence, they are executed independently from each other. Consequently, the total number of paths of a sequence block can be calculated by multiplying the number of paths in each child-block. This results in the following sequence block function:

$$F_{\rightarrow}(x_1, \ldots, x_u) = \prod_{i=1}^{u} x_i \tag{3.2}$$

3.2.3.3 Exclusive Choice

In an exclusive choice block, only one of the different blocks will be executed at a time, therefore, the number of possibilities is the sum of the number of possibilities in each of the children:

$$F_{\times}(x_1, \ldots, x_u) = \sum_{i=1}^{u} x_i \tag{3.3}$$

3.2.3.4 Parallelism

For the parallel construct, the calculations get more complex. In order to illustrate the development of this block function, consider the process tree in Fig. 3.2 which has four leafnodes with activities a, b, c and d. Determining the number of unique paths in this tree is equivalent to determining the number of unique words that can be formed by the set of activity letters {a, b, c, d}—given the constraints imposed by each child-block, which make some words, such as *bacd*, invalid. In particular, a and b are children of a sequence construct, such that b is never allowed to happen before a.

In order to solve this challenge it is important to realise the following. Originally we have a problem of determining all four-letter words with the letters {a, b, c, d}, given specific constraints. We start with four empty, undecided places in our word. Then, for each child-block, we can divide the calculation into two steps. Let's consider the sequence construct.

Firstly, we determine the number of valid orderings of the letters of the child-block, i.e. {a,b}. Secondly, we determine the number of possible ways how the two letters can be placed in a four-letter word.

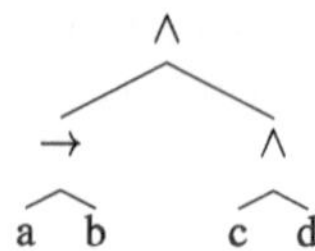

Fig. 3.2 A process tree with parallelism.

Given the example in Fig. 3.2, the two steps for the sequence construct have the following result.

1. There is only a single valid order of a and b, since these are children of a sequence node.
2. There are six possible ways to insert these letters in a four letter word, i.e.,
   - X X _ _
   - X _ X _
   - X _ _ X
   - _ X X _
   - _ X _ X
   - _ _ X X

   The number of possible ways to select two places out of a total of four—the current amount of empty places—can be expressed as the binomial coefficient $\binom{4}{2}$. This is justified because the order of the selection is not important at this point, as it was already taken into account in the previous step. Indeed, $\binom{4}{2} = \frac{4!}{2!(4-2)!} = 6$.

These steps are subsequently repeated for the next child. Firstly, determine the number of valid orderings of the letters of the second element, i.e. {c,d}. And secondly, determine the number of possible ways how these letters can be placed in the remaining empty spaces of the four-letter word. Note that this second step can be omitted for the last child, as there will be just the right amount of empty places left. Nonetheless, we will add this term for the sake of generality. For the parallel child-block of activities c and d, the steps are the following.

1. There are two valid orders in which the letters c and d can be placed, since these are children of a parallel construct. This number can actually be found by applying the same steps on this smaller parallel construct construct.
   a. The first child of this parallel construct is an activity block, and therefore contains a single path.
   b. The total number of non-silent activities in this parallel construct is equal to two. There are $\binom{2}{1} = 2$ ways to insert the first activity.
   c. The second child of this parallel construct is an activity block, and therefore contains a single path.
   d. There is only one way to insert the remaining activity in the remaining space.
   e. As a result, this parallel construct contains $1\binom{2}{1}1\binom{1}{1} = 2$ paths.

2. There is only a single way to insert the two letters into the two remaining empty spaces of the four-letter word.

To recap, the calculation of the number of distinct paths in this example is characterised by the following formula. As a result, the total number of paths in this parallel construct is 12.

$$\left[1\binom{4}{2}\right]\cdot\left[2\binom{4-2}{2}\right]=12 \tag{3.4}$$

For each child of the parallel construct, there is a term consisting of two parts: 1) the number of allowed orderings of the activities in this child, and 2) the number of ways in which the activities can be inserted in the remaining space. The first child contains two non-silent activities which can be executed in a single order (due to the sequence construct), while the second child contains two non-silent activities which can be executed in two different orders (due to the parallel construct). The first pair of activities can be placed in $\binom{4}{2}$ ways, while the second pair of activities can be placed in $\binom{4-2}{2}=1$ way in the remaining places.

In order to formalise this approach, we need some additional notation. Assume z_i to be the number of non-silent activities in child-block i. We can then express the formula above in terms of symbols as follows.

$$\left[x_1\binom{z_1+z_2}{z_1}\right]\cdot\left[x_2\binom{z_2}{z_2}\right] \tag{3.5}$$

By applying this same formula to the second child—in itself also a parallel construct—we find that $x_2=2$ as outlined above and shown in the formula below.

$$x_2=1\binom{2}{1}\cdot 1\binom{2-1}{1}=2 \tag{3.6}$$

For a generic parallel construct with u children, we can thus express this block function as follows.

$$\begin{aligned}F_\wedge(x_1,\ldots,x_u,z_1,\ldots,z_u)&=x_1\binom{\sum_{j=1}^{u}z_j}{z_1}x_2\binom{\sum_{j=2}^{u}z_j}{z_2}\ldots x_u\binom{z_u}{z_n}\\&=\prod_{i=1}^{u}x_i\binom{\sum_{j=i}^{u}z_j}{z_i}\end{aligned} \tag{3.7}$$

Note that for now it is assumed that each z_i—i.e. the number of non-silent activities in child i—is fixed. In reality this is hardly the case, as parallel branches can contain loop constructs and choices. This issue will be addressed in Sect. 3.3.

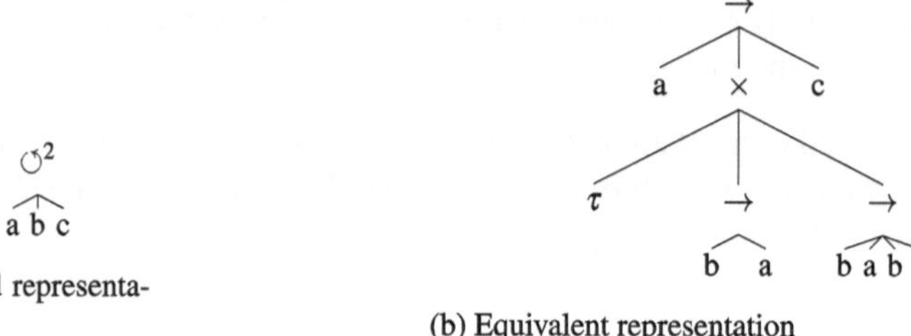

(a) Standard representation

(b) Equivalent representation

Fig. 3.3 Finite loop construct

3.2.3.5 Structured Finite Loops

A structured finite loop block is a special kind of process construct in the sense that it always contains three child-blocks.[2] The first child-block is always executed, the second child-block is executed a limited number of times (between zero and k times), each time followed by the first child-block, and finally the third child-block is executed to conclude. This structure allows us to transform a finite loop into an equivalent structure using $\rightarrow$ and $\times$ nodes, as illustrated by Fig. 3.3.

Based on the block functions $F_{\rightarrow}$ and $F_{\times}$, and the insight provided by Fig. 3.3, we can now easily see that the finite loop block function can be expressed as follows, where k represents the maximum number of loop-iterations:

$$F_{\circlearrowleft}(x_1, x_2, x_3, k) = x_1 \cdot \sum_{i=0}^{k} (x_2 x_1)^k \cdot x_3 \tag{3.8}$$

Indeed, the finite loop is a sequence of three parts, in which the middle part is actually a choice between several sequences.

3.2.4 *Limitations*

Our suggested approach holds two limitations the reader should be aware of. Firstly, there is no block function for a non-exclusive choice construct. Secondly, the parallelism block function assumes that the number of activities z_i within a child-block i is fixed. However if a child-block contains an (exclusive) choice construct or a finite loop construct, this assumption is violated.

Both limitations can be circumvented by preprocessing the process tree. As for the first limitation, non-exclusive choice constructs can be transformed into an exclusive

[2]This is so for the process tree notation. One could argue whether the third element is in fact part of the loop when considering other notations, but the point remains that it is always possible to transform a structured finite loop to a three-block construct.

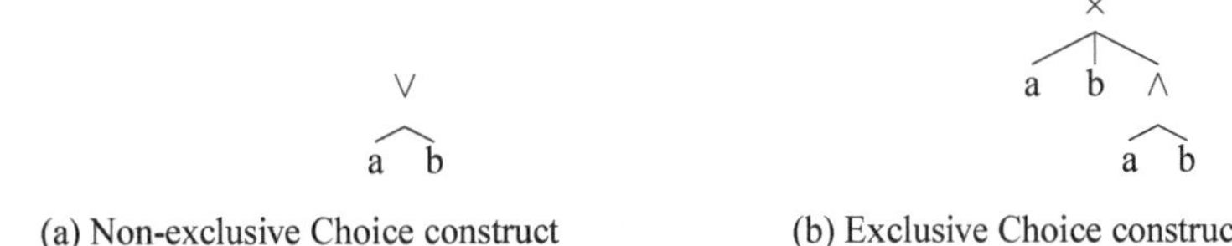

(a) Non-exclusive Choice construct (b) Exclusive Choice construct

Fig. 3.4 Transformation of non-exclusive choice construct.

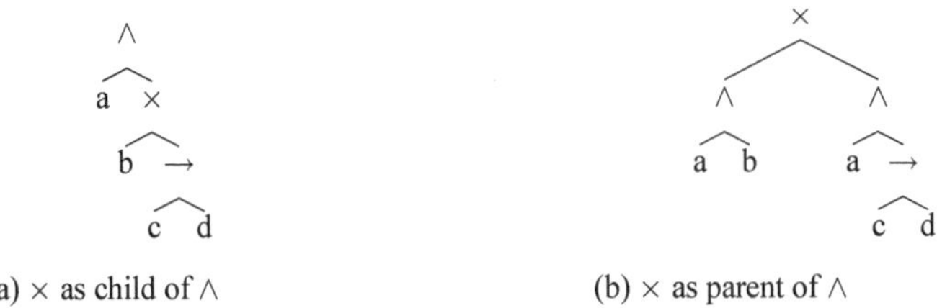

(a) $\times$ as child of $\wedge$ (b) $\times$ as parent of $\wedge$

Fig. 3.5 Transformation of process tree to remove $\times$ as siblings of $\wedge$.

choice between all possible combinations of the non-exclusive choice construct put in parallel. This is illustrated in Fig. 3.4.

As for the second limitation, we can always transform finite loop constructs (cf. Fig. 3.3) and non-exclusive choice constructs (cf. Fig. 3.4), such that we only have sequence, exclusive choice and parallelism constructs left. Subsequently, we can transform the tree by duplicating parts of the tree such that exclusive choice constructs only appear as parent and never as child of parallelism constructs. After this transformation, the number of visible activities in the parallel block children are always fixed. This transformation is illustrated in Fig. 3.5.

While these transformations allow for the sufficient application of the block functions to calculate the number of paths for any process tree, they can lead to an explosion of the tree. Therefore, a more efficient work-around to deal with these limitations which does not require explicit transformation of the process tree is possible, by using block dictionaries, as we will show in the next section.

3.3 Implementation

In this section, we conceptually show how the algorithm has been implemented. The implementation for process trees has been done in R and belongs to the process analytics tool-set `bupaR` which is further discussed in Part III. The implementation has been put available as an R-package on *github.com/gertjanssenswillen/ptR*.

In our implementation, we follow a slightly different approach than suggested above such that we do not need to transform the process tree. Instead of computing the number of unique paths for each block, we compute a *block dictionary* for each block such that the keys represent a specific path-length (i.e. the number of visible activities) and the values represent the number of unique paths of that specific length in the block. These block dictionaries are a way to provide a richer characterisation of the paths in a (sub)tree, and can make sure that varying numbers of activities in the parallel constructs pose no problems to apply the block function, as we will see further below. Formally, we define this block dictionary as

$$T = \{(z_i, x_i) | \forall (z_i, x_i), (z_j, x_j) : z_i = z_j \Rightarrow x_i = x_j\} \tag{3.9}$$

For example, a block with dictionary $T = \{(1, 3), (3, 2)\}$ contains a total of 5 paths: 3 paths of length 1 and 2 paths of length 3. To retrieve the number of unique paths in a process tree, one has to sum over all values of the block dictionary for the root block: $\sum_{i=1}^{u} x_i$. In this section, we combine these block dictionaries and the block functions described above to efficiently compute the number of execution paths. First, some additional notation is introduced.

3.3.1 Preliminaries

We define a function f_Z which returns the set of all existing path lengths in a specific block dictionary.

$$f_Z(T) = \{z \mid \exists (z, x) \in T\} \tag{3.10}$$

Furthermore, we define the function $f_X : T \times \mathbb{N} \rightarrow \mathbb{N}$, which determines how often a path of a certain length occurs in a block.

$$f_X(T, z) = \begin{cases} 0, & \text{if } z \notin f_Z(T) \\ x, & \text{else such that } (z, x) \in T \end{cases} \tag{3.11}$$

Finally, we define the operator $\biguplus$ to combine two block dictionaries T_i and T_j as follows:

$$T_i \biguplus T_j = \{(z, x) \mid z \in f_Z(T_i) \cup f_Z(T_j), x = f_X(T_i, z) + f_X(T_j, z)\} \tag{3.12}$$

Algorithm 3.1 NumberOfPaths

1: **Input:**
2: $PT = (N, r, m, c)$: A Process Tree
3: k: A maximum number of iterations for loops
4: **Output:**
5: T: a dictionary characterizing the paths in PT
6: **if** $r \in \mathscr{A}$ **then**
7: $T = (1, 1)$ ▷Tree contains one path of length one
8: **else if** $r = \tau$ **then**
9: $T = (0, 1)$ ▷Tree contains one empty path
10: **else**
11: $u = |c(r)|$
12: **for** each child c_i of PT **do**
13: $T_i = NumberOfPaths(c_i)$ ▷Call the function recursively on each of the subtrees
14: **end for**
15: **if** $r = sequence$ **then** ▷Use results and type to calculate end result
16: $T = Sequence(T_1, ..., T_u)$
17: **else if** $r = choice$ **then**
18: $T = Choice(T_1, ..., T_u)$
19: **else if** $r = parallel$ **then**
20: $T = Parallel(T_1, ..., T_u)$
21: **else if** $r = loop$ **then**
22: $T = Loop(T_1, ..., T_3, k)$
23: **else**
24: $T = Or(T_1, ..., T_u)$ ▷i.e. non-exclusive choice
25: **end if**
26: **end if**
27: **return** T

3.3.2 Algorithm

Algorithm 3.1 shows the main structure of the implementation, which implements the general idea of our approach by exploiting the block-structuredness of the model. We start with the block defined by the root-node and calculate its block dictionary based on the block-type and the block dictionaries of its children. If the root-block is a visible or silent activity, its block dictionary is respectively $\{(1, 1)\}$ or $\{(0, 1)\}$ (cf. line 6–9).

In all other cases, we first determine the block dictionaries of the child-blocks (line 10–14) by applying the algorithm recursively. Next, we apply the appropriate block function based on the block type (line 15–25). These block functions are an extension of the block functions described above, since they need to compute block dictionaries instead of scalar values representing the number of paths. In the next section, we will illustrate each extended block function by means of the process tree shown in Fig. 3.6. Note that, for the sake of clarity, this process tree is annotated, i.e. each node contains a subscript identifying the node number as well as its block dictionary.

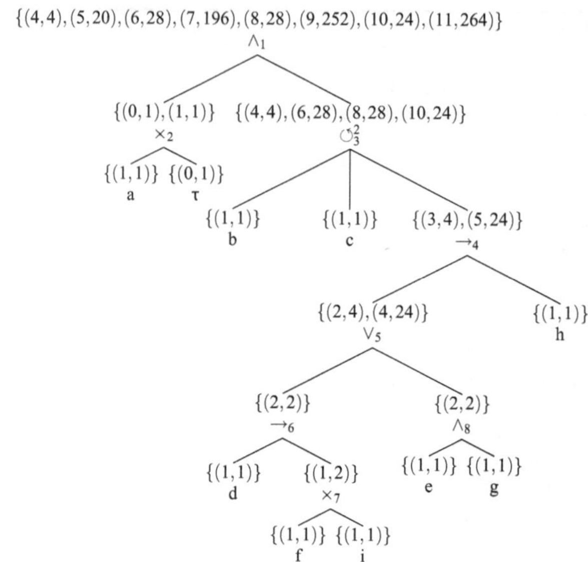

Fig. 3.6 Process tree annotated with block dictionaries.

3.3.3 Extended Block Functions

3.3.3.1 Sequence

In order to illustrate the implementation of the extended sequence block function (Algorithm 3.2), consider $\rightarrow_4$ in Fig. 3.6. This sequence block has two children, with the following dictionaries $\{(2, 4), (4, 24)\}$ and $\{(1, 1)\}$. As the sequence construct allows for all combinations between paths of different children, we have to combine every key-value pair from the first dictionary with every key-value pair from the second dictionary (line 8–9). For each combination we create a new key-value pair and add it to the parent's block dictionary (line 10–12). These new key-value pairs are constructed by adding together the number of visible activities, and multiplying the number of paths. Thus, $(2, 4)$ with $(1, 1)$ produces $(3, 4)$ and $(4, 24)$ with $(1, 1)$ results in $(5, 24)$. Note that line 10 corresponds to the general block function described in Eq. 3.2.

Note that while the block functions in Eq. 3.2 combines all u children at once, Algorithm 3.2 initially combines the first two children, and then combines that result incrementally with the next child-block, until all children have been considered. This algorithmic difference has been made for the sake of simplicity and is conceptually equivalent, as a sequence construct with u children can be rewritten as $u - 1$ nested sequence constructs.

Algorithm 3.2 Sequence

```
Input:
    {T_i | i = 1, ..., u}: u dictionaries representing paths in child-blocks of a sequence node
Output:
    T: a dictionary representing the paths in a sequence node
S = T_1
for T_i ∈ T_2, ..., T_u do
    R = {}
    for (z_r, x_r) ∈ S do
        for (z_i, x_i) ∈ T_i do
            x_0 = x_r · x_i
            z_0 = z_r + z_i
            R = R ⊎ {(z_0, x_0)}
        end for
    end for
    S = R
end for
return T = R
```

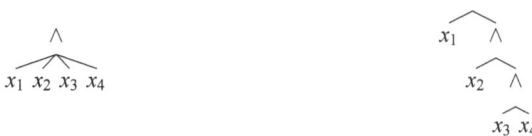

Fig. 3.7 Representing a parallel construct with more than two children as nested parallel constructs.

3.3.3.2 Parallelism

In order to illustrate the implementation of the extended parallelism block function (Algorithm 3.3), consider $\wedge_8$ in Fig. 3.6. This parallelism block has two children, with the following dictionaries $\{(1, 1)\}$ and $\{(1, 1)\}$. Since both dictionaries have only one key-value pair, we only have to combine those two key-value pairs (line 8–9). To compute the key-value pair for the parent's block dictionary we apply the formulas in line 10 and 11. Thus, $(1, 1)$ and $(1, 1)$ result in $(1 + 1, 1\binom{2}{1}1\binom{1}{1}) = (2, 2)$. Note that line 10 corresponds to the general block function described in Eq. 3.7.

The algorithm first considers the first two children of the parallel construct, iterates over all combinations key-value pairs of the children, and applies the block function to combine them. Subsequently, it combines the resulting key-value pairs with that of the next child, until all children have been considered.

Instead of considering all children at once, such as shown in Eq. 3.7, the block function is thus only used for two children at a time. This adjustment is only done for the sake of simplicity of the algorithm, as the outcome is equivalent. Indeed, a parallel construct with u children can be rewritten as nested series for $u - 1$ parallel constructs. This implicit conversion is shown in Fig. 3.7. It can be observed that both trees allow for the same behaviour, and thus have the same number of unique paths.

Algorithm 3.3 Parallel

Input:
    $\{T_i | i = 1, ..., u\}$: u dictionaries representing paths in children of a parallel node
Output:
    T: a dictionary representing the paths in a parallel node
$R = T_1$
for $T_i \in T_2, \ldots, T_u$ **do**
    $S = \{\}$
    for $(z_r, x_r) \in R$ **do**
        for $(z_i, x_i) \in T_i$ **do**
            $x_0 = x_r \cdot \binom{z_r + z_i}{z_r} \cdot x_i \cdot \binom{z_i}{z_i}$
            $z_0 = z_r + z_i$
            $S = S \uplus \{(z_0, x_0)\}$
        end for
    end for
    $R = S$
end for
return T = R

Algorithm 3.4 Choice

1: **Input:**
2:     $\{T_i \mid i = 1, ..., u\}$: u dictionaries representing paths in children of a choice node
3: **Output:**
4:     T: a dictionary representing the paths in a choice node
5: $R = T_1$
6: **for** $T_i \in T_2, \ldots, T_u$ **do**
7:     **for** $(z_i, x_i) \in T_i$ **do**
8:         $R = R \uplus \{(z_i, x_i)\}$
9:     **end for**
10: **end for**
11: **return** T = R

3.3.3.3 Exclusive Choice

To illustrate the implementation of the extended exclusive choice block function (Algorithm 3.4), consider $\times_7$ in Fig. 3.6. This exclusive choice block has two children, with the following dictionaries $\{(1, 1)\}$ and $\{(1, 1)\}$. According to the block function in Eq. 3.3, the amount of paths is the sum of the amount in each of the children. As a result, for the extended block function, this is equivalent to the $\uplus$ operator introduced above, and applied in line 8.

3.3.3.4 Finite Structured Loop

For the finite structured loop we fall back to the insight, illustrated in Fig. 3.3, that a finite structured loop can be transformed into an equivalent structure of sequence

Algorithm 3.5 Loop

```
1: Input:
2:     {T_1, T_2, T_3}: 3 dictionaries representing paths in the children of a loop node
3:     k: A maximum number of iterations for loops
4: Output:
5:     T: a dictionary representing the paths in a loop node
6: do = T_1
7: redo = T_2
8: exit = T_3
9: repeat = {(0, 1)}
10: XORset = repeat
11: for i in 1, ..., k do
12:     repeat = Sequence(repeat, redo, do)
13:     XORset = Choice(XORset, repeat)
14: end for
15: T = Sequence(do, XORset, exit)
16: return T
```

constructs and a exclusive choice construct. As a result, Algorithm 3.5 will refer to Algorithms 3.2 and 3.4 accordingly. As an illustration, we consider $\circlearrowleft_3^2$ in Fig. 3.6.

At lines 9–14 (Algorithm 3.5), we first determine the block dictionary of the exclusive choice in the transformation (cf. Fig. 3.3b), by incrementally creating a sequence of the redo and do children. At first, $XORset = \{(0, 1)\}$, which represents the invisible task. Next, a single repeat-block is added, which consists of a sequence of the redo and do parts. In our example, this results in $XORset = \{(0, 1), (2, 1)\}$. Since, the maximum iterations of the repeat-block is two, we add another block which repeats the repeat-block twice, resulting in $XORset = \{(0, 1), (2, 1), (4, 1)\}$. Finally, we calculate the block dictionary of the entire loop-block, by applying the sequence block function to the do-block, the XOR-block and the exit-block. First it combines the do and XOR-block, which results in $\{(1, 1), (3, 1), (5, 1)\}$. Next, it combines this with the exit block, which results in $\{(4, 4), (6, 28), (8, 28), (10, 24)\}$.

3.3.3.5 Non-exclusive Choice

For the extended non-exclusive choice block function, we exploit the insight that a non-exclusive choice construct can be rewritten as an exclusive choice of parallelism constructs, as illustrated in Fig. 3.4. This can be seen in the code in Algorithm 3.6 on lines 6–7.[3] Here, we iterate over all possible subsets of children, i.e. $\mathbb{P}(\{T_i\})$[4], except the empty set.[5] To illustrate, consider $\vee_5$, which has two children with block

[3]Note that when only a single of the children is executed—i.e. S only contains one path dictionary—then $R = Parallel(S) = S$ according to Algorithm 3.3.

[4]$\mathbb{P}(\{T_i\})$ refers to the set of all subsets of $\{T_1, ..., T_u\}$.

[5]At least one of the branches of a non-exclusive choice should be executed.

Algorithm 3.6 Or (non-exclusive choice)

Input:
  $\{T_i | i = 1, ..., u\}$: u dictionaries representing paths in children of an or node
Output:
  T: a dictionary representing the paths in a or node
$R = \emptyset$
for $S \in \mathbb{P}(\{T_i\}) \setminus \emptyset$ **do** ▷Iterate over all non-empty subsets of the branches
  $R = R \uplus Parallel(S)$ ▷Calculate the paths using the Parallel function
end for
return T = R

dictionaries $\{(2, 2)\}$ and $\{(2, 2)\}$. When executing this choice block, one can either execute only the first child, only the second child or both children. When executing only a single child, the resulting block dictionary will be that of the child. When executing both children in parallel, the block dictionary will be $\{(4, 2\binom{4}{2}2\binom{2}{2})\} = \{(4, 24)\}$. Next, the union is taken of the three block dictionaries, which results in the set $\{(2, 4), (4, 24)\}$.

3.3.4 Silent Transitions and Duplicate Tasks

One of the limitations of the suggested implemented approach is how it behaves in the presence of duplicate labels and silent transitions. For example, consider the trees in Fig. 3.8.

Tree PT_1 allows for a single observable activity sequence, i.e. $\langle a \rangle$, since the silent transition τ will not be observed. The algorithm will find that both sub trees can be executed in a single way (i.e. $x_1 = x_2 = 1$); the first will lead to a sequence of length 1 ($z_1 = 1$) and the second will lead to a sequence of length zero ($z_2 = 0$). Inputting these in the block function for parallel constructs, we find that the number of paths equals

$$\left[x_1 \binom{z_1 + z_2}{z_1}\right] \cdot \left[x_2 \binom{z_2}{z_2}\right] = \left[1 \binom{1}{1}\right] \cdot \left[1 \binom{0}{0}\right] = 1$$

Thus, the algorithm correctly calculates the number of distinct paths for PT_1.

Let's consider process tree PT_2 in Fig. 3.8. In this tree we can choose between the same sub trees (instead of executing them in parallel). As such, the algorithm will find that the number of paths equals

$$x_1 + x_2 = 1 + 1 = 2$$

Indeed, we can execute this tree in two different ways, leading to the sequence $\langle a \rangle$ or the empty sequence $\langle\rangle$.

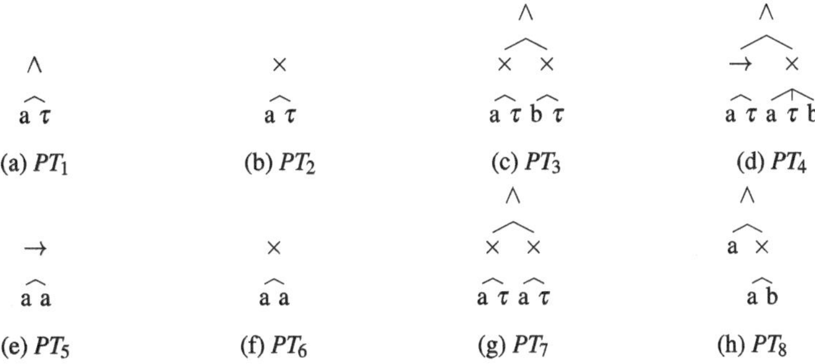

Fig. 3.8 Example process trees with duplicate tasks and/or silent transitions.

Process tree PT_3 constitutes a parallel construct with two choices as child. In the first child one can chose between activity a or skipping and in the second child one can chose between activity b or skipping. Thus, each child allows for 2 paths, one of length zero and one of length 1. I.e., we need to combine the dictionaries $\{(1, 1), (0, 1)\}$ and $\{(1, 1), (0, 1)\}$. Applying Algorithm 3.3, we then find the following path dictionary, next two which we have listed the actual observable traces.

$$\begin{aligned} \{(2, 2), \quad & \langle a, b\rangle, \langle b, a\rangle \\ (1, 2), \quad & \langle a\rangle, \langle b\rangle \\ (0, 1)\} \quad & \langle\rangle \end{aligned}$$

The algorithm thus correctly determines that there are 5 different paths.

In PT_4, a sequence of a and a silent transition is executed in parallel with a choice between a, b or a silent transition. The first child has one path of length one. The second child has two paths of length one, and one path of length zero. I.e., we need to combine the dictionaries $\{(1, 1)\}$ and $\{(1, 2), (0, 1)\}$. In accordance to Algorithm 3.3, we find the following path dictionary.

$$\begin{aligned} \{(2, 4), \quad & \langle a, a\rangle, \langle a, b\rangle, \langle a, b\rangle \quad \text{1 path overestimated} \\ (1, 1)\} \quad & \langle a\rangle \end{aligned}$$

Thus, in this case, the algorithm overestimates the number of distinct paths, as it distinguishes the order in which both a activities are executed, which leads to the same path.

Process tree PT_5 is a sequence of two activities. Obviously, the algorithm will return a single distinct path—which is correct, i.e. $\langle a, a\rangle$

The same cannot be said for PT_6. Here, the algorithm will determine that there are two paths of length one, while in reality there is only a single observable path, i.e. $\langle a\rangle$.

In process tree PT_7, process tree PT_2 is duplicated and combined by using a parallel construct. Given the calculations above, we know that each child in the parallel construct thus contains two paths, one of length one, and one of length zero.

Thus, following the path dictionary approach, we need to combine the dictionaries $\{(1, 1), (0, 1)\}$ and $\{(1, 1), (0, 1)\}$. Applying Algorithm 3.3, we then find the following path dictionary, next to which we have shown the observable paths of the tree.

$$\begin{array}{lrl} \{(2,2), & \langle a, a\rangle & \text{1 path overestimated} \\ (1,2), & \langle a\rangle & \text{1 path overestimated} \\ (0,1)\} & \langle\rangle & \end{array}$$

Strictly speaking, the parallel construct allows for 8 different executions[6], however some of them are equal. E.g., when for both choice constructs we chose a, the parallel construct can execute them in 2 orders, but this does not change the sequence we observe. Similarly, when for both choice constructs we chose τ, we can chose which τ comes first, but this does not actually make a difference for the output. The algorithm correctly recognises the last case, but cannot recognise that different orders of a and a are actually equivalent. In the intermediate case, where in one of the choice construct τ is selected and in the other a, the algorithm also distinguish two different sequences, while in reality there is no detectable difference. Thus, the algorithm finds 5 different paths, while in reality we would only observe 3 different sequences: $\langle a, a\rangle$, $\langle a\rangle$, $\langle\rangle$, and the tree can be executed in 8 different ways.

Finally, consider also PT_8. This is a parallel construct between a single activity block and a choice between two single activity blocks. Applying the block function, we get the following number of paths.

$$\left[x_1\binom{z_1+z_2}{z_1}\right]\cdot\left[x_2\binom{z_2}{z_2}\right]=\left[1\binom{2}{1}\right]\cdot\left[2\binom{1}{1}\right]=4$$

However, instead of four paths, only three can be observed: $\langle a, a\rangle$, $\langle a, b\rangle$ and $\langle b, a\rangle$. In other words, the algorithm distinguished both a activities while one cannot observe any difference.

As such, the number of distinct paths obtained by the algorithm is an upper bound to the actual number. However, it is still lower than or equal to the number of possible ways in which the tree can be executed, as it takes into account silent transitions to a certain extent. Only when tasks are duplicated, there is a chance that the actual number of distinct paths is lower than the obtained number.

The examples in Fig. 3.8 to some extent shows how problematic this limitation is. For instance, the algorithm has no problem with PT_2, which is a construct very likely to be observed in a process model—the skipping of an activity. It does has a problem with PT_6, but this is a construct which is less likely to be observed in a real case—there does not seem to exist a reason why we would like to create a choice

[6]For the sake of completeness, there would be 8 different paths in the tree if we could observe silent transitions and distinguish the duplicate tasks from each other. When we label the leaf nodes in PT_4 as a_1, τ_1, a_2 and τ_2, the tree can produce the following sequences: $\langle a_1a_2\rangle$, $\langle a_2a_1\rangle$, $\langle\tau_1\tau_2\rangle$, $\langle\tau_2\tau_1\rangle$, $\langle a_1\tau_2\rangle$, $\langle a_2\tau_1\rangle$, $\langle\tau_1a_2\rangle$, $\langle\tau_2a_1\rangle$.

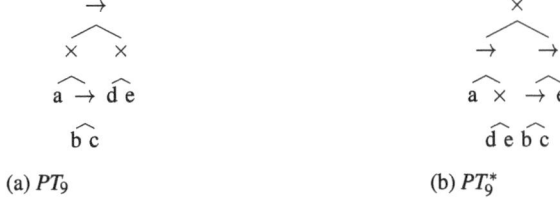

Fig. 3.9 Example long-term dependency.

between two equal elements. Also PT_7 is a construct which is not very likely to be seen in realistic processes.

Nevertheless, this limitation should be taken into account when using the algorithm. Given that the problems arise from the use of duplicates tasks, the issue is less present when using the algorithm on discovered process models, as they typically do not have duplicate tasks.

In subsequent chapters, the algorithm will however be used on simulated process trees, which can include duplicate tasks. Especially in the case that the tree has long-term dependencies. Using the approach in [91], long-term dependencies are included in process trees by duplicating the tree and creating a choice between different variants of the tree. For example, consider tree PT_9 in Fig. 3.9a. We can introduce a long-term dependency stating that activity d can only be executed if a was executed. This will be represented as shown in Fig. 3.9b. The left child of the root node displays the scenario that a is executed, and thus d or e can be chosen. The right child of the root node displays the scenario that a is not executed, and thus, only e can be chosen.

Thus, long-term dependencies are introduced in a tree T by duplicating that tree in T_1 and T_2 and applying the dependencies. Introducing these dependencies will thus inevitable introduce duplicate tasks. However, if the original tree did not contain duplicate tasks, the duplicate trees will represent disjoint sets of process behaviour—i.e. a single trace can only be observed after execution of one of the new T_i's, it can never result from multiple of the duplicate trees. This means that introducing long-term dependencies does not cause problems for the algorithm.

As an illustration, tree PT_9^* has $1 \times 2 + 1 \times 1 = 3$ paths according to the block functions. This is correct, as the observable paths are $\langle a, d\rangle$, $\langle a, e\rangle$ and $\langle b, c, e\rangle$. The duplicate activity e does not cause any problems at all, because it is the result of long-term dependency induction.

3.4 Performance

The performance of the algorithm was empirically investigated on a collection of 1000 process trees. The trees were generated using the framework described in [90]. Each of the five constructs was given an equal probability of occurrence, i.e. 20%. The occurrence of silent transitions was set at 10%. The number of visible activities

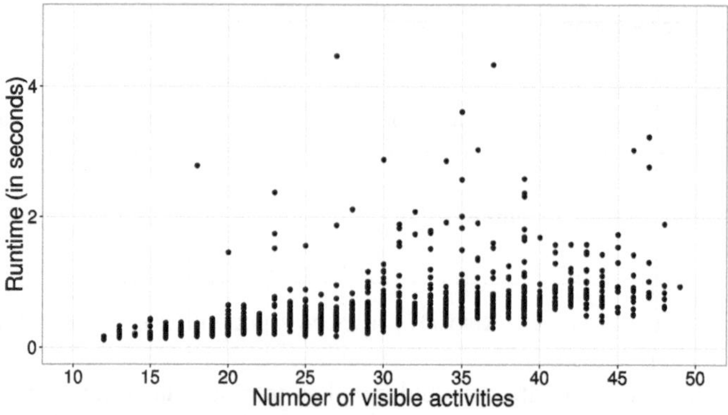

(a) Run-time in relation to the number of activities.

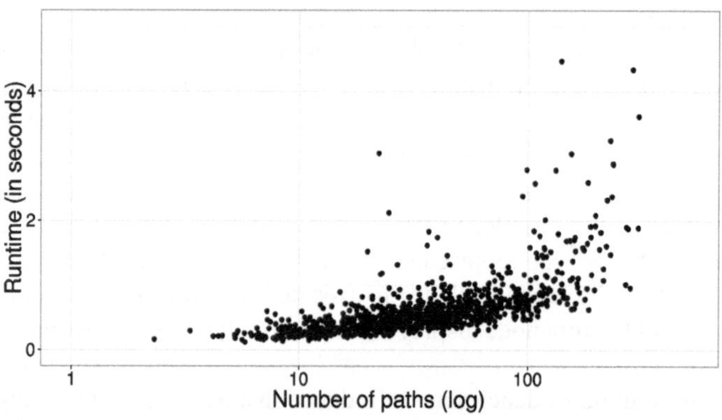

(b) Runtime in relation to number of paths

Fig. 3.10 Influence of the number of activities and number of paths on run-time.

in the trees follows a triangular distribution with minimum 10, maximum 50 and a mode of 30. All experiments were executed on a workstation with 2 processors (2.30 GHz; 4 virtual threads) and 8 GB of memory.

Figure 3.10 shows both the number of visible activities in the tree and the number of paths in relation to the run-time (in seconds). In Fig. 3.10a, it can be seen that there appears to be a linear relation between the number of visible activities and the run-time. However, the number of activities on itself is not a very precise proxy for the complexity of a tree, since the real impact stems from the operators and their relative positions in the tree. Therefore, the number of paths itself appears to be a more reliable estimate for the complexity of the tree. Figure 3.10b shows the relation between the number of paths (with logarithmic transformation), as a proxy for the complexity of the tree, and the run-time. Note that due to the logarithmic transformation, the relation is actually more linear than exponential.

Table 3.1 Log-log regression between number of paths and runtime.

	Dependent variable
	log(runtime)
log(numberOfTraces)	0.004***
	(0.0001)
Constant	−0.453***
	(0.008)
Observations	985
R^2	0.490
Adjusted R^2	0.489
Residual Std. Error	0.169 (df = 983)
F Statistic	943.526*** (df = 1; 983)

Note: *$p < 0.1$; **$p < 0.05$; ***$p < 0.01$

In order to quantify the relationship between complexity, as measured by the number of paths, and run-time of the algorithm, several linear regression models were fitted on the data. A linear-linear model, a linear-log model, and a log-log model was composed. These results showed that the log-log model fitted the data best. The result of this regression are shown in Table 3.1.

The interpretation of the regression is that when the complexity increases with one order of magnitude (i.e. an increase of 1000%), the run-time will increase with $10^{0.004}$, or 0.8%. Thus, although a positive relation exists, it can be stated that it is almost negligible.

3.5 Conclusion and Future Work

Estimating the number of execution paths in a process model is a non-trivial task. Approaches which enumerate all possible paths or traverse the state space of the model quickly become unfeasible, due to the explosion of possible paths in the presence of parallel constructs. This chapter introduced a new technique to calculate the number of execution paths for finite block-structured models. The technique has been implemented for process trees, but can easily be translated to other model notations.

Instead of enumerating all the paths, the technique constructs so-called block dictionaries for each block in the process model, which contain the number of paths per given length. The result of the algorithm is an annotated process tree, where each of the operator nodes has been allocated a block dictionary describing the number of execution paths it contains. The number of paths in the tree can then be obtained by summing over the block dictionary of the root node.

The evaluation of the performance of the algorithm showed that even for trees with more than 10^{500} different paths, the run-time does not exceed 5 s. Using linear regressions, only a negligible effect of the complexity of the model on the run-time was found.

The major limitation is that when the tree contains duplicate labels, the algorithm will only be an upper bound in certain cases. While no problem for most discovered process models—which typically do not contain duplicate transitions—this can be a problem when using the algorithm with hand-drawn or automatically generated process models.

One way to tackle this limitation is through an alternative approach, based on what was done in [115]. Starting from a petri net representation, we can calculate a reachability graph, which is an automaton of the process model. This can be done after unfolding the loops of the petri net in correspondence with the maximum number of iterations. The reachability graph can then be used to apply Johnson's algorithm [89] to find the elementary paths. The reasoning behind this approach is fundamentally different from the approach suggested in this chapter. Although it is not clear how it will compare in terms of performance, it will be better able to cope with duplicate tasks, and thus preferable in certain situations.

In the next chapters, the usefulness of this algorithm in experimental settings will be illustrated. The implementation will be further described as part of the `bupaR` suite [83] in Part III.

3.6 Further Reading

1. Janssenswillen, G., Depaire, B., Jouck, T.: Calculating the number of unique paths in a block-structured process model. In: Proceedings of the International Workshop on Algorithms & Theories for the Analysis of Event Data 2016, pp. 138–152 (2016)
2. Depaire, B.: Process Model Realism: Measuring Implicit Realism. In: Business Process Management Workshops, pp. 342–352. Springer (2014)
3. Johnson, D.B.: Finding all the elementary circuits of a directed graph. SIAM Journal on Computing **4**(1), 77–84 (1975)
4. Reißner, D., Conforti, R., Dumas, M., La Rosa, M., Armas-Cervantes, A.: Scalable conformance checking of business processes. In: OTM Confederated International Conferences" On the Move to Meaningful Internet Systems", pp. 607–627. Springer (2017)

Chapter 4
Comparative Study of Quality Measures

> The world we live in is vastly different from the world we think we live in.
>
> Nassim Nicholas Taleb

4.1 Introduction

In Chap. 2, an overview was presented of all implemented quality measures for fitness, precision and generalization. Although the existing measures have been used to compare the performance of process discovery algorithms [43], little research has been done concerning the evaluation and comparison of the measures itself. Until now, it is unclear what the differences are between measures within the same dimension: do they judge discovered process models in a similar way, or do they qualify models differently? Are some measures more optimistic or pessimistic than others? Furthermore, there is ongoing debate about the precise definition of certain dimensions, and the relationships between the dimensions.

In this chapter, we conduct an empirical study, incorporating the state-of-the-art quality metrics, with the aim to statistically analyse the relationships between measures within and among dimensions. The results of the experiments indicate:

- the feasibility of the measures, in terms of CPU-time and memory,
- whether measures measuring the same dimension agree with each other or not,
- whether the dimensions are related to each other, or independent from one another,
- to which extent some measures are more optimistic about process model quality compared to others,
- to which extent some measures are more sensitive to differences in process models quality compared to others.

The next section further introduces the problem which is investigated in this chapter. Section 4.3 discusses the experimental set up. The results of the experiment are reported in Sect. 4.4 and discussed in Sect. 4.5. Section 4.6 concludes the chapter.

G. Janssenswillen: Unearthing the Real Process Behind the Event Data, LNBIP 412
https://doi.org/10.1007/978-3-030-70733-0_4

4.2 Problem Statement

Literature on evaluating and comparing quality measures is limited, although some works should be noticed. In [118], metrics were compared on a very small scale. However, as this is one of the earliest works on process model quality, most of those measures have become obsolete. The measures based on negative events were incorporated in a comparison in [42], but also here only a small set of example models was used. Nevertheless the authors concluded that not all measures are one-dimensional and some suffer from computational inefficiency.

Experiments on a much larger scale were done in [43], although the objective of this research was to compare the performance of discovery algorithms. Therefore, no conclusions on the relationship between measures within and among dimensions were drawn. Finally, in [24], measures were compared within dimensions. Here, the hypothesis that the average of different measures within each dimension were equal was rejected. Nonetheless, no further analyses on their relationship were done.

Compared with the existing literature, the contribution of this chapter is that the state-of-the-art quality metrics are evaluated on a large set of event logs and models. The focus is not to compare discovery algorithms, but rather to compare the measurements of the quality metric itself. The gained insights can then be used to make an informed decision on which quality measures to use for the evaluation of discovered process models.

In particular, measures will be evaluated on three different aspects: feasibility, validity and sensitivity.

- **Feasibility** looks at the extent to which measures can be calculated within a certain time and memory limit. Chapter 2 already briefly mentioned some feasibility issues measures have, e.g. because of state-place explosion. However, calculating a quality measure within a reasonable amount of time with a reasonable set of computational resources is necessary in order to evolve towards mature quality tools.
- **Validity** looks at whether measures of the same dimension are actually measuring the same thing, i.e. whether they agree on the quality of a certain model along a certain dimension. Furthermore, we will also pay attention to orthogonality of dimensions, checking whether dimensions are independent from each other or not.
- **Sensitivity** concerns the more subtle differences between measures of the same dimension. We will highlight whether specific measures are more or less sensitive towards changes in model quality and which measures are rather optimistic or pessimistic, considering all measures of the same dimension.

In the next section, we will proceed with laying out the methodology for the experiment.

Table 4.1 Experimental setup.

Step	Characteristic	Value
1	Number of systems	15
3	Completeness levels	100%, 75%, 50%, 25%
	Noise levels	0%, 5%, 10%, 15%
	Number of logs	1200 logs
4	Discovery algorithms	Heuristics [138]
		Inductive [97]
		ILP [139]
		Alpha Miner [10]
		Flower Miner
	Number of models	6000 models
5	Fitness	Token-Based Fitness [117]
		Behavioural Recall [60]
		Alignment-Based Fitness [6]
	Precision	Alignment-Based Precision [6]
		Behavioural Precision [22]
		One Align Precision [12]
		Best Align Precision [12]
	Generalization	Alignment Based Generalization [6]
		Behavioural Generalization [22]

4.3 Methodology

The methodology used in this paper is based on the framework for comparing process mining algorithms presented in [135]. In particular, the experiment encompasses the steps listed below. Each of these will be discussed in more detail in the remainder of this section. The summary of the experiment can be found in Table 4.1 and a schematic overview is given in Fig. 4.1.

1. Generate systems
2. Calculate number of paths
3. Simulate logs
4. Discover models
5. Measure quality
6. Statistical analysis

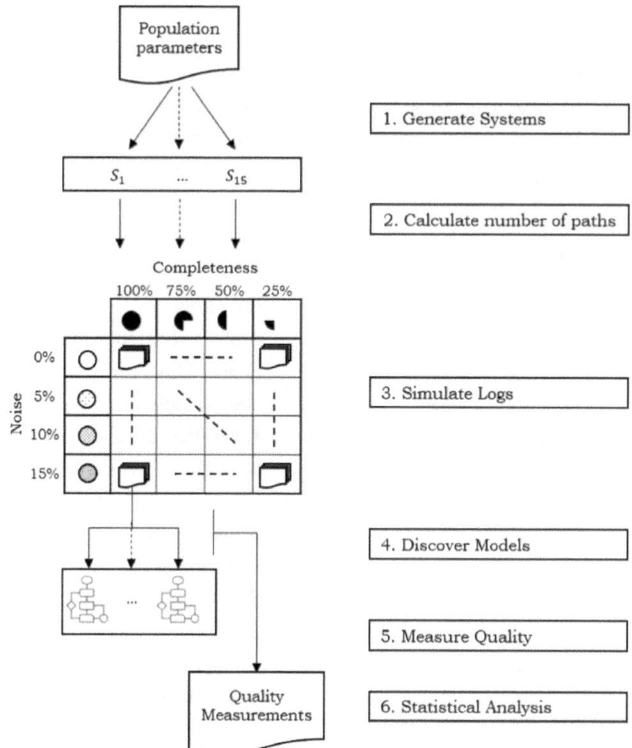

Fig. 4.1 Schematic overview of experimental setup.

4.3.1 Generate Systems

As a first step, systems are generated to act as ground truth process models. The systems were generated in the form of process trees using the methodology described in [90]. As input for this generation, different population parameters had to be set, such as the distribution for the number of leaf nodes, the distribution for the type of operator nodes and the probability for silent and duplicate tasks. Table 4.2 shows the used population parameters for each of the 15 systems. Figure 4.2 gives a graphical overview of the parameters.

The first three parameters define a triangular distribution from which the number of visible activities is randomly drawn. The next five parameters - $\Pi^{\rightarrow}$, $\Pi^{\wedge}$, $\Pi^{\times}$, $\Pi^{\circlearrowleft}$ and $\Pi^{\vee}$ - define a probability distribution over the different types of process tree operators: sequence, parallel, exclusive choice, loops, and non-exclusive choice, respectively. The probability that a silent (invisible) activity is included in an exclusive choice, loop, or choice construct is given by Π^{τ}, the probability that an activity is duplicated is defined by Π^{Re}, and Π^{Lt} gives the probability that a long-term dependency is included between two decision points.

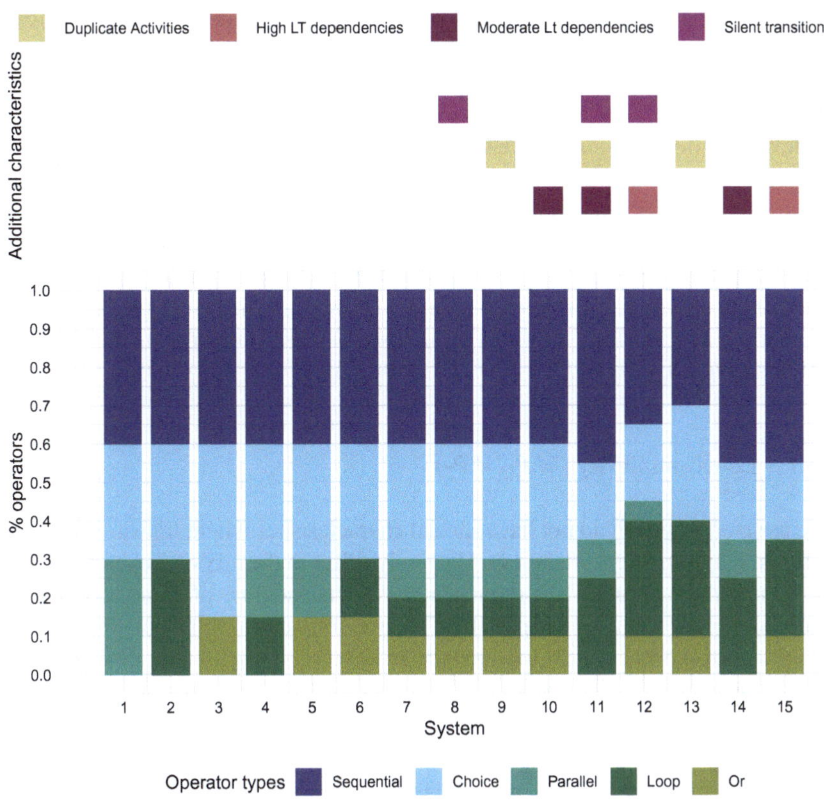

Fig. 4.2 Graphical overview of population parameters (Table 4.2).

Table 4.2 Population parameters.

Parameters	Population														
	MP_1	MP_2	MP_3	MP_4	MP_5	MP_6	MP_7	MP_8	MP_9	MP_{10}	MP_{11}	MP_{12}	MP_{13}	MP_{14}	MP_{15}
Minimum of visible activities	10	10	10	10	10	10	10	10	10	10	15	15	15	15	15
Mode of visible activities	15	15	15	15	15	15	15	15	15	15	20	20	20	20	20
Maximum of visible activities	20	20	20	20	20	20	20	20	20	20	25	25	25	25	25
Sequence ($\Pi^{\rightarrow}$)	0.40	0.40	0.40	0.40	0.40	0.40	0.40	0.40	0.40	0.40	0.45	0.35	0.30	0.45	0.45
Parallel ($\Pi^{\wedge}$)	0.30	0.00	0.00	0.15	0.15	0.00	0.10	0.10	0.10	0.10	0.10	0.05	0.00	0.10	0.00
Choice ($\Pi^{\times}$)	0.30	0.30	0.45	0.30	0.30	0.30	0.30	0.30	0.30	0.30	0.20	0.20	0.30	0.20	0.20
Loops ($\Pi^{\circlearrowleft}$)	0.00	0.30	0.00	0.15	0.00	0.15	0.10	0.10	0.10	0.10	0.25	0.30	0.30	0.25	0.25
Or ($\Pi^{\vee}$)	0.00	0.00	0.15	0.00	0.15	0.15	0.10	0.10	0.10	0.10	0.00	0.10	0.10	0.00	0.10
Silent activities (Π^{τ})	0.00	0.00	0.00	0.00	0.00	0.00	0.00	0.10	0.00	0.00	0.10	0.10	0.00	0.00	0.00
Reoccurring activities (Π^{Re})	0.00	0.00	0.00	0.00	0.00	0.00	0.00	0.00	0.10	0.00	0.10	0.00	0.10	0.00	0.10
Long-term dependencies (Π^{Lt})	0.00	0.00	0.00	0.00	0.00	0.00	0.00	0.00	0.00	0.50	0.50	1.00	0.00	0.50	1.00

In terms of parameters, three groups of systems can be observed in Fig. 4.2: systems of low complexity (MP_1-MP_7), moderate complexity (MP_8-MP_{10}) and high complexity (MP_{11}-MP_{15}). This is inspired by the findings in [43], where it was found that process discovery algorithms perform differently when the process behaviour is complex (real life event logs) instead of more elementary process behaviour (artificial event logs). As such, the obtained values for the quality measures will be more widespread over the range from zero to one.

The probabilities for sequence, parallel and choice constructs are loosely based on the work in [96]. In this work, the occurrence of sequence, exclusive choice and parallelism in a large set of real-life models is analysed, which (when normalised to 100%), are on average 46%, 35% and 19%. Based on this starting point, the following variations have been made.

4.3.1.1 Low Complexity (MP_1-MP_7)

These are models which do not have special characteristics (silent transitions, duplicate tasks, long-term dependencies). They only differ in the mix of 5 operator types. As a default, most have 40% of sequence constructs and 30% of choice constructs. The remaining 30% is used for parallel, OR, and loop constructs. Note that in case only OR constructs occur next to sequence and choice, the setting targets only 15% OR constructs, because 30% would lead to very complex models. This is balanced by allowing for more choice construcs. Apart from that, there are 7 different configurations: all remaining constructs apart from sequence and choice are of one type (1-3), a combination of 2 types (4-6) or a combination of all three types (7).

4.3.1.2 Moderate Complexity (MP_8-MP_{10})

These are variations of MP_7, with additionally added silent transitions, duplicate transitions, or a moderate amount of long-term dependencies.

4.3.1.3 High Complexity (MP_{11}-MP_{15})

These are models which have either more than one additional characteristic, and/or a very high probability of a more complex operator (especially loops).

4.3.1.4 A Discussion on Complexity

We have defined complexity here mainly in terms of the mix of constructs which are used in the systems and the occurrence of special phenomena, such as duplicate labels. The reason behind these different complexities is to have a diversified set of models, both simple and more complex models. The goal is not to compare the valid-

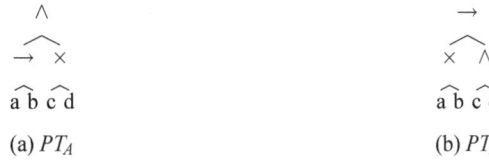

Fig. 4.3 Parameter settings as indicator of complexity.

ity and sensitivity of quality measures in relation with complexity. While interesting, the challenge in the latter case would be how to exactly define or quantify complexity. While the configuration of the systems is in accordance with intuitive expectations of quality (e.g. we expect models with more loops to be more complex that models with less loops), there are many factors which influence the actual complexity of the eventual models, many of which depend on the random results of the generation software used. For example, consider the two trees in Fig. 4.3. They have the same number of activities, the same distribution of operator types, and no additional complexities. So, do they have the same complexity? According to our definition above they do—they could very well be generated using the same parameter settings. But tree A has thrice as many paths compared to tree B, and might thus be genuinely considered to be more complex.

Complexity as discussed here is related to the simplicity of a process model, as introduced in Chap. 2—although strictly speaking we are not in a process discovery context here. As such, even though it is not trivial to target the complexity of the systems before generation, we can nonetheless use measures of simplicity, such as those described in [107], to quantify the complexity of the eventually generated system.

The systems have been included in Appendix A. The following descriptive characteristics are shown in Table 4.3.

- The number of leaf nodes ($|N_L|$)
- The number of operator nodes ($|N_O|$)
- The number of sequence nodes ($n_\rightarrow$)
- The number of parallel nodes ($n_\wedge$)
- The number of exclusive choice nodes ($n_\times$)
- The number of loop nodes ($n_\circlearrowleft$)
- The number of non-exclusive choice nodes ($n_\vee$)
- The number of silent transitions (n_τ)
- The number of recurring transitions (n_{Re})
- The number of unique labels (n_A)
- The number of distinct paths (n_P)

Table 4.3 System characteristics. All systems can be found in Appendix A.

MP	$\lvert N_L \rvert$	$\lvert N_O \rvert$	$n_{\rightarrow}$	$n_{\wedge}$	$n_{\times}$	$n_{\circlearrowleft}$	$n_{\vee}$	n_{τ}	n_{Re}	n_A	n_P
1	11	8	2	4	2	0	0	0	0	11	178
2	18	14	5	0	7	2	0	0	0	18	295
3	15	9	4	0	4	0	1	0	0	15	234
4	15	10	4	0	3	3	0	0	0	15	518
5	18	12	4	2	4	0	2	0	0	18	1344
6	18	12	4	0	5	2	1	0	0	18	924
7	14	10	3	2	3	1	1	0	0	14	2188
8	19	10	3	1	4	2	0	1	0	18	120
9	11	7	4	1	1	0	1	0	4	7	252
10	21	16	6	0	7	3	0	0	7	14	224
11	25	19	9	3	5	2	0	4	7	14	680
12	33	14	7	0	3	4	0	4	14	15	507
13	14	8	2	0	2	2	2	0	4	10	780
14	24	14	6	2	1	5	0	0	9	15	688
15	22	11	2	0	2	5	2	0	8	14	740

4.3.2 *Calculate the Number of Paths*

In order to further increase the variability in the event data, and thereby bringing about the discovery of a large set of different models, logs with a different level of completeness and noise are generated in the next step. In order to be able to target the completeness of event logs, the number of execution paths in each of the systems needs to be calculated first. The algorithm introduced in Chap. 3 was used for this end. The number of paths (n_P) for each system are shown in Table 4.3.

It can be observed that on average, the *high complexity* systems have more paths than the *moderate complexity* systems, while the latter do not necessarily have more paths than those systems labelled of *low complexity*. Of course, the complexity of a model is not equal to the number of paths. Indeed, the occurrence of silent transitions, long-term dependencies and duplicate tasks makes models more complex, but this does not necessarily mean that they can replay more behaviour.

4.3.3 *Simulate Logs*

For each of the systems, event logs with a certain level of completeness and noise have been simulated using the simulation framework in [91]. For completeness, 4 levels were considered: 100%, 75%, 50%, and 25%. These percentages measure how many of the different paths in the system, as calculated in the previous step, have been observed in the event log. Thus, for a model with 100 unique paths, a log with 75% completeness is one where 75 of the unique paths in the system have been seen.

Differing levels of completeness have been defined for two reasons. Firstly, to increase the variety in the logs and subsequently the discovered models. Secondly, in order to relate completeness to possible biases in the measures used in a later phase (see Chap. 5). Especially with respect to the second goal, defining these levels in a realistic way is important. However, it is not trivial to define what a realistic level of completeness is. In a real setting, the completeness of event data in mainly influenced by two factors. Firstly, the diversity of the process—how structured or unstructured is the process? Secondly, the *velocity* of the process—what is the frequency with which new cases *arrive*? The more unstructured the process, the less likely it is that event logs will have a high completion. Furthermore, the slower the arrival rate of new instances, the less likely it is that event logs will have a high completion.

In the current context, velocity is not relevant. Since the generation of logs is artificial, the effect of arrival rate is de facto neutralised. The level of structuredness differs from system to system, as can be seen in Table 4.3. As such, a log of x% completeness will be more or less realistic given the specific system. However, using different completeness levels for each system will only increase the complexity of subsequent analysis. Instead, it was decided to use a single set of thresholds for all systems.

In [144], several estimates for log completeness are compared. When applying these estimates on a range of real-life event logs, it is found that the completeness is expected to be less than 50%. As such levels of 25%, 50% and 75% can be regarded as *pessimistic, realistic* and *optimistic* completeness thresholds. The 100% level was added in the light of the follow-up experiment in Chap. 5, where we also want to see what happens in the case where completeness is not an issue.

Analogously, 4 different noise levels were considered: 0%, 5%, 10%, 15%. A log with 15% of noise means that 15% of the cases contain noise. The types of noise that where induced are described in [90]. The noise introduced is defined as follows.

Definition 4.1. Given a trace $\sigma = \langle a_1, a_2, \ldots, a_n \rangle$, the following types of noise are defined:

1. Missing head: remove all activities a_i with $i \in [1, \frac{n}{3}]$.
2. Missing body: remove all activities a_i with $i \in [\frac{n}{3} + 1, \frac{2n}{3}]$.
3. Missing tail: remove all activities a_i with $i \in [\frac{2n}{3} + 1, n]$.
4. Swap tasks: interchange two random activities a_i and a_j with $i \neq j$.
5. Remove task: remove random activity a_i.

This definition of noise is based on existing literature [103], and as adopted by the simulation framework [91]. While a discussion on a realistic definition of noise is out of the scope for this manuscript, we do encourage future experiments to reason more elaborately on this point and construct a better, agreed-upon definition of noise. From the viewpoint that noise refers to measurement errors or data inconsistencies, it is important that the definition of noise reflects these phenomena. According to this reasoning, swapping two random tasks (4) is not really a realistic type of noise, unless they are perhaps consecutive tasks.

Moreover, there are other possible types of noise, such as insertion of additional activities, which are not currently included in the used log simulation framework. We will return to this issue in Chap. 6, as the experimental setup is essential for future advancements in the fields.

The induction of noise is done by

1. taking a sample of the original event log,
2. adding noise to each of the sequences in the sample, according to the definition above, and
3. joining the noisy sample together with the original data.

For a target level of 15% noise in the final log, a sample of $x\%$ of the original event log is needed, such that $\frac{x}{100+x} = 15\%$. For 15%, this means that x = 17.6%. This mechanism is used to avoid that the specified completeness goes down because traces are perturbed. By combining the perturbed cases together with the original log, all the sequences in the original log are still part of the final log.

Notwithstanding this mechanism, completeness can *increase* in cases where the perturbed sequences are real sequences which were not observed in the log before. This is because the noise as defined above does not check whether the resulting sequence is actually not present in the system.[1]

As a result, both the completeness and noise level should be regarded as a *conservative* upper bound: completeness can be higher than the stated threshold, while noise can be lower than the stated threshold.

For each of the systems (15) and each of the noise (4) and completeness (4) levels, 5 different logs were generated. This amounts to a total of $15 \cdot 4 \cdot 4 \cdot 5 = 1200$ logs. Descriptive characteristics of the simulated logs are shown in Table 4.4 and Table 4.5. These statistics are based on the Structural Log Metrics in [64] and are defined as follows.[2]

[1] While not possible at the time the experiments were conducted, advancements in methodology do allow to check this [19].

[2] Note that three of the metrics defined in [64] are omitted. Firstly, the Time Granularity (G) is not relevant given the fact that all timestamps are artificially generated. Secondly, the Balance (B) is not computed as it requires an *event importance* defined by a domain expert, which is not applicable in our case. Thirdly, Affinity (A) was not included as a metric because of computational difficulties given the scale of the experiments. Affinity requires to compare the directly follows relationships between all the cases, and then compute the overlap between each pair. The Affinity is then the mean overlap over all cases in the log. Even after simplifying the computations (i.e. only compute them once for each pair of unique variants and then multiplying with the frequency of that pair, and considering all event logs of the same system at once – thereby avoiding to compute the overlap for the same trace pairs multiple times – this computation is very hard given the number of logs, their size, and – especially – the amount of paths which are possible. I.e. based on Table 4.3, a complete log for system 7 would require 2188 * (2187)/2 = 2 392 578 comparisons of traces. Even with the most efficient strategy, we would need to make 19 236 598 comparisons or traces, for all systems combined.

Table 4.4 The average Magnitude, Support, Variety, Level of Detail and Structure for logs by system.

System	Ma	SP	V	LoD	ST
1	9465.41	2652.20	11.00	3.59	0.46
2	8137.91	1566.12	18.00	4.17	0.87
3	15279.14	3864.39	15.00	3.96	0.77
4	18173.64	2716.62	15.00	3.44	0.83
5	106131.40	13561.91	18.00	7.83	0.74
6	25383.60	2292.68	18.00	8.88	0.74
7	83124.96	17642.46	14.00	3.44	0.81
8	2319.61	169.94	18.00	10.98	0.91
9	17184.05	2453.11	7.00	5.71	0.39
10	4399.26	597.75	14.00	5.36	0.82
11	18759.44	1723.45	14.00	7.84	0.48
12	17658.95	910.15	15.00	10.72	0.50
13	8338.94	1021.10	10.00	5.38	0.40
14	17536.75	1066.55	15.00	9.91	0.51
15	21814.36	2490.50	14.00	5.16	0.59

Table 4.5 Summary statistics of Magnitude, Support, Variety, Level of Detail and Structure.

Metric	Min	Q1	Median	Mean	Q3	Max	St.Dev
Magnitude	247.00	3998.50	10704.50	24913.83	26854.75	530203.00	52985.15
Support	31.00	382.50	1133.00	3648.60	3015.00	69190.00	7881.90
Variety	7.00	14.00	15.00	14.40	18.00	18.00	3.05
Level of Detail	3.02	4.01	5.64	6.42	8.70	11.98	2.65
Structure	0.08	0.44	0.75	0.65	0.83	0.93	0.23

- Magnitude (Ma): the number of events
- Support (SP): the number of cases[3]
- Variety (V): the number of activities
- Level of Detail (LoD): the mean variety of all cases (V/SP)
- Structure (ST): the inverse relative amount of directly-follows relations in the log, compared to the maximal number of directly-follows relations possible (V^2)

Table 4.5 shows that there is a wide variety of logs according to these metrics. The Magnitude—the number of events—varies between very small logs (247 events) and very large logs (5mio events). Likewise, the number of process instances varies between only 31 and circa 70 000. Note that in sharp contrast with these extreme

[3]The support $SP(L)$ defined in [64] is different from the *supp* L defined in Chap. 2. The support SP is actually the size $|L|$ of an event log, while *supp* L is the set of unique traces.

minimum and maximum numbers, the boundaries of the interquartile range are much more moderate. 50% of the logs contain between 4000 and 27 000 events according to Magnitude, and between 382 and 3000 cases according to Support.

The Variety refers to the number of distinct activities. These are of course in close correspondence with the characteristics of the systems in Table 4.3. The level of detail on the other had refers to the average number of distinct activities per case, which is much lower in comparison.

Finally, the Structure is a ratio in terms of directly-follows relations, where a value close to one indicates that there are very few distinct directly-follows relations in the log compared to the maximum possible of relations. A value close to zero means that almost all possible directly-follows relations did occur. Given the minimum value of 0.08 and the maximum of 0.93 it can be said that there are logs from both ends of the extreme in the experiment.

In Fig. 4.4, a graphical representation of the distribution of Magnitude, Support, Level of Detail and Structure is provided. This shows the very strong right skewness of the distributions for both Magnitude and Support, indicating that the very large log files are rather the exception. However, it can hardly be said that the majority of log files is small. The distribution of Structure shows that the range from 0 to 1 is well covered, with a higher concentration near one (very structured logs) and another large number of logs centred around 50%.

Note that for all systems, it was possible to generate an event log which is 100% complete, i.e. they have as many traces as the process tree used has distinct paths according to the approach described in the previous chapter. As such, the limitations which regards to duplicate activities can be nuanced. Indeed, this proves that, for the 15 trees used, there was no overestimation of the number of distinct paths due to the occurrence of duplicates tasks. If the latter was the case, it would not be possible to generate a 100% complete log. This corroborates the assumption that this problem is mainly due to very coincidental constructions of process trees, and that the inducement of long-term dependencies cause no problems herein.

4.3.4 Discover Models

Subsequently, the simulated logs were used for the discovery of process models. For each log, five different process discovery algorithms were applied: the Alpha Miner [10], the Heuristics Miner [138], the Inductive Miner [97], the ILP miner [139] and the Flower Miner. Note that the goal of the experiment is not to evaluate the performance of these miners. However, a variety of mining algorithms has been selected in order to avoid algorithm-specific biases. The main goal of the process discovery step is thus to provide a large variety of models for which the quality can be measured by different measures. Each of the algorithms returned a Petri Net, of which the quality is measured in the next step. ProM 6.5 was used for the discovery of the process models. Default values were used for all parameters. In total, $1200 \text{ logs} \cdot 5 \text{ algorithms} = 6000$ models were discovered.

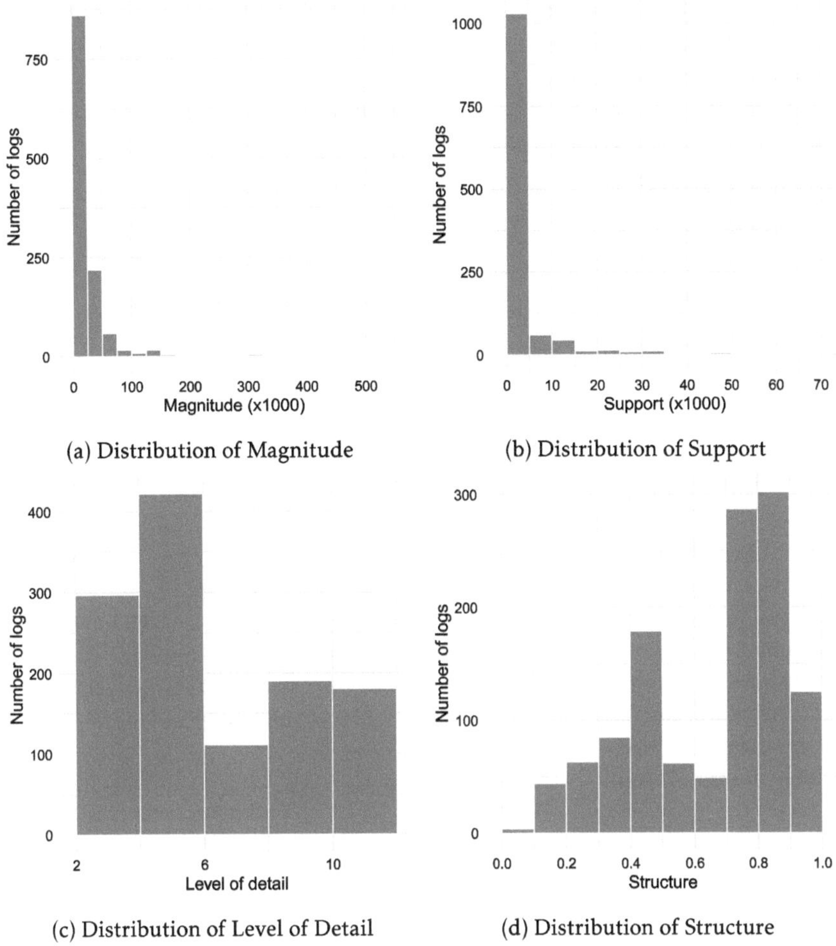

(a) Distribution of Magnitude

(b) Distribution of Support

(c) Distribution of Level of Detail

(d) Distribution of Structure

Fig. 4.4 Visual representation of log statistics.

4.3.5 Measure Quality

The measures used for quality measurement in this experiment are those indicated in Table 4.1. The measures were selected first and foremost based on their expected type of model input, as all discovery algorithms used return a Petri Net. Furthermore, the initial coarse-grained measures such as Proper Completion and (Advanced) Behavioural Appropriateness are not included. While Behavioural Precision was included, Behavioural Specificity was not considered, as it is defined slightly different compared to other precision measures, as stated in [23]. Since the discovery algorithms used do not guarantee a perfect fitness, also ETC-precision is not taken into account, while the alignment-based versions Best Align Precision and One Align

Precision are. Finally, in relation to the large scale of the experiments, only measures supported by the Comprehensive Benchmarking Framework CoBeFra [23] were selected for technical reasons.

Each of the metrics was calculated for each model against the event log it was discovered from. The resulting values will be the input for the experimental analysis. All calculations were performed using the benchmarking framework CoBeFra [23], each time using the default values for parameters.[4] In total, 6000 models $\cdot$ 9 metrics = 54000 metrics were computed.

4.3.6 *Statistical Analysis*

The obtained values are thereafter statistically analysed. In particular, the measures will be investigated on three desirable properties: feasibility, validity and sensitivity.

4.3.6.1 Feasibility

One should be able to assess the quality of a model within a reasonable amount of time and without excessive memory requirements. In order to test this, the calculations are performed with a limited, though not unreasonable amount of resources. In particular, a maximum working memory of 1 Gb is used and computations are not allowed to last more than one hour.

It should be remarked that the feasibility analysis reflects the implementation of the measures in CoBeFra v2015, which was the state-of-the-art at the moment the experiments were executed. Improvements in the implementations, particularly for alignment-based measures have been made since then. Furthermore, feasibility of the measures also relates to the parameters used. Both points will be revisited in subsequent discussions of the results.

4.3.6.2 Validity

The validity of the measures will be assessed, i.e. whether they measure what they are supposed to measure. In order to do this, the relationships between measures within and among dimensions will be analysed by means of a correlation analysis and a factor analysis.

The analysis of correlations will reveal whether measures within a specific dimension are positively correlated with each other or not. Furthermore, by examining the correlations across different dimensions, the relations between the dimensions will become clear.

---

[4]The version from 2015 of CoBeFra was used.

Secondly, an Exploratory Factor Analysis (EFA) [65] will be conducted. Since the set of dimensions is not unanimously accepted in literature, an Exploratory Factor Analysis (EFA) is chosen instead of a Confirmatory Factor Analysis. This will allow non a priori specified factors to be found. In order to decide on the number of factors to construct, a scree plot will be composed to find the number of factors that explain the most variability in the data. In order to make the factors more interpretable, a rotation will be applied. A Promax rotation is chosen [37]. This is an oblique, non-orthogonal rotation, which assumes that factors are possibly correlated. Since it is not clear whether dimensions (or their implementations) are orthogonal or not, an oblique rotation is the safest option.

4.3.6.3 Sensitivity

Finally, the sensitivity of the measures will be investigated. Both the analysis of factors and correlations implicitly assume that the relations between different measures are the same for the complete range of values. Nonetheless, it is not impossible that measures agree on the precision of very precise models, while they judge the precision of less precise models differently. By comparing all measures pairwise, it will become clear whether some measures are more pessimistic than others. Furthermore, it will clarify whether certain measures observe differences between models where others do not, and thus are more sensitive.

For each pair of measures X and Y within a dimension, the relationship will be analysed by drawing a scatter plot and fitting a Lowess smoothing line onto it [33]. This smoothing line can then be compared to the diagonal. Some hypothetical Lowess curves are shown in Fig. 4.5. When the smoothing line approximates the diagonal, as in Fig. 4.5a, the two measures at hand score models equally. However, when the smoothing line falls below the diagonal as in Fig. 4.5b, measure Y is more pessimistic. When it sits above the diagonal, measure Y is more optimistic. Moreover, when the *slope* of the Lowess curve significantly differs from the diagonal, it can be said that there is a difference in sensitivity. I.e. when the Lowess curves forms a horizontal plateau or vertical wall, it can be said that measure Y or X, respectively, becomes insensitive to differences in quality compared to the other measure. In Fig. 4.5c, measure Y is insensitive compared to the metric on the x-axis is the lower range of possible values.

Optimism, pessimism, and insensitivity will be analysed using two metrics, in addition to the visual analysis. Firstly, the *level of optimism (pessimism)*, and secondly the *stability of optimism (pessimism)*, which is a proxy for insensitivity.

The level of optimism of measure Y compared to measure X, is defined as the average value of $Y - X$. The average difference of $Y - X$ is the expected amount of optimism (pessimism). For Fig. 4.5a, this average will be close to zero. For Fig. 4.5b it will be negative, indicating that measure Y is pessimistic compared to measure X. For Fig. 4.5c, a positive level of optimism will be found.

The stability of the optimism is defined as the correlation of the Y - X with the value for measure X. E.g., it shows whether the distance between Y and X (i.e. the

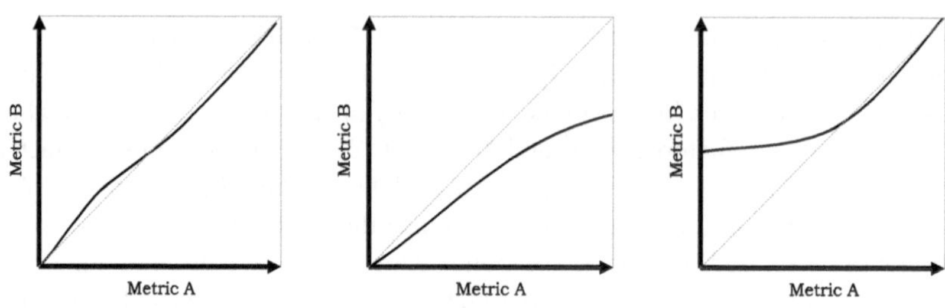

(a) Metrics behave similar. (b) Metric A is more pessimistic than B. (c) Metric B is insensitive in the lower range.

Fig. 4.5 Hypothetical Lowess curves.

amount of optimism) correlates to the level of X. If the obtained correlation is close to zero, it means that the amount of optimism is stable. If close to 1, it means that measure Y will get more optimistic compared to X as X increases. If close to -1, it means that measure Y will get less optimistic (or more pessimistic) compared to X as X increases—which is the case in both Fig. 4.5b and 4.5c. This instability is a proxy for insensitivity.

4.4 Results

4.4.1 Feasibility

During the computation of the measures, it turned out that some of the computations could not be completed because of excessive requirements in memory or CPU time. For each computation 1 Gb of working memory was available and computations were aborted after 1 h. In total, for 11.69% of the log-model-metric combinations we were unable to obtain a quality measure. Figure 4.6 shows the relative number of missing values for each measure. It can be seen that some measures had more feasibility problems than others. The measures with most problems are those which rely on alignments, especially Best-Align Precision and Alignment-Based Fitness.[5]

Figure 4.7 shows the relationship between the system and the percentage of missing values. It can be observed that there is a relationship between the expected complexity of the systems, as discussed in Sect. 4.3 and the number of failed computations. However, exceptions can be noted, such as system 10. Of all systems, this has the least percentage of missing values, while based on the population parameters it was not expected to be a simple model.

[5]As noted before, performance improvements have been developed since the experiments were conducted.

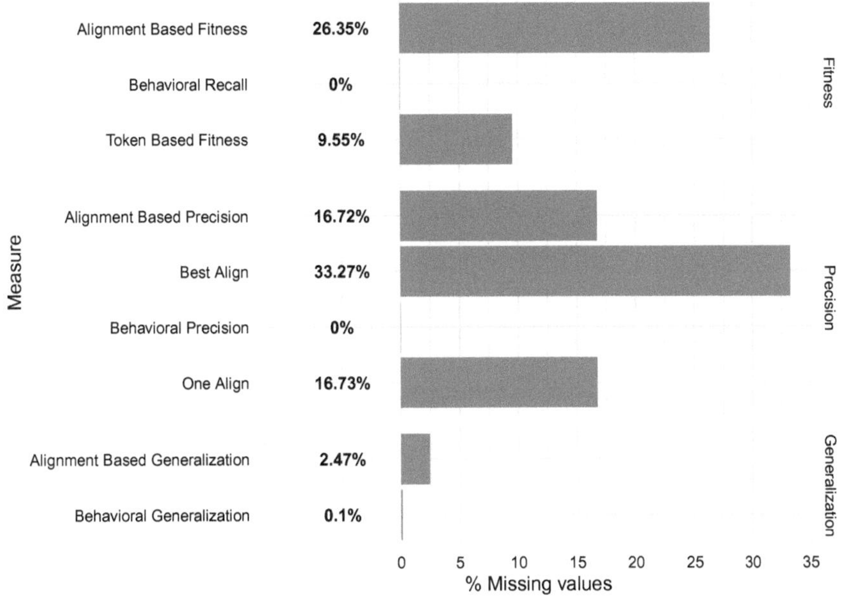

Fig. 4.6 Number of missing values by measure.

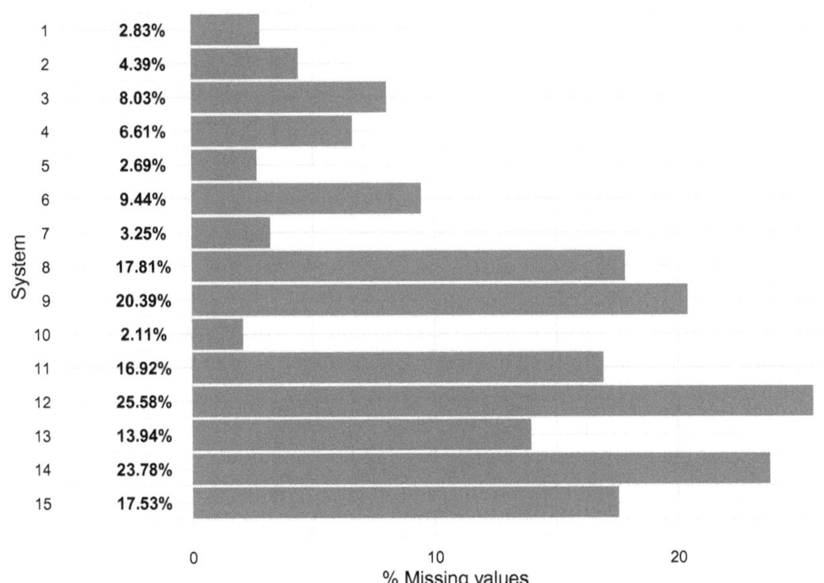

Fig. 4.7 Relationship between missing values and system characteristics.

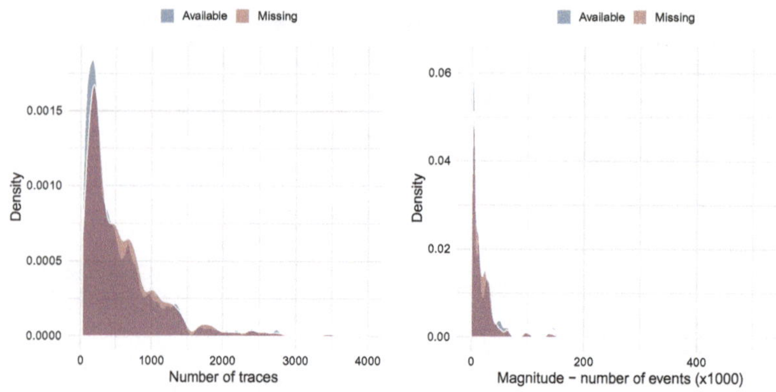

(a) Density of number of traces for available and missing values.

(b) Density of Magnitude for available and missing values.

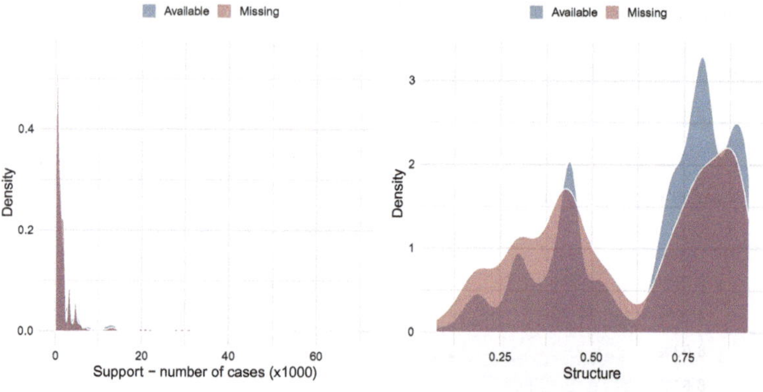

(c) Density of Support for available and missing values.

(d) Density of Structure for available and missing values.

Fig. 4.8 Relationship between missing values and log characteristics.

In order to investigate the root causes of computational difficulties, Fig. 4.8 relates the missing values with four log characteristics: number of traces, Magnitude, Support and Structure. For each of these characteristics, the density of problematic cases is shown in red can be compared with the density of non-problematic cases in blue. It can be seen that the two densities mostly overlap for the amount of traces, cases and events. As such, these do not appear to strongly influence the feasibility. A different conclusion can be made with regards to Structure. Here, the density of problematic cases in higher for lower Structure values, while the density for non-problematic cases is higher for logs with a high Structure. Recall that Structure depends on the directly-follows relations which were observed. The more possible relations were seen, the higher the probability that the measure cannot be obtained.

Thirdly, Fig. 4.9 compared the number of missing values for different discovery algorithms. Especially models discovered using the Heuristics miner and the Induc-

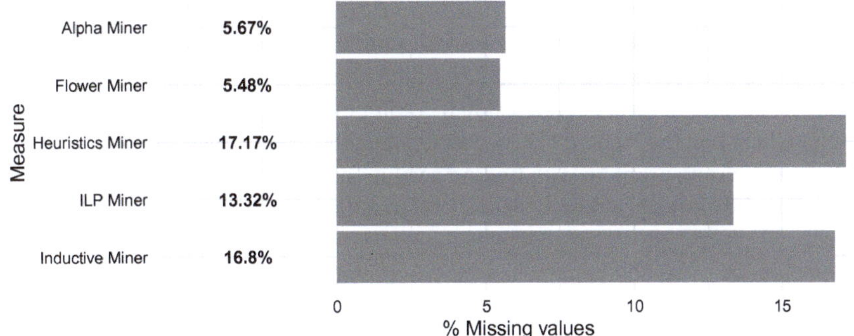

Fig. 4.9 Relationship between missing values and discovery algorithm used.

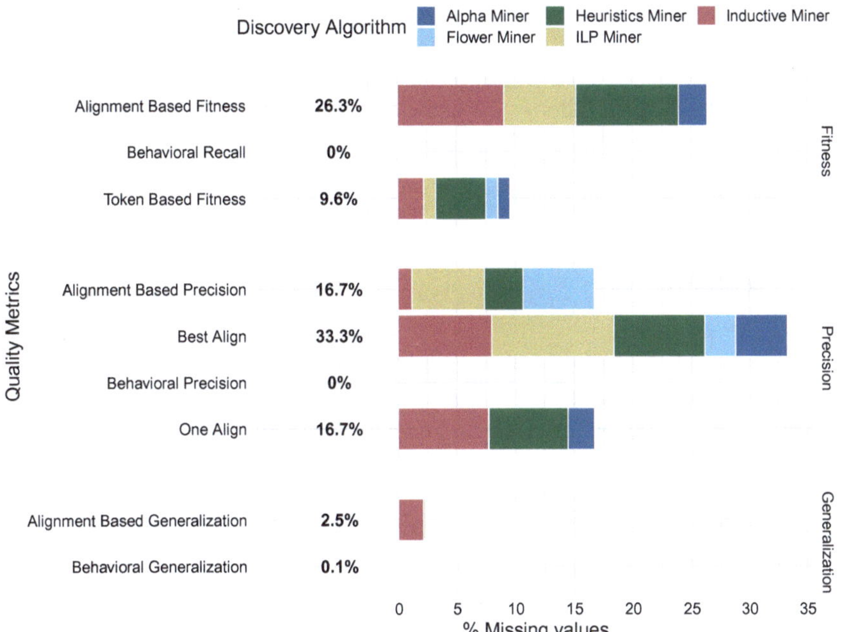

Fig. 4.10 Missing values by metric and discovery algorithm.

tive Miner can run into trouble during the calculation of quality measures. However, there is also a link between these algorithms and the measures used, as shown in Fig. 4.10. Here, it can be observed that One-Align Precision has problems with models from Inductive Miner and Heuristics Miner, but not with models from ILP Miner. However, Best-Align Precision has mostly problems with ILP miner.

It is clear the missing values are not spread randomly among the miners, but instead, some of the miners create models for which quality measurement by some of the measures gets practically unfeasible. For example, the problems with Alignment-

Based Precision and Best Align Precision are mainly related to models discovered by the Flower miner, ILP miner and Heuristics miner. This can be explained because these algorithms tend to discover models which allow for too much behaviour (discussed in more detail further). As a result, it is computationally hard to find the optimal alignment between the log and the model. On the other hand, the Behavioural Precision measure has no problem with finding a value for these models, while One-Align Precision mainly has a problem with models from the Heuristics miner and Inductive miner.

It can thus be concluded that, when the complexity of the behaviour is high, some of the measures are less suitable to be used in practice, especially in combination with certain discovery algorithms. In particular, for models which contain a large number of different activity execution sequences, measures which rely on alignments experience difficulties to quantify precision. The One Align Precision measure is the best alignment-based measure in this situation.

Overall, the percentage of missing values was 11.69%. For 2952 (49.2%) models all values were obtained, i.e. for all 9 metrics. Only these *complete* observations will be used in the remainder of the analysis. Since the missing values are related to specific types of models (i.e. imprecise) models, it would be unfair to use partial observations in the analysis.

4.4.2 Validity

The spread of the obtained values for each of the measures can be observed in Fig. 4.11. Each grey dot depicts one observation, i.e. a value for a quality measure concerning a specific log and a specific model. The blue dots in the figure indicate the mean value for each measure.

For the fitness measures, it can be seen that the distributions of the observation are similar, but there are some minor exceptions. For example, there are no instances for which Token-Based Fitness was lower than 0.125. Furthermore it is clear that the mass of the distribution for Behavioural Recall and Token-Based Fitness is mostly close to one, while values for Alignment-Based Fitness are slightly more uniformly spread.

Concerning the precision measures, the mean values are rather different from one another—Behavioural Precision being a lot more balanced than Alignment-Based Precision. Furthermore it can be seen that certain measures have denser areas, with lots of observations, notably Alignment-Based Precision and One Align Precision in the vicinity of one. On the contrary, such dense areas do not exists for Behavioural Precision and Best Align Precision measures. These dense areas can indicate that said measures are more insensitive and less balanced.

Finally, the spread of values for the generalization measures are quite different. Alignment-Based Generalization has a left skewed distribution with most values close to one. There are only a few values lower than 0.25. The spread of observations

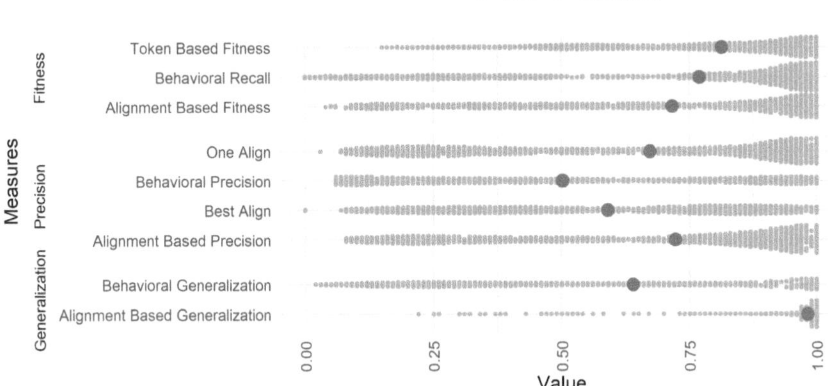

Fig. 4.11 Distribution of values for different quality metrics

for Behavioural Generalization on the other hand does not contains gaps, and is much more evenly spread over the range from zero to one.

These first high level results indicate there are differences within each of the dimensions. However, to get a detailed view of their differences, one needs to connect all observations related to a specific log and model. In the next sections, additional insights will be gained using correlation analysis and factor analysis.

4.4.2.1 Correlation Analysis

In order to analyse the relations between the different measures within and among dimensions, a correlation analysis was done. Ideally, measures within the same dimension should by positively correlated, while measures from different dimensions should not be correlated.

The obtained correlation coefficients are visualised in Fig. 4.12. Some very interesting remarks can be made. When considering measures within each dimension, there is a clear difference between fitness and precision on the one hand, and generalization on the other hand. Firstly, it is very clear that all fitness measures are positively correlated with each other, with for each pair a correlation higher than 0.81. While precision measures are also positively correlated, the coefficients for some pairs are slightly lower compared to fitness. For generalization metrics, the situation is very different however. Here, no relationship is found between the two measures. The main reason for this is probably the lack of variability for Alignment-Based Generalization, as was already indicated in Fig. 4.11.

When looking at relations across dimensions, two important results should be noted. Firstly, there are substantial negative correlations between fitness measures and precision measures. As such, models with a good fitness typically have a low precision, and vice versa. Secondly, Alignment-Based Generalization is not correlated

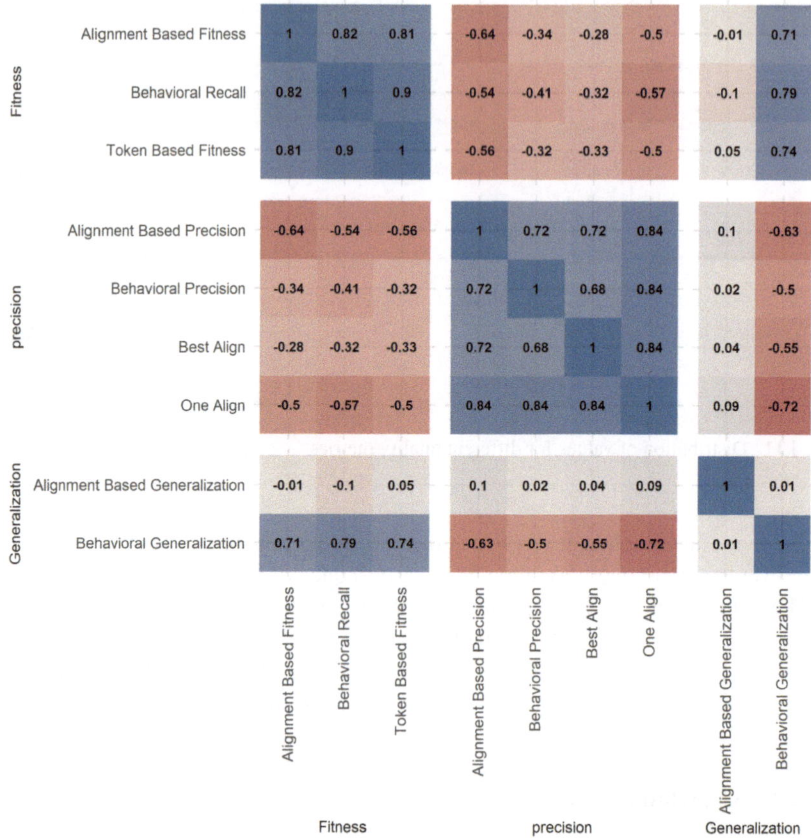

Fig. 4.12 Correlation matrix.

with either fitness or precision measures, while Behavioural Generalization behaves somewhat like a fitness metric. Indeed, the latter is positively correlated with fitness measures and negatively correlated with precision measures. In the following paragraphs we will inspect both phenomena more closely.

The fact that a generalization measure leans toward fitness measures should not come as a total surprise—it is logical that a model with a low fitness will also perform bad when seeing new observations, and vice versa. Also the conceptual formalisations introduced in Chap. 2 show that both are similar to some extent—only the event log L is replaced by system S. In Chap. 5 we will further look into these relations.

Secondly, the negative correlation between fitness and precision measures is not necessarily a characteristic of the dimensions itself. The conceptual analysis in [26] shows that both dimensions are theoretically independent from each other. The negative correlations which were found can be explained by the mix of process discovery algorithms used.

A correlation analysis for each of the algorithms individually, displayed in Fig. 4.13, shows that the negative correlation between fitness and precision metrics is to some extent prevalent for the Alpha miner models (Fig. 4.13a) and the Heuristics miner models (Fig. 4.13c), while a positive relation can be seen for the ILP miner (Fig. 4.13d) and Inductive miner (Fig. 4.13e). The correlation matrix for the Flower miner (Fig. 4.13b) does not show any correlations values for fitness metrics and Behavioural Generalization, because both are constant over all models, i.e. equal to one. The same is true for Behavioural Recall for the ILP miner models.

However, the results for individual mining algorithms are not always consistent. For the Alpha miner for instance, it can be seen that the precision measures are much less correlated. Moreover, the Alignment-Based Precision is negatively correlated with fitness measures, the Behavioural Precision is slightly positively correlated, while for the Best Align and One Align precision measures mostly only weakly negative correlations can be found. The pattern for the Heuristics miner models is similar, although the strength of the relations differ.

Another peculiarity can be seen for the ILP miner models, where all precision measures are strongly positively correlated, except for Alignment-Based Precision. The latter has a weak negative correlation with other precision metrics. Furthermore, while the other measures are positively correlated with fitness measures, Alignment-Based Precision is not correlated with Token-Based Fitness, and slightly negatively correlated with Alignment-Based Fitness. Finally, the two generalization measures are much higher correlated for these models than for the overall set of models.

These matrices thus show that the relations between different measures is highly dependent on the type of models considered in the experiment—i.e. the discovery algorithm used—which is not desirable. In order to shed more light on these relationships, we visualised the search space of each discovery algorithm in terms of fitness and precision in Fig. 4.14. In this figure models are distributed in terms of their *average* fitness and precision value, i.e. the average of the different measures[6]. The saturation of the colours indicate where the mass of the discovered models is located for each algorithm. The coloured lines represent a linear regression between mean fitness and mean precision for each of the algorithms.[7] The dashed black line represents the negative linear regression for all miners combined, which reflects the negative correlations between fitness and precision measures in Fig. 4.12.

[6]The average fitness and precision was used for the sake of simplicity, and justified since they were mostly found to be strongly related. Nevertheless, similar figures for each pair of individual fitness and precision measures are included in Appendix A.

[7]Note that is was not possible to draw a regression line for the Flower Miner, since each of these models had a fitness equal to one.

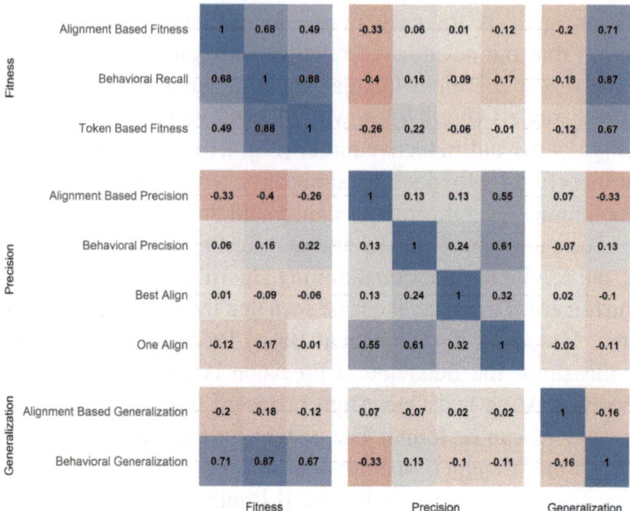

(a) Correlation matrix Alpha miner.

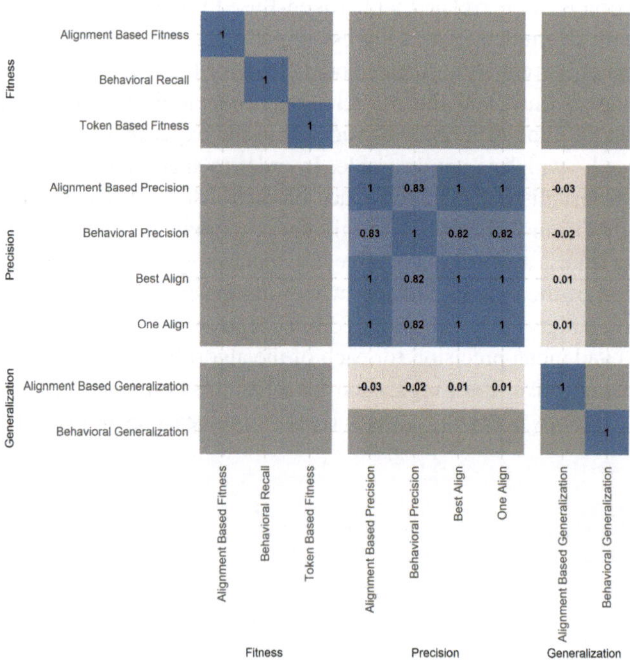

(b) Correlation matrix Flower miner.

Fig. 4.13 Correlation matrix for each discovery algorithm.

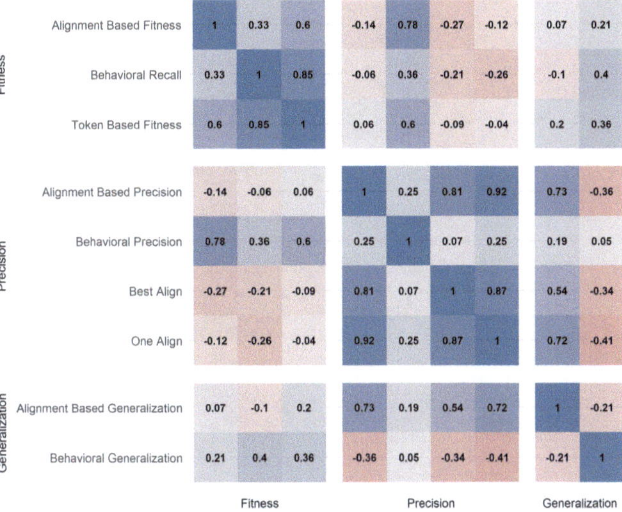

(c) Correlation matrix Heuristics miner.

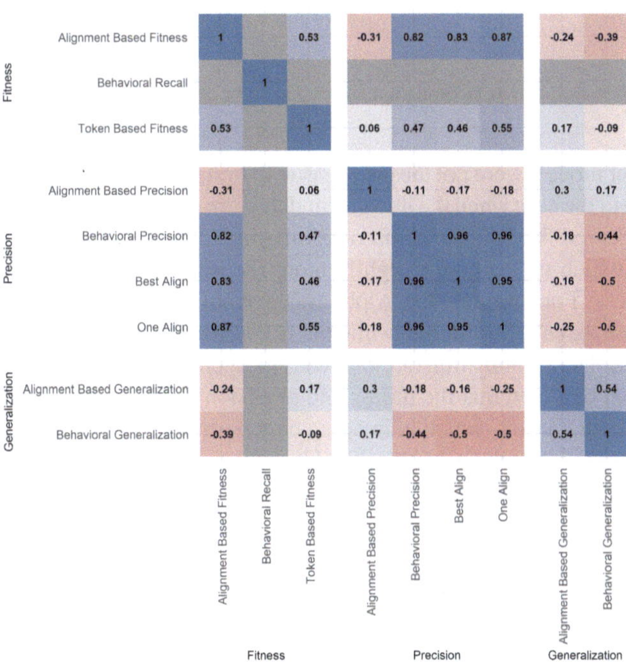

(d) Correlation matrix ILP miner.

Fig. 4.13 (continued)

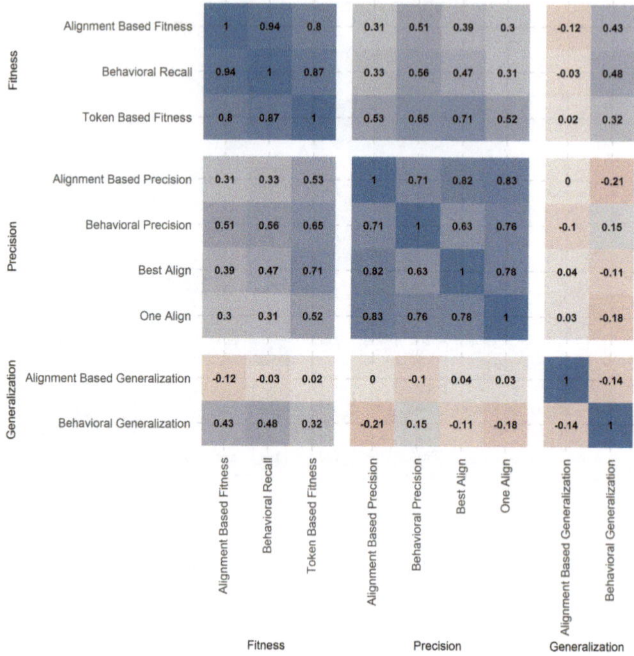

(e) Correlation matrix Inductive miner.

The flower models were not the only reason to find an overall negative correlation, as this was still the case when the flowers models were omitted from Fig. 4.12. Rather, it can be observed that it is the result of combining the search space of the different algorithms, which typically are slightly more focused towards either precision, or towards fitness. For instance, the Alpha miner tends to find models which have a high precision, but a lower fitness, while the ILP miner finds models with the reverse characteristic. The combination of those leads to a perceived negative correlation. As a result, it can be stated that the fitness and precision dimensions are not negatively correlated per definition, which is in agreement with the theoretical foundations of the dimensions. Rather, their relationship depends on which discovery algorithms are taken into consideration. Furthermore, this also impacts the extent to which different measures of the same dimensions correlate.

4.4.2.2 Factor Analysis

In order to further investigate the relationship between measures within and across quality dimensions, an Exploratory Factor Analysis was done [65]. In order to decide on the number of factors to construct, a scree plot was composed to find the appropriate number of factors which explain the most variability in the data. This suggested

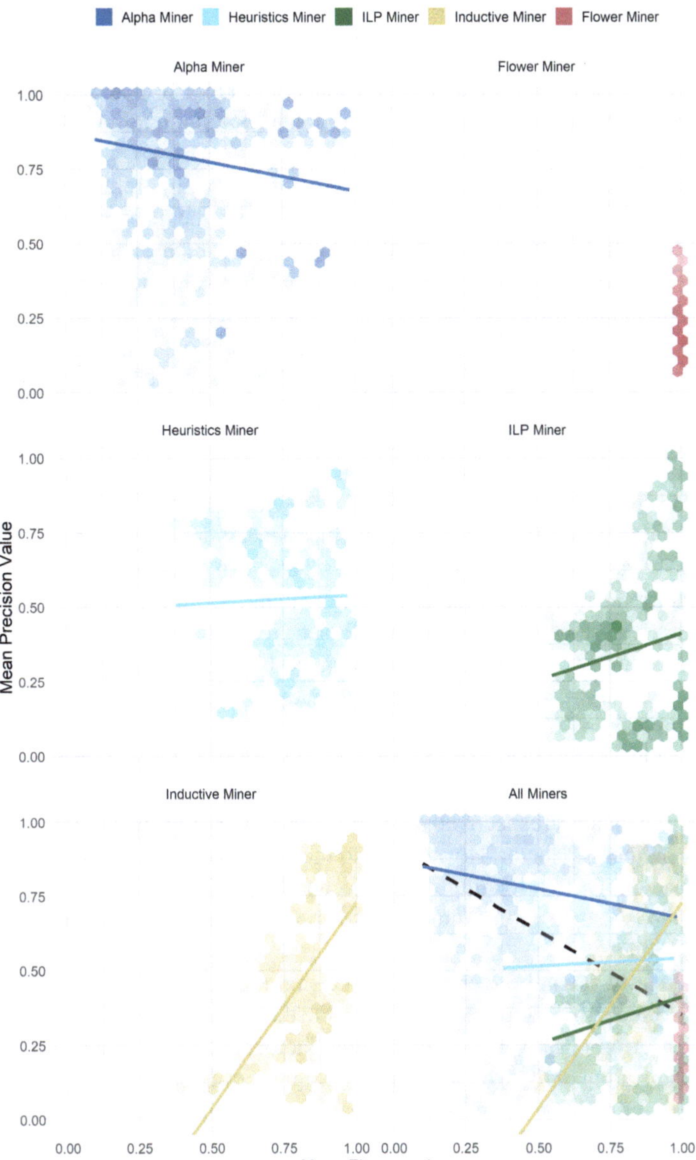

Fig. 4.14 Relation between mean fitness and precision for different discovery algorithms, averaged over different fitness and precision measures, respectively. The saturation of the colour indicates the mass of the observations. Coloured lines resemble the correlation between mean fitness and precision for each algorithm. The dashed lines resembles the correlations for all miners combined.

that 2 or 3 factors would be most suitable. A factor analysis with 2 factors was chosen, based on the observation that a third factor did not have any significant loadings. As was stated in Sect. 4.3, a Promax rotation was used to increase the interpretability of the factors. As this is an oblique, non-orthogonal rotation, it allows for the fact that factors might be correlated.

The quality of the factor analysis can be assessed using Table 4.6. The Kaiser-Meyer-Olkin statistic (KMO) [65], which displays the proportion of variation between the different metrics, was equal to 0.7838, which is adequate. The Measures of Sampling Adequacy (MSA), which depict this proportion for each of the metrics individually are also quite high for most metrics. Only the Alignment-Based Generalization has a remarkably low value for this metric. However, this does not pose problems, as the overall KMO value is high enough. The Root Mean Squared Residual (RMSR) is equal to 0.0370, and thereby well below the suggested maximum of 0.06 [113]. The Bartlett's test of Sphericity was done to test whether the correlation matrix was equal to a unity matrix, and thus factor analysis would be useless. However, this hypothesis was rejected with a p-value smaller than 0.0001.

The communalities for each of the specific metrics, shown in Table 4.6, show the proportion of variance for each of the metrics that is explained by the factor [65]. This shows that for the majority of the metrics more than 70% of the variance is explained by the factors. Also here, the Alignment-Based Generalization is the only metric for which almost none of the variance is explained by the factors. Nonetheless, it can be concluded that the quality of the factor analysis is good and it is meaningful to interpret the factors.

The loadings of the factors that were found are shown in Fig. 4.15 for each of the dimensions separately. It is clear that Factor 2 and Factor 1 represent the fitness and precision dimensions, respectively. All three fitness measures have a loading of more than 0.80 on the first factor. However, also the Behavioural Generalization measure has a considerably high loading on this factor. This means that, to a certain extent, it behaves in the same way as fitness metrics, which was also evident by looking at the correlations.

Subsequently, it can be seen that all precision measures load reasonably high on Factor 2. As such, this factor seems to resemble the concept of precision. Behavioural Generalization is negatively loaded on this factor, but the loading is too small to attach any meaning onto it. The loading for Alignment-Based Precision is less strong than for other precision metrics. This was also apparent in the correlation analysis, especially for the models of the Alpha and ILP miner.

Furthermore, it is important to observe that Alignment-Based Generalization did not have significant loadings on any of the factors, and this did not change when the number of factors was increased. This is unsurprisingly, due to the fact that there is very little variance among the values obtained by this metric, as was shown in Fig. 4.11. As such, it will require a large amount of factors before one would address this limited amount of variance.

The fact that Behavioural Generalization has a high loading on the fitness-factor confirms the conclusion that was found earlier based on the correlation matrix. Again, the relationship between fitness and generalization should not appear eccentric. A

Table 4.6 Quality assessment factor analysis.

(a) Communality and MSA-value per metric		
Metric	Communality	MSA
Alignment-Based Fitness	0.7426	0.8221
Alignment-Based Generalization	0.0085	0.0609
Alignment-Based Precision	0.7260	0.7819
Best Align Precision	0.7292	0.8481
Behavioural Generalization	0.7590	0.9112
Behavioural Precision	0.7154	0.8170
Behavioural Recall	0.9160	0.6994
One Align Precision	0.9950	0.7906
Token-Based Fitness	0.8920	0.7539

(b) Overall quality summary.	
Characteristic	Value
Total Communality	0.7204
KMO	0.7838
RMSR	0.0370
Bartlett's p-value	0.0000

model with a good generalization is able to replay unobserved behaviour. As a result, it appears logical that such a model can also replay observed behaviour. The other way around, a model that cannot replay observed behaviour, is unlikely to be able to replay unobserved but realistic behaviour. This conceptual relationship between fitness and generalization is further discussed in Chap. 5.

It can thus be concluded that both fitness measures and precision metrics agree with each other, respectively. As a result, the validity of these measures is approved. On the other hand, generalization measures do not measure the same thing. The fact that one of the generalization measures, i.e. Behavioural Generalization, loads reasonably high on the fitness-factor is expected to a certain extent. The Alignment-Based Generalization metric seems to be a very insensitive metric, as the variance is very low.

4.4.3 Sensitivity

The analysis of correlations and factors implicitly assume that the relations between different metrics are similar along the whole range, i.e. as well for models with a high quality as for models with a low quality. However, it is not impossible that some measures tend to be more optimistic or more pessimistic. Moreover, measures might

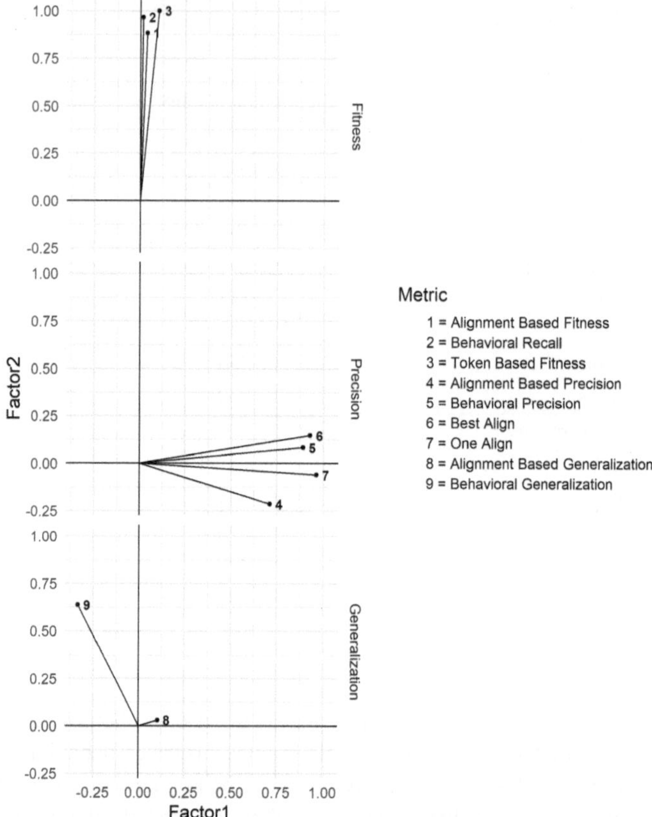

Fig. 4.15 Factor loadings for a factor analysis with 2 factors and promax rotation.

undoubtedly agree on models with a very good or very bad fitness, but might judge models with intermediate fitness differently.

In order to examine the relationships between metrics on a more local level, scatter plots were drawn for each pair of measures in each dimension. Upon these, Lowess Smoothing lines were fitted [33]. The distance and difference in slope of the Lowess Smoothing in relationship with the diagonal line, as well as patterns in the underlying scatter plot, shows which of the two measures is more sensitive and more optimistic or pessimistic.

In Fig. 4.16a, Lowess smoothing lines are shown which describe the relationships between the fitness measures. The position and shape of the smoothing line tells us something about the sensitivity and the level of optimism/pessimism.

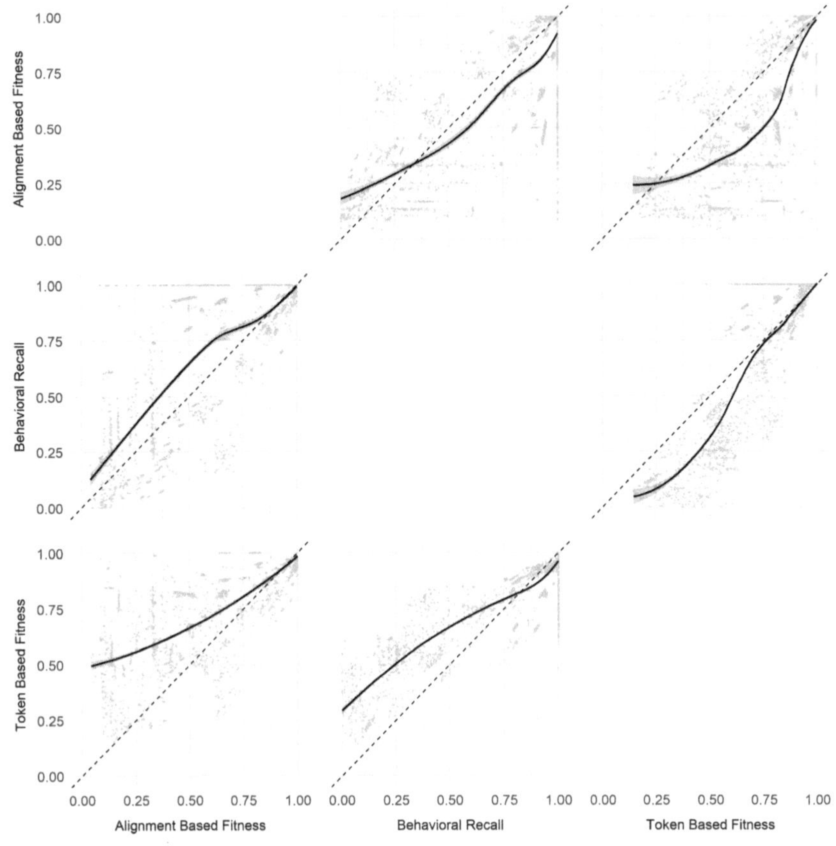

(a) Lowess smoothings for Fitness.

Fig. 4.16 Lowess smoothings for pairs of metrics within the dimensions Fitness, Precision and Generalization.

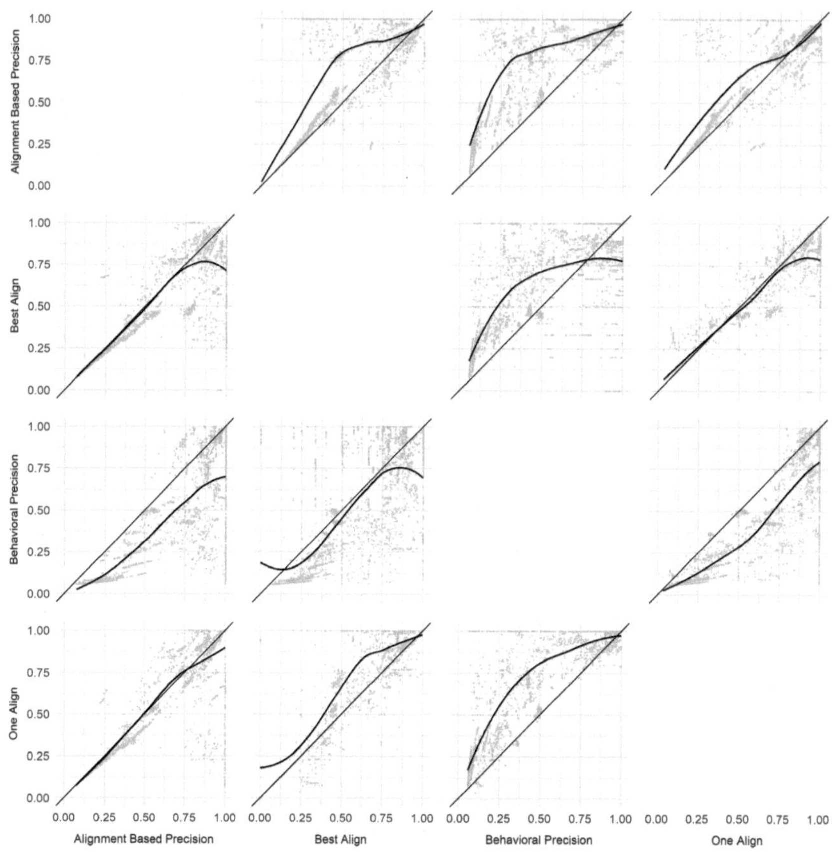

(b) Lowess smoothings for Precision.

Fig. 4.16 (continued)

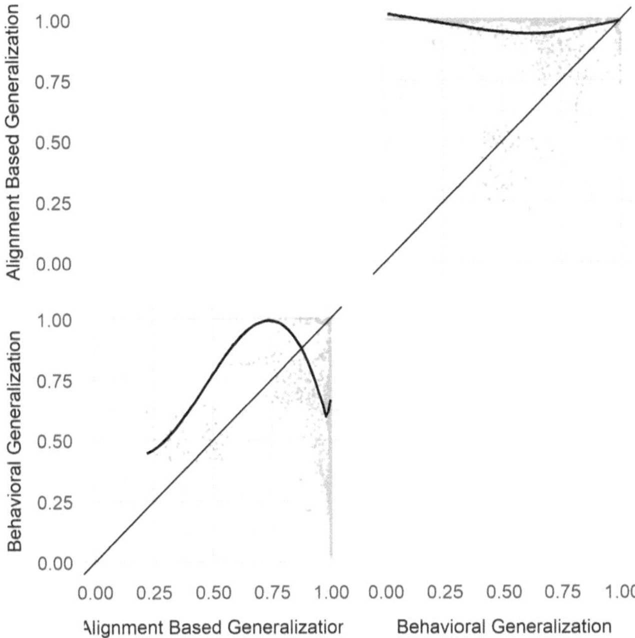

(c) Lowess smoothings for Generalization.

When the smoothing line approximates the diagonal, the two measures at hand score models equally. However, when the smoothing line falls below the diagonal, the y-axis measure is more pessimistic. When it sits above the diagonal, the y-axis measure is more optimistic. Moreover, when the *direction* of the Lowess curve significantly differs from the diagonal, i.e. it is remarkably steep or flat, it can be said that there is a difference in sensitivity. I.e. when the Lowess curves turns toward a specific measure, as is the case in the lower left of Fig. 4.16a, it can be said that this measure becomes less sensitive compared to the other measures.

4.4.3.1 Fitness

In Fig. 4.16a it can be seen that the smoothing line between Behavioural Recall and Alignment-Based Fitness is close to the diagonal, which indicates a good correspondence. When models have a higher fitness, Behavioural Recall and Alignment-Based Fitness score models equally, while Behavioural Recall stays more optimistic as fitness decreases. According to Table 4.7, the average difference between Behavioural Recall and Alignment-Based Fitness is 0.529. This optimism decreases when the value for Alignment-Based Fitness increases. The stability reported in Table 4.8 of 0.2809 means that there is only a slightly negative correlation between the value of

Table 4.7 Level of optimism (pessimism) for pairs of fitness measures.

Measure	is more optimistic/pessimistic compared to		
	Alignment-Based Fitness	Behavioural Recall	Token-Based Fitness
Alignment-Based Fitness		−0.0529	−0.0965
Behavioural Recall	0.0529		−0.0436
Token-Based Fitness	0.0965	0.0436	

Table 4.8 Stability of optimism (pessimism) for fitness measures.

The level of optimism of measure	correlates with level of		
	Alignment-Based Fitness	Behavioural Recall	Token-Based Fitness
Alignment-Based Fitness		−0.3236	0.2005
Behavioural Recall	−0.2809		0.4629
Token-Based Fitness	−0.7367	−0.7976	

Alignment-Based Fitness and the optimism of Behavioural Recall. As such, there are no obvious signs of insensitivity in one of the two metrics.

Nonetheless, the horizontal line of measurements at the top of the chart shows that many models have a perfect fitness for Behavioural Recall while not so according to Alignment-Based Fitness. Closer analysis of these data points showed that all these referred to models discovered using the ILP miner. As such, this artefact in the data is the result of a specific characteristic of the ILP miner—most probably an abundance in silent transitions and/or source transitions—which causes a problem in terms of fitness for Alignment-Based Fitness, but not for Behavioural Recall.

Although Token-Based Fitness and Alignment-Based Fitness agree on models with perfect fitness, Token-Based Fitness appears to be more optimistic than Alignment-Based Fitness when the fitness of a model is lower. The average surplus in Token-Based Fitness is 0.0965. Furthermore, there is a strong negative correlation between that surplus and the value of Alignment-Based fitness, meaning that Token-Based fitness seems to be far less sensitive, as the gap between the Lowess curve and the diagonal increases when Alignment-Based Fitness goes to zero.

Finally, Token-Based Fitness also seems to be more optimistic than Behavioural Recall. However, for models with a good fitness, the two measures correspond nearly perfect. The vertical line of dots shows that Token-Based Fitness is more sensitive then Behavioural Recall.

Table 4.9 Level of optimism (pessimism) for pairs of precision measures.

Measure	is more optimistic/pessimistic compared to			
	Alignment-Based Precision	Best-Align Precision	Behavioural Precision	One-Align Precision
Alignment-Based Precision		0.1328	0.2203	0.0490
Best-Align Precision	−0.1328		0.0874	−0.0839
Behavioural Precision	−0.2203	−0.0874		−0.1713
One-Align Precision	−0.0490	0.0839	0.1713	

Table 4.10 Stability of optimism (pessimism) for precision measures.

The level of optimism of measure	correlates with level of			
	Alignment-Based Precision	Best-Align Precision	Behavioural Precision	One-Align Precision
Alignment-Based Precision		−0.2934	−0.4923	−0.3725
Best-Align	−0.4511		−0.5694	−0.4753
Behavioural Precision	−0.2565	−0.2096		−0.2057
One-Align	−0.1931	−0.0848	−0.3631	

4.4.3.2 Precision

The same Lowess smoothing lines for precision measures are shown in Fig. 4.16b. Compared to Alignment-Based Precision, Best-Align Precision and One-Align Precision have a perfect correspondence most of the time. Table 4.9 shows a small amount of optimism compared to One-Align Precision, while it is higher for Best-Align Precision. This is mainly due to differences when Alignment-Based Precision value are high. When this is the case, Best Align Precision seems to be very insensitive and pessimistic, as the Lowess curve gets nearly horizontal. Behavioural Precision appears to score models more pessimistic on their preciseness compared to Alignment-Based Precision in all of the cases. The vertical lines of dots that can be seen in each plot for Alignment-Based Precision, show that the measure is more insensitive compared to the other precision measures, as many models which appear perfectly precise by Alignment-Based Precision are judged more pessimistic by other measures.

Best-Align Precision correlates very well with One Align Precision for almost all models, although One Align Precision is slightly more optimistic (on average by 0.0839). Compared to Behavioural Precision, Best-Align Precision scores models equivalently when precision is moderate. However, when Best-Align returns a high

Table 4.11 Level of optimism (pessimism) for generalization measures.

Measure	is more optimistic/pessimistic compared to	
	Alignment Based Generalization	Behavioural Generalization
Alignment Based Generalization		0.3424
Behavioral Generalization	−0.3424	

precision value, Behavioural Precision will be more pessimistic. On the other hand, when Best-Align Precision scores the precision of a model to be very low, Behavioural Precision tends to be more optimistic. Finally, it can be observed that One-align returns more optimistic precision values than Behavioural Precision, except towards the extremes of the range. The horizontal lines of dots that can be observed when comparing One Align on the one hand, with Best Align and Behavioural Precision on the other hand, indicate that One Align is less sensitive than the latter two. In conclusion, Behavioural Precision and Best Align Precision are the most sensitive measures, followed by One Align Precision. Alignment-Based Precision scores the least on sensitivity.

Remarkable is the fact that all correlations in Table 4.10 are negative, which means that discrepancies between each measure Y and X always get larger as X gets larger. In other words, measures do not agree on the precision of more precise models, while they agree more on the precision not so precise models.

4.4.3.3 Generalization

At last, Fig. 4.16c shows the relation between the two generalization measures. In accordance with earlier results, most values for Alignment Based Generalization are in the vicinity of one. As a result, this measure is very insensitive and always more optimistic than Behavioural Generalization. However, the factor analysis showed that these measures do not measure the same aspect anyhow.

Table 4.11 shows that the average level of optimism of Alignment-Based Generalization is 0.3424. Furthermore, in Table 4.12, it can be seen that there is an almost perfect negative relationship between this discrepancy and the level of Behavioural Generalization. The higher the latter number, the lower the distance between that number and the value for Alignment-Based Generalization. This is only logical, as the latter acts as a *flat ceiling*.

Table 4.12 Stability of optimism (pessimism) for generalization measures.

The level of optimism	correlates with level of	
	Alignment Based Generalization	Behavioural Generalization
Alignment-Based Generalization		−0.9751
Behavioural Generalization	−0.2160	

Table 4.13 Summary of the results.

Metric	Feasibility	Validity	Sensitivity
Alignment-Based Fitness	✗	✓	✓
Behavioural Recall	✓	✓	⚠
Token-Based Fitness	⚠	✓	✓
Alignment-Based Precision	⚠	⚠	✗
Behavioural Precision	✓	✓	✓
Best Align Precision	✗	✓	✓
One Align Precision	⚠	✓	⚠
Alignment-Based Generalization	✓	✗	✗
Behavioural Generalization	✓	✗	✓

4.5 Discussion

Since the number of quality measures introduced in Chap. 2 keeps growing, it is increasingly important to know how they perform, and how they relate to each other. Such information is not only needed to be able to select appropriate measures and interpret them correctly during conformance checking, but also for process discovery and conformance checking to evolve towards a stable and mature research discipline.

In this chapter, we looked at feasibility, validity and sensitivity of state-of-the-art quality measures. An overview of the results on each of these criteria can be found in Table 4.13.

Alignment-Based Fitness scores good on both validity and sensitivity, but has problems in terms of feasibility, especially when models tend to be complex. Token-Based Fitness has less problems with feasibility, although it is still unable to find a result in 10% of the cases with reasonable effort. Behavioural Recall does not have any problems at all with feasibility, but scores lower on sensitivity. Especially, it tends to give models a perfect score while the other measures will be more pessimistic.

Behavioural Precision was found to be the single precision measure to score highly on all three criteria. Best Align Precision scored remarkably bad on feasibility—having trouble with one out of every three models—while scoring similarly good as Behavioural Precision on validity and sensitivity. Alignment-Based Precision has some problems regarding the validity, showing a low correlation with other precision measures. Also on feasibility, it was slightly less performing, having problems with one in every six models. Moreover it was found to be remarkable insensitive compared to the other measures. Finally, One Align Precision also had issues with insensitivity, although to a lesser extent. With regards to feasibility, it also had problems with one out of every six models.

For generalization there were no problems with feasibility, but validity and sensitivity are problematic. None of the two measures appeared to measure a distinct concept, Alignment-Based Generalization containing a very low amount of variance and Behavioural Generalization strongly related to fitness. The latter observation can be corroborated with the conceptual definitions of the quality dimensions.

As most research is focused on the performance and effectiveness of process discovery algorithms, existing literature on the performance of quality measures itself is limited. Although this chapter only scratches the surface, it indicates that there is room for improvement and increased understanding in this area. Moreover, the relation between generalization and fitness should be further investigated, as well as the relation between fitness and precision. Finally, further research is needed to find why certain metrics are more sensitive than others, and whether this relates to certain characteristics of the behaviour, for instance in terms of work-flow patterns.

4.6 Conclusion

In the context of process discovery, being able to evaluate the quality of obtained process models as a representation of the process at hand is essential. In order to do this, different quality dimensions were introduced and for each of the dimensions several measures were implemented. However, only limited empirical evidence exists on the behaviour of these measures and their relationships both within and across different quality dimensions. Nonetheless, the feasibility, validity and sensitivity of quality metrics are important aspects that need to be considered. In this chapter, a large experiment was conducted in order to evaluate these characteristics.

In terms of validity and sensitivity, the results seem to be most problematic in the case of generalization. This brings us back to the problem of even appropriately defining this concept which we encountered in Chap. 2. Therefore, in the next chapter, we will take a step back and focus not primarily on the measures but foremost on the dimensions. In particular, we ask ourselves whether the classical dimensions are sufficient, and whether we can improve the overall quality measurement framework. For this, we will contrast the current dimensions with classical data analysis and statistics.

Some limitations of the experiment should be addressed. In order to get an as diverse as possible set of measurements, particular choices have been made while defining the methodology of the experiment presented above. Each of these decisions has specific implications on the results.

Firstly, the event logs were simulated using 15 different systems, which were drawn from 15 different model populations. Among these populations, a distinction was made between populations of differing complexity. The aim here was to have a set of systems which were very diverse in terms of process constructs and overall complexity, and at the same time realistic. Judging by the spread of log statistics and quality measurements, this aim was clearly accomplished.

However, because of the limited number of systems used, we cannot draw definitive conclusions about differences between model populations. It might for instance very well be that certain measures perform better in terms of feasibility when there are relatively less parallel constructs. However, in order to draw such conclusions, we would need to generate more models with a lower and higher number of these constructs, and then compare the feasibility of the measures. Future research would be needed to see whether the validity and sensitivity of measures depends on process characteristics.

Secondly, the event logs were simulated along different completeness and noise levels. Here, the definition of noise, and the way it was induced certainly has its implications on the obtained measures. Since we consider noise to refer to measurements errors or data inconsistencies (and not just infrequent, but correct, behaviour), adequate attention should be given on how to simulate these errors. Furthermore, one should take careful consideration of the impact of noise on completeness levels. In the current experimental set up, both threshold have been defined to be conservative: the actual completeness could be higher than stated, and the actual amount of noisy traces could be lower than stated.

While these choices have had their impact on the measurements, their implications are inconsequential for the experiment at hand. In fact, varying the completeness and noise of event logs was only done to diversify the event logs used. Since the levels itself have not been used in the analysis itself, it is less critical that they are either optimistic or pessimistic. On the other hand, it is critical that noise is introduced in realistic ways, such that the results can be generalised to real-life situations. As such, the precise definition of noise should be taken into account when interpreting or generalising the results. More future research will be necessary in order to understand whether the definition of noise, or perhaps the different types of noise, has a consequential impact on the feasibility, validity and sensitivity of the measures considered.

Finally, five different process discovery algorithms were used, in order to have a diverse set of models for quality measurements. Theoretically, the origin of a process model is irrelevant to its quality measurement. However, it has already been shown that the specific mix of models used does impact the analysis, because of their specific search space. For example, while fitness and precision are in reality independent concepts, the mix of algorithms in Fig. 4.14 makes it appear as if they are not. In order to mitigate the effects of certain (combinations of) discovery algorithms, we have made sure to consistently test whether results discussed in Sect. 4.4 also applied when controlling for the discovery algorithm, and indicated if they did not.

It can clearly be seen in Figs. 4.11, 4.14 and 4.16 that these methodology choices have resulted in a very diverse set of event logs and models, and thus a very diverse set of measurements, as intended. As a result, we can confidently say that the conclusions for each of the measures are representative of their general behaviour, and not only for a narrow segment of models or event logs.

4.7 Further Reading

1. Janssenswillen, G., Donders, N., Jouck, T., Depaire, B.: A comparative study of existing quality measures for process discovery. Information Systems **71**, 1–15 (2017)
2. vanden Broucke, S.K.L.M., Delvaux, C., Freitas, J., Rogova, T., Vanthienen, J., Baesens, B.: Uncovering the relationship between event log characteristics and process discovery techniques. In: Business Process Management Workshops, pp. 41–53. Springer (2014)
3. De Weerdt, J., De Backer, M., Vanthienen, J., Baesens, B.: A critical evaluation study of model-log metrics in process discovery. In: Business Process Management Workshops, pp. 158–169. Springer (2011)
4. DeWeerdt, J., De Backer, M., Vanthienen, J., Baesens, B.: A multi-dimensional quality assessment of state-of-the-art process discovery algorithms using reallife event logs. Information Systems **37**(7), 654–676 (2012)
5. Jouck, T., Depaire, B.: Generating Artificial Data for Empirical Analysis of Control-flow Discovery Algorithms: A Process Tree and Log Generator. Business & Information Systems Engineering pp. 1–18 (2018)
6. Rozinat, A., De Medeiros, A.K.A., Günther, C.W., Weijters, A.J.M.M., Van der Aalst, W.M.P.: Towards an evaluation framework for process mining algorithms. In: BPM Center Report BPM-07-06. BPM Center (2007)
7. Weber, P., Bordbar, B., Tino, P., Majeed, B.: A framework for comparing process mining algorithms. In: GCC Conference and Exhibition, pp. 625–628. IEEE (2011)

Chapter 5
Reassessing the Quality Framework

> Once you have accepted a theory, it is extraordinarily difficult to notice its flaws.
>
> Daniel Kahneman

5.1 Introduction

The results of process discovery and consecutive analyses are often directly based on a sample of event data that may not have captured all possible/actual behaviour correctly or completely. However, the question whether these results also apply to the real, underlying process typically remains unanswered. In order to solve this, there is a need for unbiased estimators of the quality of a discovered model as a representation of the underlying process. The adequacy of the established quality dimensions fitness, precision and generalization is typically only demonstrated using a limited set of special cases, such as flower models or models enumerating one or more traces [50, 117]. Hence, a critical analysis of these classical dimensions, both on theoretical and empirical grounds, is missing and certainly necessary for process discovery to evolve towards a mature research discipline.

In this chapter, we take a step back from the measures and focus instead on the framework of dimensions itself. We extend the established distinction between exploratory and confirmatory data analysis from traditional statistics to process discovery. As a result,

- we propose a new paradigm to quantify the quality of discovered process models, depending on the type of analysis and discuss its necessity,
- we empirically analyse the difference between the perspectives and investigate possible biases when using metrics for a different purpose than the one they were designed for.

G. Janssenswillen: Unearthing the Real Process Behind the Event Data, LNBIP 412
https://doi.org/10.1007/978-3-030-70733-0_5

5.2 Exploratory Versus Confirmatory Process Discovery

The data science field largely originated from the discipline of statistics during the last decades of the 20th century [132]. Within statistics, the emphasis has historically been on confirmatory analysis, relying on the well known paradigms of testing and estimation [59], to *confirm* or reject a stated hypothesis. However, confirmatory techniques are not designed to find hypotheses. Only when one has a certain clearly formed idea or hypothesis and data which can be exploited to elucidate that idea, one can use confirmatory statistics to investigate whether or not the idea is justified in light of the evidence [54].

With the arrival of more computational power, and the increase of readily available data, the field of exploratory data analysis (EDA) emerged [131]. Exploratory analyses are typically the starting point for a line of research, when no specific statistical hypotheses are specified. It mainly encompasses methods to plot your data and transform it. Even when the question to be answered is perfectly clear, the analysis can benefit from exploratory analysis to test whether underlying assumptions for the confirmatory tests are met and by highlighting and subsequently neutralizing other variables which might have an impact on the question asked.

Exploratory and confirmatory methods are not each other's competitors, but rather go hand in hand. Exploratory analysis will both lead to new ideas to be tested, and perhaps new data to be collected. Moreover, it will form the groundwork for the confirmatory analysis. In confirmatory analysis, it is investigated whether the insights learned from the sample can be applied to the population as a whole. While confirmatory analysis can be seen as the work conducted in a law court to determine guilt based on evidence, exploratory analysis can be seen as the indispensable detective work that has to be performed in advance. Through exploring data, one wants to find clues, get ideas and follow up on them in search for new hypotheses [54]. It is clear that one cannot exist without the other, but they are complimentary, and can be used in alternation or parallel.

The concept of a *sample* from statistics finds its equivalent in process mining as the *event log* L. On the other hand, we defined the *system* S [26] as the *population* of process behaviour. The system thus refers to the underlying process, the way work is done. Just as in traditional statistics, the system and event log are not equal, as the event log is only a sample and can contain noise, i.e. measurement errors and inaccuracies. This was shown conceptually in Figure 2.6, originally introduced in [26]. In the following paragraphs, we introduce 4 conceptual dimensions which can be used instead of the classical dimensions for exploratory or confirmatory analysis.

5.2.0.1 Model-Log Similarity

In the case of exploratory analysis, it is important that there is a tight correspondence between the event log and the model. The fit between an event log and a process model is monitored by two ratios [26], *log-fitness* and *log-precision*. Given event log L, the *log-fitness* and *log-precision* of a model M can be defined as follows. In these definitions, we assume that the amount of behavior in S, M and $supp(L)$ is *countable*, which is reflected by a count function $\#(\ldots)$, just as in Chap. 2.

Definition 5.1 (Log-fitness). Log-fitness is a function $F^L : \mathbf{M} \times \mathbf{L} \rightarrow [0, 1]$, which quantifies how much of the behavior in the event log is captured by the model. This can be defined conceptually as [26]:

$$F^L = F^L(M, L) = \frac{\#(\text{supp } L \cap M)}{\#(\text{supp } L)} \tag{5.1}$$

Definition 5.2 (Log-precision). Log-precision is a function $P^L : \mathbf{M} \times \mathbf{L} \rightarrow [0, 1]$, which quantifies how much of the behavior in the model was recorded in the event log. This can be defined conceptually as [26]:

$$P^L = P^L(M, L) = \frac{\#(\text{supp } L \cap M)}{\#(M)} \tag{5.2}$$

Only when both log-fitness and log-precision are equal to 1, then $supp(L) = M$, i.e. the event log and the model represent exactly the same behaviour. These metrics are orthogonal to each other, which makes it possible to construct models which score poorly on one criterion and excellent on the other. Acting as complementary forces, maximising log-fitness and log-precision simultaneously maximises the *fit* between the model and the event log. Note that log-fitness and log-precision coincide with the classical definition of fitness and precision introduced in Chap. 2.

5.2.0.2 Model-System Similarity

For confirmatory analysis, one would like to reject or *accept* hypotheses such as *Model M_1 is more likely than Model M_2 to be the real underlying system*. In order to do this, it is necessary to estimate how well a model M represents the system S.

By drawing the analogy, it is evident that two similar dimensions are needed to quantify the match between the model and the system. Firstly, there is a need for a metric that ensures the selection of models that contain all possible real behaviour. Secondly, a metric that favours the selection of models that only contain real behaviour is needed. Therefore, given the system S, the *system-fitness* and *system-precision* of a model M can be defined as:

Definition 5.3 (System-fitness). System-fitness is a function $F^S : \mathbf{M} \times \mathbf{S} \rightarrow [0, 1]$, which quantifies how much of the behaviour in the system is captured by the model. This can be defined conceptually as [26]:

$$F^S = F^S(M, S) = \frac{\#(S \cap M)}{\#(S)} \tag{5.3}$$

Definition 5.4 (System-precision). System-precision is a function $P^S : \mathbf{M} \times \mathbf{S} \rightarrow [0, 1]$, which quantifies how much of the behavior in the model is part of the system. This can be defined conceptually as [26]:

$$P^S = P^S(M, S) = \frac{\#(S \cap M)}{\#(M)} \tag{5.4}$$

While there are some similarities between system-fitness and generalization, the latter as defined in Chap. 2, there is no counter part for system-precision in the original framework, a gap in the quality dimensions which was noted earlier in [45].

5.2.1 Problem Statement

In a real-life process mining project, there is an inherent difference between log-measures and system-measures because of sampling error and observational errors. Given the complexity of business processes, it is unlikely that all the possible behaviour and dependencies in a process can be recorded in a reasonable time span. As a result, log-precision might be lower than system-precision because the model allows for unrecorded but correct behaviour. On the other hand, there can be measurement errors in the data. These can lead to a log-fitness which is lower than system-fitness, because the model is penalised for not being able to replay behaviour which turns out to be incorrect. Furthermore, measurement errors can have an opposite impact on precision, and sampling error can have an opposite impact on fitness. However, system-based measures cannot be computed since the system is generally unknown in reality. As a result, the question is whether the existing log-based measures are good estimators of their system-based counterparts. To this end we define

$$\Delta F(L, M, S) = F^L(M, L) - F^S(M, S) \tag{5.5}$$

ΔF can be computed for each of the existing fitness metrics. For example, to investigate the quality of Token-Based Fitness as an estimator of system-fitness, we inspect $\Delta F_{tb}(L, M, S) = F_{tb}(M, L) - F_{tb}(M, S)$. By using the Token-Based Fitness measure itself in the calculation of the system-fitness, any measure-dependent effects are ruled out.

The same analysis is conducted for precision, where we define ΔP as

$$\Delta P(L, M, S) = P^L(M, L) - P^S(M, S) \tag{5.6}$$

Using an empirical analysis, we will examine whether the existing quality log-based measures are indeed unbiased estimators of system-quality. Formally, the next two hypotheses are tested for each existing measure:

$$H_0 : \Delta F = 0 \qquad H_1 : \Delta F \neq 0 \tag{5.7}$$

$$H_0 : \Delta P = 0 \qquad H_1 : \Delta P \neq 0 \tag{5.8}$$

The methodology of the empirical examination is detailed below.

5.3 Methodology

In order to analyse the quality of the introduced measures as unbiased estimators of the fit between a discovered model and the underlying system, an experiment is conducted consisting of the following steps:

1. Generate systems
2. Calculate number of paths
3. Simulate logs
4. Discover models
5. Measure log-quality
6. Measure system-quality
7. Statistical analysis

A schematic overview of the methodology is shown in Fig. 5.1 and details can be found in Table 5.1. Note that the methodology is based on the proposed methodology in [135], just as in the previous chapter. Note that for step 1 till 5, we rely on Chap. 5. As such, we will only briefly discuss these steps were needed. For more details about the systems and the logs, we refer back to the descriptive statistics shown in Chap. 4.

5.3.1 *Generate Systems*

Systems 1 till 10 from Chap. 4 were used for the experiments in this chapter. Systems 11 until 15 will not be used further given the issues with feasibility. Only for 12% of these models the complete set of measures were obtained. Given the fact that even more measures are needed in this experiment—i.e. system measures—it can be expected that this number will even be lower. As such, we will focus on system 1 until 10 instead.

5.3.2 *Simulate Logs*

Next to the logs that were already simulated in the previous Chapter, a additional set of ground truth event logs were generated for each systems—i.e. logs which are complete and have no noise. For each system, five ground truth logs were created for the measurement of system-quality. It was chosen to use five logs instead of a

Table 5.1 Experimental setup.

Step	Characteristic	Value
1	Number of systems	10
3	Completeness Levels	100%, 75%, 50%, 25%
	Noise levels	0%, 5%, 10%, 15%
	Number of logs	800 logs
4	Discovery algorithms	Heuristics [138]
		Inductive [97]
		ILP [139]
	Number of models	2400 models
5	Fitness	Token-Based Fitness [117]
		Behavioural Recall [60]
		Alignment-Based Fitness [6]
	Precision	Alignment-Based Precision [6]
		Behavioural Precision [22]
		One Align Precision [12]
		Best Align Precision [12]
	Generalization	Alignment Based Generalization [6]
		Behavioural Generalization [22]

single log to limit the influence of sampling. While all ground truth event logs are guaranteed to contain the same amount of behaviour, there can be differences in the frequencies of traces because of the random simulations.

5.3.3 *Discover Models*

In contrast to the experiment in Chap. 4, the Flower Miner and Alpha Miner are not used for this experiment. In particular, Flower Miner does not provide very realistic models, which would make its inclusion in this experiment irrelevant. The Alpha Miner was not considered further because of the poor quality of the discovered models.

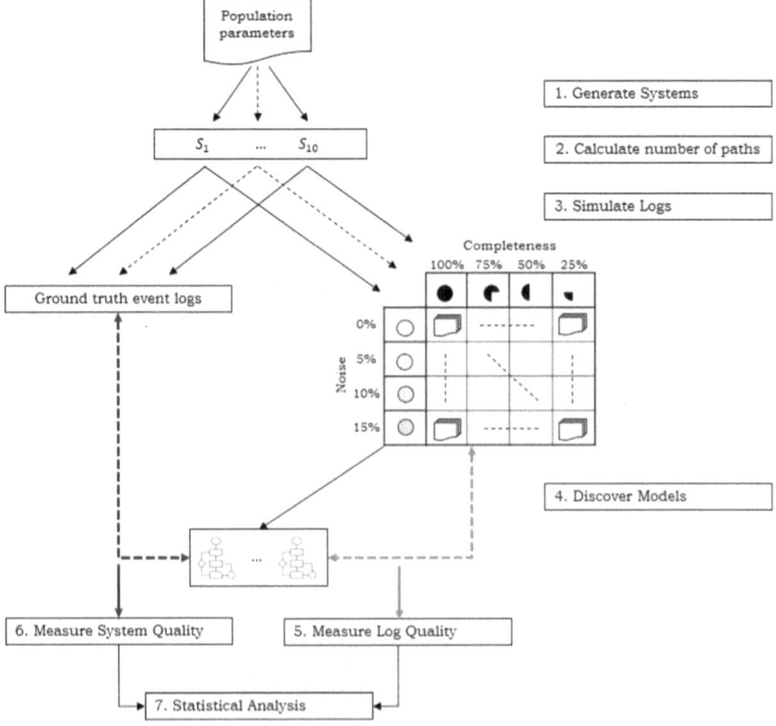

Fig. 5.1 Schematic overview of methodology

5.3.4 Measure Log-Quality

After the event logs are generated and the models are discovered, the same quality measures as those in Chap. 4 are applied to each discovered process model and the event log it was learned from. Since there are 2400 process models and 9 quality measures, this results in a total of 21600 measurements.

5.3.5 Measure System-Quality

Next to the log-quality, also the system-quality of process models is measured. This is done by applying each of the fitness and precision measures with respect to the ground truth event log for each of the systems, as to compute system-fitness and system-precision of these models. This means that for each model there are actually 3 system-fitness measures and 4 system-precision measures.

Note that the ground truth event logs of the systems are used for several reasons. Firstly, there are no metrics for quantifying a notion of fitness and precision between two process models, which is solved by representing one of them as an equivalent event log. Secondly, the systems are better candidates to be represented by a ground truth event log than the models, as the latter may not be sound. Deadlocks or livelocks might cause problems when simulating the models. Also, the calculated number of paths is essential to assure the ground truth event logs are complete. Calculating the number of paths in the discovered models might not be feasible for all discovered models, as the technique in [82] requires block-structuredness, which is not guaranteed by ILP-miner and Heuristic miner. Finally, from the viewpoint of comparing log-measures with system-measures, it appears more logical to use the discovered model in the same appearance (i.e. as a process model) in both measurements. The system-quality of each model is determined by computing the measures between the model and each of the five ground truth event logs, and averaging over the obtained number. While all ground truth event logs are guaranteed to contain the same amount of behaviour, there can be differences in the frequencies of traces because of the random simulations.

5.3.6 *Statistical Analysis*

The analysis of the results consists of two parts. The first part analyses the difference between log-measures on the one hand, and system-measures on the other hand. The aim here is to see whether log-fitness is an adequate proxy for system-fitness, as well as whether log-precision is an adequate proxy for system-precision. The second part analyses the relationship between generalization measures and system-fitness.

5.3.6.1 Log Versus System-Perspective

In order to analyse the difference between log-fitness and system-fitness, and log-precision and system-precision, we investigate whether the existing fitness and precision measures can be used as an unbiased estimator for system-fitness and system-precision, respectively. This means that

$$E[\Delta F] = 0 \tag{5.9}$$

and

$$E[\Delta P] = 0 \tag{5.10}$$

regardless of the amount of noise or level of completeness of the log. Recall that ΔF and ΔP are defined as follows:

$$\Delta F(L, M, S) = F^L(M, L) - F^S(M, S) \tag{5.11}$$

$$\Delta P(L, M, S) = P^L(M, L) - P^S(M, S) \tag{5.12}$$

The distribution and expected values of ΔF and ΔP under different circumstances in terms of noise and completeness are analysed both visually and using t-tests.

5.3.6.2 Generalization

Although the concept of generalization, as discussed in Sect. 2.2, does not directly fit in the perspectives proposed in Sect. 5.2, it is to some extent related to system-fitness. As a result, next to log-fitness metrics, generalization metrics might be a viable candidate as estimators for system-fitness. In order to analyse the quality of generalization metrics as unbiased estimators, we compare their value with system-fitness. In this analysis, Alignment-Based Fitness is chosen as the reference system-fitness, as it is considered as a state-of-the-art fitness-metric and also scored good on validity and sensitivity in the previous chapter. Formally, we define

$$\Delta G(L, M, S) = G^L(L, M) - F^S_{ab}(M, S) \tag{5.13}$$

The distribution of ΔG is analysed in the same way as those related to fitness and precision, i.e. both graphically and using t-tests. Not only will the generalisation measures be compared with each other to see which is the best predictor of system-fitness, but we will also compare them to fitness measures, in order to examine whether generalization measures actually provide added value in the estimation of system-quality.

5.4 Results

5.4.1 Log Versus System-Perspective

5.4.1.1 Fitness

Figure 5.2 shows that the influence of completeness and noise on the distribution of ΔF is quite different. Note that in this and subsequent figures, there is a data point for each combination of simulated event log, discovered model, and quality metric used. In Fig. 5.2a it can be seen that, if the completeness of the log decreases, log-fitness measures remain unbiased estimators of system-fitness, but their precision as estimator decreases.

On the other hand, when the amount of noise in the event log increases—keeping completeness constant—both the variance of ΔF increases and its expected value decreases. In the presence of noise, log-fitness measures are thus biased estimators of system-fitness; they underestimate real system-fitness.

Table 5.2 shows the extent of the biases in more detail for each of the measures. T-tests were conducted to see whether the mean ΔF was equal to zero or not, under

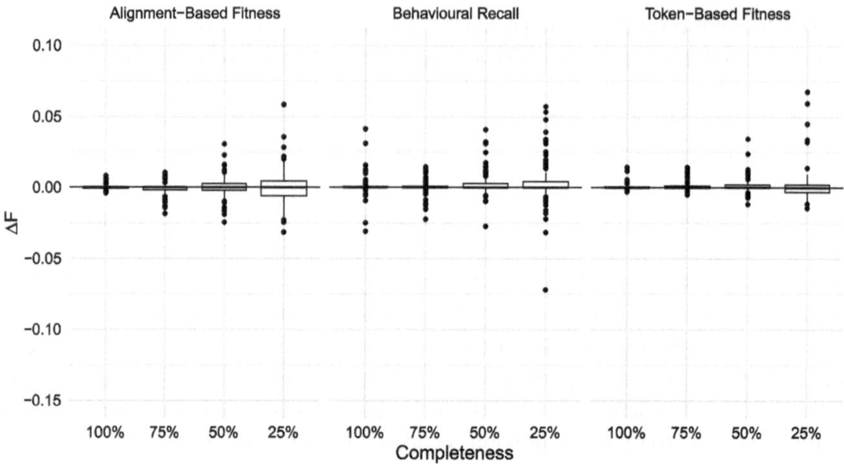

(a) Distribution of ΔF for different levels of completeness, while noise is constant at 0%.

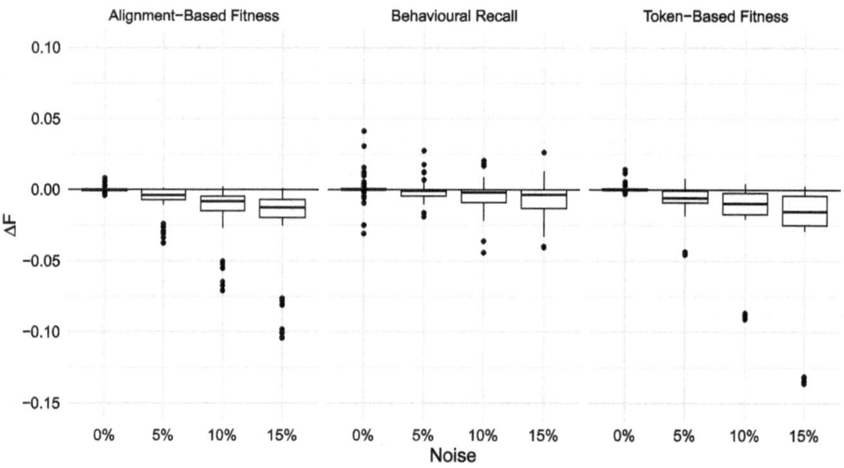

(b) Distribution of ΔF for different levels of noise, while completeness is constant at 100%.

Fig. 5.2 Impact of completeness and noise on ΔF.

the various circumstances. The annotated $*$'s indicate whether ΔF is significantly different from zero in a certain situation. In order to correct for multiple testing, the Bonferroni correction was applied. It can be observed that the impact of incompleteness (in the absence of noise) is limited, with only a few statistically significant differences. However, when the logs contain noise, there are statistically significant underestimations of system-fitness. It should be noted that Behavioural Recall is more robust for noise, having a remarkably lower bias compared to the other two metrics. On the other hand, it has a greater bias in the absence of noise. As such, in case where only completeness is known to be a problem, it would be more safe to

Table 5.2 Mean ΔF for fitness metrics under differing noise and completeness levels.

		Noise			
Metric	Completeness	0%	5%	10%	15%
Alignment-Based	100%	−0.0002	−0.0071***	−0.0144***	−0.0212***
Fitness	75%	−0.0013	−0.0081***	−0.0158***	−0.0217***
	50%	0.0002	−0.0066***	−0.013***	−0.0209***
	25%	0.0011	−0.0051*	−0.0115***	−0.0181***
Behavioural	100%	0.0011**	−0.0017***	−0.0047***	−0.0069***
Recall	75%	0.0003	−0.0017***	−0.0049***	−0.0076***
	50%	0.0024***	−0.002***	−0.0043***	−0.008***
	25%	0.0033**	0.0011	−0.0034***	−0.0057***
Token-Based	100%	0.0007	−0.0069***	−0.0155***	−0.023***
Fitness	75%	0.0011	−0.0049***	−0.0106***	−0.0195***
	50%	0.0016	−0.0037***	−0.011***	−0.017***
	25%	0.0024	−0.0014**	−0.006***	−0.0082***

Note: *p < 0.1; **p < 0.05; ***p < 0.01
Based on Wilcoxon signed rank test with Bonferroni correction

use Alignment-Based Fitness or Token-Based Fitness, while Behavioural Recall is a better option when the log is known to be noisy.

5.4.1.2 Precision

Figure 5.3a shows that when event logs are incomplete, precision measures are increasingly underestimating system-precision, while Fig. 5.3b shows that they overestimate system-precision in case of noisy logs. The mean ΔP for different levels of noise and completeness is shown in Table 5.3. In this case, both noise and completeness have a statistically significant impact on ΔP.

In general, it can be stated that incompleteness of the event log always leads to an underestimation of system-precision, while noise results in an overestimation. Log incompleteness means that models are compared with fragmentary process behaviour. Consequently, the precision of the model when compared to the fragmentary log will be lower than when compared to the full system. Logs that contain noise appear to have more behaviour. Log-precision will therefore be inflated. The analysis shows that both effects are statistically significant. However, making assumptions about the completeness and the amount of noise of a given event log is a non-trivial task. As a result, quantifying the bias in a particular case would not be straightforward.

Table 5.3 Mean ΔP for precision metrics under differing noise and completeness levels.

		Noise			
Metric	Completeness	0%	5%	10%	15%
Alignment-Based Precision	100%	−0.0002	0.0415***	0.0453***	0.0597***
	75%	−0.0032***	0.0339***	0.043***	0.049***
	50%	−0.0101***	0.0268	0.0379***	0.0384***
	25%	−0.0225***	0.0018*	0.0093	0.0122
Best Align Precision	100%	0.0013	0.0412***	0.0538***	0.0636***
	75%	−0.0066***	0.0201***	0.0161***	0.0308***
	50%	−0.015***	0.0085	0.0118	0.0104
	25%	−0.0394***	−0.015	−0.0063	−0.0111
Behavioural Precision	100%	−0.0012***	0.0595***	0.0728***	0.0837***
	75%	−0.0055***	0.0265**	0.0425***	0.053***
	50%	−0.0101***	0.0157	0.0185	0.0246
	25%	−0.0254***	−0.0073	−0.0088	−0.0047
One Align Precision	100%	−0.0004	0.0334***	0.042***	0.0467***
	75%	−0.0049***	0.0174***	0.0262***	0.0315***
	50%	−0.0156***	0.0069	0.012**	0.0152**
	25%	−0.0381***	−0.0124***	−0.0064	−0.0013

Note: *p < 0.1; **p < 0.05; ***p < 0.01
Based on Wilcoxon signed rank test with Bonferroni correction

Table 5.4 Mean ΔG under differing noise and completeness levels.

		Noise			
Metric	Completeness	0%	5%	10%	15%
Alignment-Based Generalization	100%	−0.0001**	0.0101***	0.0099***	0.0175***
	75%	−0.0052***	0.0053***	0.0066***	0.0077
	50%	−0.0141***	−0.0048***	0.0046***	0.0038***
	25%	−0.0291***	−0.0298***	−0.0275***	−0.0278***
Behavioural Generalization	100%	−0.0054	−0.244***	−0.2487***	−0.2529***
	75%	−0.0075	−0.2323***	−0.2527***	−0.2574***
	50%	−0.0073***	−0.194***	−0.2241***	−0.2431***
	25%	−0.0126**	−0.1466***	−0.1807***	−0.2***

Note: *p < 0.1; **p < 0.05; ***p < 0.01
Based on Wilcoxon signed rank test with Bonferroni correction

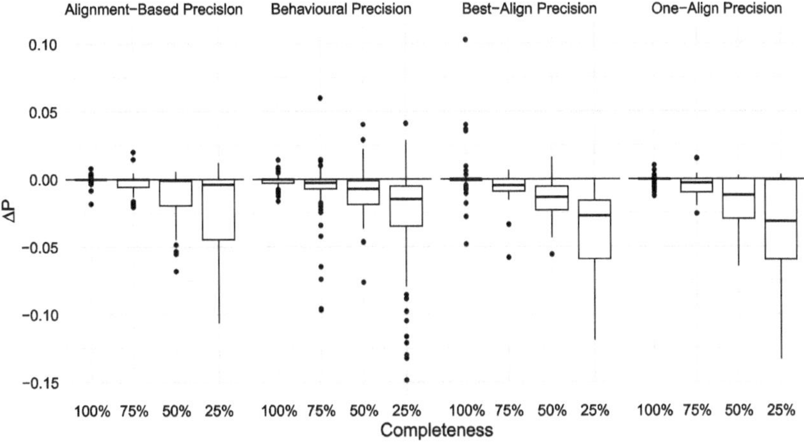

(a) Distribution of ΔP for different levels of completeness, while noise is constant at 0%.

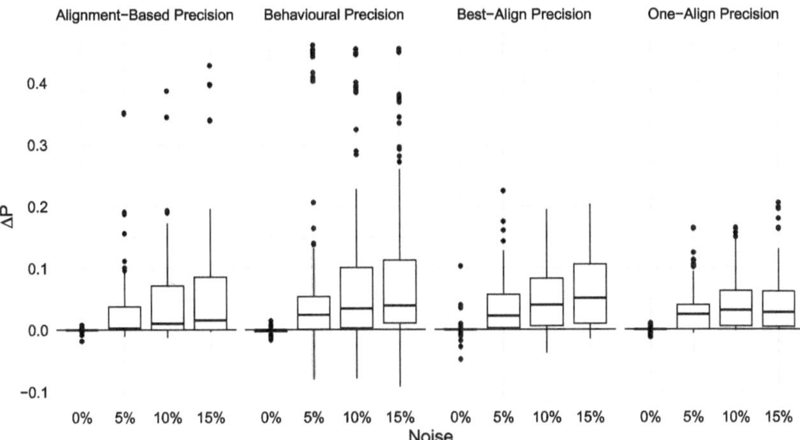

(b) Distribution of ΔP for different levels of noise, while completeness is constant at 100%.

Fig. 5.3 Impact of completeness and noise on ΔP.

5.4.2 Generalization

Figure 5.4 shows the impact of both incompleteness (Fig. 5.4a) and noise (Fig. 5.4c) on ΔG. It can be seen that there is a clear distinction between the Alignment-Based Generalization and Behavioural Generalization. Although ΔG is more or less stable for both metrics when the completeness of event logs decreases, this is not the case when the amount of noise increases.

Moreover, the impact of noise does not seem to be linear. For Alignment-Based Generalization there is a sudden increase in ΔG when the amount of noise is increased

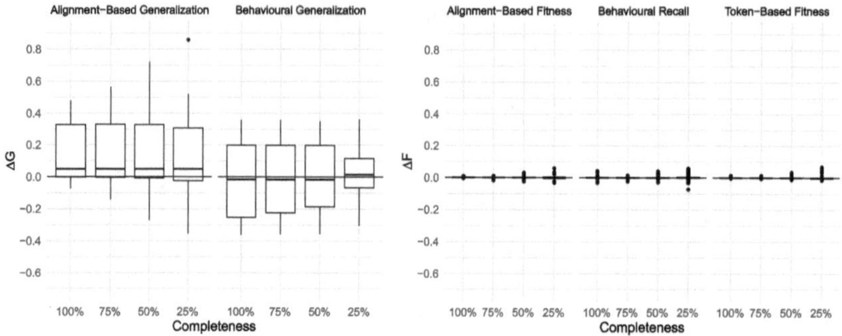

(a) Distribution of ΔG for different levels of completeness, while noise is constant at 0%.

(b) For comparison, distributions of ΔF for different levels of completeness, while noise is constant at 0% (Figure 5.2a).

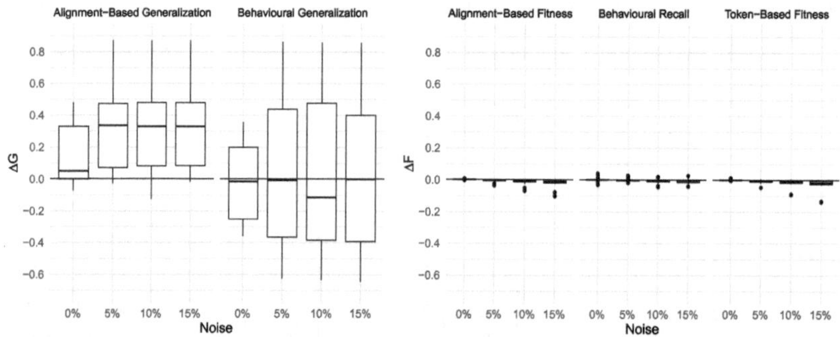

(c) Distribution of ΔG for different levels of noise, while completeness is constant at 100%.

(d) For comparison, distribution of ΔF for different levels of noise, while completeness is constant at 100% (Figure 5.2b).

Fig. 5.4 Impact of completeness and noise on ΔG.

from 0% to 5%. As a result, this generalization metric overestimates system-fitness. However, when noise increases further than 5%, there is no increase in the overestimation. On the other hand, the pattern for Behavioural Generalization is more erratic, with a strange underestimation for logs with 10% noise, while the bias remains limited at other levels of noise.

For comparison, the distributions of ΔF shown in Fig. 5.2 are repeated next to the distributions of ΔG for completeness (Fig. 5.4b) and noise (Fig. 5.4d). It can be seen that the fitness measures clearly are better at estimating system-fitness than the generalisation measures are, in terms of the size of the bias as well as the variation of the bias.

The mean values of ΔG in Table 5.4 show that for both metrics, ΔG is statistically different from zero in nearly all situations where noise or incompleteness is the case. This indicates that Behavioural generalization is consistently underestimating system-fitness, even in the absence of noise and for complete event logs.

5.5 Discussion

When assessing the quality of a process model, often the implicit goal is to find out whether it reflects the underlying, unknown process, on the basis of the sample of event data that has been collected. However, the ability of current metrics to assess the similarity between a process model and the underlying system has never been explicitly tested. As a result, one should be careful when interpreting the obtained measures.

The empirical analysis described in this chapter shows that the fitness and precision measures are indeed biased estimators of system-fitness and system-precision in realistic circumstances, i.e. in the presence of noise and incomplete event data.

Noise leads to overestimation of system-precision and underestimation of system-fitness, while incompleteness has the opposite effect. While the direction of the biases are intuitive, the empirical study has shown how severe they are in terms of the level of noise and incompleteness used. Nonetheless, estimating what the amount of noise or the level of log completeness is in a specific practical context is a difficult task.

It can thus be concluded that, given the measures which are available today, we are not able to confidently quantify which model is the best representation of the underlying process under consideration, which is definitely an obstacle to evolve towards confirmatory process discovery. It is therefore important not to derive too many conclusions when using fitness and precision metrics, as they only assess the log-perspective.

If one would still like to have an estimate for system-fitness, the results suggest that Behavioural Recall is much more robust against the influence of noise than the other two measures, while those can better cope with incompleteness. Furthermore, the fitness measures are much better positioned to estimate system-fitness than the generalization measures are, which are strongly biased. Finally, it seems that Alignment-Based Precision has the smallest bias when used for estimating system-precision, both with regards to the impact of incompleteness and noise.

5.6 Conclusion

Since the emergence of the process mining field, the focus has been largely on exploratory and descriptive data analysis. In other words, the main emphasis was on the sample of event data under consideration, while limited to no efforts have been done to statistically confirm findings. For process discovery to mature as a research field and in order to increase adoption of process discovery techniques in industry, the latter step is however essential.

In this chapter, we connected the process discovery context with the traditional concepts and exploratory and confirmatory analysis in statistics and data science. In particular, when checking the quality of discovered process models, it is important to be aware whether the conclusions of process discovery techniques only apply to the sample of the event data, or conversely apply to the broader context of the process itself. In order to make these kinds of assertions about the system, it is shown that new quality dimensions are needed.

An empirical analysis showed that current fitness and precision metrics, which are targeted towards log and model, are biased estimators of the resemblance between model and the underlying system. As a result, although they are fine for measuring the quality of a model as a representation of the log, they should not be used when the goal is to make statements about the real process. Furthermore, the generalization dimension has been identified as a vaguely defined concept which is unable to properly grasp the relation between model and system. The implemented generalization metrics are moreover unfit to estimated system-fitness or system-precision.

The experiment described in this chapter has some limitations. Firstly, although the empirical analysis was performed using a set of systems generated with various parameter settings, the instances are too limited to compare the impact of individual parameters on the measurement biases. Further research would be needed to see whether the biases can be linked to characteristics in the process, and thus be analysed in increased detail. Moreover, while the results can be generalised to the populations described in Table 4.2, additional research is needed to determine the whether these parameters adequately represent realistic process models.

Secondly, since the algorithm for noise induction does not strictly ensures that the resulting traces are incorrect, the noise threshold is an upper bound and the completeness threshold is a lower bound. While this creates difficulties in interpreting the results of the experiment, it is less relevant from a practitioners point of view, in which the amount of noise and completeness is unknown in any case.

Thirdly, only three discovery algorithms were used in the experiment, each with default settings. While the aim of the experiment was not to compare different algorithms, further research is needed to verify whether the biases can be generalised to other sets of models.

We believe that additional insights from fields such as statistics and machine learning can facilitate the finding of solutions. Traditional statistical inference could provide answers when event logs are regarded as sets of traces with individual quality measures over which a standard deviation can be computed. Moreover, a promising track for further research would be to compare a set of possible models using Bayesian inference, in order to estimate the likelihood that they represent the underlying system, given the data.

5.7 Further Reading

1. Janssenswillen, G., Depaire, B.: Towards confirmatory process discovery: making assertions about the underlying system. Business & Information Systems Engineering, pp. 1–16 (2018)
2. Janssenswillen, G., Jouck, T., Creemers, M., Depaire, B.: Measuring the Quality of Models with Respect to the Underlying System: An Empirical Study. In: M.L. Rosa, P. Loos, O. Pastor (eds.) Business Process Management, pp. 73–89. Springer International Publishing (2016). doi: 10.1007/978-3-319-45348-4_5
3. Buijs, J.C.A.M.: Flexible Evolutionary Algorithms for Mining Structured Process Models. Ph.D. thesis, Technische Universiteit Eindhoven, Eindhoven (2014)

Chapter 6
Towards Mature Conformance Checking

Forward movement is not helpful,
if what is needed is a change of
direction.

David Fleming

This chapter formulates the overall conclusion of Part II, providing a synthesis of previous chapters in Sect. 6.1, together with challenges and recommendations for future research in Sect. 6.2.

6.1 Synthesis

A summary of the results of the previous chapters is shown in Table 6.1. In the subsequent Sections, the results will be described in more detail for each dimensions, and recommendations on the usage and future development of measures will be given.

6.1.1 Fitness

For fitness, three measures were analysed in detail: Alignment-Based Fitness [6], Behavioural Recall [22] and Token-Based Fitness [117]. It was found that Alignment-Based Fitness had the biggest issues with feasibility—the required time and storage needed to calculate the measure—followed by Token-Based Fitness, which had fewer problems, while Behavioural Recall had no problems at all.

A factor and correlation analysis both indicated that the three measures are highly related. Nevertheless, when compared in detail, it was found that Behavioural Recall is relatively insensitive for some fitness problems—scoring models with perfect fitness in contradiction to the other measures. Furthermore, it was found that Token-

G. Janssenswillen: Unearthing the Real Process Behind the Event Data, LNBIP 412
https://doi.org/10.1007/978-3-030-70733-0_6

Table 6.1 Summary of the results of Chap. 4 and 5. F = Fitness, P = Precision, G = Generalization, ab = Alignment-Based, ne = Behavioural, tb = Token-Based, ba = Best Align, oa = One Align.

	Measure	Feasibility	Validity	Sensitivity	Unbiased estimator
F	ab	✗	✓	✓	⚠
	ne	✓	✓	⚠	⚠
	tb	⚠	✓	✓	⚠
P	ab	⚠	⚠	⚠	⚠
	ne	✓	✓	✓	✗
	ba	✗	✓	✓	✗
	oa	⚠	✓	⚠	✗
G	ab	✓	✗	✗	✗
	ne	✓	✗	✓	✗

Based Fitness is more optimistic than Alignment-Based Fitness and Behavioural Recall.

When used as estimators for the fitness with the underlying process, i.e. system-fitness, biases exist under the influence of noise and incompleteness of the event log. In general, it appears that the bias as a result of incompleteness is limited for Alignment-Based Fitness and Token-Based Fitness, while Behavioural Recall is more robust to noise.

In conclusion it can be said that there is a trade-off between sensitivity and practical feasibility of the measures. In case that the event log and model are not of exuberant complexity, it is advised to use Alignment-Based Fitness, whereas in the case that the complexity poses problems in terms of memory and time constraints, one can opt for Behavioural Recall. The latter however is insensitive for certain fitness issues and should be used with caution. While Token-Based Fitness has less problems with both feasibility and insensitivity, it suffers strongly from representational bias—an issue not specifically addressed in the experiments. It should therefore also be used with caution, especially when comparing two or more models—in which case any reported difference might be the result of a different Petri Net representation, and not necessarily of different behaviour.

The above recommendations should be taken into account in the first place with regards to measuring the similarity between model and log. When estimating system-fitness it should further be noted that each of the measures is biased, especially when the event log contains noise.

It should be noted that further research to optimise the feasibility of alignments is being done, e.g. [49], and clearly needed. Moreover, additional empirical analysis is required to investigate the root cause of Behavioural Recall's insensitivity in certain cases in order to find out how to correct this, if needed.

6.1.2 Precision

For precision, four measures were investigated: Alignment-Based Fitness [6], Best Align Precision [12], Behavioural Precision [22], and One Align Precision [12]. Among those, most practical issues were observed with Best Align Precision, followed by Alignment-Based Precision and One Align Precision. Again, no issues at all surfaced for Behavioural Precision.

The correspondence between the precision measures was found to be remarkably less strong compared to the correspondence between fitness measures, and furthermore appears to depend on the discovery algorithm used. While the measures strongly agree on models discovered by the flower miner and inductive miner, they agree less on models discovered by the alpha, heuristics and ILP miner. The most probable reason for this difference is that the latter do not guarantee that the discovered models are sound, which can lead to strange effects in the model. For the ILP miner, it could be seen that Alignments-Based Precision returns atypical results, while for the heuristics miner deviating results were found for Behavioural Precision. For the Alpha miner, all 4 measures were less strongly related in general, although the most notable difference here was found for Behavioural Precision, Alignment-Based Precision and Best Align Precision.

With regards to the sensitivity, Alignment-Based Precision was found insensitive compared to all other measures. Furthermore, One Align Precision was found insensitive compared to Best Align and Behavioural Precision, and Best Align Precision is slightly insensitive when compared to Behavioural Precision. Behavioural Precision and Best Align Precision are the least insensitive of all precision measures as a result.

With regards to their ability to estimate the precision with respect to the underlying process, i.e. system-precision, each of the measures is biased when the log is incomplete and/or contains noise. However, it can be observed that the Alignment-Based Precision's bias is generally smaller compared to the other metrics, as well for noisy as for incomplete logs.

For measuring log-precision, using the Behavioural Precision is most advisable. The other measures—all alignment-based—suffer from limitations with regards to feasibility or are to certain extent insensitive for particular phenomena. Compared to fitness measure, the precision measures score much worse as unbiased estimators of system-precision, and should not be used as such. The only slight exception here is Alignment-Based Precision, which shows smaller biases. Peculiar here is that this measure was also found to be weakly correlated to other precision measures in certain cases. An interesting question for future research is therefore why this is the case, and whether the approach taken by Alignment-Based Precision is more suited for measuring system-precision than log-precision, and can be optimised as such.

6.1.3 Generalization

The story for generalization is much different from that of fitness or precision. Firstly, remarkably less implementations exists for generalization, and the ones that do use very different approaches. The metrics considered in the experiments in previous chapters are Alignment-Based Generalization [6] and Behavioural Generalization [22].

Both metrics were found to be very different from each other, having a nearly zero correlation. Alignment-Based Generalization did not significantly correlate with any other measure at all, while Behavioural Generalization was found to be relatively strongly correlated with fitness measures—though not as strongly as fitness measures are correlated with each other. When generalization is interpreted as system-fitness, the latter observation does not come at a surprise—log-fitness and system-fitness should clearly be expected to be correlated. However, Behavioural Generalization does not perform better as an unbiased estimator of system-fitness when compared to the use of fitness measures. As a result, it is not advised to use these measures at all, and future research related to generalization is much required. The following section will further elaborate specifically on this subject, among other things.

6.2 Future Research

The experiments of previous chapters and their conclusions indicate several important challenges to be tackled by future research—related to process quality measurement itself as well as to the empirical evaluation—which are further described in the next paragraphs.

6.2.1 System-Fitness and System-Precision

Since the moment that system-fitness and system-precision were firstly recognised as two different distance measures between model and system in [26], they have not received the status they deserve. The claim in [26] that system-precision is irrelevant when fitness, precision and generalization—i.e. system-fitness—are taken into account, partly explains why system-precision is largely overlooked. Similarly is the inadequacy of existing literature to guide practitioners in balancing the different quality dimensions, a balance which is often mentioned but never elaborately discussed.

The allegation that system-precision is irrelevant is unfounded. As Chap. 5 illustrated, there are two orthogonal criteria to measure the similarity between event log and model, and equivalently two orthogonal criteria are needed to measure the similarity between model and system. Furthermore, given the fact that log and system will

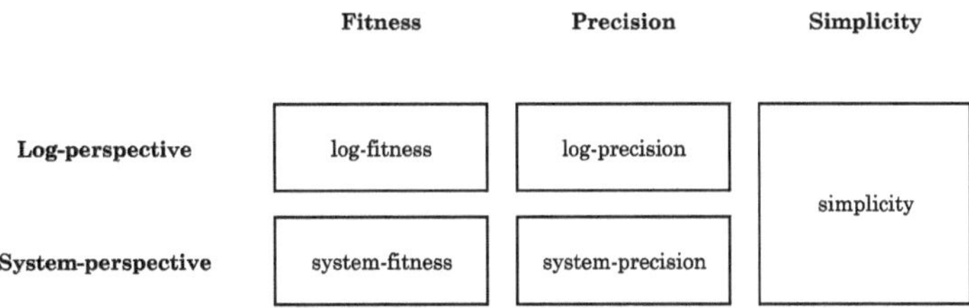

Fig. 6.1 An adjusted paradigm for process model quality measurement.

not be identical in typical situations, it is impossible to optimise both log-precision and system-fitness—i.e. generalization—at the same time. When the event log is incomplete, it is not feasible to have a model that is both precise with respect to the log—not allowing for additional behaviour—and also fitting the same—allowing for all system behaviour, both seen and unseen. Likewise is it unreasonable to maximise log-fitness and system-precision simultaneously. A model cannot at the same time perfectly fit with an event log, including all measurement errors, and also allow for real system behaviour only.

Instead, distinguishing between a log and system perspective—as proposed in Chap. 5—is crucial in order to recognise the existing trade-off in the measurement of process model quality, and will facilitate future development of appropriate quality measures.

As such, we strongly recommend an adjusted set of quality dimensions as shown in Fig. 6.1 in which both fitness and precision take on different interpretations based on the perspective taken, while simplicity takes the place of a third dimension which only takes into account the model characteristics. While the concept of generalization is still relevant and embedded in the proposed paradigm, its use as a separate one-dimensional quality dimension is illogical and incomplete, of which the analyses in foregoing chapters provide ample evidence.

In order to evolve towards this new framework, some important challenges can be recognised. Firstly, there remains the question on how to measure system-fitness and system-precision. Secondly, also the orthogonality of different dimensions, i.e. fitness versus precision, is of relevance. Both are discussed below.

6.2.1.1 Measuring System-Quality

Based on existing literature on similar problems, three different approaches to measuring system-quality can be distinguished. The first approach would be to simply distinguish between log and system-quality, under the assumption that there is no bias, and log measures are good, unbiased estimators of system measures. The second approach would be to develop separate measures, that through incorporating certain assumptions and workarounds aim to solve the biases that exist and provide reliable estimates of system-quality. The third approach would be to use k-fold cross-validation.

The first approach—using log-measures as estimates of system-measures—was investigated in this thesis and was found to be unsatisfactory, as discussed in Chap. 5. The same goes for the second approach, which resembles the use of generalization measures. The existing generalization measures are even outperformed by the used of log-measures as estimates, and thus do not have added value in the assessment of a models quality.

The third approach, k-fold cross validation, which was considered out of the scope of this thesis, remains as the most hopeful one and certainly merits further attention. The idea here, as illustrated in [14], is to split the event log into k parts—for example assume k equals 3. Subsequently, a model is mined from 2 parts, and fitness is measured with respect to the third part. This procedure is repeated until each of the three parts have been hold out once. Precision is measured at each time between the model—discovered from 2 of the parts—and the complete log.

The fact that both fitness and precision are measured in the k-fold cross validation is compatible with system-fitness and system-precision. Limitations of the approach are practical issues for high k values, given the feasibility problems with existing measures—which makes advancements on this level even more welcome. Furthermore, it is unclear whether the approach also works well to assess the quality of a single model, i.e. when we no longer discover models by repeatedly holding out folds, but keep the model fixed at all times. Nevertheless, given the evidence on quality measures gathered in previous chapters, we recommend further research on the usefulness of this technique in the context of process discovery and quality measurement.

6.2.1.2 Orthogonality of Dimensions

Another issue is the orthogonality of dimensions. The conceptual formalisations show that both fitness and precision are orthogonal in theory, i.e. the fitness of a model is in principle not related to the precision of that model. However, the results in Chap. 4 showed that instead relations do exist between fitness and precision measures. Two important remarks are to be made here.

First is the fact that many precision measures use alignments to transfer a non-fitting event log into a fitting log. It need not be illustrated that this transformation creates an artificial relationship between fitness and precision, which is undesirable. By replacing unfitting traces with traces of the model, there is a considerable risk that the precision of the model is inflated. As a result, it is ambiguous whether the model is precise because its behaviour has been observed, or because something similar has been observed. Given the fact that precision should be independent from fitness, it is recommended that the exact impact of this alignment approach is investigated.

Secondly, it was found that the relationship between fitness and precision measures highly depends on the characteristics of the models taken into account, in particular the used discovery algorithm. Different discovery algorithms have markedly different *search spaces* which has a great impact on any analysis of the quality measures. Future research is needed to examine to which extent the analysis of discovery algorithms and of process model quality can be separated.

The above-mentioned issues related to measuring system-quality and the orthogonality of dimensions certainly require attention, but are not sufficient by themselves in order to proceed to a more mature conformance checking discipline. Among the important concerns that need to be investigated, and which did not get substantial attention in previous chapters are parameter settings of quality measures. Most measures come with abundant parameters which can have far-reaching impacts on the obtained quality values, while little guidance exist on how to decide on the appropriate setting of parameters.

6.2.2 *Improving the Experimental Setup*

Next to these concerns, challenges also remain related to the empirical analysis of process model quality.

6.2.2.1 Improved Benchmarking Framework

The calculations of the quality measures in the experiments were performed using the Comprehensive Benchmarking Framework for Conformance Checking (CoBeFra) [23]. Such framework, which centralises several metrics and allows for batch processing—i.e. multiple models and logs can be compared in a single set-up, greatly adds to the feasibility of large-scale experiments. However, several issues remain which prohibit such a framework of realising its full capacity.

Firstly, the framework is conceived using a graphical interface, which forms an important drawback towards large-scale experiments. While the framework can be employed using a command line interface, such work-flow requires in depth familiarisation with the source code and is not supported by documentation.

Secondly, the same graphical user interface limits the possibilities to interactively reproduce calculations. While the option to save input files is provided, they cannot be easily changed e.g., in case one wants to adjust some of the parameters.

An implementation of the framework in a scripting environment, such as Python, would not only remove said limitations, but would also be more inviting for peers to contribute with new metrics, or with updates to old metrics, as well as create more transparency on the framework. For example, it is unclear whether updates with regards to the complexity of the alignment-based measures such as described in [49] are currently implemented by the framework.

Furthermore, more attention should be spend on *how* to design conformance checking experiments. For example, which types of models to be used, which types of noise to be simulated, how to reproduce experiments, how to distinguish between analysis of conformance measures and analysis of process discovery, as they two are so strongly linked. There are many questions and decisions that need to be solved or taken in performing experiments for which currently little guidance or formality exists.

6.2.2.2 Evaluating Conformance Measure Using Propositions

In Chap. 4, measures were compared using correlation analysis, factor analysis and Lowess curves to see whether they are similar and to examine differences in sensitivity and optimism versus pessimism. However, the precise root causes of these differences were not investigated. E.g. why is fitness measure A more pessimistic than fitness measure B, or why is precision measure A more sensitive than precision measure B?

Most measures do not have an intuitive interpretation—they just return a value between 0 and 1, and it is difficult to judge whether the difference between 0.70 value and a 0.75 value is equivalent to a difference between a 0.80 value and a 0.85 value. As such, the information on correlation, insensitivity and pessimism/optimism is relevant from the perspective of a user.

Nevertheless, more insights about the precise characteristics of measures—their strengths and their weaknesses—is warranted. First attempts towards the definition of *propositions* have been made [5]. These propositions are intuitive requirements to which measures should adhere. Currently, it is only checked whether these propositions always hold, or whether there can be situations in which they are violated. By testing the propositions on realistic models and logs, a more nuanced evaluation would be possible—e.g. a proposition might hold in the majority of cases and only be violated in specific exceptional cases. Knowing which are these cases would be useful information in order to check when it is *safe* or not to use specific measures. Conversely, an empirical analysis has a higher chance of finding violations than an ad-hoc search for counter examples.

Related to this, we also strongly recommend that when new measures are developed, their publication is accompanied by an adequate analysis of their behaviour and comparison with the existing state-of-the-art similar to the experiments done in previous chapters and by matching their behaviour with the propositions mentioned above.

Part III
Process Analytics

Chapter 7
Reproducible Process Analytics

> Reproducibilty is actually all about being as lazy as possible.
>
> Hadley Wickham

7.1 Introduction

Part II examined ways to increase process realism through conformance checking. As a result, the focus has so far been mainly on process models, and how to measure their quality. In this part, we will shift focus towards the process data itself. Indeed, as a process is more than control-flow alone, progressing towards a realistic understanding of a process requires more instruments than process models and quality measures alone.

In this part we will envision a new tooling framework to extract insights from process data. The starting point for this will be an overview of existing process analytics tools, both open-source and commercial, and their limitations. As noted in Chap. 1, the focus for this framework will be on three aspects: flexibility, connectivity and transparency. Based on these aspects, from which requirements with respect to design and functionality will be derived as described in this chapter, the framework `bupaR` will be introduced. `bupaR` is an extensible set of R-packages for business process analysis, developed in order to support flexible, reproducible and extensible process analytics. As an evaluation of the framework, subsequent chapters will describe two case studies of this tool, in order to evaluate the added value of the tool, as well as its limitations.

In the next section we will further describe the problem, followed by the definition of the requirements for the new tool in Sect. 7.3. The design and development of the tool will be discussed in Sect. 7.4 and demonstrated in Sect. 7.5. Section 7.6 will discuss the final design and development in light of the requirements. Section 7.7 will conclude the chapter. The evaluation of the tool will be done in Chap. 8 and 9, by

G. Janssenswillen: Unearthing the Real Process Behind the Event Data, LNBIP 412
https://doi.org/10.1007/978-3-030-70733-0_7

using the developed framework in two real-life process analysis context. In particular, Chap 8 will discuss the use of process analytics in an educational context, while Chap. 9 displays the advantages of process analytics in a transportation context.

7.2 Problem Statement

Simultaneously with the increasing amount of literature produced in process mining, a large set of tools has been developed to implement the various algorithms and provide them to end users. The tools that were developed are both academic and commercial in nature, and are diverse concerning their ability to be customised, architecture, and the techniques they support. An overview of the existing tools in shown in Table 7.1.

The existing tools have several drawbacks which may limit their adoption for certain uses, and the adoption of process mining as a part of the data science field in general. Firstly, the majority of tools does not provide the possibility of creating work-flows which can be reused at a later point in time to reproduce the results. Secondly, since they aim to support any possible process, most tools are not (easily) customised, besides some commercial tools requiring a significant vendor lock-in. Finally, the majority of tools are stand-alone programs, solely supporting process mining techniques. As a result, they have no interface to more general or related data mining tools, which might also proof useful in a process analysis setting.

Subsequently, there is a void in the existing tool base, as there are no tools that are 1) conveniently connected to a broader data science ecosystem, 2) can be used in an iterative, reproducible manner, and 3) are easy to extend. This gap is illustrative of the field's youthfulness state, and it is imperative to overcome this limitation in order for the field to mature and facilitate the transfer of new techniques from research institutes towards practitioners. In the next paragraphs, we will discuss each of these aspects in more detail.

Firstly, most tools are conceived as standalone environments, at most as part of a bigger process or work-flow tool. While this can be explained by the fact that process mining evolved relative isolated from the broader data science field, this has important ramifications for industry adoption. The need for better evidence-based decision making in modern companies transcends the somewhat limited scope of process analytics. Not only will standalone tools for different use cases require higher investments from companies—especially small to medium sized ones—there is a risk for major inefficiencies whereas considerable synergies are possible across different domains. The very first tool to recognise this was RapidProM [8], which enables one to combine process analytics functionalities with a large set of general purpose data analysis and machine learning techniques. Integration with other analysis tools is also found to be one of the most important aspects of a process mining tool in a recent comparative study [25].

Table 7.1 Overview of process mining software (The list of the commercial software tools in this table is based on Gartner's Market Guide for Process Mining [94]. The open source tools include bupaR—introduced in this chapter—but also the more recent PM4Py.).

Tool	Vendor	Type	Website
Apromore	Apromore	Open source, Commercial	apromore.org
bupaR	—	Open source	bupar.net
PM4Py	—	Open source	pm4py.org
ProM	—	Open source	promtools.org
RapidProm	—	Open source	rapidprom.org
Aris	Software AG	Commercial	ariscommunity.com
Celonis	Celonis	Commercial	celonis.com
Disco	Fluxicon	Commercial	fluxicon.com/disco
EverFlow	Icaro Tech	Commercial	icarotech.com
Kofax Insight	Kofax	Commercial	kofax.com
Lana Process Mining	Lana Labs	Commercial	lana-labs.com
Minit	Minit	Commercial	minit.io
myInvenio	Cognitive Technology	Commercial	my-invenio.com
PAFnow	Process Analytics Factory	Commercial	pafnow.com
ProcessGold	ProcessGold	Commercial	processgold.com
ProDiscovery	Puzzle Data	Commercial	puzzledata.com
QPR ProcessAnalyzer	QPR Software	Commercial	qpr.com
Signavio Process Intelligence	Signavio	Commercial	signavio.com
StereoLogic Process Analytics	StereoLOGIC	Commercial	stereologic.com

Secondly, most tools are built for ad-hoc analysis of processes, and are not very well-suited for iterative, reproducible and interactive use. With reproducibility, we refer to the possibility to easily rerun analysis, while interactivity refers to the possibility to easily adapt analyses interactively. Both are complimentary qualities that are required to facilitate iterative process analysis, which is natural in a data analysis context. However, many existing tools have limited interactivity and reproducibility features.

ProM, for example, is one of the most extensive and open-source process mining framework to date [133]. While containing an incredible amount of plug-ins to support all sorts of process analyses, its graphical user interface largely restricts its use as an interactive tool. In particular, it is impossible to save a specific analysis setup to be used later, at the same time limiting the tool to be used interactively and iteratively. Other established tools, such as Disco, have started to introduce features to facilitate reproducing analysis. In particular, Disco introduced the concept of *recipes*, allowing you to save and reuse filter settings. While very useful, the focus on filters only, and the overhead in managing and reusing recipes, limits its added value. More heavy-weight tools, such as Celonis, offer more functionalities geared towards reproducibility. Among other things, they provide means to create reproducible ETL workflows and deploy reusable dashboards. However, the graphical interface for end-users is still not fully appropriate for true interactive usage.

Thirdly, the open-source tools that exist are not easy to extend. Given the relative novelty of the field, being able to add new functionality at a regular interval is critical. While the open-source ProM framework is extensible in theory, it requires a considerable time investment to do so, as one has to be familiar with the source code of the central framework. For these reasons, extension have come exclusively from the academic community whereas contributions from industry are non-existent. For the commercial tools, the users are fully dependent on the vendors for extensions of functionality.

Other concerns, raised in a recent comparative study of Disco, ProM and Celonis, are a lack of documentation and intuitiveness [47]. For a more in depth discussion of the commercial software tools, we refer to the Gartner's Market Guide for Process Mining [94] and a recent comparative study [25].

In the next section, these concerns will be taken into account when defining the requirements for the new tool-set to fill the void in the process mining software landscape. It should be noted that of the tools listed in Table 7.1, next to the solution suggested in this chapter, also the more recently developed `PM4Py` mitigates the identified issues, as both are very similar from a technical point of view.

7.3 Requirements Definition

The requirements of a new tool for reproducible and interactive process analytics can be divided in two parts: required functionalities and requirements about design.

7.3.1 Functionality Requirements

While functionalities were not discussed explicitly in the problem statement in Sect. 7.2, the comparative study in [25] noticed that tools can be placed on a wide spectrum according to the functionalities they support. On the one hand there are tools such as Disco, which provide relatively few functionalities - mainly import/export, process map visualisations, filter methods, overall statistics, and variant analysis. On the other hand there is ProM, which contains nearly each and every technique which originated from academic research over the past decade.

While it is infeasible to mirror the functionalities provided by ProM, a distinction can be made between basic functionalities and advanced functionalities. One way to do this is by looking at the flow of a process mining project as described by the PM^2-workflow [52] in Fig. 7.1. Three phases are particularly important from the perspective of a process analytics tool, which are 2) extraction, 3) data processing and 4) mining and analysis. Within each of these steps we define a certain basic functionality that should be present. Advanced functionality can be added later by making it sufficiently easy to extend the tool through appropriate design requirements (See Sect. 7.3.2).

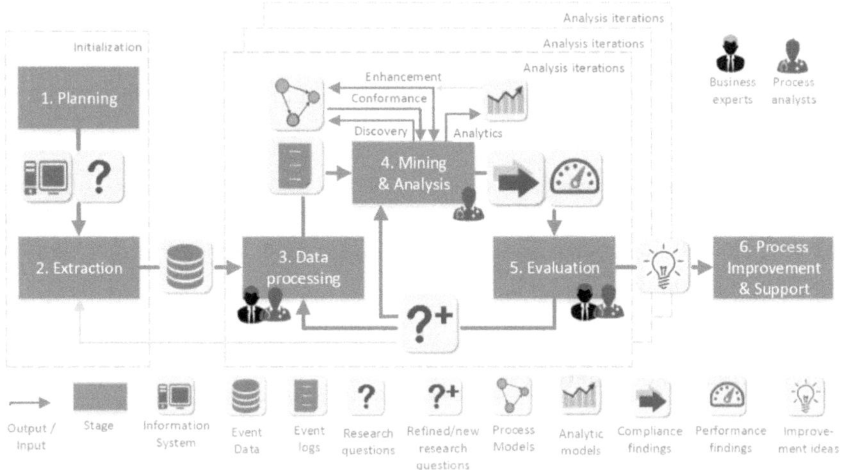

Fig. 7.1 Overview of the PM^2 methodology [52].

7.3.1.1 Extraction

Basic extraction functionality for the tool would mean to have an interface with the eXtensible Event Stream standard notation (XES) [133]. Furthermore, it is important to provide a minimum of support to transform event data into the right format.

7.3.1.2 Data Processing

Under data processing, four different tasks are considered [52]: creating views, aggregating events, enriching logs, and filtering logs.

Creating Views

One can look at the same event data from very different angles, by changing how cases, activities, etc., are defined. Creating views in practice is strongly related to the phase of extracting data and building event logs [72], and will further be considered part of this functionality.

Aggregating Events

Often, alterations to the level of granularity of events is needed to perform analysis at a higher level of abstraction [20]. Two important aggregation types are suggested in [52]: part-of and is-a aggregations. While deemed necessary, it is important to note that this is only a high-level categorisation, as there are many different ways to perform either aggregation.

Filtering Logs

The importance of data filtering cannot be underestimated, as it allows the user to drill-down to certain problems. As such, a large set of filtering methods is required.

Enriching Logs

Flexible enrichment of event data is not provided by most existing tools—often one will need to export the data, enrich it using a more generic data processing tool, and import it again. Being able to do so within one work-flow is therefore an important requirement for our tool.

7.3.1.3 Mining and Analysis

While the data extraction and processing phase can be considered largely as basic, essential functionality, the mining and analysis phases is much broader. Covering all existing techniques and algorithms for mining and analysing event data would be an extremely strong requirement. Instead, we list a set of basic required functionalities below.

- basic statistics about different aspects of the event-data (control-flow, time, resources),
- process map visualizations,
- dotted chart visualizations.

It can be observed that these minimal requirements are mostly focused on the *analysis* part, and less on the *mining* part. Disregarding the terminology, it can be said that these minimal requirements coincide with the functionalities that are offered by some commercial tools, such as Disco among others. Next to that, the analysis functionality can be greatly expanded through the design requirements, discussed in the next section. These will allow the use of general purpose techniques (classification, clustering, inferential statistics), as well as facilitate the contribution of additional process analysis techniques by users and academics.

7.3.2 Design Requirements

Next to requirements on functionality, we also formulate requirements about the design and architecture of the tool. Most of the problems listed in Sect. 7.2 relate to this aspect.

1. The tool-set should be embedded or connected with a general-purpose data analysis software, such that synergies can be made by linking existing data analysis and/or statistical techniques with process analysis applications.
2. Creating extensions should be straightforward, and well-supported through documentation.

3. The tool-set should allow to reproduce analyses, thereby facilitating iterative analysis
4. The tool-set should have a clear documentation and impose guidelines for the documentation of extensions.

In the next section, the actual design and development of the tool based on both the functional and design requirements is discussed.

7.4 Design and Development of Artefact

In this section, the framework `bupaR` is introduced as an answer to the requirements set out in the previous paragraphs. The term framework is used, because it is conceived as a modular set of packages, each having their own functionalities, which can be extended indefinitely.

In order to create a link between process analysis functionality and general-purpose functionalities, an existing general main-stream data analysis ecosystem was choosen. The statistical programming language R was selected as ecosystem for the new framework, because of its powerful IDE, Rstudio[1], the ease with which to make reports using Rmarkdown, and dashboards using Shiny. Furthermore, the rules for publishing packages with the Comprehensive R Archive Network (CRAN) ensure that all packages are well-documented. Moreover, CRAN and the wider R-community provide many useful materials to guide the development of new packages, thereby making it very easy to extend the framework.

While a comprehensive comparison between R and other candidate ecosystems, such as Python, for a new framework is out of the scope of this manuscript, as well as unreasonable[2], it is important to stress the increasing amount of possibilities to connect the two. As a result, it would be possible to connect R-based process analysis functionalities with future process analysis functionalities developed as Python libraries, thereby creating an integrated process analytics tool-set embedded in two general purpose data analysis ecosystems.

An overview of the different packages contained by the bupaR framework is given in Table 7.2. Note that the name *bupaR* refers to the overall framework as well as to the central package for supporting event data. We will generally use the term to refer to the overall framework, unless we explicitly state otherwise. In the next paragraphs, the functionalities of each of the packages is described briefly. More information on

---

[1] www.rstudio.com.

[2] Both R and Python are two widely-used ecosystems for data science, each with their own distinguishing strengths. While Python is increasingly well-known for it's machine learning techniques, R offers an extremely large repertoire of statistical techniques, and is powerful in the field of data visualisation. In recent years, it is believed by many scholars and practitioners that neither R nor Python will emerge as a predominant language. Instead, the two are increasingly being connected with each other. IDEs such as RStudio are now able to execute both languages, among others such as SQL. Rmarkdown documents even allow one to combine both R and Python code chunks within the same document.

Table 7.2 Current packages in the bupaR framework. *Latest version on 2018-10-08.

Package	Version*	Functionality	Availability
bupaR [75]	0.4.0	Creation and handling of event log objects and basic preprocessing tasks	gitHub, CRAN
edeaR [87]	0.8.0	Calculate descriptive process metrics	gitHub, CRAN
eventdataR [76]	0.2.0	Contains example event data	gitHub, CRAN
xesreadR [80]	0.2.2	Read and write .XES-files	gitHub, CRAN
processmapR [78]	0.3.2	Draw process map and other process specific visualization	gitHub, CRAN
processanimateR [102]	0.1.1	Animate process maps	gitHub, CRAN
petrinetR [73]	0.1.0	Read and handle Petri Nets	gitHub, CRAN
processmonitR [74]	0.1.0	Create interactive dashboards for process analysis	gitHub, CRAN
processcheckR [77]	0.1.0	Check declarative rules	gitHub, CRAN
ptR	0.1.0	Support for Process Trees	gitHub
discoveR	0.1.0	Process discovery algorithms	gitHub

how the toolset supports the different stages of the PM^2 methodology described above is given in Sect. 7.5, demonstrating the artefact.

7.4.1 Core Packages

The five packages below can be considered as the *core* of the `bupaR`-framework, supporting the basic functionalities described in Sect. 7.3.1.

7.4.1.1 bupaR

The `bupaR`-package [75] is the core package of the framework, which implements an S3-object class for event data. It provides functions to create these objects, as well as support for common transformations. Auxiliary functions to seamlessly change the classifiers of the event data are made available, and event log versions of common `dplyr` [143] functions for data manipulation are implemented, such as `filter`, `group_by` and `mutate`, among others. These functions can be used to preprocess event data. Some specific preprocessing tasks are supported explicitly by functions, such as aggregations of activity labels.

7.4.1.2 edeaR

`edeaR` [87] stands for Exploratory and Descriptive Event data Analysis, and contains a set of process metrics to describe and explore event logs. The process metrics are based on Lean Six Sigma literature [127] and can be analysed and visualized at different levels of granularity. Additionally, `edeaR` contains an extensive collection of event data specific filters.

7.4.1.3 eventdataR

`eventdataR` [76] is a data-package which provides easy access to event logs for testing and experiments. Currently, both artificial event data, e.g. `patients`, as well as real-life event data, such as the Sepsis dataset [101], are included.

7.4.1.4 xesreadR

In order to be compatible with the eXtensible Event Stream IEEE standard [133], the `xesreadR` package [80] allows to read and write XES-files. `Eventlog` objects created with `bupaR` can be directly written to a XES-file without additional transformations.

7.4.1.5 processmapR

Process data specific visualizations, such as process maps and dotted charts [125], are provided by `processmapR` [78]. As a result, `processmapR` is complementary to `edeaR` for exploring and describing process data, where the latter focuses more on numeric results and `processmapR` on visualizations.

7.4.2 Supplementary Packages

The packages below are extensions beyond the basic requirements.

7.4.2.1 processanimateR

By extending processmapR, processanimateR [102] allows to easily animate process maps using token replay. It supports several ways to customize the animations, in terms of size of colors of tokens.[3]

7.4.2.2 processmonitR

In order to facilitate the creation of dashboards using shiny [31], processmonitR [74] provides a limited set of process dashboards, focussed on a specific aspect, e.g. performance, resources, etc. These can be used in a permanent, real-time fashion, as well as for interactive data analysis. While still in an experimental phase, the goal is to extend this package to allow for easy building of custom process dashboards. Furthermore, built-in support for online analysis using partial cases and using event streams can be added in the future.

7.4.2.3 petrinetR

While all the packages above are centered around process data, petrinetR [73] is the first package to introduce a notion of process models in R. Currently, the main functionality is to create, read and write Petri Nets, to adjust them, visualize them, but also to perform token replay and parse transition sequences. While this package does not allow to discover Petri Nets from event logs, the goal is to link this package with the other packages by means of process discovery and conformance checking in the future. The first steps have been taken by the—so far experimental—discoveR package, discussed below.

7.4.2.4 processcheckR

Rule-based conformance checking can be done using the processcheckR package. It supports a range of declarative rules [112] which can be checked for each case, and the result is immediately added to the event data as a calculated variable.

7.4.2.5 ptR

ptR is a package for support of process trees in R. Its main functionality is the reading and writing of PTML files, and visualizing process trees in R. It also contains the algorithm for calculating the number of distinct execution paths, described in Chap. 3.

[3] It should be noted that processanimateR is an extension which was contributed by Felix Mannhardt [102].

7.4.2.6 discoveR

The `discoveR` package is a new package which provides process discovery algorithms. Currently it is still in an experimental stage, only avaliable on github, containing a very limited set of discovery algorithms.

7.5 Demonstration of Artefact

In this section, a short demonstration will be given on how the proposed framework supports tasks in the three phases: data extraction, data processing and mining & analysis (see Fig. 7.1). Note that this demonstration is by no means comprehensive, and only aims to show that the functional requirements defined above are met. A comprehensive list of functions is included in the Appendix (corresponding to the versions as listed in Table 7.2).

In subsequent chapters, more extensive case studies will be used to evaluate how the software can be used to gather valuable insights in real-life scenarios. These chapters will illustrate how it can be use for customised analyses and visualisations, as well as discuss any limitations compared to conventional tooling.

7.5.1 Event Data Extraction

Extracting event data is a complex process by itself, and necessitates many decisions to be made which have important consequences in the analysis stage. Common questions are: What is the process instance we want to analyse? What are the activities? How do we tackle correlation of events? A conceptual procedure for building an event log from a relational database is described in [71]. Besides deciding on what the event log should look like, it also has to be prepared. This can be straightforward if the enterprise management information system in place explicitly logs cases and events. However, when this is not the case, such transformations can be challenging. Several practical techniques and tools are available to help in this task, such as **onprom** [29], which is both a tool and methodology to extract event data from relational data sources. Other research has investigated more specific challenges, such as how to link different segments of process instances from multiple data sources which do not share a common process instance identifier [114].

Since an elaborate description of the particular steps and decisions needed in building event logs is out of the scope of this manuscript, this section focusses instead on the required structure for event data to be used in `bupaR`—which is linked with existing data structures such as XES [1]—and gives some guidelines to transform, create and handle event data in R.

Figure 7.2 shows the conceptual model for event data used by `bupaR`. An event log describes one specific process, which consists of a set of activities. An instantiation

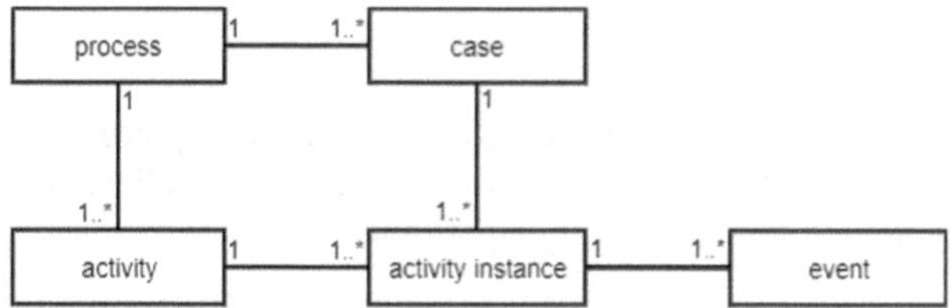

Fig. 7.2 Conceptual data model of an event log.

of the process is called a case, and consists of one or more instantiations of activities, which are called activity instances. An activity instance in turn consists of one or more events, which are atomic registrations of actions.

As will be discussed below, data in the eXtensible Event Stream notation can be seamlessly transformed to this format and vice versa using functions provided by bupaR. Futhermore, it should be noted that the conceptual model allows for actual data structures which have less details, e.g. where each activity instance is equivalent to a single event.

As an illustration, consider the example in Table 7.3. The event log shown contains data about a claims management process at an insurance company. When a client runs into an accident, it files a claim with the insurance company. The latter will then perform several checks in order to decide whether to accept or reject the claim. Each row in Table 7.3 is an event in the process.

In this example, each claim is an instance of the process, i.e. a case. Two claims are shown in Table 7.3, one consisting of seven activity instances and a second consisting of 13 activity instances. Each activity instance has an activity type (indicated by the activity column). Note that in this example all activity instances within a case have a unique activity label, but this is not required. In general, there can be multiple activity instances in a case with the same label. Some of the activity instances, e.g. the Check Contract - 12009, consist of more than one event. This means that more than one time registration is related to this activity instance. Events are always atomic, i.e. they do not have a duration, while activity instances can have a time duration.

Next to these four data elements (case, activity, activity instance, and timestamp), `bupaR` ideally expects two more data attributes: a transactional lifecycle status and a resource. When an activity instance consists of multiple events, the transactional lifecycle status gives an interpretation to each of the events. In the example, we can see that Check Contract - 12009 *started* on the 20th of June, while it was *completed* on the 21st of June. While a detailed standard transactional lifecycle is available (see Fig. 7.3 [3]), typically only complete events are recorded. Occasionally, both start and complete events are available. In the claims data, most activity instances only have a complete event, while some also have a start event. Of course, the more different statuses are recorded for a single activity instance, the more detailed analyses can be performed.

Table 7.3 Example event log about claim management.

	claim_id	act_ins	Activity	Status	Date	Resource
1	160	12007	Accident	Complete	2008-06-09	Client x
2	160	12008	File Claim	Complete	2008-06-17	Client x
3	160	12009	Check Contract	Start	2008-06-20	Assistant 5
4	160	12009	Check Contract	Complete	2008-06-21	Assistant 5
5	160	12010	Franchise?	Complete	2008-06-21	Assistant 5
6	160	12011	Covered?	Complete	2008-06-23	Assistant 5
7	160	12012	Acceptance Decision	Complete	2008-06-28	Manager 2
8	160	12013	Reject Claim	Complete	2008-07-01	Manager 2
9	262	13279	Accident	Complete	2008-09-19	Client x
10	262	13280	File Claim	Complete	2008-09-27	Client x
11	262	13281	Check Contract	Start	2008-09-30	Assistant 7
12	262	13281	Check Contract	Complete	2008-10-01	Assistant 7
13	262	13282	Franchise?	Complete	2008-10-01	Assistant 7
14	262	13283	Covered?	Complete	2008-10-03	Assistant 7
15	262	13284	Acceptance Decision	Complete	2008-10-08	Manager 2
16	262	13285	Start Investigation	Complete	2008-10-20	Assistant 7
17	262	13286	Appoint Lawyer	Complete	2008-10-29	Manager 2
18	262	13287	Appoint Expert	Complete	2008-10-29	Manager 2
19	262	13288	Receive Conclusion Expert	Complete	2008-11-18	Assistant 7
20	262	13289	Receive Conclusion Lawyer	Complete	2008-11-28	Assistant 7
21	262	13290	Pay Back Decision	Start	2008-12-08	Manager 2
22	262	13290	Pay Back Decision	Complete	2008-12-09	Manager 2
23	262	13291	Pay Claim	Complete	2009-01-23	Assistant 7

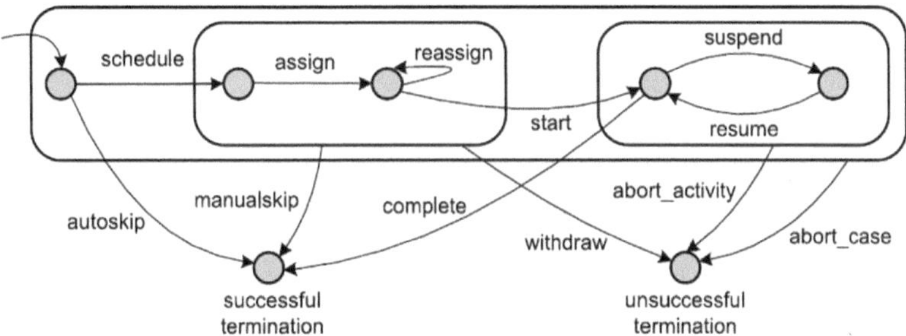

Fig. 7.3 Standard transactional lifecycle model [3].

Finally, also a resource variable is—ideally—expected by the event log constructor. This variable indicates which resource was responsible for the event. The concept of a resource can refer to process participants, software systems, or equipment [51].

Additional data attributes can be present, depending on the context of the process. These can be defined at the level of a case, i.e. *case attributes*, or at the level of a single event, i.e. *event attributes*. An example of a case attribute in the claims management process could be "Outcome", which records the final outcome of the claim (Reject, Refund or No refund). An example of an event attribute in this process could be "Cost", which records the cost which was incurred while executing an activity instance, if any.

To summarise, ideally six different data attributes should be available for each event in order to create an event log:

- Case identifier
- Activity identifier
- Activity instance identifier
- Timestamp
- Lifecycle status
- Resource identifier

Given a data.frame with event data in R, an event log object can then be generated as shown in Code Extract 7.1. The `eventlog` creator function expects a data.frame object with event data, including a column for each of the six identifiers. These column names are mapped to the appropriate argument in the `eventlog` function.

Code Extract 7.1 Creating eventlog object.

```
eventlog <- eventlog(data,
                     case_id = "claim_id",
                     activity_id = "activity",
                     activity_instance_id = "activity_instance",
                     lifecycle_id = "status",
                     timestamp = "date",
                     resource_id = "resource")
```

During the creation of the object, a few checks will be performed on the configuration of the object. Firstly, each specified parameter obviously must be a variable in the data.frame. Secondly, the timestamp variable must be of the class *POSIXct* or *Date*. Thirdly, the activity instance identifier cannot be related to more than one case or more than one activity label.

These checks should be regarded as minimal checks and certainly do not guarantee that the object is a proper event log. This allows some flexibility in working with very unstructured event logs, e.g. not all activity instances have to contain the same statuses, there is no formal check on the statuses allowed, etc. A formal check would as such be problematic to cope with many possible variations found in event logs.

However, in real-life scenario's not all of these attributes might be available. When this is the case, one can resort to the *minimal requirements* to create an event log, which are the following:

- Case identifier
- Activity identifier
- Timestamp

In the latter case, the notion of activity instances and transactional lifecycle information is lost, which means that each event is regarded as a single execution of an activity. Furthermore, the resource attribute is not strictly required. An example of how to create these event logs in a simplified way is shown in Code Extract 7.2.

Code Extract 7.2 Creating simplified eventlog object.

```
eventlog <- simple_eventlog(data,
                            case_id = "claim_id",
                            activity_id = "activity",
                            timestamp = "date")
```

It is important to note that the output of this constructor will be an `eventlog` object as well, i.e. there is no distinct class for these *simple* event logs. This means that this constructor will automatically provide the additional dummy variables: activity instance identifier, life cycle identifier, and resource identifier. Since in a minimal event log each event is an activity instance, the activity instance identifier will be a new column with a unique key for each row. New columns will also be added for both the resource and the life cycle identifier, only containing the place holder value *undefined*. As a result, the `simple_eventlog` constructor will free the user of performing some typical data manipulations in case of less complex event data, and at the same time guarantees a proper configuration of the resulting `eventlog`. Event logs which only adhere to these minimal requirements will however not yield useful insights for some of the analysis techniques which will be discussed in the remainder of this chapter, such as processing time.

Next to `eventlog` and `simple_eventlog`, bupaR itself supports a few common transformations. One of those can be used in the situation where each activity instance is stored as a single observation but contains multiple time attributes representing multiple events. Such an *activity log* can easily be transformed to an eventlog using the `activities_to_eventlog` function. Similar functions are provided for the situation where each case is stored as a single row with multiple timestamps.

Instead of starting from regular data.frames, one can also import event data from XES-files using the `read_xes` function. Event data can be exported to XES-files using `write_xes`. For a detailed description of the IEEE XES standard, we refer to [1].

Finally, one can resort to other data manipulation packages in R to perform the needed transformations in case the tools offered by `bupaR` are not sufficient. Especially interesting here are packages such as `dplyr` and `tidyr` [141]. Packages such as `stringr` [142] can be used for string manipulation, which is sometimes required to correlate events, such as described in [114]. While not exhaustive, some example transformations are shown on the website of `bupaR`. In order to decide on the appropriate transformations needed in a specific situation, one can use [29] or [72] as a starting-point.

7.5.1.1 Different Views on Event Data

Changing the view on an event log with bupaR is done easily by using the eventlog constructor with an eventlog object and only specifying the mapping attributes that you want to change, as shown in Code Extract 7.3. Returning to the example of the claims, we can for example change the view as follows. The column *claim_id* is now used as resource identifier while the column *resource* is used as a case identifier. This means that the newly created event log will consider all the events belonging to a specific resource as one case. The arguments which are not specified are left untouched.

Code Extract 7.3 Changing view of event data.

```
claims_eventlog_resource <- eventlog(claims_eventlog,
        resource_id = "claim_id",
        case_id = "resource")
```

In case only a single element of the mapping needs to be changed, one of the individual *set* functions can be used, as shown in Code Extract 7.4 for the resource identifier.

Code Extract 7.4 Changing a single identifier.

```
claims_eventlog_resource <- set_resource_id(claims_eventlog,
                                            "claim_id")
```

While adjusting the view using the mapping attributes of an event log allows for every possible view, it should be noted that some very common views are built-in. For example, the resource_map function provided by processmapR (see further) is equivalent to the process_map function applied on an event log where the focus is on resources instead of activities. By providing built-in functions for this common alternative view on event data, the end user is able to save precious time for actual analysis instead of data preprocessing.

7.5.2 Data Processing

When the data is extracted, additional transformations are often needed to proceed to the analysis stage. The data processing step will transform the event data extracted, to make sure that it is optimally prepared for the analysis stage. This is often an iterative process. Below we discuss the three main types of data processing: aggregating, enriching, and filtering. Furthermore, some generic event data processing functions are introduced.

7.5.2.1 Aggregating Event Data

Aggregating event data can be seen as *zooming out* of the process by changing the granularity level of activities. Activities that are similar or belong together can be united or collapsed into a single activity, respectively.

Is-a Aggregation

An *is-a aggregation* means that two or more different activity labels are replaced with one unique label. As such, it allows to go from fine-granular activity labels to more general activity labels. In practice, this can be easily done using the `act_unite` function. This function expects one or more named character vectors containing activity labels. The labels in each vector will be replaced with the name of the vector. Alternatively, it is also possible to recode individual levels one by one with `act_recode`. As an illustration, Code Extract 7.5 unites the activities "Receive Conclusions Expert" and "Receive Conclusions Lawyer".[4]

Code Extract 7.5 Uniting activities.

```
claims_eventlog % > %
  act_unite("Receive Conclusion" = c("Receive Conclusion Expert",
                                     "Receive Conclusion Lawyer"))
```

Part-of Aggregation

The example above replaces the labels *Receive Conlusion Expert* and *Receive Conclusions Lawyer* with the unique label *Receive Conclusion*. This is useful when similar activities are defined at a too specific level. However, there also might be situations in which several low-level activity instances that belong together should be grouped to form a single higher level activity instance. This is what is called a *part-of* aggregation.[5]

If we look at the activity labels in the claims event log, we see the activities *Start Investigation*, *Appoint Lawyer*, *Appoint Expert*, *Receive Conclusion Expert* and *Receive Conclusion Lawyer*, which together form the *Investigation*. A part-of aggregation will replace the instances of these activities with a single instance of the *Investigation* activity, with a start event at the first timestamp (the *Start Investigation* instance) and an end event at the last timestamp (the last receipt of conclusions). For example, the activities relating to the investigation in the claims management process can be collapsed in a single "Investigation" activity, as shown in Code Extract 7.6.

---

[4]Note that the % > %-symbol is called the *piping symbol*, and is used to pass-through an object as first argument to the following function [16].

[5]One might prefer to keep the original, low-level activity instances as events of the newly created activity instance. However, this is not done by the default aggregation, since these low-level events will not fit the transactional lifecycle (Fig. 7.3), as is usually the case when an activity instance contains more than one event—e.g. as the start and complete events of several instances in the example in Table 2.1. In cases where retaining the original activity instances as underlying events is favourable, it is advised to perform a custom aggregation using the general event data processing tools discussed in Sect. 7.5.2.4.

Code Extract 7.6 Collapsing activities.

```
claims_eventlog %>%
  act_collapse("Investigation" = c("Start_Investigation",
                                   "Appoint_Lawyer",
                                   "Appoint_Expert",
                                   "Receive_Conclusion_Expert",
                                   "Receive_Conclusion_Lawyer"))
```

Note that collapsing part-of activities into a single activity is not straightforward in case where the sub process is iterated over multiple times, or in case when it happens in parallel with other activities. In these cases, it is important to correctly distinguish different instances of the same sub process. To this end, different strategies are provided by the `act_collapse` function. More information on these strategies can be found in the accompanying documentation.

The difference between both aggregations can be explained more detailed as follows. The *is-a* aggregation retains all activity instances, such that the frequency of the new label is the sum of the original labels. The *part-of* aggregation collapses different activity instances into one. As a result, the *Investigation* activity will only have 2244 activity instances, even though it represents 5 lower-level activities, or 2244×5 activity instances (under the assumption that all cases have the same 5 activity instances).

7.5.2.2 Enriching Event Data

While the aggregation methods discussed above change the labels of activities and merge activity instances, the data can also be enriched by adding event or case attributes. Enrichment of event data can be done in several ways. One way is to calculate or define new variables based on the existing attributes. Another is to compute metrics about the process and to add them to the event data. We will discuss an example of both options below.

Calculated Variables

New variables can be added using `mutate` from `dplyr` [143] in the traditional way. For instance, suppose we want to add a logical case attribute which denotes whether a refund was made or not. The cases in which a refund is made contain the *Pay Claim* activity. As a result, we can use `str_detect` from `stringr` [142] to detect whether any activity has the name Pay Claim, and add this as the variable `refund_made` as shown in Code Extract 7.7. More information on `mutate` and related functions for more generic data processing is given further below.

Code Extract 7.7 Adding new variables using mutate.

```
claims_eventlog %>%
  group_by_case %>%
   mutate(refund_made = any(str_detect(activity,
        "Pay_Claim"))) -> claims_eventlog
```

Add Metrics

Another option is to add a predefined process-related metric to the event data.[6] Suppose we want to add the throughput time of the cases as an attribute. We can do this by calling the `throughput_time` function with the arguments `level` set to `case` and `append` set to TRUE, as shown in Code Extract 7.8. The last argument indicates that we want to append the throughput time to the original data. Leaving this argument to FALSE (the default), the function will only return a list of cases with their throughput time and drop the event data. The metrics are further elaborated upon in Sect. 7.5.3.

Code Extract 7.8 Appending metrics.

```
claims_eventlog %>%
  throughput_time(level = "case", append = TRUE)
```

7.5.2.3 Filtering Event Data

Several methods for filtering event data are included in `edeaR`. All filtering methods take an `eventlog` as input, together with some arguments, and return an `eventlog` as output. The arguments differ depending on the method used, although there are some common arguments. For example, all filtering methods have a `reverse` argument to negate the conditions that are specified.

There are two different types of filtering. One group contains methods to filter at the level of entire cases, while the other group contains methods to filter parts of cases, i.e. at the level of events. Each of the groups will be discussed in more detail.

Case Filters

An overview of the case filters is shown in Table 7.4. All filters are implemented as S3-generic functions with methods for both the `eventlog` and `grouped_eventlog`. In the latter case, the filters are applied to each group in the event log independently. As a result, one can use these as *stratified* filters.

Filter Activity Presence

This functions allows to filter cases that contain certain activities. It requires as input a vector containing one or more activity labels and it has a `method` argument. The latter can have the values *all*, *none* or *one_of*. When set to *all*, it means that all the specified activity labels must be present for a case to be selected, *none* means that they are not allowed to be present, and *one_of* means that at least one of them must be present. For example, we can subset the part of the claims event data to find the cases which were either rejected or not refunded using this method as shown in Code Extract 7.9.

[6]For an overview of available metrics, see further in Sect. 7.5.3.

Table 7.4 Case filtering methods

Functions	Filters cases...
`filter_activity_presence`	... in which a (set of) activity(ies) is present
`filter_case`	... based on their id
`filter_endpoints`	... based on their start and end activities
`filter_precedence`	... based on precedence constraints
`filter_processing_time`	... based on their processing time
`filter_throughput_time`	... based on their throughput time
`filter_time_period`	... based on a time period
`filter_trace_frequency`	... based on the frequency of the related trace
`filter_trace_length`	... based on the number of activity instances

Code Extract 7.9 Filter activity presence.

```
claims_eventlog %>%
  filter_activity_presence(activities = c("Reject_Claim",
                                          "No_Refund"),
                           method = "one_of")
```

Filter Case

The case filter allows to subset a set of case identifiers. As arguments it only requires a vector of case id's. The selection can also be negated using `reverse = T`, thus removing the listed case identifiers.

Filter End Points

The `filter_endpoints` method filters cases based on the first and last activity label. It can be used in two ways: by specifying vectors with allowed start activities and/or allowed end activities, or by specifying a percentile. In the first case, it will only retain cases if they have a specific first and/or last activity. As such, this filter is very helpful in distinguishing unfinished cases from finished cases (by filtering on the last activity), or for distinguishing different types of cases based on the initiating activity.

In the latter case, using a percentile, preference will be given to more common start and end activities. As such, it will discard cases with a deviating start or end activity. The percentile value will be used as a cut off. For example, when set to 0.9, it will select the most common endpoint pairs which together cover at least 90% of the cases, and filter the event log accordingly. In both cases, the filter can also be reversed.

Filter Precedence

In order to extract a subset of an event log which conforms with a set of precedence rules, one can use the `filter_precedence` method. There are two types of precedence relations which can be tested: activities that should *directly follow* each other, or activities that should *eventually follow* each other. The type can be set with the *precedence_type* argument. Further, the filter requires a vector of one or more antecedents (containing activity labels), and one or more consequents. Finally, also a *filter_method* argument can be set. This argument is relevant when there is more than one antecedent or consequent. In such a case, you can specify that all possible precedence combinations must be present (*all*), or at least one of them (*one_of*).

Code Extract 7.10 Filter by precedence.

```
claims_eventlog %>%
        filter_precedence(antecedents = c("Appoint_Expert",
                                          "Appoint_Lawyer"),
              consequents = c("Receive_Conclusions_Expert"),
              precedence_type = "eventually_follows",
              filter_method = "one_of")
```

The example in Code Extract 7.10 filters those cases in which at least **one of** the following conditions hold:

- Appoint Expert is eventually followed by Receive Conclusion Expert.
- Appoint Lawyer is eventually followed by Receive Conclusion Expert.

Filter Processing Time, Throughput Time and Trace Length

There are three different filters which take into account the *length* of a case:

- **processing time:** which is the sum of the duration of the activity instances contained in the case.
- **throughput time:** which is the time between the first event and the last event of the case.
- **trace length:** which is the number of activity instances contained in the case.

Each of these filters can work in two ways, similar to the endpoints filter: either by using an interval or by using a percentile cut off. The percentile cut off will always start with the shortest cases first and stop including cases when the specified percentile is reached. The processing and throughput time filters also have a *units* attribute to specify the time unit used when defining an interval. All the methods can be reversed by setting `reverse = T`.

Filter Time Period

Cases can also be filtered by supplying a time window to the method `filter_time_period`. There are four different filter methods, of which one can be used as argument[7]. The selection can also be reversed.

- **contained:** retains all cases which are completely contained in the time period.
- **start:** retains the cases which started in the time period, regardless of their end point.

[7] Note that there is a fifth filter method for the time period filter, i.e. *trim*, but this is actually an event filter and will thus be discussed in the next section.

Table 7.5 Event subsetting methods

Function	Filter events...
`filter_activity`	... based on activity labels
`filter_activity_frequency`	... based on frequency of activity label
`filter_attributes`	... based on conditions
`filter_resource`	... based on resource labels
`filter_resource_frequency`	... based on the frequency of resource label
`filter_time_period`	... which occurred within a time period
`filter_trim`	... in the head or tail of a case

- **complete:** retains the cases which were completed in the time period, regardless of their starting point.
- **intersecting:** retains the cases which have at least one event within the time period.

Filter Trace Frequency

The last case filter can be used to filter cases based on the frequency of the corresponding trace. A trace is a sequence of activity labels, and will be discussed in more detail in Section 7.5.3. There are again two ways to select cases based on trace frequency, by interval or by percentile cut off. The percentile cut off will start with the most frequent traces. This filter also contains the reverse argument.

Event Filters

The filters described below filter individual events, i.e. they do not necessarily select cases as a whole. An overview of event filters is given in Table 7.5. Note that the output of cases and event filters does not differ from a technical viewpoint—both return `eventlog` objects. The only difference is conceptual. The case filters will never select only segments of cases, while event filters will.

Filter Activity or Resource Identifiers

In order to filter on activity and resource identifiers, the methods `filter_activity` and `filter_resource` can be used in a similar way as `filter_case` filters on case identifiers. They have an activities and resources argument, respectively, to which a vector of identifiers can be given. The selection can be negated with the reverse argument.

Filter on Activity or Resource Frequency

Instead of filtering events on the labels of resources or activities, they can also be filtered based on their frequency. The two approaches to do this are already familiar by now: defining a frequency interval or setting a percentile threshold. The selection can again be negated by setting `reverse = T`.

Filter on Attributes

The `filter_attributes` method can be used to filter event data using conditions. It is a wrapper around the `dplyr::filter` function. In general it is an event filter, although it can also be used as a case filter when the conditions only use case attributes.

Filter by Time Period

The `filter_time_period` method, which was introduced before, can be used as an event filter when the filter_method is set to `trim`. In that case, it will only retain events that occurred within the time period. If reverse is set to `T`, it will retain events which occurred outside of the time period.

Filter by Trimming

Finally, one can *trim* cases by removing one or more activity instances at the start and/or end of a case. Trimming is performed until all cases have a start and/or end point belonging to a set of allowed activity labels. This filter requires a set of allowed start activities and/or a set of allowed end activities. If one of them is not provided it will not trim the cases at this edge. Also here, the selection can be reversed, which means that only the trimmed events at the start and end of cases are retained. As such, this argument allows to *cut* intermediate parts out of traces.

Filter Interactively

Due to the abundance of available filters and their variety in arguments, each filter can be used interactively with a Shiny gadget. As a result, the user will easily see which are the required arguments for the selected filter. In order to do this, one needs to prefix the function name with an `i` (for interactive), and only supply the event log as argument. A Shiny gadget will launch asking to provide the other arguments.

7.5.2.4 Generic Event Data Processing

Besides aggregating, filtering and enriching functionalities, data processing can also be done in a very generic way. Towards this end, many of the *`dplyr` verbs* have been implemented to be used on event logs, and some special event data oriented functions are created. An overview of these functions is given below.

select, arrange, filter, mutate, group_by
Some of the main `dplyr` verbs received S3-methods for the `eventlog` class. The workings of select, arrange, filter and mutate are similar as for ordinary data.frames, with the exception that they return an object of the class `eventlog` instead of a `tbl_df`. The method for `group_by` is quite different, in the sense that it returns an object with class `grouped_eventlog`. As will be shown in the next section, this will have an impact on the results of other `bupar`-functions. There are also the shortcuts `group_by_case`, `group_by_activity`, and `group_by_resource`, which group on the appropriate column as specified in the mapping of the event log.

Note that no S3-method for the `summarize` function was made. This means that when summarizing an `eventlog` object, you will obtain an ordinary `tbl_df` and the `summarize` function will just perform the same manipulations as on a normal data set. The absence of a S3-method for event data is straightforward, as this function will typically change the entire structure of the data, both in terms of observations and in terms of variables. Consequently, the result will no longer be a proper `eventlog`.

The implementation of methods for `dplyr` generics has been set up to provide a maximal interface with `tidyverse` packages [141], containing general purpose data manipulation tools. Next to these, all functions related to `bupaR` can be easily used in combination with the %>%-symbol [16]. As a result, process analysis workflows can be created with ease.

sample_n, slice, first_n, last_n
Within `dplyr`, the `sample_n` function is used to sample n rows from a data.frame. The method for event logs does **not** sample n events, but instead samples n *cases*. In practice this will be a more useful sampling approach than sampling events, i.e. rows, from an event log. In the latter scenario, one would end up with parts of cases, or even part of activity instances, which is undesirable in the analysis of processes.

Similarly, the `slice` function for event data does not slice the dataset based on row indexes, but rather based on case identifiers. The order of the cases will be defined based on the position of the first event belonging to the case in the dataset. The shift from row-slicing to case-slicing is motivated in the same way as was done for the `sample_n` function: it makes much more sense to take a slice of one or more cases than to take a slice of one or more events, which will probably lead to the disruption of process instances.

In some cases however, it might be needed to take a slice of activity instances, or even of events. For these situations, the functions `slice_activities` and `slice_events` have also been created.

Moreover, the heads and tails of an event log can be selected using the `first_n` and `last_n` functions. The desired length can be configured using the `n` argument. In combination with `group_by_case`, this can be done on a case basis.

7.5.3 Mining and Analysis

The mining and analysis stage entails the actual analysis of the process. There are four different perspectives along which a process can be analysed [3]:

- The **control-flow** perspective which focusses on the analysis of precedence relations between activities. It includes, among others, techniques for process discovery, conformance checking, etc.
- The **time** perspective which focuses on the time dimension of process data. It therefore contains the analysis of throughput time, processing time, waiting time, etc.

- The **organizational** perspective which zooms in on the organizational context of a process, and mainly looks at the resources in the process.
- The **data** perspective: which includes both the application of traditional data mining techniques on the event and trace attributes and mining decisions related to choices in the control-flow.

Note that these perspectives can be analysed in isolation, or in combination with each other. For example, combining the time perspective with the organisational perspective can answer research questions such as: Which of the resources are overloaded with work? Which of the resources perform certain activities the fastest?. Another typical analysis requires that control-flow, time or organisational perspectives are analysed in relationship with different data attributes, e.g. which cases have a higher throughput time than others?

For each of the perspectives, a distinction between *numerical* and *visual techniques* can be made. Numerical techniques, from this point onward also referred to as *metrics*, typically return a data.frame with results, while visual techniques consist of process-specific visualizations. However, all numerical results can also be visualized using traditional plots. S3-methods for the generic `plot` function have been implemented to do so. Each metric is implemented as a S3-generic with methods for both `eventlog` and `grouped_eventlog` objects. Most visual techniques also distinguish between grouped and ungrouped event logs, unless stated otherwise.

7.5.3.1 Control-Flow Perspective

Control-flow refers to the order of activities in a process. Although an event log consists of a finite number of different activities, there are infinitely many orders in which they can occur and they can do so multiple times within the same case. The sequence of activities which are executed in a case is called the *trace*.[8] For example, the trace of the claim 160 in Table 7.3 is *Accident, File Claim, Check Contract, Franchise?, Covered?, Acceptance Decision, Reject Claim.*

There are different levels to analyse *traces* or structuredness in general. Firstly, one can look at the structuredness of an event log at a high level, i.e., whether the behaviour is very diverse rather than systematic. Secondly, one can look at typical patterns within cases.

Visual Techniques

A first visual technique to analyse the control-flow in an event log is to create a *process map*. This is a directed graph where each node refers to an activity label, and nodes are connected with edges to represent flows from one activity to another. Both nodes and edges can be annotated with (relative) frequencies. The default process map can be generated as shown in Code Extract 7.11 (see output in Fig. 7.4).

---

[8] It's important to note that throughout `bupaR` the term *trace* is used to refer to a unique sequence of activity labels—also known as a process variant. It is different from the term *case*, which refers to a single, unique execution of the process.

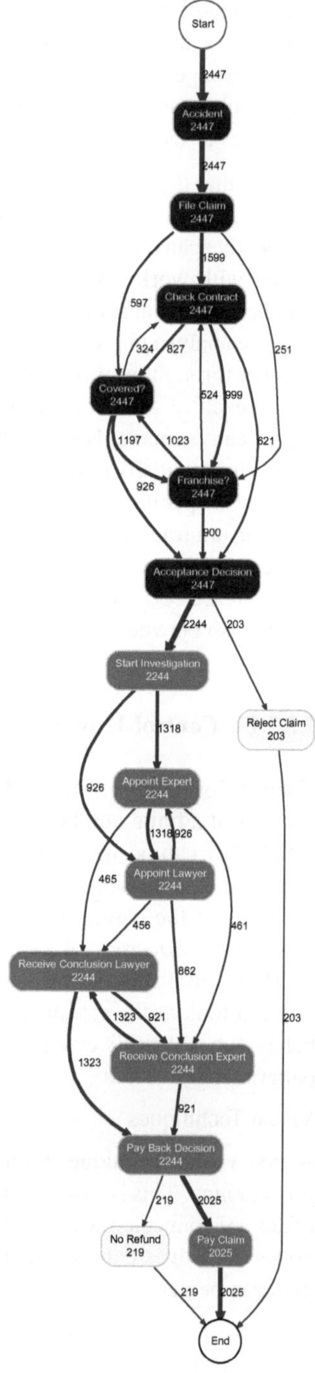

Fig. 7.4 Process map of claims event log.

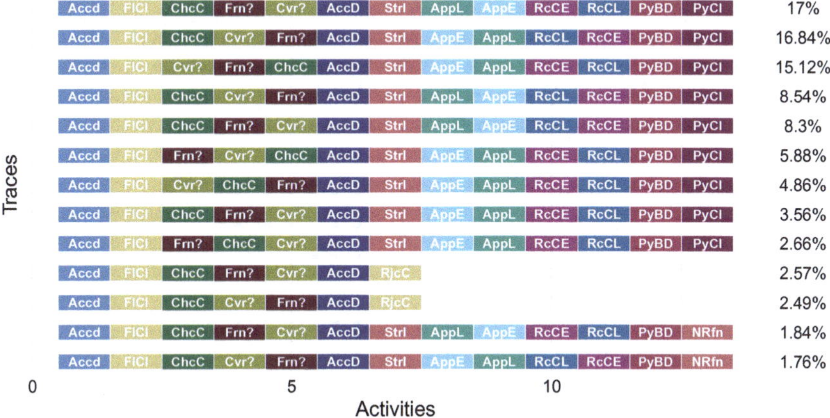

Fig. 7.5 Trace explorer output for the claims event log.

Code Extract 7.11 Creating process map.

```
claims_eventlog %>%
     process_map()
```

This process visualisation, shows that the process is fairly structured, almost sequential. In general, processes tend to look more *spaghetti-like*. Creating an understandable process map therefore typically is an iterative process, involving the use of one or more subsetting methods discussed in Sect. 7.5.2.3. The underlying data (frequencies etc.) can also be retrieved and further analysed through the `precedence_matrix` function, of which the output can be visualised using the `plot` function.

Although process maps have the ability to show *local* structures in the process, they are not well suited to visualise the different unique paths in a process from start to end. For instance, the fork after *File Claim* might have an impact on the path taken at the fork after *Appoint Lawyer*. However, these types of dependencies are not clear from this graph. An alternative is to analyse traces in a more grid-like way, which can be done using the *trace_explorer* function (Fig. 7.5). It can be seen that the first trace has a coverage of about 17%, while the coverage of subsequent traces rapidly decreases. The *coverage* argument states that this graph covers at least 90% of the traces in the event log. Visualising more traces would lead to an illegible graph. Code Extract 7.12 shows how to create the trace explorer output.

Code Extract 7.12 Creating trace explorer graph.

```
claims_eventlog %>%
    trace_explorer(coverage = 0.9)
```

Numerical Techniques

Numerically, the control-flow can be analysed using various *metrics*. The set of metrics are inspired upon Lean Management and Six Sigma literature. In this section,

Table 7.6 Methods for the numerical analysis of control-flow at different levels of granularity: Log (L), Trace (T), Case (C), Activity (A), Resource (R) and Resource-activity (RA).

Aspect	Method	L	T	C	A	R	RA
Trace coverage	`trace_coverage`	•	•	•			
Trace length	`trace_length`	•	•	•			
Start & end activities	`start_activities`	•	•		•	•	•
	`end_activities`	•	•		•	•	•
Activities	`activity_frequency`	•	•	•	•		
	`activity_presence`						
Self-loops	`number_of_selfloops`	•	•		•	•	•
	`size_of_selfloops`	•	•		•	•	•
Repetitions	`number_of_repetitions`	•	•		•	•	•
	`size_of_self-loops`	•	•		•	•	•

the discussion is limited to the implementation of each metric, although an overview of the different metrics and their fundamental groundings can be found in [127]. The metrics related to control-flow can be roughly classified in the following six aspects

- **Trace coverage:** analyse (the variability of) the support of the traces.
- **Trace length:** analyse the distribution of the number of activity instances per case.
- **Start and end activities:** analyse the entry and exit points of the process.
- **Activities:** analyse the frequency of activities.
- **Self-loops:** analyse immediate reoccurences of activities.
- **Repetitions:** analyse delayed reoccurences of activities.

Each aspect can be looked into with one or more methods and at different levels of granularity, of which an overview is shown in Table 7.6. Only one method, `activity_presence`, does not have an adjustable level of granularity. This method will always result in a list of activities. For the other methods, the result depends on the level of granularity, and will either be summary statistics (log), or a list of cases, traces, activities, resources or resource-activity pairs, respectively.

All the metrics that can be applied at *case*, *activity*, *resource*, or *resource_activity*-level have an `append` argument. If set to TRUE, this will return the original event log with the metric appended as additional case attributes. When the level of granularity is activity, resource, or resource-activity, it will append the metric as event attributes (e.g. values will vary for different events within the same case). When the level is log or trace, the argument will be ignored. Appending the metric output to the event log provides an easy way to enrich the event data or to perform more advanced filtering (see also Sect. 7.5.2). Some of the methods have additional arguments which can be set to configure the desired outcome.

Each of the metrics is implemented as a S3-generic with methods for objects of both `eventlog` and `grouped_eventlog`. In the latter case, results will be shown for each of the levels of the grouping variable(s) separately. The outputs of the methods have their own specific object class, and for each of these, an S3-method for the `plot` function is implemented to create a default visualization of the metric.

The example in Code Extract 7.13 shows the trace length at the general log level, grouped on the `refund_made` variable which was created earlier. It shows that for cases where a refund is made, there are always 13 activity instances. For cases in which refunds are not made, the amount of instances varies between 7 and 13. This result again shows the fairly structured nature of this process.

Code Extract 7.13 Computing trace length for grouped event log.

```
claims_eventlog %>%
    group_by(refund_made) %>%
    trace_length(level = "log")

 # A tibble: 2 x 9
   refund_made   min    q1 median     mean    q3   max
         <lgl> <dbl> <dbl>  <dbl>    <dbl> <dbl> <dbl>
 1        TRUE    13    13     13 13.00000    13    13
 2       FALSE     7     7     13 10.11374    13    13
```

7.5.3.2 Time Perspective

In order to analyze the time perspective, `processmapR` [78] provides functions for creating a dotted chart and a performance process map. Furthermore, numerical analysis of the time perspective is supported by `edeaR` [87].

Visual Techniques

A performance-variant of the process map discussed in the previous section can be created by adjusting the arguments of the `process_map` function. In particular, the `type` argument can be configured with an object of class `process_map_profile`. There are currently three ways to generate this profile object: using the `frequency` function (the default, which was used implicitly in Sect. 7.5.3.1), using the `performance` function, and using the `custom` function for custom attribute profiles. In order to analyse time, we use the performance profile, as shown in Code Extract 7.14, where we can configure the function to be applied on the time interval (defaults to `mean`) and the time units to be used. The result of this is shown in Fig. 7.6. The coloured nodes indicate activities with a duration, where red nodes have the heighest average duration. The many nodes wih a neutral colour do not have a duration—for these only a single event was recorded, as can also be seen in the example log in Table 2.1. The flows between activities are annotated with their average duration, which is also reflected in the thickness of the arrows.

Code Extract 7.14 Creating performance map.

```
claims_eventlog %>%
    process_map(type = performance(FUN = mean, units = "hours"))
```

The *dotted chart* is a process data visualization [125] which aims to show several aspects of the event data at once. Although configurations can differ, by default it

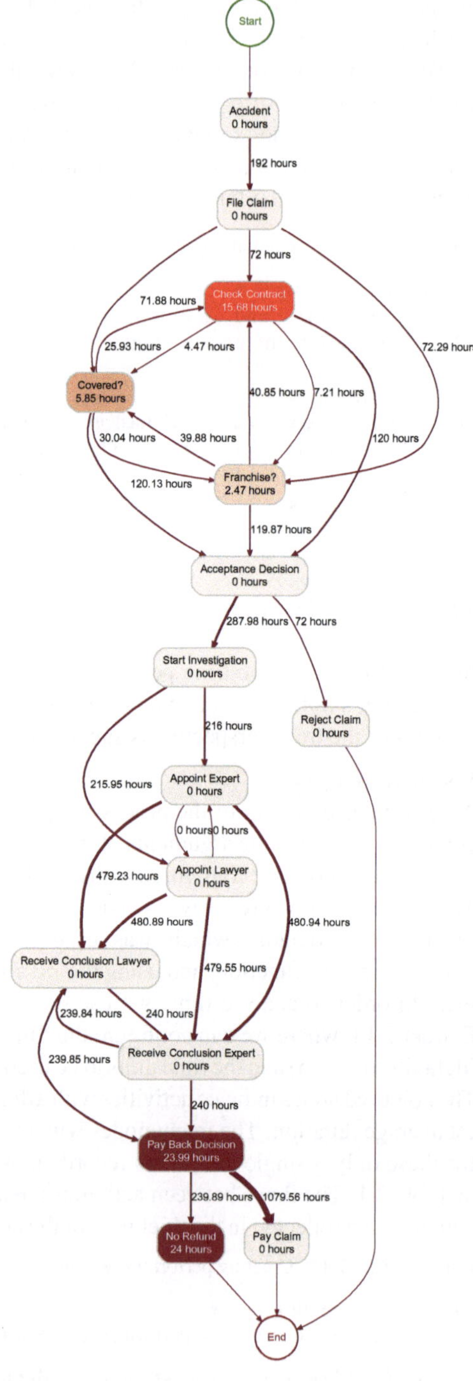

Fig. 7.6 Performance process map of claims event log.

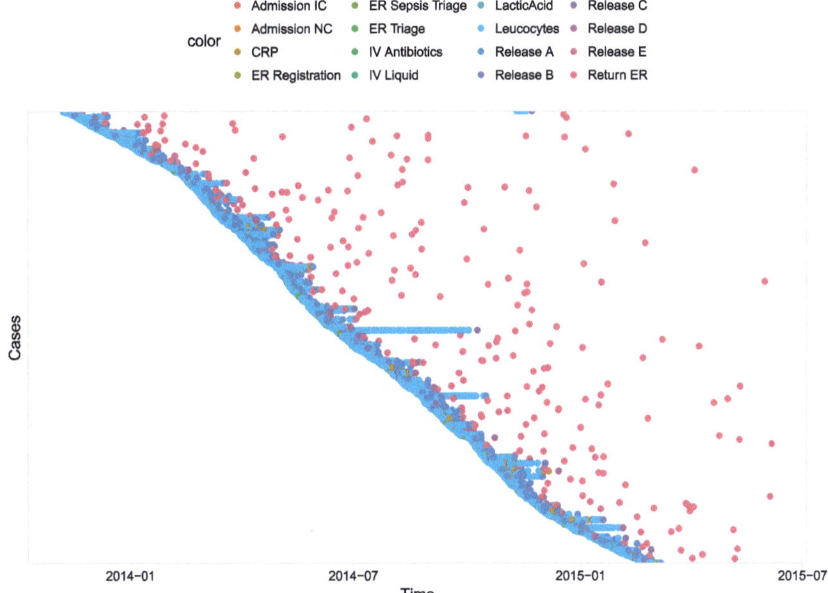

Fig. 7.7 Dotted chart for sepsis event log.

plots activities as a scatter plot with time on the x-axis and the cases along the y-axis. Cases are in this configuration typically ordered according to their first event, which results in the dotted chart shown in Fig. 7.7.

Another common configuration is by changing the x-axis argument to `relative`, i.e. the time difference between the start of the activity instance and the start of the case, and ordering the cases according to their duration, as displayed in Code Extract 7.15, which results in the dotted chart shown in Fig. 7.8.

Code Extract 7.15 Creating dotted chart.

```
sepsis %>%
    dotted_chart(x = "relative",sort = "duration")
```

It can be seen that the majority of cases have a relatively short duration while there is a long tail. It is also clear that the *pink* activities always occur at the end of the process, while the *blue* and *green* activities typically occur at the start.

Colours are typically used to visualize activity labels, although any other attribute can be mapped on the colour. Other configurations for the x-axis are the time difference since the start of the day, and the time difference since the start of the week. These show whether there are any patterns over time can be found, in days or in weeks, respectively.

Note that while this visualization mainly focusses on the time perspective, due to its many configuration options it can also be used to look at control-flow or resources, or a combination of different perspectives.

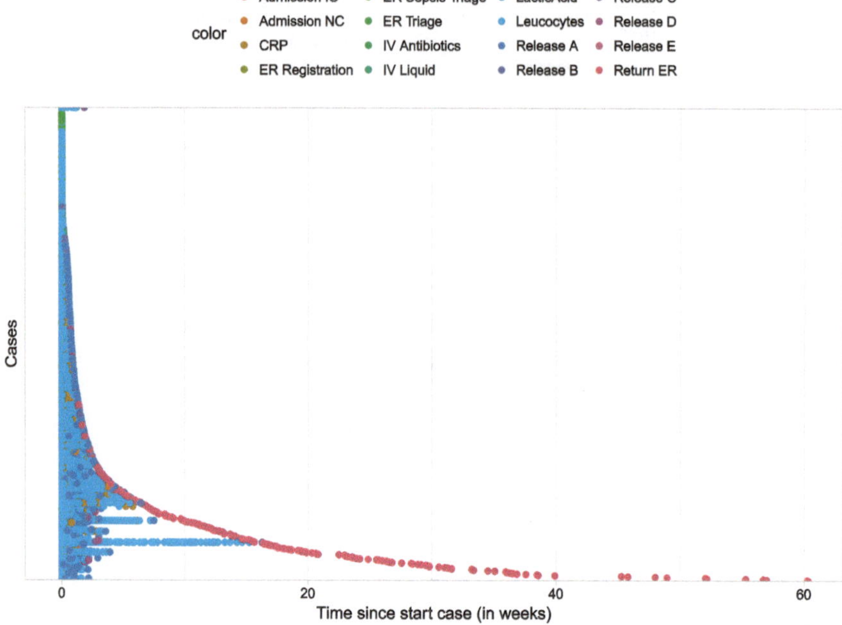

Fig. 7.8 Dotted chart for sepsis event log using relative time.

Numerical Techniques

For a numerical analysis of the time perspective, three different metrics can be studied, which are introduced in [127]. The implementation of these metrics is equivalent to those discussed before. The list of metrics and their granularity levels is shown in Table 7.7. The three metrics are defined as follows:

- **Throughput time**: the time passed between the first event and the last event of a case.
- **Processing time**: the sum of the duration of all activity instances. The duration of an activity instance is the time passed between the first event and the last event of the instance.[9]
- **Idle time**: the sum of the time spans in which no activity instance is active.

7.5.3.3 Organisational Perspective

Visual Techniques

To visually analyse the organisational perspective of a business process, a handover-of-work network can be constructed [126]. This is a directed graph that shows

[9]Note that the duration of an activity instance with only one event is equal to zero.

Table 7.7 Methods for the numerical analysis of time at different levels of granularity: Log (L), Trace (T), Case (C), Activity (A), Resource (R) and Resource-activity (RA).

Aspect	Method	L	T	C	A	R	RA
Throughput time	`throughput_time`	•	•	•			
Processing time	`processing_time`	•	•	•	•	•	•
Idle time	`idle_time`	•	•	•		•	

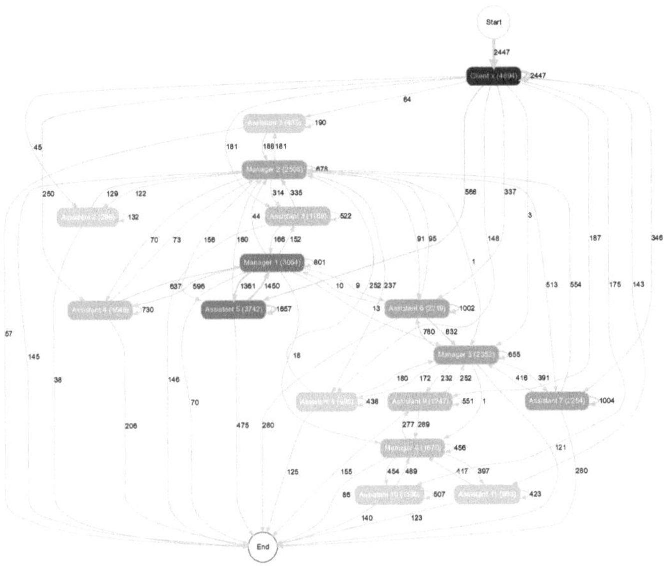

Fig. 7.9 Resource handover-of-work map for claims event log.

how cases are *handed over* from one resource to the next. With `processmapR`, such a network can be created using the `resource_map` function, as shown in Code Extract 7.16. The result is shown in Fig. 7.9.

Code Extract 7.16 Creating resource map.

```
claims_eventlog %>%
    resource_map()
```

Numerical Techniques

For a numeric analysis there are three resource metrics, as listed in Table 7.8, which are based on the work in [128]. Their implementation is again equivalent to the implementation of the earlier discussed control-flow and time metrics. Furthermore, note that also the *resource* and *resource-activity* levels of other metrics can be used to analyse the organisational perspective.

Table 7.8 Methods for the numerical analysis of resources at different levels of granularity: Log (L), Trace (T), Case (C), Activity (A), Resource (R) and Resource-activity (RA).

Aspect	Method	L	T	C	A	R	RA
Frequency	`resource_frequency`	•		•	•	•	•
Involvement	`resource_involvement`	•		•		•	•
Specialization	`resource_specialization`	•		•	•	•	

7.5.3.4 Data Perspective

The data perspective in process analysis mainly refers to the application of traditional data mining and statistical techniques on event data. As a result, conventional tools can be used for these types of analysis and these are not further discussed in this paper. Examples are

- **clustering** cases based on their attributes.
- **classification** of cases according to a certain variable (e.g. predicting claims with refund vs. without refund).
- **descriptive analysis** of event or case attributes.

7.6 Discussion

The above description of the design and the functionalities shows that the requirements are met. To recapitulate, the following design requirements were defined.

1. The tool-set should be embedded or connected with a general-purpose data analysis software, such that synergies can be made by linking existing data analysis and/or statistical techniques with process analysis applications.
2. Creating extensions should be straightforward, and well-supported through documentation.
3. The tool-set should allow to reproduce analysis, thereby facilitating iterative analysis
4. The tool-set should have a clear documentation and impose guidelines for the documentation of extensions.

With regards to the first requirement, the link with existing data analysis techniques is straightforward as the tool-set is conceived as a suit of packages in the R ecosystem. The fact that many known `tidyverse` functions for data manipulation [141] are supported makes sure that there is a solid interface between the packages discussed in this chapter and existing packages used for generic data analysis, making it straightforward to treat event logs also as conventional data sets.

As a corollary from this, also the ease of extensibility is provided. Over the past decade the R community has put in place many procedures to help the publication of packages—such as `devtools`[10]—or automatic checking procedures, as well as documentations to guide new programmers in this endeavour. It is therefore no coincidence that the number of packages published on CRAN has increased tenfold over the past 10 years.

Next to the guidance provided by the R community it should also be noted that the ease to contribute with new packages or functions is higher compared to other extensible tools, such as ProM, since using the packages for analysis is very similar to writing new functionalities. The transfer from *using R* towards *contributing R* is therefore much lower than the transfer from, for example, using ProM to contributing to ProM. For the latter, the graphical user interface to use it is markedly different from the underlying source code one has to be familiar with in order to contribute. This makes contributions to `bupaR` by users which do not necessarily have a very technical background more likely, as is illustrated by the large amount of issues and pull request the packages receive from users via github.

Thirdly, concerning the reproducibility, the choice for a scripting language is paramount. While other approaches toward reproducibility are possible, such as the workflow approach used by RapidProM, the chosen solution has some important benefits. Firstly, it improves the transparency of the analysis, as parameters for the analysis are visible and not obscured in various operator nodes. Secondly, it greatly increases the ease to interactively adjust the analysis by quickly changing the order of different commands, skipping or repeating certain commands, etc. Thirdly, the choice for R, which comes with useful tools such as Rmarkdown documents and Shiny dashboards, not only ensure reproducibility of analyses, but also reproducibility of reports.

Finally, the documentation of the packages is ensured by the very strict rules which are in order for published packages on CRAN. Not only do all functions and their arguments have to be adequately described, the packages have to be provided with examples or vignettes on how to use them. Additionally, packages such as `pkgdown`[11] help to create a dedicated, up-to-date website for R-packages, which is also used by www.bupar.net.

Concerning the functional requirements, the above description of functions for data extraction, data processing and data analysis shows that these are met. Important for the functionalities are also the combinations with other, existing techniques which are possible. Subsequent chapters will showcase some of these combinations with, among others, clustering techniques, statistical techniques (regression, correlation), but also the power of custom preprocessing tasks and other data manipulations.

Also important to note in this respect, is the recently developed python library for process mining `PM4Py`.[12] From a design perspective, `PM4Py` is similar to `bupaR`, in that it is also linked with a general purpose data analysis ecosystem, in this case Python, is easy to extend and supports reproducibility. The main difference between the two is the focus on functionality: where `PM4Py` focuses more on the mining

[10]https://cran.r-project.org/web/packages/devtools/index.html.

[11]https://pkgdown.r-lib.org/.

[12]http://pm4py.org/.

aspect, providing various algorithms for discovery, conformance checking, etc., the focus of `bupaR` has so far been on data processing and manipulation and exploratory and descriptive analyses. A promising avenue for future research will be to investigate how these two tool-sets can be combined as complimentary frameworks.

7.7 Conclusion

In this chapter, we introduced a suite of R-packages which were designed to support the different analytical stages within process analysis, from the data extraction to the analysis and mining. It is the first effort to support the handling and analysis of process event data in R. While the preceding sections focused primarily on the technical aspects of the implementations, more practical guidance can be found on the website www.bupar.net and a comprehensive function index is available in Appendix B.

Making process analysis possible in R will improve the reproducibility of process analyses. Reusable analysis scripts can be combined with the interpretation of the analysis as well as with meta-data (who did the analysis and when?). Furthermore, it will allow process analysts to easily create custom analysis tools, and will enlarge the adoption and publicity of process mining in industry. Future developments of the framework will include the introduction of process models in R, such as Petri Nets. As a result, additional techniques which use both process data and process models can be implemented.

While the demonstration of functionalities in this chapter was limited to an isolated enumeration of different functions, the following chapters will provide a more in-depth evaluation of the framework. Using two different case studies, it will be illustrated how the functionalities can be used in a real-life setting to create added value. Both case studies will show how different functionalities can be combined with each other and with existing tools. Chap. 8 will discuss a case study on learning trajectories in higher education, while Chap. 9 will describe an application of process analytics to detect reroutings in a railway environment.

7.8 Further Reading

1. Janssenswillen, G.: bupaR: Business Process Analytics in R (2018). URL https://bupar.net. R Package version 0.4.0
2. Janssenswillen, G., Depaire, B., Swennen, M., Jans, M.J., Vanhoof, K.: bupar: Enabling Reproducible Business Process Analysis. Knowledge-Based Systems **163**, 927–930 (2019)
3. Janssenswillen, G., Depaire, B.: bupaR: Business Process Analysis in R. In: Business Process Managements: Demos (2017)

4. Swennen, M., Janssenswillen, G., Jans, M.J., Depaire, B., Vanhoof, K.: Capturing Process Behavior with Log-Based Process Metrics. In: Proceedings of the 5th International Symposium on Data-driven Process Discovery and Analysis (SIMPDA), Vienna, pp. 141–144 (2015)
5. Swennen, M., Martin, N., Janssenswillen, G., Jans, M.J., Depaire, B., Caris, A., Vanhoof, K.: Capturing Resource Behaviour From Event Logs. In: Proceedings of the 6th International Symposium on Data-driven Process Discovery and Analysis (SIMPDA), Graz (2016)
6. Devi, A.T.: An informative and comparative study of process mining tools. International Journal of Scientific and Engineering Research **8**(5), 8–10 (2006)
7. Jans, M.J., Soffer, P., Jouck, T.: Building a valuable event log for process mining: an experimental exploration of a guided process. Enterprise Information Systems **0**(0), 1–30 (2019). doi: https://doi.org/10.1080/17517575.2019.1587788
8. Jans, M.J., Soffer, P.: From Relational Database to Event Log: Decisions with Quality Impact. In: Business Process Management Workshops, pp. 588–599. Springer, Cham (2017)
9. van Eck, M.L., Lu, X., Leemans, S.J.J., van der Aalst, W.M.P.: PM^2: A Process Mining Project Methodology. In: International Conference on Advanced Information Systems Engineering, pp. 297–313 (2015)
10. Kerremans, M.: Market guide for process mining. Tech. rep., Gartner (2018)

Chapter 8
Student Trajectories in Higher Education

> Learning isn't a way of reaching one's potential but rather a way of developing it.
>
> K. Anders Ericsson

In this chapter, we evaluate the use of `bupaR` in the context of education. This chapter is different from the demonstration of functionalities in the previous chapter, as it does not discuss functions in isolation, but uses them in combination with each other and existing techniques, to get useful insights and answers to specific questions. In particular, this chapter will analyse student trajectories in terms of successful and failed courses. The following questions will be addressed:

1. How is the behaviour of students aligned with the prescribed program?
2. What is the impact of failures on the trajectories and which are common failure patterns?
3. How do students take decisions about the amount of credits to take in each semester, and how to balance mandatory and elective courses?

A short introduction on learning analytics and the combination with process mining is given in the next section. In Sect. 8.2, the data will be introduced, together with some basic descriptives. Section 8.3 will discuss the alignment between student behavior and the prescribed program, where one major will be used as a prototype. In Sect. 8.4, the impact of failure will be investigated, while in Sect. 8.5 certain trajectory decisions are analysed from a quantitative point of view. In Sect. 8.6 we will discuss the findings, limitations, and lessons learned with respect to the use of `bupaR` for process analysis. Section 8.7 concludes the chapter.

G. Janssenswillen: Unearthing the Real Process Behind the Event Data, LNBIP 412
https://doi.org/10.1007/978-3-030-70733-0_8

8.1 Learning Analytics and Process Mining

Learning analytics is a relatively young domain, which focuses on the measurement, collection, analysis and reporting of data about learners. It aims to understand and optimise learning and the environment in which it occurs [32]. It emerged as a combination of various related fields, such as technology enhanced learning, data mining, statistics and visualisation [55]. Learning analytics developed particularly as a response to the rise of e-learning, such as Massive Open Online Courses (MOOC), and the new challenges and opportunities that came with this shift.

The application of process analytics in this area is not brand-new. Process mining techniques have been used on MOOC data to distinguish different learning styles [100] as well as to relate behaviour with final grades [108]. However, the scope of learning analytics is not limited to e-learning. In [58] process mining was already used in the context of blended learning, where e-learning and traditional learning are mixed.

But learning analytics can also be interesting at a higher meta-level, where students are not followed throughout a course, but throughout their education trajectory. Courses do not exist in isolation from each other, and the way that study programmes are constructed has important ramifications towards phenomena such as students attrition and postponement of graduation [69]. In subsequent sections, these phenomena will be analysed using a process analytics approach. The analyses done in this chapter should not be seen as a full-fledged solution to these problems, but nonetheless provides a conceptual example for process analytics in higher education trajectories, while simultaneously also highlighting limitations of the taken approach.

8.2 Data Understanding

The data used describe the trajectories of engineering students who started their higher education in 2013 at a large university (circa 27.000 students, divided over 18 faculties).[1] In total, information for 5 years is available, each consisting of two regular semesters and a summer period, for students of one specific faculty. The program contains 400 credits, which should ideally be taken in chunks of 50 credits in each regular semester over the course of 4 years. A total of 644 students enrolled in 2013. Relatively few students terminated the program prematurely in the first 2 years (49 students, 7.6%). 515 students (80%) were still active in the second semester of the 5th year, i.e. one year after the foreseen completion of the program.

For each student, the following information is available.

[1]For data privacy reasons, the origin of the data for this chapter is not disclosed. References to particular students are anonymized and references to courses are replaced with fictitious course names.

- Each course ever taken by the student, including:
  - which semester it was taken;
  - the final grade that was obtained;
  - the number of credits of the course.
- Educational history, including:
  - the region and type of high school;
  - the year of graduation in high school;
  - the way of entering the university.
- Choices about specialization, including:
  - chosen major, if already chosen;
  - chosen minor, if already chosen;
  - chosen track within major, if applicable.

In total, 1073 courses have been taken by the students over the course of 5 years. This very high number of courses can be explained by the large amount of different specialisations that can be selected, as well as the large amount of external, optional courses which students can take. More than 50% of the courses were taken less than 4 times in 5 years, while the 100 most taken courses represent 77.4% of all the trajectories.

8.3 Followed Versus Prescribed Trajectories

In this section, we will analyse whether students obey the prescribed course program or not. For this, we will look at one specific major in particular as a proof of concept. The major contains ten courses, which should be taken from the 4th until the 8th semester, as shown in Table 8.1.

In Fig. 8.1, the order of completion of the different semesters is shown using a process map with relative frequencies. It can be seen that 77.14% of students first completes the courses in the 4th semester, while others first complete semester 5 (22.86%). Furthermore, only 28.57% finished semester 6 directly after semester 5, while 14.29% do so after they finished semester 4, and a considerable group of students do so only after they already finished semester 7 (48.57%) or 8 (8.57%). As such, it seems that the semesters are not completed by students as the program prescribes.

If we take into account the entire end-to-end completion sequence of students, we get the results as displayed in Fig. 8.2. It can be seen that the *correct* completion order only occurs for 20% of the students, while the largest group of students (40%) completes semester 7 before 6.

Given these results, two follow-up questions can be asked. Firstly, which specific course(s) can be identified as the reason(s) for diversions between the prescribed and followed program? Courses can lie at the root of these diversion because of two

Table 8.1 Prescribed major program. (Note that actual course id's and names have been anonymised.)

Semester				
4	5	6	7	8
[Course 4.1] [Course 4.2]	[Course 5.1]	[Course 6.1] [Course 6.2] [Course 6.3]	[Course 7.1] [Course 7.2]	[Course 8.1] [Course]

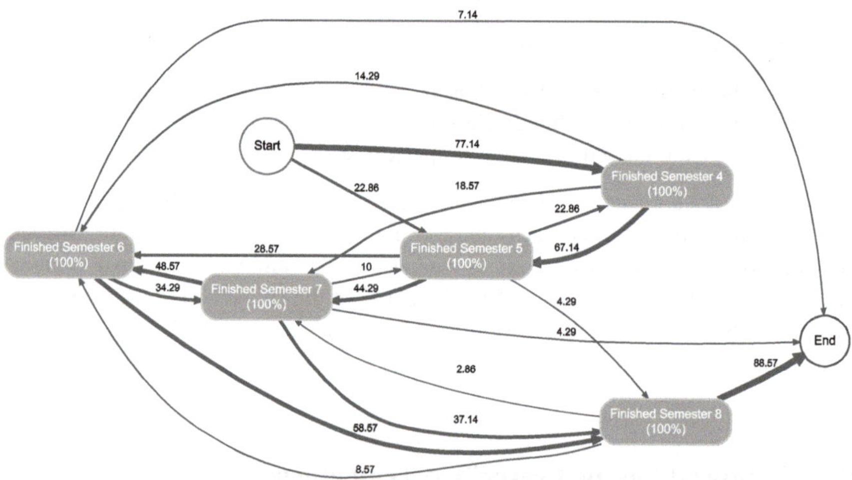

Fig. 8.1 Recorded completion order of semesters of major.

Traces	1	2	3	4	5	
	4	5	7	6	8	40%
	4	5	6	7	8	20%
	5	4	6	7	8	12.86%
	5	4	7	6	8	8.57%
	4	7	5	6	8	7.14%
	4	5	7	8	6	4.29%
	4	7	5	8	6	2.86%
	5	4	6	8	7	1.43%
	4	5	8	6	7	
	4	5	6	8	7	

Activities

Fig. 8.2 Completion sequences of semesters of major.

reasons. They either have a high failure rate, thereby impeding completion of the program, or they are intentionally delayed by students.

Secondly, do the student's diversions have a positive or negative impact on the overall study performance? In case the impact is positive, this information could be used to adjust the prescribed study program for the major. In case it is negative, one could devise some control measures to increase the compliance of the program.

8.3.1 Root Causes

In Fig. 8.3, the actual point in time that a course is completed by students is compared with the prescribed moment. The red lines indicate the semester in which a course should be completed, while the black dots show the actual average point in time it is completed. The grey areas show the distribution of the actual completion time.

Two courses in particular stand out here, i.e., [Course 4.1] and [Course 6.2]. For these courses, it can be seen that the average completion time is much later than the prescribed semester in which these courses should be completed. Comparing the place of these courses in the program with the results in Fig. 8.2, it can be concluded that [Course 4.1] is the main reason for untimely completion of semester 4 (22.86% of students), while [Course 6.2] is the main reason for delayed completion of semester 6 (64.29% of students).

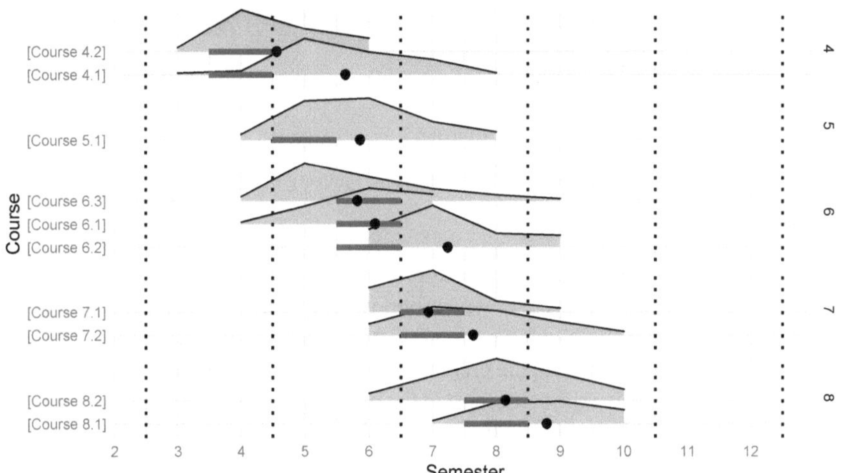

Fig. 8.3 Comparison of prescribed and actual moment a course is completed. The prescribed period in which a course should be taken is indicated with a red line, while the actual distribution of when the course is taken by students is indicated by the grey density line. The black dots indicate the average actual point in time each course is completed.

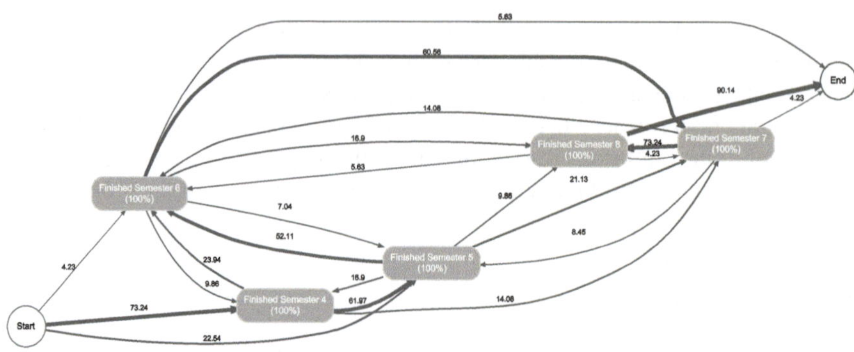

Fig. 8.4 Recorded completion order of semesters of major, ignoring [Course 6.2].

Activity 1	Activity 2	Activity 3	Activity 4	Activity 5	Traces
4	5	6	7	8	43.66%
5	4	6	7	8	14.08%
4	5	7	6	8	11.27%
5	6	4	7	8	5.63%
6	4	5	7	8	4.23%
4	7	5	8	6	2.82%
4	7	5	6	8	2.82%
4	6	7	5	8	2.82%
4	6	5	8	7	2.82%
4	6	5	7	8	2.82%
4	5	7	8	6	2.82%
5	4	7	6	8	1.41%
5	4	6	8	7	1.41%
4	7	6	5	8	1.41%

Fig. 8.5 Completion sequences of semesters of major, ignoring [Course 6.2].

If we ignore [Course 6.2]—which appears to be the primary diversion—in the process map and trace explorer shown earlier, we get the results displayed in Fig. 8.4 and Fig. 8.5, respectively. It can be observed that, when ignoring [Course 6.2], there is markedly less diversion from the prescribed program. The largest group of students (43.66%) now completes the semesters in the appropriate order, and late completion of semester 6 is only a problem for about 21.14% of students (compared to 64.29% before).

When looking at the failure rate for these two courses, we see that for [Course 4.1] 78.5% passes the course in the first attempt, while for [Course 6.2] 97.4% of students passes the course in the first attempt. As a result, the delay of [Course 4.1] can partly be explained by the struggles students are having to complete this course. In contrast, students do not seem to struggle to succeed for [Course 6.2]. In the latter case, the delay is thus almost exclusively due to intentional postponement by students.

8.3.2 Impact

Having identified the main root causes for students not following the major as prescribed, the next logical step is to see what the impact is of those diversions on the overall student performance. However, analysing this impact is a non-trivial task because of several reasons.

Firstly, quantifying student performance is not straightforward, as this is a multifaceted concept. One can measure the performance of a student in terms of the average grade obtained, in terms of timely graduation, or a combination of both. However, both measures can only be examined reliably when students have obtained their degree. In the current context, only a minority of students has reached this point. Alternatively, one could look at the student performance of the major only, instead of the entire program. Nevertheless, a bias will still exist, as not all students of the same cohort who elected this major have completed it.

Secondly, one should be cautious not to confuse correlation with causation. A diversion from the prescribed program can lead to a lower average grade, but there might also be a third variable which causes both a lower grade and the likelihood to deviate, such as previous educational programs followed. Indeed, these concepts are strongly influenced by other factors, such as previous education the students received, the social situation of students, but also the ambition and goals of the students. As a result, any found relation between performance and recorded behaviour should be interpreted with considerable care.

The regression results in Table 8.2 show that the average score obtained in the major is almost perfectly linear to the global score obtained for the other courses throughout the educational program, the major courses excluded. The fit between the behaviour and the prescribed major program[2] has a positive relationship with the score for the major. However, as stated above, these result should be interpreted very cautiously. Ideally, a more elaborate analysis should be performed at a time when all students have terminated their program.

---

[2]The fit between the behaviour and the prescribed major program was calculated by taking the correlation between on the one hand the semesters that courses were completed in, and on the other hand the semesters courses should have been completed in. A fit of 1 means a perfect correlation between those, while a fit of -1 means that a student took courses in completely the opposite order.

Table 8.2 Regression of the average score on the major in terms of global score and fit between behaviour and prescribed program.

	Dependent variable:
	Score major
Fit with program	0.722*
	(0.413)
Global score Excluding courses from major	0.825***
	(0.093)
Constant	0.192
	(0.515)
Observations	43
R^2	0.716
Adjusted R^2	0.702
Residual Std. Error	0.239 (df = 40)
F Statistic	50.534*** (df = 2; 40)

*Note:**$p < 0.1$; **$p < 0.05$; ***$p < 0.01$

8.4 Failure Patterns

A second subject that was investigated are students failing courses. Understanding the existing patterns in this area is important in two different ways. Firstly, the high-level understanding of students' struggles gives an idea of the overall performance of the students. Comparing this for different cohorts might also indicate long-term trends.

Secondly, also the low-level understanding is important, i.e., how does failing a certain course relate to other courses? This detailed information can be used to provided tailored support and advice to students with a certain track record.

In this section we will propose the concept of *bags* as a method to analyse patterns of failing students, including some guidelines on how this method can be used to answer specific research questions.

8.4.1 Bags

When a student fails a course, this can be seen as a burden that he will carry on to the subsequent semester. In such a case, we can metaphorically speak of a *bag* that a student is carrying. Each bag has a *weight* which varies over time, depending on the amount of courses the student fails (*added* to his bag) as well as the amount of courses in the bag he eventually succeeds (*taken* from his bag). The concept of bags was introduced before in [120, 121].

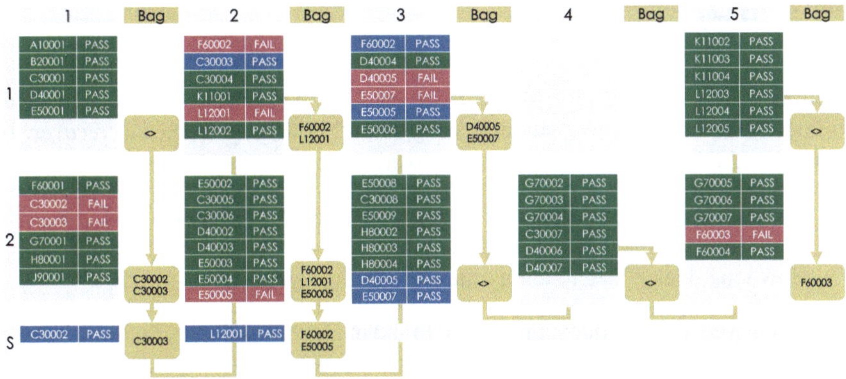

Fig. 8.6 Hypothetical example of student trajectory with bags.

Figure 8.6 shows an example of a hypothetical student.[3] Columns one through five list the different years of the students trajectory, while the rows show the different periods (1st semester, 2nd semester, and summer semester). For each period, it can be seen which courses the student took, and the result for each course. Green courses are those for which the student passes immediately. Red courses are those for which the student failed (added to bag, if not already included). Blue courses are those for which the student passes after having failed originally (removed from bag). The evolution of the bag for this student can be seen next to the list of courses. The heaviest bag the student held was after the 2nd semester of the 2nd year. At that point, he had a bag of three courses.

When a student holds a bag for subsequent periods, this is considered as a *single* bag, notwithstanding that the content and the weight might be changing continually. The time during which a bag is held by a student is called the *length* of the bag.

For the student trajectory in Fig. 8.6, the student has held 2 bags, over the course of 5 years. The first bag was started in semester 2 of the first year and lasted until semester 1 of the third year. The second bag was started in the last semester shown in Fig. 8.6, and not emptied (yet).[4]

In the paragraphs below, we will use the concept of bags to look at student patterns at two levels. Firstly, a high-level analysis is done in Sect. 8.4.2. Here, the main focus is on the number, weight and length of bags. This provides a high level understanding of the burden students are carrying. Secondly, a low-level analysis is done in Sect. 8.4.3, where a proof of concept is presented on how to use the notion of bags at the level of individual courses, with the goal to understand relations between courses, which can be used to support students and remedy problems.

---

[3] All course id's in this example are hypothetical and have no significance.

[4] Note that only data for 5 years was available for the analysis in this chapter.

8.4.2 High-Level Analysis

In this Section, we will look at three very specific bag-related questions in order to understand how *frequent* students struggle and how long it takes to *recover*. In particular, the following questions are answered.

1. How many bags do students on average hold over the 5-year period?
2. How heavy are the bags students hold?
3. How long does it take to empty the bags on average?

The answers to these questions can be found in Fig. 8.7. In Fig. 8.7a, it can be seen that most students have had one or two bags over their 5 years of education. Only 1 out of every 5 students has had no bag, i.e. never failed a course.

Most of the time these bags are not very heavy, as is shown in Fig. 8.7b. While there are rare examples of bags containing up to 9 different courses, more than half of the time only one course is in the bag. It's important to note that the bag weight is not constant, but can increase or decrease over the period of the bag. Figure 8.7c shows the distribution of the average weight of all bags. The average weight for 50% of the bags is between 1 and 2 courses.

Finally, the length of the bags is shown in Fig. 8.7d. While the maximum is 13 periods (the theoretically possible maximum is 15), the majority only lasts a single period.

It can be concluded that really *problematic* bags—long and heavy ones—are rare. Most bags do not exist for a long time and are not so heavy. On the other hand, it is likely that a student soon or late has one.

This high-level analysis provides a snapshot of the overall performance of a cohort of students. Comparing the results for different cohorts can reveal trends of the overall difficulty students are having with the program. While the discussion above is done for the complete data, more targeted analysis can also be done, i.e. for a certain group of courses (e.g., a major) or a specific group of students (e.g., depending on previous studies).

Nonetheless, the high level analysis comes with several drawbacks. Firstly, it should ideally be done after all students have finished, or dropped out, their studies. Otherwise, both the length and the number of bags are slightly biased by the better performing students. This makes it difficult to act on the results, because there is a large lag between student actions and the analysis. Moreover, changes to study programs happen more frequent, which means that the analysis should be interpreted with care.

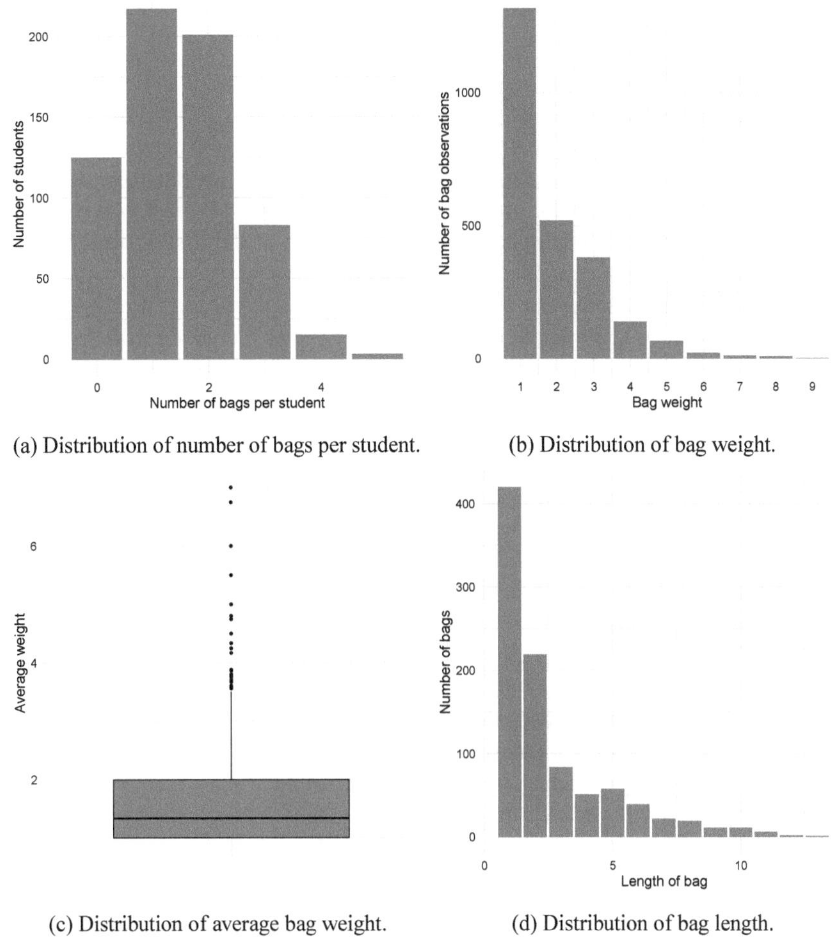

(a) Distribution of number of bags per student.

(b) Distribution of bag weight.

(c) Distribution of average bag weight.

(d) Distribution of bag length.

Fig. 8.7 High-level analysis of the number, length, and weight of bags.

Secondly, additional information of the student curriculum for each student is necessary to know when a student eventually drops a course (if possible). When this happens, it might appear that the course is still in his bag because he never completed it, while in fact he has chosen to change its curriculum. Analysis at a lower level can to a certain extent resolve both shortcomings. Therefore, we will look at lower-level patterns in the next section.

8.4.3 Low-Level Analysis

At a lower level of analysis, we can have a look at the impact of a specific course. Using the concept of bags, we can answer questions such as *how often is this course the reason for starting a bag?* and *if a student starts a bag with this course, how long does it take before it is emptied.* Moreover, links between courses can be investigated and frequent patterns observed. In the next paragraphs, we will use a course called *Statistics I* as a prototype example.[5] This course is part of the first semester for all students, and typically poses some problems.

Of all 943 bags which were observed, 213 (22.5%) contained the Statistics I course. In most cases (209 bags), the course was already included in the bag from the start. This is unsurprising, as it is one of the first courses the students should take.

Comparing the length of bags of those that started with this course and those that did not, no difference was found. The average length was 2.65 periods for those bags starting with the course, while 2.59 periods for those bags that did not. However, differences were found in the average weight of the bag. For those that started with this course, the average weight was 2.16 courses. The average weight of bags for other bags was only 1.48 courses. In other words, failing the Statistics I course will not lead to an unusually long recovery period, but is nevertheless related to a heavy backlog of courses. This heavy weight when failing the course under consideration can already be seen at the first period that the student carries the bag. More than 50% of the students who fail Statistics I, will fail 2 or more other courses.

Subsequently, we can investigate *which* courses are frequent problem cases, together with the Statistics I course. Analysis shows that 69.4% of the students also failed Introduction to Data Analysis, and 62% failed Management Accounting. This helps to identify the context in which students find themselves struggling.

Furthermore, one can also look at the future. Which courses are students more likely to fail after failing Statistics I, for instance? For example, we can observe that 9% of these students eventually failed Econometrics, and 6.7% of these students failed Database Management. Nevertheless, putting these figures in the correct context is very important, and not necessarily trivial. It should be taken into account what the overall fail rate is for these courses, but also the fall-out of students should be considered (e.g. students that drop out of the program, or that elect a major without these specific courses). It is therefore recommended to start from clear research questions, concerning specific courses, and test all the assumptions needed in order to formulate an answer. The found results can then be useful when providing guidance for students in a certain context.

[5]The course names in this section are fictitious, although the results refer to actual courses.

8.5 Understanding Trajectory Decisions

In the previous sections we mainly looked at the student trajectories from a *result* point of view—i.e. what are the trajectories students have eventually taken. However, these are the result of a series of decisions students made based on certain events that occurred. Investigating the results of these decisions is more straightforward than investigating the decisions itself. However, understanding how certain things came about is often essential to comprehend the whole scene.

Therefore, in this section, we will have a look at decisions made by students in the process of getting their degree, in order to further understand the patterns which can be seen on the surface. In order to do so, event attributes will be used. While often ignored by process mining techniques, they can provide very useful information. Using `bupaR`, this information is more easily incorporated.

The specific topic which will be considered is that of *elective courses*. Each student enrolled in the program should take a set of elective courses for a total of 80 credits, which are ideally uniformly divided over the 8 semesters. These courses can be seen as *general education* and cover a broad range of topics, including sports, religion, philosophy, etc.

The distribution of the number of elective credits taken by students in each semester is shown in Fig. 8.8. The median value in all semesters lies at the pre-

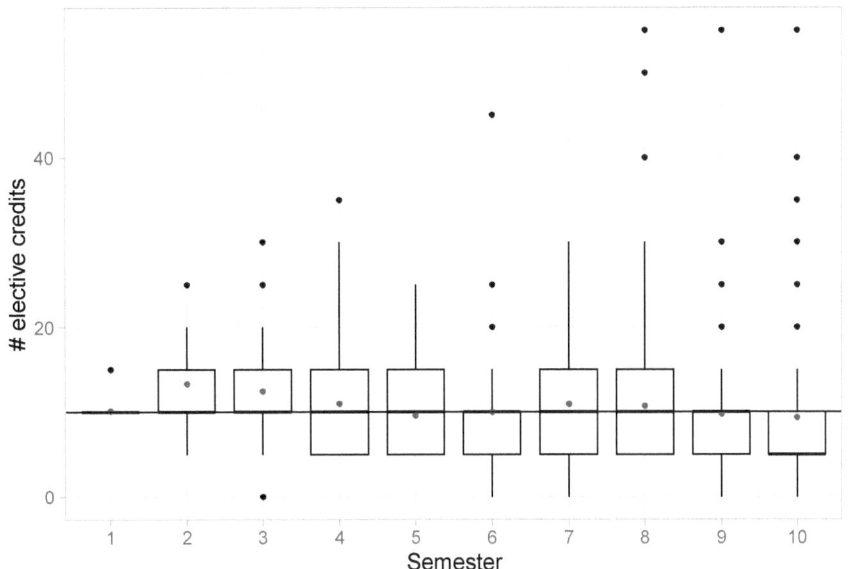

Fig. 8.8 Distribution of Elective Credits taken by students in regular semesters. Average number of credits are indicated with red dot.

scribed amount of 10 credits—except for the last semester. Nevertheless, a large variation can be seen in the number of elective credits taken by students. Also the average amount of credits—indicated by the red dots in Fig. 8.8—is markedly higher than the prescribed 10 credits during semesters 2 and 3. The aim of the university is to understand the reasons why students take more or less elective credits in a specific semester.

In order to analyse this, the event log used in previous sections was aggregated so that a single event for each student in each semester remained. For each events, the following attributes were calculated:

- the total number of normal credits taken,
- the total number of elective credits taken,
- the difficulty[6] of the normal courses taken,
- the difficulty of the elective courses taken,
- the number of normal credits failed,
- the number of elective credits failed.

The goal of the analysis is to understand which of these concepts correlate to the number of elective credits taken in a semester. However, not only the correlation at a fixed moment in time is important, but also the correlation over time. Indeed, the hypothesis of the university is that a high number of failed courses in a semester will lead to a higher number of elective credits taken in the **next** semester. The rationale behind this hypothesis is that elective courses—which in general are less difficult—are used as a counterbalance to cope with the recuperation of failed courses.

Figure 8.9 displays the correlations between the number of elective credits in each semester, shown along the x-axis, and other characteristics, shown along the y-axis, are displayed. Among these are both characteristics of the previous and of the current semester. It can be seen that the correlations between the current number of elective credits and the characteristics of the previous semester are very weak to non-existent. This rejects the hypothesis that students take up less elective credits in response to failed courses in the previous semester.

On the other hand, relatively strong correlations can be seen between the number of optional credits in a semester and other characteristics in the same semester. In the first two years, there is a positive correlation with the difficulty of the normal courses the student takes. This means that students will take more elective courses if they are expecting a more difficult semester. On the other hand, there is a negative correlation with the amount of normal credits. In other words, if the number of normal credits increases, they will take less elective credits. As such, it seems that the number of elective credits in a given semester is the result of a balancing exercise between the amount and difficulty of other courses taken in the same semester, and has nothing to do with reacting to failures in the previous semester.

---

[6]The difficulty of a course is expressed based on the average number of attempts students need to pass as well as the average score students obtain. The lower the obtained score, or the higher the number of attempts needed, the more difficult a course is. The final score for difficulty is the normalised average of these two variables.

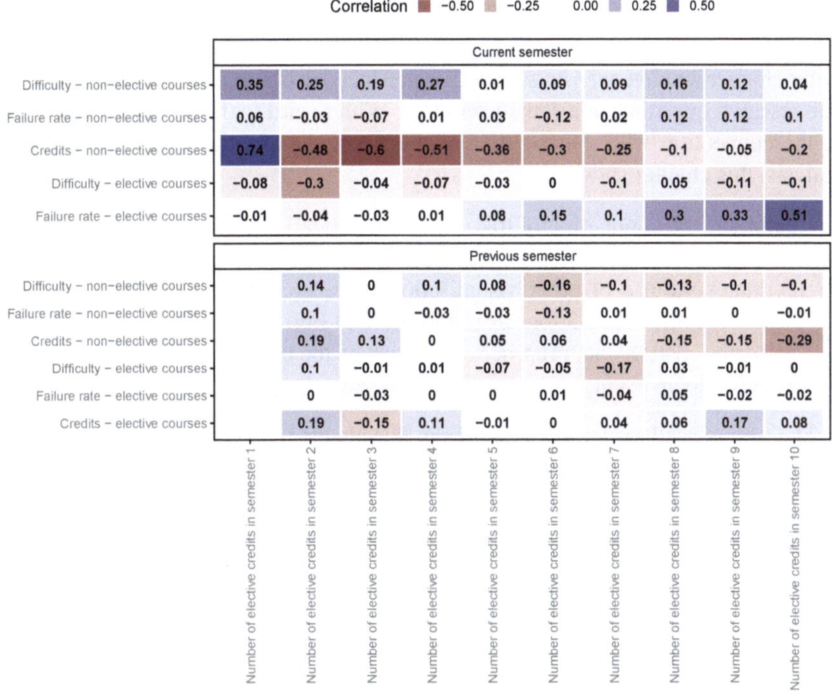

Fig. 8.9 Correlation between the amount of elective credits in a given semester and other characteristics of that particular and the previous one.

One anomaly in Fig. 8.9 is the strong positive correlation between the amount of normal credits and the amount of elective credits in the first semester. However, this artefact in the data is the direct result of the default study program, which most students still have in their first semester. In this semester, almost all students take the prescribed 50 normal credits and 10 elective credits, while only a handful of students takes more than 10 elective credits. This results in a strong positive correlation.

Another peculiarity in the correlations is the increasing correlation between the amount of elective credits failed and the elective credits in the final semesters, which is not prevalent in the first 3 years. It thus seems that students who are taking up more elective credits tend to have a higher failure rate. The fact that this correlation surfaces in later semesters is mostly the result of exuberant amounts of elective credits taken by students in those semester, as can be observed in Fig. 8.8.

While these correlations should not be confused with causal relationships, they are able to characterise the different phenomena which play in the context of the students as well as disprove pre-existent hypothesis on the students' motives. From a technical viewpoint, this example shows the flexibility of `bupaR` to perform non-standard analyses.

8.6 Discussion

In this chapter we have seen how `bupaR`, introduced in Chap. 7, can be used to investigate research questions in a specific context. With regard to the design requirements on the connection with generic data analysis tools and ability to perform custom analysis, this chapter shows that `bupaR`:

- facilitates the application of traditional (statistical) techniques in a process context, such as regression analysis (Table 8.2) and correlation analysis (Fig. 8.9);
- facilitates the use of other visualisation software such as `ggplot2` [140] to create custom visualisations as in Fig. 8.3 and Fig. 8.8;
- facilitates custom data preprocessing, such as the transformation of the original event log to an event log containing bags (Sect. 8.4).

The scripts used to create the figures in this chapter can be found in Appendix C. While they show how each of the above-mentioned combinations and customisations can be achieved, it should also be noted that none of these come for free. Instead, a certain familiarity with R and some of its packages is required to really enable these synergies. In the end, *"there is no such thing as a free lunch"*.[7]

In relation to the case study itself, the chapter has shown that process analysis can create valuable insights into the trajectories of students. However, some limitations have to be considered.

Firstly, when looking at student trajectories over a long-term, considering courses in a study program instead of exercises in a course, analysis of end-to-end student progress and performance requires a rather long period of data. As a result, conclusions can be made only at after several years of data gathering. In the increasingly fast changing world of education such a time window might proof too long, such that its already to late to act on the conclusions. Most of the time, student curricula are changing faster, which not only makes results about the end-to-end process obsolete before they are obtained, but also reduces the reliability of said results, as the environment is changing constantly during the data gathering. Nevertheless, analysis of *local* patterns, concerning a certain course, or a segment of the curriculum can still be valuable.

A second limitation is the flexibility of student programs. In modern times, students have almost unique, individual student trajectories—all of them pursuing different interests and studying in different circumstances. This flexibility makes it increasingly difficult to provide students with appropriate and reliable guidance. Indeed, how to advice a student if you cannot learn from other students with a similar trajectory, because they don't exist? As a result, some analyses in this chapter, such as the low-level analysis using bags (Sect. 8.4.3) are only reliable in segments of the data where there are enough observations—such as the typical common first year of a student program, where all students start on the same plane and haven't decided on any specialisations yet. The issues with very low structured processes is

[7] Robert Heinlein, The Moon is a Harsh Mistress.

by no means a new problem in process mining, and most certainly also applies in this context.

8.7 Conclusion

In this chapter, the process analytics framework introduced in the previous chapter was used in the context of high-level learning analytics. In particular, three different topics where discussed. Firstly, to which extent are students following the prescribed program, and where do they deviate from it? Secondly, how fast do students recover from failing a course, and how heavy is the burden of failed courses? And finally, which elements are related to the number of elective credits selected by students in a particular semester.

The examples showed the suitability for a process-oriented view in the analysis of higher education trajectories, as well as the flexibility with which `bupaR` allows for non-standard analyses and visualisations. The scripts used for the figures in this chapter can be found in Appendix C.

8.8 Further Reading

1. Chatti, M.A., Dyckhoff, A.L., Schroeder, U., Thüs, H.: A reference model for learning analytics. International Journal of Technology Enhanced Learning **4**(5-6), 318–331 (2012)
2. Ferguson, R.: Learning Analytics: Drivers, Developments and Challenges. International Journal of Technology Enhanced Learning **4**(5/6), 304–317 (2012)
3. Gelan, A., Fastré, G., Verjans, M., Martin, N., Janssenswillen, G., Creemers, M., Lieben, J., Depaire, B., Thomas, M.: Affordances and limitations of learning analytics for computer-assisted language learning: a case study of the VITAL project. Computer Assisted Language Learning **31**(3), 294–319 (2018)
4. Hovdhaugen, E.: Do structured study programmes lead to lower rates of dropout and student transfer from university? Irish Educational Studies **30**(2), 237–251 (2011)
5. Mukala, P., Buijs, J.C., Leemans, M., van der Aalst,W.M.P.: Learning Analytics on Coursera Event Data: A Process Mining Approach. In: Proceedings of the 5th International Symposium on Data-driven Process Discovery and Analysis, pp. 18–32 (2015)

Chapter 9
Process-Oriented Analytics in Railway Systems

> There are so many different kinds of normal.
>
> Becky Albertalli

9.1 Introduction

Improving the punctuality of railway operations is one of the most important objectives of rail infrastructure managers. In reaching this goal, they are restricted by safety constraints and capacity limitations. As for the latter restriction, optimising capacity planning and monitoring constitutes a major necessity. In this chapter, we show how process analytics can be of added value in a railway operations managing context.

The contribution of this chapter is twofold. Firstly, metrics are proposed to evaluate train scheduling by using train describer data. The metrics allow to identify areas in the train schedule where re-routings are frequent, and will provide guidelines to consequently improve the scheduling of trains. In particular, we will use metrics from process mining and business process management to quantify to following aspects.

- How frequent do deviations occur on a particular train route?
- How diverse are these deviations?
  - In terms of width (*horizontal diversity*), i.e. the amount of diversity at a certain location.
  - In terms of location (*vertical diversity*), i.e. do all deviations occur at the same place or on a varied number of places.
- Can we recognise patterns in the deviations which can be used as input for train scheduling?

G. Janssenswillen: Unearthing the Real Process Behind the Event Data, LNBIP 412
https://doi.org/10.1007/978-3-030-70733-0_9

Train describer data recorded by the Belgian railway infrastructure manager Infrabel will be used to illustrate the workings of the suggested metrics. Train Describer systems record the position and movement of trains throughout a railway network, with the aim to monitor train traffic and to secure safety regulations. Next to recording train movements, the systems also allow user interventions, such as modifying the trajectory of a train.

Secondly, the chapter illustrates the large potential of process analysis techniques to analyse train describer data. Not only does it show how `bupaR`, introduced in Chap. 7, can be useful in visualising processes and quantifying certain characteristics—it moreover shows, analogously to Chap. 8, how the toolset can be easily customised to a very specific context, and how it can be used in combination with regular data analysis techniques, such as clustering, as well as traditional statistics, such as analysis of variance.

The next section will introduce the problem further and describe related work. Consequently, a set of metrics will be developed in Sect. 9.3, together with a methodology to use them. In Sect. 9.4, the results of this methodology will be illustrated using train describer data recorded by the Belgian railway infrastructure manager Infrabel. Finally, in Sect. 9.5 lessons learned about both process analytics in a railway context and process analytics with `bupaR` are described.

9.2 Problem Statement and Related Work

In order to bridge the gap between railway scheduling and execution, it is necessary to analyse to which extent traffic operators make decisions to deviate from the planned capacity allocation. Consequently, it needs to be examined whether these decisions were favourable, thereby possibly pointing at flaws in the railway planning, or not. While a lot of research on train scheduling and real-time rescheduling exists, little literature is available on the ex post analysis of capacity usage. Most research in this area is focused on train delays and ensuing conflicts, while limited consideration has been given to the evaluation of train rescheduling. Nevertheless, railway infrastructure managers possess tremendous amounts of data about the railway operations, which are recorded in so-called train describer systems. Because of the abundance of data, extracting knowledge from it is a complicated task.

Improving the punctuality of railway operations starts with the development of a robust train schedule. In this area, the work in [130] should be noted. The author provides an overview of 48 techniques for railway scheduling. These techniques were categorised according to the plan perspective, the supported infrastructure, the goal, the level of evaluation and the control strategy. It demonstrates that most attention in literature goes to techniques for tactical scheduling and less to operational scheduling. Moreover, a considerable amount of techniques can only be applied on line-infrastructures, and not on more complex and realistic network-infrastructures.

More recently, robust scheduling in a more complex railway infrastructure was investigated in [48]. The main focus of this research was on the robustness of the complex station area of the North-South connection in Brussels. The author identified the different elements which determined the robustness of a train schedule, and hereupon defined an approach to improve the robustness, by taking into account routing decisions, train sequences and platform allocation.

Once railway schedules are put into service, the performance of the operations needs to be monitored and evaluated. Train conflicts and delay propagations have been studied extensively in literature of transportation and operations research. The Belgian train describer data used in this chapter were analysed before with respect to train delays [36]. Using frequent item-set mining, patterns between train delays were detected. If train A has a delay of x minutes or more, train B will also have a delay with x minutes or more, with a certain confidence y.

The use of train describer data for data analysis has been done in [92] and [93]. In this work, the authors aimed at the adaptive prediction of train event times, i.e. taking into account not only delay but also predicted route conflicts, braking and acceleration times.

In [34], three different types of delay propagation were identified: propagation along the same train, propagation between trains due to required connections, and propagation between trains due to shared use of scarce infrastructure capacity. The last type of delay propagation is better known as *knock-on delays* [30, 68, 145]. These three types of propagations were analysed through the use of stochastic models.

Related to the work of [34, 56] presents efficient algorithms to detect both resource conflicts and delays from maintained connections, within large scale data sets. Further steps which are proposed are a statistical examination and to extend the approach to global dependencies. The latter could for instance lead to the construction of networks of conflicts between trains.

In the same area, [39] focused on real-time dispatching. The objective of this research has been to develop a decision support system for real-time management of railway traffic. The resulting tool, called ROMA, *Railway traffic Optimisation by Means of Alternative graphs*, assists traffic managers in choosing the *best* trajectory, ordering of trains and the optimal speed of trains. The recommendations done by the system are based on simulations of the resolution of traffic after certain decisions are taken.

In [136], the authors advocate that it is important to have feedback from operations to planning, to close the control loop. In order to achieve this, the performance of the railway operations in the Dutch railway are analysed and this is used as input towards a better planning. In The Netherlands, train describer data have been used to identify route conflicts. The TNV-conflict tool introduced in [38] defines a train conflict as the situation in which a train comes within sight distance of a signal which is not open, i.e. obliging the train to slow down or halt. Both conflicts due to scarce capacity and required train transfers were identified, in accordance with the different delay propagations proposed in [34]. The additional tool TNV-statistics has been developed to look into the conflicts with more detail, and to link them together in conflict chains or trees [62].

In [122], several data mining techniques are applied on a large set of sensor data generated by railway infrastructure and rolling stock. The aim of the analysis is to use temporal sequences of recorded events to predict failure of equipment, as to improve maintenance scheduling. Although not related to routing conflicts, it shows how much can be learned from analysing the great amount of data which is available.

Apart from the TNV-statistics tool and the work in [36, 122], little attention has been directed to the analysis of recorded data. Nevertheless, event data such as train describer data can be used to extract process-related knowledge using process mining. For example, train trips can be regarded as process instances, while activities are specific types of events. For instance, activities related to a train trip can be the passing of a signal, or the adjustment of its trajectory. Other attributes may be available, which can be related to the event as well as to the case. Typical additional event attributes relate to resources. As such, the passing of a signal may also record which signal was passed. Case attributes can contain any characteristic information about the process instance, for instance, the type of rolling stock or the number of carriages. In this chapter, we will adopt a process-oriented view for the analysis of train describer data.

9.3 Methodology

The main focus of the analysis in this chapter is to analyse how recorded train routes deviate from the planned route. Thus, two routes are needed for each train: the planned route and the actual route. In our analysis, the planned routes refer to the routes which are communicated to the signal area before the arrival of the train in the area, or before the departure of the train (in case it departs in a station within the area). Note that hereby, anticipated changes to the capacity allocation, e.g. due to known infrastructure works, are neutralised. Both planned and actual routes have been defined at the level of signals. In order to describe the complete path, also the final track segment has been taken into account. This is the track where the train arrives in the destination station or where it leaves the signal area. Considering this track segment is essential since the train might have different routes after passing the last signal. Reroutings on this point of the route often include platform changes, and therefore should not be ignored. Formally, we define the actual and planned route as follows. An overview of the terminology used in this chapter is provided in Table 9.1.

Definition 9.1 (Preliminaries). We define $\mathscr{S}$ as the alphabet of signals and $\mathscr{T}$ as the alphabet of track segments. $\mathscr{S}^*$ is the set of al finite sequences over $\mathscr{S}$.

Definition 9.2 (Actual route). The actual route of a train i, denoted by σ_i, is defined as a sequence of signals plus the destination track segment of the train within the area. Given $s \in \mathscr{S}^*$ and $t \in \mathscr{T}$, we can define σ_i as $< s, t >$.

Definition 9.3 (Planned route). The planned route of a train i, denoted by π_i, is the allocated route of a train 30 min before it enters the signalling area (or before it

Table 9.1 Terminology used in this chapter.

Terminology	Description
Route	A route of a train is a sequence of signals, when needed supplemented with additional details, such as track segments
Planned route	The planned route of a train, based on planning and apriori known disruptions.
Actual route	The actual route of a train, based on train describer data
Rerouting	The situation when the actual and planned route of a train differ
Connection	A connection refers to all train trips from station A to station B. This does not take into account whether the train stops in all station or just in major cities. In case there are multiple routes between A and B, intermediate points are used to distinguish them
Relation	A relation refers to all train trips from station A to station B, **and vice versa**. This does not take into account whether the train stops in all station or just in major cities. In case there are multiple routes between A and B, intermediate points are used to distinguish them

departs, in case the departure is within the area). It consists of a sequence of signals plus the destination track segment of the train within the area. Given $s \in \mathscr{S}^*$ and $t \in \mathscr{T}$, we can define π_i as $< s, t >$.

Given the planned and actual route, rerouting can be formally defined as follows:

Definition 9.4 (Rerouting). A rerouting, or deviation, of a train i is defined as the case where a difference exists between the planned route of a train and the actual route of a train, i.e. $\sigma_i \neq \pi_i$.

Using process maps, recorded process behaviour can be easily visualised as a directed graph. Graphs G_1 and G_2 in Fig. 9.1 show the visualisation of two fictitious groups of train trips. The hypothetical underlying infrastructure is shown in Fig. 9.2. In the directed graphs, each node refers to a signal which was passed by one or more trains, and each edge refers to a route from one signal to the next that was taken by at least one train. In other words, trains are the cases, or process instances, and signal passings are the activities. The darkest path throughout the graph, i.e. the most frequent path, corresponds to the planned route in this example. When all trains visualised in a graph have the same planned route, reroutings become readily noticeable.

Based on an exploratory inspection of the recorded train routes and interviews with business experts, two dimensions seemed relevant to quantify train reroutings. Firstly, the *severity* of the reroutings should be measured. This refers to both how many deviations occurred and how long they are. Upon inspection of both graphs in Fig. 9.1, one can see that more reroutings occurred in G_1 compared to G_2. Furthermore, reroutings in G_2 seem to be less severe, as they take up at most two signals. In contrast, in G_1, only about three quarters of the trains passed through signal AD as

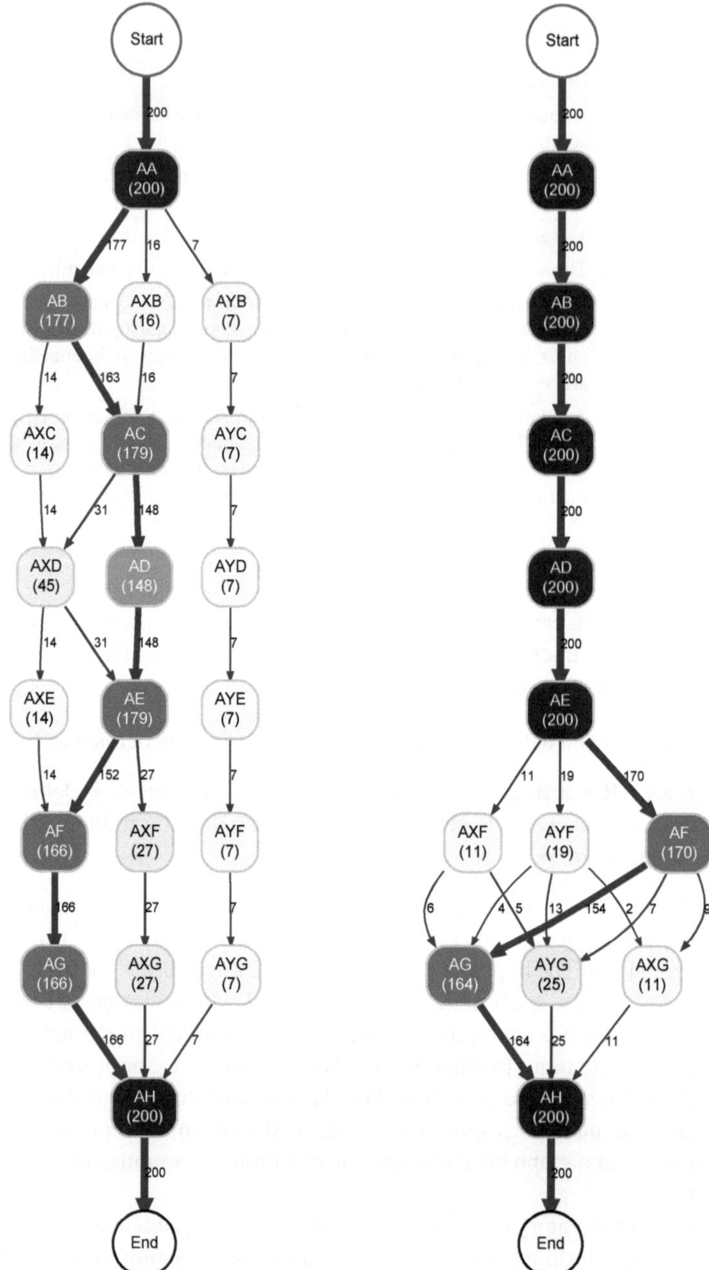

Fig. 9.1 Fictitious actual routes for two sets of 200 train trips with planned route AA → AB → AC → AD → AE → AF → AG → AH. Referred to as G_1 (left) and G_2 (right).

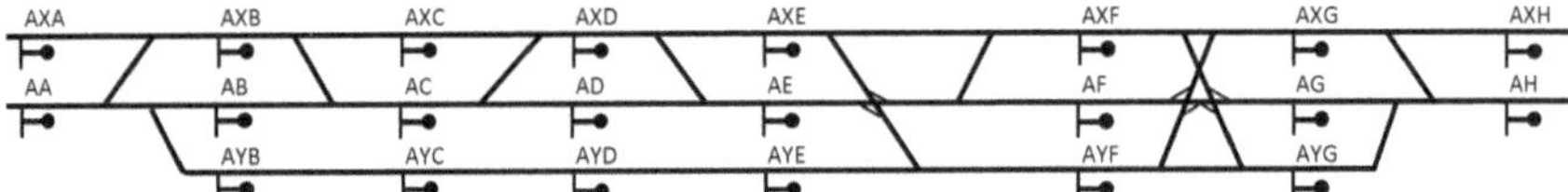

Fig. 9.2 Example infrastructure.

planned, and only 2 signals of the planned routes were never deviated from. The severity of reroutings will be referred to as the *rerouting severity*.

Secondly, the complexity and structuredness of the graphs are relevant, as they represent how many *different* reroutings have occurred. In Fig. 9.1, the model on the left is clearly less complex than the model on the right. The complexity of the model will be used as a proxy for *rerouting diversity*.

Visual inspection of all planned routes would, however, be a cumbersome task. Therefore, the next paragraphs suggest metrics to quantify the severity and diversity of reroutings and to single out the routes which should be examined more closely.

9.3.1 Rerouting Severity

In order to measure rerouting severity, we draw upon insights of conformance checking within process mining, as introduced in Chap. 2. Given a process model, conformance checking determines whether the events that were recorded can be *replayed* by the process model [3]. For example, the *Alignment-Based Fitness* measure has been defined (see also Sect. 2.3), which is one of the best-known metrics within conformance checking. In general terms, each case is *aligned* to the most optimally corresponding execution trace of a process model, according to a cost-function. For cases which are allowed by the model, the cost of the alignment is obviously zero. For cases which cannot be replayed by the model, corrections have to be made. A correction can be an insertion of an event, a deletion of an event, or the substitution of an event. Note that multiple alignments can be made, which each have their own cost. Using default values, a single insertion or deletion has a cost of 1, while a substitution is allocated a cost of 2. The most optimal alignment will be used to compute the overall fitness between the recorded behaviour and the model.

In the context of train deviations, suppose we have a group of k trains which were allocated the same planned route. Let π_L be the planned route of the trains and let $L = \{\sigma_1, ..., \sigma_k\}$ refer to the set of the actual routes of the trains. For train i, given the actual route $\sigma_i \in L$ and π_L, we define $\lambda_{\pi_L}(\sigma_i)$ as the optimal alignment for the actual route σ_i and $\delta(\lambda_{\pi_L}(\sigma_i))$ as the corresponding cost. It should be noted that, while there are multiple optimal alignments possible in general, there is only a single way to align the actual route with the planned route. This is because the *model*, i.e. the planned route, is only a single sequence of signals. As a result, computing the Alignment-Based Fitness will be straightforward, and will not suffer from the

Table 9.2 Example of an alignment between actual route σ_1 and planned route π_L.

π_L	AA	$\perp$	AB	AC	$\perp$	AD	$\perp$	AE	AF	AG	AH
σ_1	AA	AXB	$\perp$	AC	AXD	$\perp$	AXE	$\perp$	AF	AG	AH

feasibility issues mentioned in Chap. 4. The fitness for train i is defined as

$$f(\sigma_i, \pi_L) = 1 - \frac{\delta(\lambda_{\pi_L}(\sigma_i))}{|\sigma_i| + |\pi_L|} \tag{9.1}$$

where $|\sigma_i|$ and $|\pi_L|$ refer to the length of the actual route and planned route, respectively. In the worst-case scenario, a train followed a completely different sequence of signals throughout the network. To align such a route, all signals that were passed by the train need to be removed, while all signals on the planned route need to be inserted. Consequently, the total cost will equal the nominator, resulting in a fitness value equal to zero. In the optimal case, when $\sigma_i = \pi_L$, then $\delta(\lambda_{\pi_L}(\sigma_i)) = 0$, yielding a fitness value of one. Given the fitness values for all individual trains, the overall fitness value can be computed for a set of train trips L as follows[1]:

$$Fitness\ F(L) = \frac{\sum_{\sigma_i \in L} f(\sigma_i, \pi_L)}{|L|} \tag{9.2}$$

Table 9.2 shows a fictitious example alignment between planned route $\pi_L = \langle AA, AB, AC, AD, AE, AF, AG, AH\rangle$ and actual route $\sigma_1 = \langle AA, AXB, AC, AXD, AXE, AF, AG, AH\rangle$. Three signals of the planned route were not passed and were thus deleted from the route, as indicated with the $\perp$-symbol. Furthermore, three signals were visited, although they didn't belong to the planned route, which results in three insertions. Notice that, in this case, each consecutive pair of one insertion and one deletion can also be regarded as a substitution, which would yield an equivalent optimal alignment according to the default cost-function. However, in general, it is not obligatory to have one deletion for each insertion, or vice versa. Since the planned route, as well as the actual route, consists of 8 signals, Eq. (9.1) results in a fitness value of 0.625.

The overall fitness values for each of the planned routes will be used as a proxy for the rerouting severity. The lower the fitness value, the more sensitive the route

[1]Note that these formulas are equivalent to those introduced in Chap. 2. Calculating Alignment-Based Fitness normally requires the computation of the optimal alignments, which is not trivial. However, given the constraints imposed by the infrastructure and the fact that our *prescriptive model* is fully sequential, only a single alignment exists. The corresponding cost will always be equal to the number of signals planned but not visited, plus the number of signals visited but not planned. As such, it is equivalent to the Levenshtein distance for strings. Given this simplification, the fitness could be easily computed using bupaR. Computing alignments was not straightforward in bupaR (or its precursors used for the initial analysis). However, through integrating bupaR and PM4Py, computing alignments is possible at the time of writing.

is towards train reroutings. In Fig. 9.1 it was already clear that, weighted by the frequencies, slightly more reroutings occurred in G_1 compared to G_2. Indeed the Fitness-metric for the set of train trips G_1 is 0.8844, while for G_2 it is 0.9175.

For the sake of interpretability, we will refer to rerouting severity as the complement of fitness from this point onwards. It is thus said that G_1 has a rerouting severity of 0.1156 while G_2 has a rerouting severity of 0.0825.

An analysis of variance can be performed to see whether deviation severity differs significantly among different groups of trains. These groups can be composed in different ways, depending on the purpose of the analysis: e.g. comparing trains on different itineraries, comparing trains at different times of the day, etc. Pairwise differences between groups and corresponding p-values can then be used to identify which specific groups perform significantly worse or better.

Once the interesting cases have been identified, the reroutings can be scrutinised further. For instance, are there only a limited number of distinct deviations, or are there many different ones? How are they distributed along the route? How many distinct reroutings generally happen at one specific point of the route, on average? In order to answer these questions, the dimension of *rerouting diversity* will be further defined in the next paragraph.

9.3.2 Rerouting Diversity

The aim of this second dimension is to investigate whether trains on a certain route always deviate in a similar manner or have many different reroutings over time. In order to measure diversity, we take a new look at the directed graphs displaying all recorded behaviour, as those shown in Fig. 9.1. The complexity of these models can be used as proxy for the deviation diversity.

Based on the visual inspection of a series of graphs, it was observed that diversity cannot be measured in a single metric. For instance, in the lower part of G_2, about 8 different routes have been observed from signal *AE* to signal AH. This is remarkably more than the number of different routes observed at any point in G_1. It is therefore said that the reroutings of G_2 are *wider*. This type of diversity will be referred to as *horizontal diversity*. Conversely, deviations in G_1 have occurred in a larger part of the itinerary, i.e. on all signals except for the first and the last. This type of diversity will be referred to as *vertical diversity*. Two different process complexity metrics have been adapted to the specific context of this paper, both taking into account one specific type of diversity. Both metrics are discussed in the following paragraphs.

9.3.2.1 Horizontal Diversity

The *Extended Cyclomatic Metric (ECyM)*, or *cyclomatic complexity* has been defined by Thomas J. McCabe [104] as a means to estimate the testability and maintainability of software systems. It uses a directed graph as input, consisting of *nodes* and *edges*.

Given the number of edges e, the number of nodes n and the number of connected components p, ECyM was defined as

$$ECyM(e, n, p) = e - n + 2p \tag{9.3}$$

Note that the formula for the cyclomatic complexity differs from the formula for the cyclomatic number, which is equal to $e - n + p$. The cyclomatic number only has a logical interpretation in the context of strongly connected graphs[2]. In contrast, the cyclomatic complexity is primarily directed towards graphs which are not strongly connected, but which have clear start and end points, as in our case. However, the cyclomatic complexity is equal to the cyclomatic number of a graph in which an extra edge was added from the end to the start of every component, in order to make the components strongly connected [134]. As a result, $e - n + p + p = e - n + 2p$. As stated in [104], in a strongly connected graph, the cyclomatic number is equal to the maximum number of linearly independent circuits. Consequently, $ECyM$ is meant to quantify *horizontal diversity*.

9.3.2.2 Vertical Diversity

In order to measure *vertical diversity*, Separability (Π) is introduced. [107] defined the notion of Separability, referring to the number of cut-vertices in a graph. A cut-vertex can be defined as a node which *separates* the graph into two parts when it would be deleted. As such, it provides an estimate of the modularity of a process model. Formally, given a set of actual train routes L,

$$\Pi = |\{s \in \mathscr{S} \mid \forall \sigma_i \in L : s \in \sigma_i\}| \tag{9.4}$$

In other words, the number of signals through which all trains in L pass. When more cut-vertices are present, it means there is a higher proportion of the planned route which is never deviated on. However, this only holds under the assumption that each signal on the planned route was passed by at least one of the trains. If this does not hold, a cut-vertex can also be a signal through which all trains have passed, although it did **not** belong the planned trajectory. Yet, to measure diversity, it is irrelevant whether the cut-vertex belongs to the planned route or not.

9.3.2.3 Impact of Trajectory Length

Complexity, as measured by the metrics discussed above, tends to increase as the size of the graph increases. This is indeed a desirable property of complexity measures in the context for which they have been defined. However, longer routes will therefore be negatively biased, i.e. obtaining higher complexity scores. To take this into account,

[2]A graph is strongly connected if there is a path from each node to any other node.

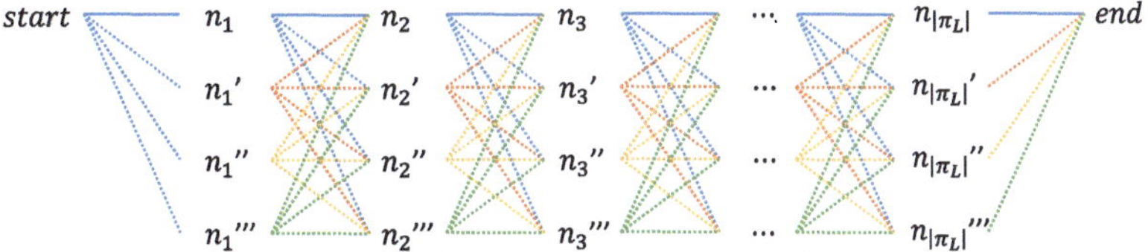

Fig. 9.3 Example of maximum number of possible deviations on a strongly-connected 4-track railway line.

both metrics were corrected for the length of the planned route. Furthermore, the complement of the separability metric is taken, so that higher values correspond to a higher diversity, as is the case with $ECyM$.

$$ECyM'(e, n, p) = \frac{e - n + 2p}{|\pi_L|} \tag{9.5}$$

$$\Pi' = 1 - \frac{|\{s \in \mathscr{S} \mid \forall \sigma_i \in L : s \in \sigma_i\}|}{|\pi_L|} \tag{9.6}$$

While values of Π' are generally in the range from 0 to 1, values of $ECyM'$ are not. For a planned trajectory of length $|\pi_L|$, the maximum possible $ECyM'$ is a function of the total number of nodes n and the number of edges e between those nodes. Although the maximum number of nodes in the graph will depend on the length of the trajectory, it is not straightforward to express this dependency mathematically. If the deviation occurs in between station areas, there can no more than 3 alternative signals for each signal deviated from, since there are never more than 4 parallel tracks in the railway infrastructure under consideration. However, if the deviation occurs within a station area, there might be more than 3 alternative signals for each signal, because a station might have more parallel tracks. Finally, when the deviation is not local, i.e. the train is forced to change its itinerary via other cities or railway connections to reach its destination, the number of alternatives becomes virtually unlimited. If the number of nodes is known, the number of edges depends again on the infrastructure, which determines whether is signal is directly reachable from another signal.

For the sake of simplicity, assume that 3 alternative signals exist for each signal on the route, and assume that after each signal, each of the next for signals is reachable, as is shown in Fig. 9.3. The maximum number of actually visited signals—i.e. the maximum value for n—is then equal to $4 \times |\pi_L| + 2$ (including the entry and exit points). The maximum number of edges e is equal to $4(|\pi_L| - 1) \times 4 + 2 \times 4$ (including the entry and exit possibilities). The maximum possible $ECyM'$ is then equal to $\frac{4(|\pi_L|-1)\times 4 + 2\times 4 - (4\times|\pi_L|+2)+2}{|\pi_L|} = \frac{12|\pi_L|-8}{|\pi_L|}$, which approximates 12 for long trajectories.

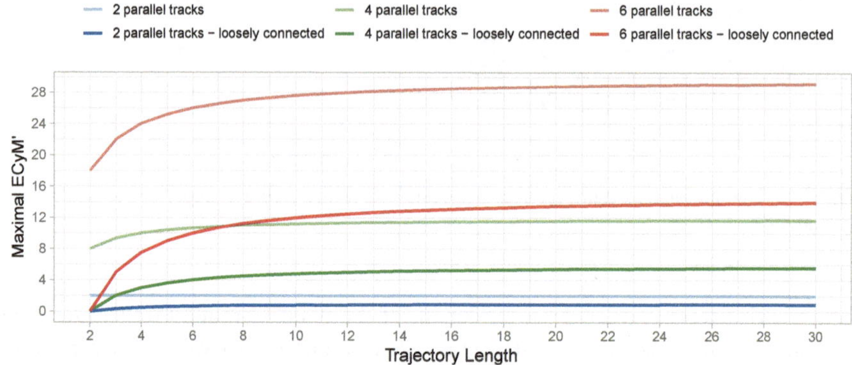

Fig. 9.4 Relation between maximal ECyM and trajectory length.

However, if there is only 1 alternative signal, i.e. a 2-track railway line, the maximum $ECyM'$ will be equal to 2. If there would be 6 parallel tracks, the maximum will approximate 30 for long trajectories. Next to the number of parallel tracks, also the number of connections between those tracks has a large impact. If, for instance, you can only switch to another track after every 2 signals, the maximum $ECyM'$ will be lower.

The maximum $ECyM'$ in function of the length of the trajectory for these 6 different scenario's—2, 4 and 6 parallel tracks, both strongly and loosely connected is shown in Fig. 9.4. For each scenario it can be seen that the maximal $ECyM'$ number quickly stabilises if the trajectory length increases, and is only depended on this length for small trajectory. However, the level at which is stabilises depends on the infrastructure. The more parallel tracks there are, and the easier they are to reach, the more diverse the deviations can be.

As a result, caution is needed when comparing the level of deviation diversity of different trajectories, as some might have more potential to deviate in diverse ways. Since the infrastructure under consideration does not neatly fall within a specific infrastructural type such as the ones shown in Fig. 9.4, it is not straightforward to normalise the metric appropriately. Indeed, the infrastructure under consideration is very complex and differs highly from location to location—some parts of a trajectory will allow for more diverse deviations than others. However, it can be argued that the difference will be less extreme than those in Fig. 9.4. In the next section, it will be shown that many of the trajectories will pass through the same railway corridor, i.e. between Brussels and Leuven. Furthermore, it can be observed that the infrastructure in the remainder of the area is similar to some extent: mostly there are 2 parallel tracks and 3 to 4 tracks in station areas. As such, the resulting $ECyM'$ values will be largely comparable. We will return to this issue when discussing the limitations of the approach later in this chapter.

9.3.2.4 Running Example

In order to calculate the $ECyM'$ of each graph in Fig. 9.1, the number of nodes and edges needs to be counted. G_1 contains 20 nodes and 25 edges, while G_2 contains 12 nodes and 18 edges[3]. Thus, $ECyM'(G_1) = 0.875$ and $ECyM'(G_2) = 1$. As we know the infrastructure for this fictitious example (Fig. 9.2), we can compute that the maximal $ECyM'$ equals 1.875 ($\frac{35\text{ edges}-22\text{ nodes}+2}{8}$).

To compute the adjusted separability-measure Π', it can be seen that G_1 contains only 2 cut-vertices, while G_2 contains 6. As a result, $\Pi'(G_1)$ is equal to 0.750 and $\Pi'(G_2)$ is equal to 0.250.

This illustration shows that both measures of diversity take into account different aspects of the reroutings which occurred. The reroutings in G_2 are assessed by Π' to have a much lower diversity, as they only occur at the end of the trajectory. However, G_2 is allocated a higher diversity score by $ECyM'$, as the reroutings in the lower part of the graph are judged to be *broader* then those in G_1. It can indeed be observed that G_1 is more structured, whereas the lower part of G_2 is more dense.

In order to further illustrate the meaning of $ECyM'$ and Π', Fig. 9.5 shows graphs with combinations of low and high values for both metrics. The x-axis depicts the level of horizontal diversity while the y-axis depicts the level of vertical diversity. In the upper right graph, reroutings are wide and well spread along the route, resulting in high values for both the metrics. Meanwhile, in both lower graphs, reroutings are not spread along the whole route, yielding a low value for separability. The graphs in the right part of the table are relatively wide, leading to a high value for the $ECyM'$ metric.

After having identified the instances which are the most sensitive to rerouting, their values for the diversity metrics can be computed. Consequently plotting them on a xy-scatterplot allows the data analyst to map the different instances to the different types of graphs in Fig. 9.5. As such, one can have a preliminary idea of how the different graphs look like, without having to look at each of them individually. The analyst can then decide which instances are the most interesting to inspect further.

9.3.3 *Discovering Patterns*

So far, the methods and metrics proposed are able to both identify which groups of trains are the most sensitive to reroutings and to map different groups of trains to different types of graphs. Finally, the question might be asked which patterns can be found in the reroutings? In other words, under what circumstances are certain reroutings occurring? For instance, do specific types of deviations always occur at the same time of day?

[3]Note that the *Start* and *End* nodes, as well as their connecting edges, are not taken into account in the calculation of $ECyM'$ and Π', as they are not really part of the routes. They only have an aesthetic function in the visualisation.

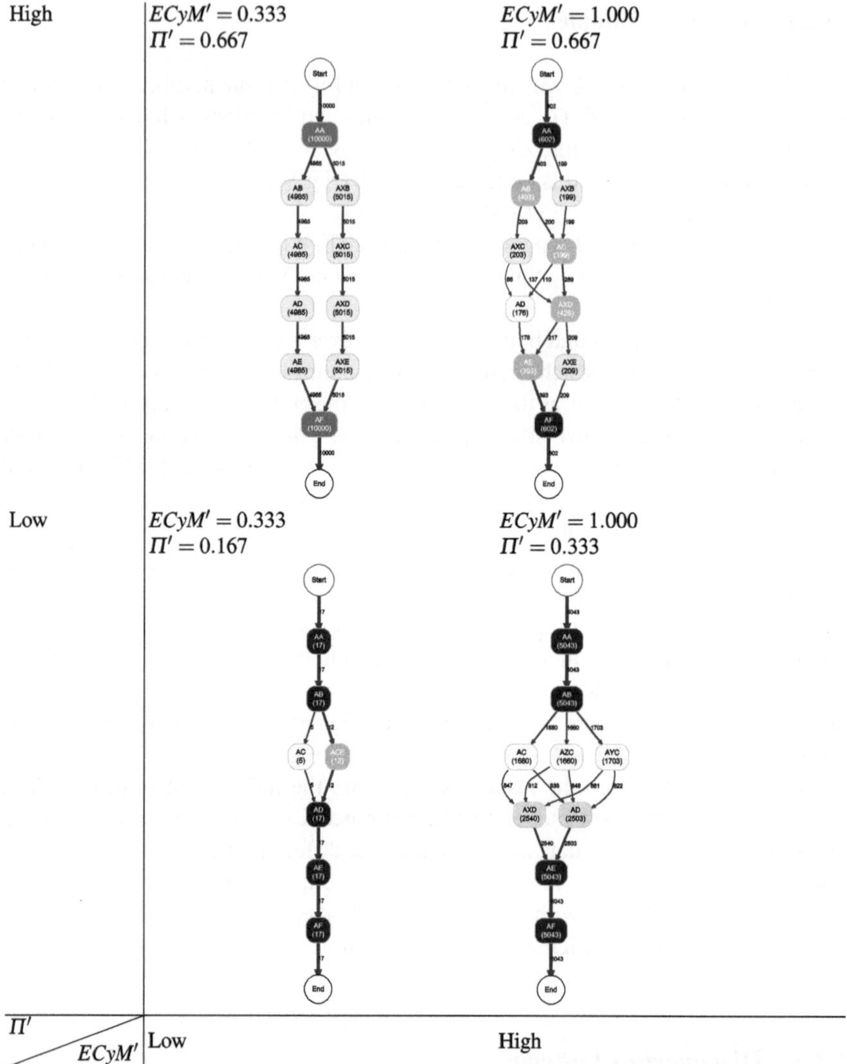

Fig. 9.5 Typical graphs for low and high values of the diversity metrics. Π' indicates vertical diversity and $ECyM'$ indicates horizontal diversity.

When the diversity is low, e.g. like in the lower left graph in Fig. 9.5, it is very easy to see which reroutings occur when, since there are only a limited number of distinct reroutings. However, when moving to the upper right graph in Fig. 9.5, distinguishing the different types of reroutings gets more difficult. However, using clustering techniques, reroutings can be grouped into different clusters of similar instances. This can be done using a hierarchical clustering design, in which the distance between two routes is measured using the Levenshtein distance. The Levenshtein distance calculates the difference between two sequences based on the number of insertions and deletions that have to be performed on one sequence, in order to be equal to the other sequence. An hierarchical clustering can be conducted using *average linkage*, where the number of clusters can be decided for each clustering by inspecting the dendogram. The clusters can subsequently be compared to each other along different characteristics: the time of day, day of week, type of rolling stock, etc. This will yield a first understanding as to when and why certain deviations occur. In the next section, the discussed methods will be illustrated using data from the Belgian train describer system, provided by infrastructure manager Infrabel.

9.4 Results

In the context of the Belgian railway network, the need to optimize capacity usage is amplified by several factors. Firstly, the railway network, as shown in Fig. 9.6, has a high density, containing many bifurcations within short distances from each other, and it is star-shaped with Brussels at its gravity centre. Every day, 57% of the railway passengers travels to or through Brussels. Secondly, the amount of passengers has risen steadily over the last decades, mounting up to 230 million a year in 2013. Meanwhile, annual punctuality has been decreasing gradually over the last couple of years until 2013. The complexity of the network makes it a non-trivial task to identify the causes of certain delays. As stated in [36], it might not be clear whether a structural delay is the result of ordinary busy traffic or of certain decisions that are made consistently by traffic operators who are unaware of its negative impact.

The data selected for the analyses conducted in this paper were recorded in the signal area of Leuven. With on average 32.247 departing passengers each day (2014), the station of Leuven is the 6th most important railway station in Belgium. Furthermore, the signal area constitutes an important *gateway* to Brussels, and is also responsible for all trains to and from the national airport. The data were recorded during the period from 15 December 2013 to 15 March 2014. The logbook used for the analyses consists of three main categories of events: train movements, user commands and auxiliary functions. The train movement events were used to reconstruct the actual trajectory of the train. On the other hand, specific user commands conveyed the planned trajectory of a train.

A total amount of 5.36 million train describer events were recorded during the three month period. Together, these records describe the history of 75 382 trains trips. On average, circa 950 train trips through the signal area were recorded on a working day,

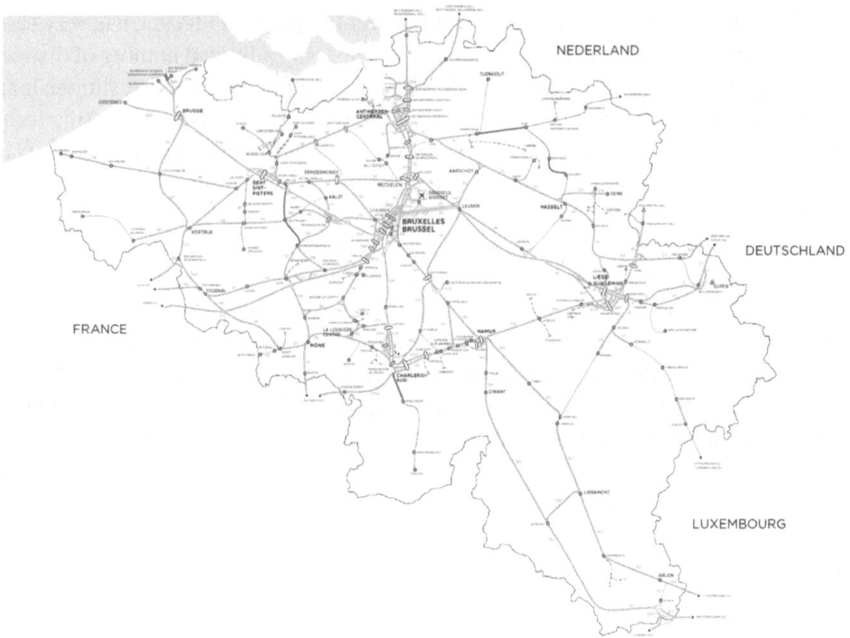

Fig. 9.6 Overview of Belgian railway network.

and approximately 600 train trips on a typical weekend day. Given this abundance of available data, there is a clear need for scalable methods in order to produce useful insights about the railway operations. The actual train trajectories covered a total number of 394 different signals and approximately 160 track segments. Note that this area only covers a small percentage of the total railway infrastructure in Belgium. Nevertheless, since the used methods require no a priori knowledge of the infrastructure, scalability of the approach is a clear advantage.

Different types of train movement recordings, related to signals on the one hand and to track segments on the other, were transformed into one standardized format. These events constitute the building blocks of the actual train routes. Table 9.3 shows the events which are related to train number 1234 on the 10th of January 2014.[4] Each train trip is considered as one *instance* or *case* of the process. Each case is identified by the date and the train number.[5] Each row in Table 9.3 is an event, which has both a timestamp and a location attached to it. The location may refer to both a signal, which is a combination of letters, or a track segment, which is a number. Recall that only the destination segment is taken into account.

Next to the actual routes, the planned routes are extracted from specific communication messages. These messages deliver the planned trajectory to the traffic

[4]Both train numbers and signals have been anonymised.

[5]Note that on a given day, each train ride has a unique train number. For example, the train from Genk to Bruges at 8:07a.m. has number 1531 while that of 9:07a.m. has number 1532.

Table 9.3 Trajectory of train 1234 on January 10th, 2014.

Date	Train number	Timestamp	Location
2014-01-10	1234	6:23:17	AB
2014-01-10	1234	6:24:15	AC
2014-01-10	1234	6:25:49	AD
2014-01-10	1234	6:27:02	100

Table 9.4 Example extraction of the planned trajectory.

Date	Train nr.	Time	Message	Planned trajectory
2014-01-10	1234	5:54:36	2E1234 :AB *>> AC *>> AD 20K *>> 100 AE	AB,AC,AD,100

control system as the train approaches the area. Table 9.4 shows this record for the corresponding train. The message column contains the original encapsulation of the planned route, while the last column shows the route after the extraction and cleaning. This route was sent to the signal box at 5:54am, about 30 min before the arrival of the train in the area.

The analysis of rerouting severity and diversity can be conducted at different levels of abstraction. The rerouting severity can be calculated at the level of a planned route, at the level of a connection, or at the level of relation. A relation contains all trains between two specific locations, in either direction. For example, all trains from Mechelen to Leuven, and vice versa. Each relation can be further divided into two connections, by taking into account the direction of the train. E.g., all trains from Mechelen to Leuven form one connection, and all trains from Leuven to Mechelen form a second one. For each connection, one or more planned routes might exists. As these are defined at the very low level of signals and tracks, they can differ based on the time of the day, or because of planned maintenance works. An overview of the terminology can be found in Table 9.1.

The selection of the appropriate abstraction level encompasses a certain trade-off. Focussing on a low level, i.e. planned route, will yield very precise results, but there can be an abundance as many planned routes might exist. Focussing at the higher level of relations will limit the number of instances, but might create the risk that certain problem cases remain hidden. Indeed, when a relation consists of 10 planned routes, of which one has an extremely high severity of reroutings, while the other 9 hardly contain reroutings, the problematic route will probably remain unnoticed in a high-level analysis. A recommended approach would be to start the analysis at a high level, and subsequently lowering the unit of analysis, while at each step discarding the most uninteresting cases from the analysis, at all times being aware that there might be interesting outliers.

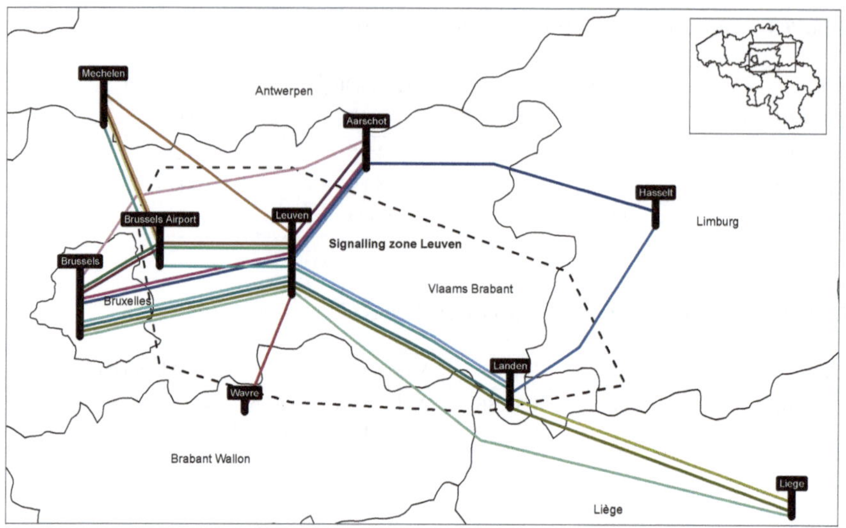

Fig. 9.7 Schematic overview of considered train relations.

The planned route was extracted for all regular trains, excluding empty train rides, freight trains, and working trains. This resulted in the selection of 58,042 train trips. Consequently, these were grouped based on their planned route. For each group, a set of train describer records, i.e. an event log, was constructed containing the actual route. In order to make sure the results of the analysis were reliable, only those groups which contained at least 50 instances were considered. The resulting selection contained 54,635, i.e. 94.13%, of all regular trains. Among these trains, 7.75% contained reroutings. For each planned route, a corresponding model was constructed. Both the model and the actual trajectories in the event log are the main input to the analysis conducted in the next section.

A total number of 109 different planned routes were considered—i.e. regular trains trajectories with more than 50 instances. They were categorized along 22 relations. The relations considered are listed in Table 9.5 and schematically visualized in Fig. 9.7. For some pairs of locations multiple relations exist, which are distinguished by certain intermediate points.[6] Note that in this analysis only the trajectory is used to distinguish train trips, and not their stops or the type of the train (regional trains vs intercity, etc.). In the remainder of the analysis, the specific connections are treated anonymously. Next to the 109 different planned routes, 590 different actual routes were found. Thus, for each planned route, on average 5.73 reroutings existed, with a minimum of zero (no reroutings) and a maximum of 29. The length of the routes varied between 2 and 23 signals, with an average of 8 signals.

[6]Notice that some of the intermediate points indicated in Table 9.5 are not visually distinguished in Fig. 9.7, since they are very local in nature, most commonly in the dense corridor between the National Airport and Brussels.

Table 9.5 Train connections considered in the analysis.

Relation			# trains
National airport	↔[d]	Brussel	6301
Mechelen	↔	Leuven	5980
Luik	↔[c]	Brussel	5562
Aarschot	↔	Leuven	5418
Leuven	↔	Brussel	4841
Hasselt	↔	Brussel	3108
Luik	↔	Brussel	2657
Mechelen	↔	Brussel	2246
Aarschot	↔	Brussel	1982
Landen	↔[b]	Mechelen	1937
Mechelen	↔[c]	National airport	1897
Leuven	↔[b]	Brussel	1747
National airport	↔[a]	Brussel	1301
Luik	↔	Landen	1039
Leuven	↔[b]	Brussel	872
Leuven	↔	National airport	465
Aarschot	↔[a]	Brussel	461
Waver	↔	Leuven	457
Landen	↔	Aarschot	370
Landen	↔	Brussel	169
Hasselt	↔	Landen	117
Mechelen	↔[b]	Leuven	114

[a] Via fast track [b] Via National airport [c] Via high speed line [d] Via default track

Table 9.6 shows some statistics for the rerouting severity and diversity metrics for the different relations, which are visualised in Fig. 9.8. It can be observed that on average, the rerouting severity of the different relations is quite low, with an average severity-value of 0.016. By comparing the mean and the median, it can be observed that the distribution is right-skewed, with the mass of the observations in the close vicinity of zero. As such, most relations only contain a limited number of reroutings, while some unfavourable outliers exist.

The values for Horizontal diversity are located in the range from 0.181 to 1.761, with a mean of 0.601. It is not unsurprisingly to find diversity levels to be low for the majority of the connections, as they are dependent on the extent that reroutings have occurred on these connections. The values for vertical diversity are distributed between 0.085 and 0.869. On average, 52.7% of the planned signals is deviated from by at least one train.

The pairwise correlation coefficients between the different metrics are shown in Table 9.7. It can be seen that, like expected, a positive correlation is found between

Table 9.6 Measures of locality and spread for the deviation severity and diversity measures.

	Rerouting severity	Rerouting diversity	
		Horizontal	Vertical
Min	0.001	0.181	0.085
Mean	0.016	0.601	0.527
Median	0.006	0.508	0.631
Max	0.122	1.761	0.869
Std. Dev.	0.032	0.405	0.279

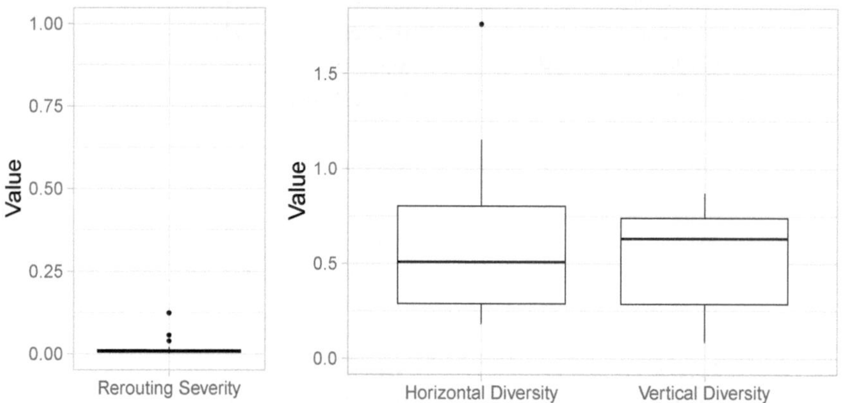

Fig. 9.8 Boxplots showing the distribution of the metrics.

Table 9.7 Pairwise correlations between deviations severity and diversity measures.

	Rerouting severity	Horizontal diversity	Vertical diversity
Rerouting severity	—		
Horizontal diversity	0.526***	—	
Vertical diversity	0.191	0.614***	—

Note: *** $p < 0.001$

deviation severity on the one hand, and both horizontal and vertical diversity on the other hand. As such, when rerouting severity increases, the rerouting diversity increases. However, the correlation between severity and vertical diversity was not found to be statistically significant. Finally, both measures for diversity were found to be significantly positively correlated, which seems legitimate.

9.4.1 Rerouting Severity

In order to identify relations with a remarkable severity of reroutings, an analysis of variance can be done for the fitness values, to analyse differences between group means. This means that all trains are grouped according to their relation, and for each train the fitness is computed using Eq. (9.1). However, two of the underlying assumptions for ANOVA were not satisfied [70]: (1) the dependent variable (i.e. fitness) is not normally distributed within each group and (2) the population variances of the fitness values within each group are not equal. For these reasons, the Kruskal-Wallis test, a non-parametric alternative, was used [95]. Since this test is rank-based, it disregards the magnitude of the differences in fitness. The Kruskal-Wallis test has theoretically less power than the parametric ANOVA when the ANOVA's assumptions are met. However, this is not necessarily true when they do not hold [44].

The test was able to reject the null hypothesis that there were no differences in rerouting severity among the different relations at a 0.001 significance level. Consequently, a post-hoc Nemenyi test was conducted [111], of which the pairwise results are visualised in a heatmap in Fig. 9.9. The bar chart on the right shows the deviation severity for each relation, ordered from best to worst. The matrix on the left demonstrates whether pairs of relations are significantly different from each other in terms of rerouting severity. As such, it allows us to see which relations are significantly more problematic than others.

A pair of relations with a red cell has a statistically significant difference in rerouting severity at the 0.001 significance level. All the pairs with a green cell are not found to be significantly different with regards to the rerouting severity. It can be concluded that relation 2 has a far higher severity to deviations than all the other connections, followed by connection 3 and 8. These connection are thus identified as the main problem cases requiring further analysis.[7]

Important to note in this respect that we are analysing only the observable *system dynamics*. We do not look at dependencies between different trains. Certainly, a deviation for a specific train might cause one or more deviations for other trains. Or, a train just being late might cause deviations for other trains. However, in process mining, different process instances are often considered in isolation from each other. Analysis of the event data in a more generic setting—i.e. not within the straitjacket of a process view—would probably lead to more diverse insights, also on the dependencies between different deviations or other events. We will return to this remark in the discussion section.

[7]Note that for data privacy reasons these relations will be treated anonymously. We will not refer to them using the descriptions used in Table 9.5.

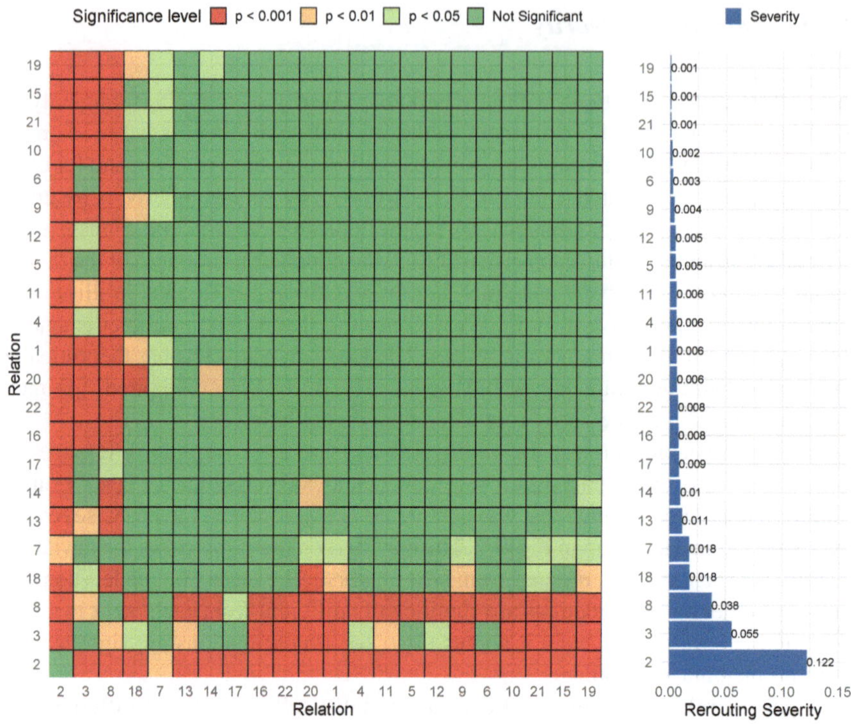

Fig. 9.9 Heatmap of post hoc Nemenyi test for rerouting severity.

9.4.2 Rerouting Diversity

Figure 9.10 shows a scatter plot based on the horizontal and vertical diversity measures. The horizontal and vertical line display the mean of both metrics. The size of the points refers to the rerouting severity; bigger points having a higher severity. Comparing this plot to Fig. 9.5 gives an overall idea of how the graphs containing the actual behaviour within each relation look like. It can thus be observed that graphs like the one in the lower right of Fig. 9.5 do not seem to occur. Furthermore, the low diversity of reroutings along relation 3 is remarkable in this figure, as it is the second most sensitive to reroutings. As such this will provide a very interesting case, as the low diversity indicates the existence of a limited set of deviations which occur very often. In the remainder of this section, these results will be drilled-down further.

As pointed out before, relations are composed of two connections, one in each direction. In Fig. 9.11 the diversity values are shown for each connection within the selected relations. Connections are distinguished with the letters *A* and *B*. This shows that the two diversity metrics are not always in agreement with each other within a relation, especially for relation 2. E.g. Connection 2A has a higher horizontal diversity than 2B according, but lower vertical diversity. As such, reroutings on 2A

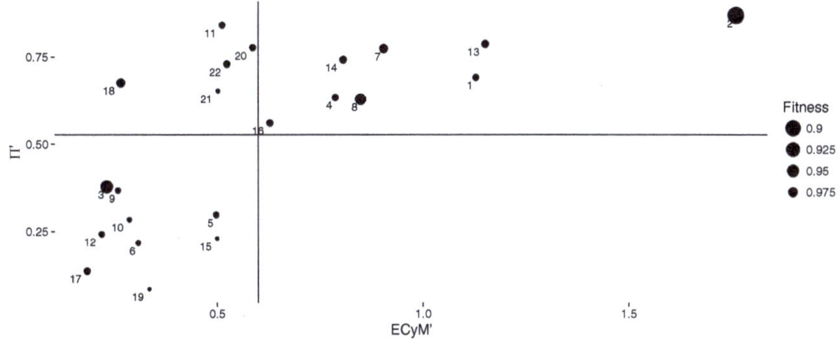

Fig. 9.10 Scatterplot of rerouting diversity metrics.

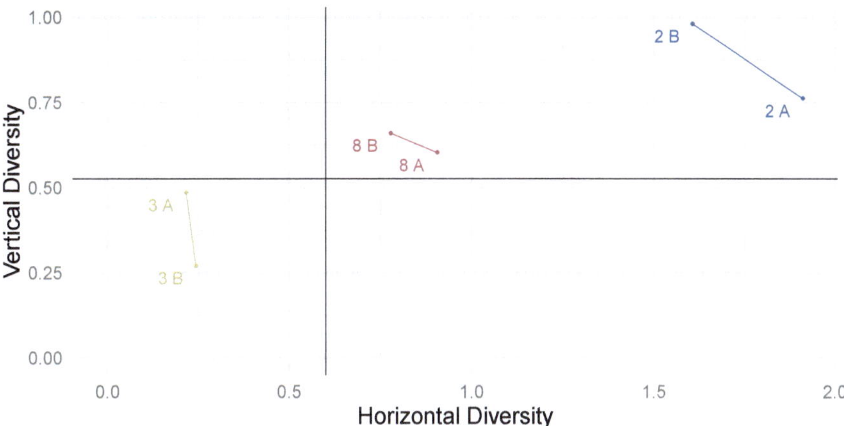

Fig. 9.11 Diversity of connections within selected relations.

are expected to differ more in their *width* but are slightly more concentrated along the route, compared to 2B. Furthermore, it can be seen that both connections of relation 3 have a relatively low diversity.

Figure 9.12 contains two graphs of actual routes, one belonging to each direction of relation 2, each having a similar level of rerouting severity. The graph on the left, belonging to direction *A* is indeed wider than the graph belonging to direction *B*. However, the right graph displays reroutings on every signal, while in the left graph the first three signals are never deviated from. It is clear that both graphs fall into the upper right category of Fig. 9.5, having both a relatively high horizontal as well as vertical diversity.

In the right graph, some reroutings appear to be relatively systematic. For example OYD > MYD > CYE is taken 8.5% of the cases. Definitely, an in depth analysis should be performed to reveal when and why this rerouting occurs.

Analogously, Fig. 9.13 shows graphs of two routes belonging to connection 3, one in both directions. As was apparent from Fig. 9.10, relation 3 has a very low diversity of reroutings. Indeed, it can be observed that in both directions only one single rerouting has occurred, albeit relatively often. It therefore corresponds to the lower left category in Fig. 9.5. The above-average rerouting severity in accordance with a low deviation diversity yields some interesting inquiries: are there any patterns in the occurrence of this deviation? Why does it occur so often? And were the occurrences beneficial for the operations?

The first question can be easily answered by looking at the data. For instance, it could be observed in the data that about 70% of the reroutings in the left graph in Fig. 9.13 took place at six in the morning. The reason for the deviation can be discovered in different ways. Firstly, one could focus on the detailed infrastructure at the location of the rerouting and *simulate* the movement of the trains in this area at the time of rerouting. As such, replaying history can give insights about why certain decisions were taken. Secondly, observations and interviews at the signal box can be clarifying.

The last question, whether the rerouting was beneficial for the overall performance of the network, is much more harder to assess. It involves the linking of reroutings with each other and with impacts on performance measures, such as train punctuality.

Finally, a closer look will be given to relation 8. Just as relation 3, it has an above-average severity to rerouting. While the diversity of reroutings was still rather low, there did not seem to be only a single rerouting. For instance, along one of the planned routes, still 10 different deviations occurred. Nevertheless, relating rerouting to specific characteristics of both train and time can still be meaningful. In order to do so, all rerouting along the planned routes underlying the relation were clustered.

On the routes of connection *8A*, four different clusters were found, each containing a set of similar deviations. For simplicity's sake, the precise composition of the clusters is abstracted from. The distribution of the clusters over the timespan of a day is shown in Fig. 9.14. It can be observed that reroutings belonging to cluster 3 are more likely to occur in the evening, while reroutings from cluster 0 are more likely to occur in the early morning. It could be further investigated why these reroutings occurred a their specific moments, by replaying history and interviewing business experts, and how they influenced the network operations.

When clusters of deviations are very common at specific points in time—such as during the evening rush in this case—it would be interesting to see what the root cause of the deviations are. It might be that the location where trains in this cluster deviate is generally very crowded during these hours, so that deviations are inevitable. On the other hand, the deviations might be caused by a specific (set of) train(s) which are either late or also deviating. Thirdly, it may also be the case that there is no specific problem on the planned route, but the operators decide to deviate anyhow. This can be a way to prevent a certain risk for delay or conflict which might exists if the planned route is taken, or even just because it is a *habit* of the operators—*"we always did it that way"*. These cases—with a large amount of deviations but a limited amount of diversity—lends itself extremely well to look for patterns and subsequently for root causes.

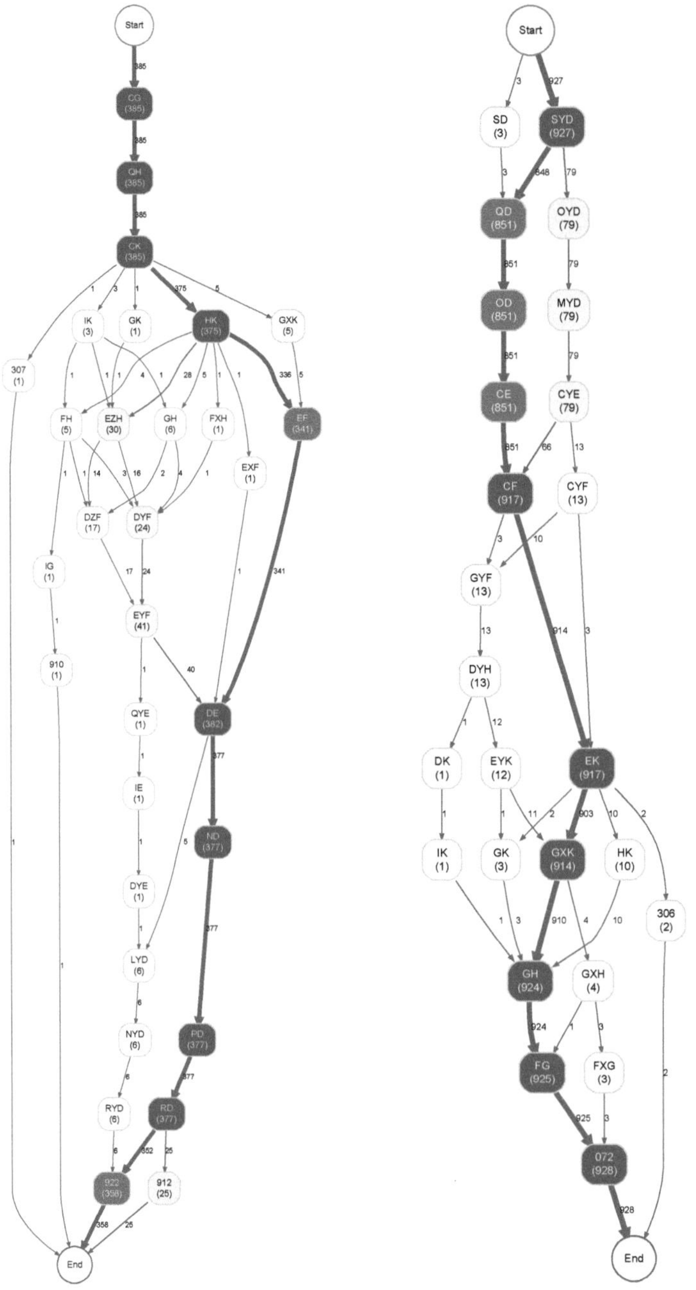

Fig. 9.12 Actual routes on relation 2 along direction A (left) and direction B (right). Only the most frequent planned route for each direction is selected.

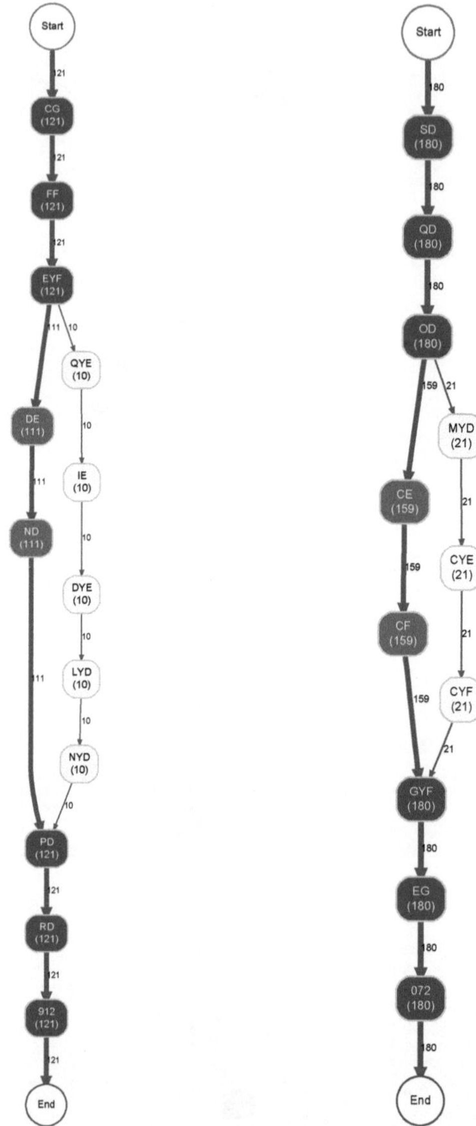

Fig. 9.13 Actual routes on relation 3 along direction A (left) and direction B (right). Only the most frequent planned route for each direction is selected.

9.5 Discussion

The case study in this chapter again evaluates the use of `bupaR` as a process analytics tool in an applied setting. It was shown how

- custom metrics such as ECyM, Separability and the Levenshtein distance can be implemented and analysed,

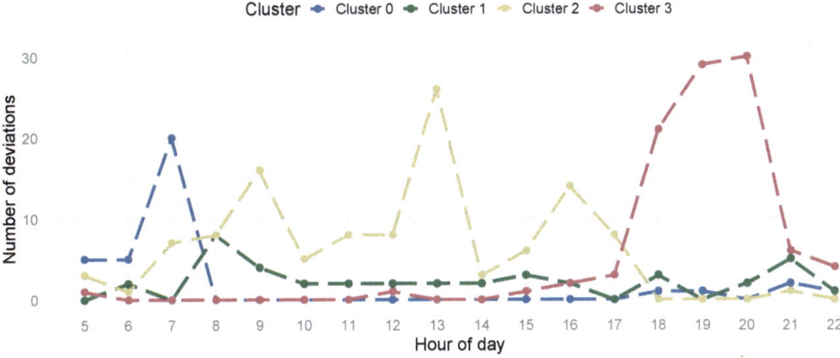

Fig. 9.14 Distribution of clusters of reroutings on connection 8A over the timespan of a day.

- statistical tests such as Kruskal-Wallis can be performed on process related data,
- general clustering techniques can be used on process data, and
- custom visualisations can help to gather insights in the process.

The scripts underlying the different tests and figures in this chapter can be found in Appendix D.

Furthermore, this chapter illustrated how process analysis can contribute towards more data-driven decision making in a railway management context. The results of these analyses provide a basis for potential improvements of the capacity allocation. Nonetheless, closer investigation by business experts is needed in order to decide whether the reroutings have been beneficial for the overall performance or not. As a first step in understanding the detected reroutings, a cluster analysis has been suggested. By clustering similar deviations into different groups, patterns can be found in their occurrences.

The main advantage of the techniques used in this chapter is that they are largely independent of the underlying railway infrastructure. As the infrastructure is not required as input, the techniques can be easily reused on new cases. Moreover, this allows the metrics to be used on every sort of infrastructure, whereas many existing algorithms are typically limited to a certain set of infrastructure characteristics.

Notwithstanding their proper functioning, some improvements to the metrics can still be made. One would be to allocate costs to the different signals, as a means to make certain reroutings more severe than others. These costs can be determined based on expert knowledge, thereby implicitly requiring input about the infrastructure. Alternatively, costs can be determined based on the data. For instance, signals which are located in an area with a lot of traffic might get a higher cost attributed to it, as reroutings in these areas might have more far-reaching consequences.

Another improvement might be needed in order to accommodate the $ECyM$ metric—used for measuring horizontal diversity—with a proper scale. In order to scale the metric between 0 and 1, an upper bound needs to be calculated. This upper bound can be determined by looking at the infrastructure, i.e. what would be the maximum number of nodes n and edges e when all possible reroutings would have occurred. When the information on the infrastructure is not provided, these numbers can be estimated by looking at all the behaviour which has occurred, on the condition that data is recorded over a sufficient amount of time.

It should also be noted that the use of process mining has some drawbacks. In the context of trains travelling on a dense, highly-connected infrastructure, it is very likely that the behaviour of one train impacts that of another. While high level information is certainly interesting—e.g. train A deviates almost daily at a certain location—it is even more interesting to link these to other events—e.g. train A deviate almost daily at a certain location, because train B is always late, or because train C is deviating and preventing A from passing, or maybe even without there being an obvious reason.

There are of course certain techniques with *do* look at the relation between different process instances, for instance in order to detect bottlenecks, or to detect similarities, but few techniques really look at the impact of events upon each other. While one mainly talks about *event data* in the context of process mining, it would often be more accurate to talk about *process data* instead. Indeed most analysis which are done are heavily focused on a *process view*, and not really consider events in relation with other events outside of their cases. Too often, it seems that event data are only analysed with a relatively strict process instances .

9.6 Conclusions

This chapter proposed and illustrated a set of metrics and methods from a process analysis perspective which can be used as a guide for an exploratory analysis of train reroutings, using train describer data. The techniques suggested are able to highlight interesting cases and to point out various paths to conduct further analysis. To this end, measures used in process mining and process modelling were applied to quantify the severity of train reroutings, entitled *reroutings severity*, as well as the variation of the reroutings which occurred, referred to as *reroutings diversity*. The analysis was centred around different train relations. A Kruskal-Wallis test was able to detect differences in the severity to reroutings among the different train relations. Subsequently, inspection of the most remarkable connections validated the correct assessment of the proposed metrics.

Simultaneously, the analysis constitutes a second evaluation of `bupaR` which concludes this part on process analytics. The last two chapters have not only shown that the requirements concerning both design and functionality of the introduced tool-set are satisfied, but also that it is able to lead to precise and insightful results when used in a particular business context. As such, `bupaR` fills a gap in the existing landscape of process analysis tools by enabling reproducible analysis, facilitating combinations of process-oriented techniques and generic data analysis techniques, and providing relatively easy ways to customise the analyses as well as to extend the tool.

9.7 Further Reading

1. Janssenswillen, G., Depaire, B., Verboven, S.: Detecting Train Reroutings with Process Mining. EURO Journal on Transportation and Logistics **7**(1), 1–24 (2018)
2. Conte, C., Schöbel, A.: Identifying dependencies among delays. Ph.D. thesis, Niedersächsische Staats-und Universitätsbibliothek Göttingen, Germany (2008)
3. Cule, B., Goethals, B., Tassenoy, S., Verboven, S.: Mining train delays. In: Advances in Intelligent Data Analysis X, pp. 113–124. Springer (2011)
4. Daamen, W., Goverde, R.M., Hansen, I.A.: Non-discriminatory automatic registration of knock-on train delays. Networks and Spatial Economics **9**(1), 47–61 (2008)
5. Dewilde, T.: Improving the robustness of a railway system in large and complex station areas. Ph.D. thesis, KULeuven (2014)
6. Flier, H., Gelashvili, R., Graffagnino, T., Nunkesser, M.: Mining railway delay dependencies in large-scale real-world delay data. In: Robust and Online Large-Scale Optimization, pp. 354–368. Springer (2009)
7. Goverde, R.M., Meng, L.: Advanced monitoring and management information of railway operations. Journal of Rail Transport Planning & Management **1**(2), 69–79 (2011)
8. Kecman, P., Goverde, R.M.: Online data-driven adaptive prediction of train event times. IEEE Transactions on Intelligent Transportation Systems **16**(1), 465–474 (2015)
9. Yuan, J., Hansen, I.A.: Optimizing capacity utilization of stations by estimating knock-on train delays. Transportation Research Part B: Methodological **41**(2), 202–217 (2007)

Part IV
Conclusions

Chapter 10
Conclusions and Recommendations for Future Research

> Puzzles are sort of like life because you can mess up and rebuild later, and you're likely smarter the next time around.
>
> Adam Silvera

At the start of this thesis, we set out on a quest for process realism: viewing and representing processes as they really are, as distinguished from the speculative. Lastly, we will revisit the research objectives and envisioned contributions we laid out at the beginning of this thesis, and outline itineraries for future advancements.

10.1 Process Model Quality

The research objective of the first part, with a focus on process model quality, was to analyse quality measures to examine their usefulness in terms of validity, sensitivity and feasibility, as well as their ability to quantify the quality of the model as a representation of the underlying process.

An inventory of the existing quality measures showed that there are clear evolutions to be noticed. Firstly, there has been a move from specific process model notations to the more general and formal Petri Net notation. Secondly, measures have clearly become more sophisticated, especially when comparing alignment-based measures or negative event measures with the earlier naive, course-grained measures. The fact that precision can be measured regardless of the fitness level, by way of using aligned event logs, increases the applicability of said measures, but at the same time leads to a dubious inter-dependency between two otherwise orthogonal concepts—on which more in the following paragraphs.

So far, little research has been done concerning the evaluation and comparison of the measures itself. Until now, it is unclear what the differences are between measures within the same dimension: do they judge discovered process models in a similar

G. Janssenswillen: Unearthing the Real Process Behind the Event Data, LNBIP 412
https://doi.org/10.1007/978-3-030-70733-0_10

way, or do they qualify models differently? Are some measures more optimistic or pessimistic than others? The empirical analyses done in this thesis had the objective to elucidate this poor comprehension, which lead us to the first contribution.

10.1.1 Lessons Learned

10.1.1.1 Improved Understanding of Quality Dimensions and Measures

The analysis shows that there are important differences between the measures for all dimensions. For measuring fitness, Alignment-Based Fitness is the most recommended measure based on the analysis of sensitivity. However, its feasibility is limited, running into problems with large models or event logs. In the latter case, Behavioural Recall can be used, although it must be said that it is insensitive to some fitness issues, such as those common in models discovered by ILP miner.

For precision, the suggested measure is Behavioural Precision, the others having either feasibility or insensitivity issues. Moreover, Alignment-Based Precision was found not to be consistently measuring the same as other precision measures.

The two generalization measures that were investigated did not correlate with each other. It was found that Alignment-Based Generalization carries very limited information, with a remarkably low variation in the values, all very close to one. Behavioural Generalization one the other hand was observed to be strongly related to fitness measures.

If we assume that the generalization dimension refers to the ability of models to replay unobserved but real behaviour, we can calculate the actual value by measuring the fitness between model and system—a concept we identified as *system-fitness*. Comparing the actual generalization measures with our calculated system-fitness values illustrated that the generalization measures are biased and extremely imprecise estimates of system-fitness.

However, we noted that this definition of generalization is insufficient to accurately measure the quality of a process model as a representation of the underlying process. Whereas the model should allow for unobserved but real behaviour, it should not allow for unobserved but unreal behaviour. In order to quantify the latter quality, the concept of system-precision was identified.

System-fitness and system-precision are two aspects that cannot be directly quantified in practical settings, since the underlying process is not known. Therefore, the ability of existing log and precision measures to estimate their system counterparts was investigated. Yet, only in very limited, ideal situations did these lend themselves to be used as unbiased estimates. Especially precision measures were problematic in this regard, while fitness measures—although biased—outperform generalization measures in estimating system-fitness. Be that as it may, it has to be concluded that current measures are unable to quantify the quality of a model as an accurate description of the underlying process—the system.

10.1.1.2 Experimental Setup

Beside an improved understanding of the dimensions and measures, there are also lessons learned with regard to performing experiments. Recently, frameworks have been introduced to generate models and logs at a large scale, such as the one in [91] which was used in this dissertation, but also the procedure discussed in [28]. Furthermore, benchmarking initiatives such as CoBeFra [23] facility conformance checking experiments to a large extent.

Nonetheless, some issues still remain. In particular,

- What are appropriate parameter settings to obtain realistic process logs?
- How to decide on the appropriate amount of observations needed?
- What are realistic types and amounts of noise?
- How to cope with parameter settings of discovery algorithms and quality measures?

In the following paragraphs, we aim to transform the lessons learned as well as the further identified problems into recommendations for future research.

10.1.2 Recommendations for Future Research

Given the analyses performed, and the evidence gathered, the following recommendations are made, both with respect to the matter at hand itself, and with respect to the execution of experiments. Recommendations reflect both the lessons learned in this dissertation, as well as topics that were not explicitly considered given the scope, but are nonetheless necessary for the field to evolve.

10.1.2.1 Towards a New Quality Framework

While the importance of generalization should not be ignored—in fact, its goal lies at the very heart of what we defined as *process realism*—its characterisation as a single, one-dimensional quality dimension falls short of its actual aim. Progressing to a framework where generalization is broken down into two separate qualities, namely system-fitness and system-precision rightly acknowledges the dual meaning of generalization, and even more importantly increases the awareness about the much needed separation between log and system-oriented quality. Since neither fitness and precision measures, nor generalization measures can be used to accurately estimate system-fitness or system-precision, we further recommend future research towards a k-fold cross validation approach for process model quality.

In addition, we will discuss several specific research challenges and ideas which are able to contribute towards a new and mature quality framework below. Firstly, it might be desirable to defined more targeted, granular measures instead of a single measure for each dimensions. Secondly, orthogonality between dimensions should receive more consideration. Fitness and precision are independent qualities and measures for one of them should not depend on the other one. Thirdly, we discus the need for notions of confidence and uncertainty, which are especially relevant in the context of system-quality. Finally, also parameter settings of metrics encompass important challenges.

Granularity and Propositions
We should be careful not to put too much emphasis on a single number. Instead, it might be helpful to broaden our view and create more nuanced measures, which quantify a specific aspect. In Chap. 4 it was shown that we can characterise an event log using 7 different metrics [64]. Why then should we try to quantify fitness or precision with a single one? A good starting point might be the axioms or propositions as defined in [5] and [129]. These have already shown that quality measures do not satisfy all propositions by far. More specific, targeted measures instead of a one-size-fits-all measure might be able to provide more detailed insights. Relatedly, these propositions should also be validated more rigorously, beyond the theoretical examinations performed in [5] and [129].

Orthogonality of Dimensions
Fitness and precision—be they measured with respect to either log or system, and as a single metric or a combination of multiple ones—are two independent dimensions. Yet, the experiments have shown that strong negative correlations exist between the two. While this negative connection can partly be explained by the use of different process discovery algorithms and their respective search space, more appears to be going on here. Of particular interest in this respect is the alignment-approach most of the precision measures use in case logs have imperfect fitness. However, aligning logs before measuring precision means that the data is tampered to measure precision by replacing non-fitting traces, thereby possibly inflating the obtained precision value. As such, the question to be asked is why precision measures should depend on alignment in case of non-perfect fitness when the two are in fact independent, and how consequential this alignment approach is to the reliability of the obtained measures.

Confidence and Uncertainty
In making the analogy with traditional statistics, we have already seen that generalisation aims to tell us something about the *population* of process behaviour, instead of the sample data. Sometimes it is even defined as a *probability* or a *confidence level*. Apart from definitions, the implementations do not have a notion of confidence or uncertainty, but rather try to measure generalization with a single point estimate. If we are able to define confidence interval on log-fitness and log-precision, those intervals can be used as a proxy for system-quality.

Parameter Settings
Finally, parameter settings of quality measures have received little attention so far. In the experiments in this dissertation, all default values where used for pragmatic reasons. Currently, there is little guidance about how these parameters should be

used, and what consequences can be regarding, for example, feasibility and sensitivity. This is mainly due to the fact that implementations continuously evolve and the information about the measures and their parameters get fragmented over different publications. Furthermore, there is little available documentation on using the measures, a point that will be addressed further in the context of the experimental setup.

Ideally, we should be able to define relations between parameter settings and the outcome of the measures, and even add some intelligence in setting the measures. For example, if an event log has a certain size or unstructuredness, this could be automatically translated to adjusted settings so as to make sure that the measure is still feasible to compute. Discovering these patterns will require further experiments. In order to be able to perform those, also the experimental setup needs further consideration.

10.1.2.2 Towards a Reproducible Experimental Setup

In order to facilitate large experiments such as the ones performed in this thesis, significant improvements can be made with regards to experimental setup, both with regard to decisions on the setup and to the executions. While some of them are already discussed above (such as the need to better understand parameter settings of measures), in this section we elaborate further on experimental design and execution from angles not necessarily related to quality measures.

Sample Size

One of the major decisions that needs to be taken during the design of experiments, be it about quality measurement or something else, is the sample size that is needed in order to evaluate a certain aspect. While in conventional statistics, there are ways to estimate sample size based on the required power of the statistical tests, defining the number of observations needed in a process mining context is a bit more challenging. Indeed, sample size in process mining is a combination of different aspects: it refers to the amount of different systems, as well as the number of logs for each system that is required, as even to the number of cases within logs. Evidently, an experiment based on 1000 logs generated from the same process model is not the same as an experiment based on 200 logs generated from each of 5 different models. The question that needs to be asked is: what is a right and balanced amount of data to use?

The fact that this question is not trivial and has been largely left unanswered, illustrates the many different approaches used in various research papers, from the use of rather anecdotal process models and logs [50] towards the use of larger collections of data and more elaborate statistics [43]. While recently more attention has been given towards experimental design [19, 91], those were mainly targeted towards workflow and tools for generating artificial data, and less about statistical argumentation. Definitely, the latter is paramount as a next step towards better experimental design.

Defining Realistic Processes

Related to the question of how many observations that should be used in experiments, it is also needed to decide on how those observations should look like. In [43], it was observed that real-life event logs lead to significantly different results than artificially generated event logs—mainly because the artificial logs that were used did not appear to be of adequate, realistic complexity. However, for many types of experiments and evaluations, artificial event logs are necessary. Indeed, we do not know the actual process which underlies real-life logs, which makes them unfit to test certain aspects—like the biases of measures in Chap. 5. As a result, these findings have inspired more complex frameworks for generating process models and logs, most notably those described in [28] and [91]. However, the ability to create more complex processes and models, has brought with it the necessity to decide on more parameter settings which should be decided upon. While large-scale surveys and studies such as [96] indicate to some extent what the balance between different components in process models typically is, it is insufficient to decide on the plethora of possibilities that we can use in model and log simulation today.

Noise

Another important decision that needs to be made in order to generate realistic logs is the inducement of noise. Firstly, there is still debate on the exact definition of noise. While sometimes referred to as exceptional, but truthful behaviour, the definition used in this dissertation is that of measurement errors and data inconsistencies.

The types of measurement errors and inconsistencies that were induced in the experiments in this dissertation were based on the tools used, which—as mentioned before—do not necessarily reflect realistic types of noise. An overview of problems and issues found in real logs could provide a more truthful starting point for different types of noise.

At this point, the different types of noise are all defined within the context of a single case: missing some parts, having some parts swapped, etc. This misses some of the data issues which are encountered in real-life, such as the difficulty to relate events to cases. In the spirit of the issues tackled in [114], another realistic way to induce noise is to perturb the case identifiers of some events, i.e. linking them to the wrong cases. Another alternative noise-induction can be to artificially change the activity labels. By replacing an activity a with different versions $a1$, $a2$ and $a3$, we can imitate the real-life issues and challenges to find appropriate granularity levels of activities. However, both these proposed alternative noise inductions are at this point only based on one person's idiosyncratic experience with analysing real logs. If we can somehow make these experiences and challenges in event data processing and cleaning—which are encountered by the complete process mining field, consisting of both academics and industry—more tangible, we can learn from them to create more realistic noise during experiments. This will be necessary to evaluate new techniques in a realistic setting.

Reproducible Tools

Finally, some future work is needed with regard to reproducible work-flows. Both the tool used for process discovery (ProM) [133] and for the computation of the quality measures (CoBeFra) [23] do not lend themselves well for large-scale experiments because of their graphical user interface, which leads to time consuming experiments, which are difficult to reproduce. While for both the source code can be accessed with the aim to automate the experiments, these approaches are error-prone and not supported through documentation. Future developments in the spirit of `bupaR` and `PM4Py` are strongly recommended to make experiments as these easier and more transparent. Also RapidProM [8] mitigates these issues, but still lacks important functionalities.

10.2 Process Analytics

Next to the objectives with regard to process model quality, we also advocated the development of a novel process analytics tool-set. After further analysis of the problem, it was defined that this new tool-set should

1. be embedded or connected with a general-purpose data analysis software, such that synergies can be made by linking existing data analysis and/or statistical techniques with process analysis applications,
2. facilitate the creation of extensions, and adequately support them through documentation,
3. allow to reproduce analyses, thereby facilitating iterative and interactive analyses, and
4. have a clear documentation and impose guidelines for the documentation of extensions.

As an answer to these requirements, `bupaR` was developed, which is an extensible framework for process analytics in R. Next to the above requirements with regard to the design, also minimal requirements with respect to the functionalities were defined. Following a detailed introduction of the design and the functionalities, the usefulness of the tool-set was evaluated by means of case studies, as described in the next paragraphs.

10.2.1 Lessons Learned

Reproducible analysis is an important requirement for tools in current times. It is relevant for both academics—allowing them to reproduce experiments—as for industry—to rerun analyses on new data, or using new assumptions. Reproducibility can be obtained using different approaches. One is to support the creation of graphical work-flows, such as RapidMiner and other graphical data analysis environments do. Another approach is through scripting, which was the approach taken by `bupaR`. As a consequence of the scripting approach, the need for documentation is amplified.

Because of a large investment in documentation, tutorials, examples and a website, as well as through a straightforward API design, many actions have been made to make bupaR as accessible as possible. At the moment of writing, more than 100.000 downloads for the packages have been registered by CRAN (thus not including the installations of the packages on github). Also presentations at both R and process mining venues, and the development of an online course, have improved the adoption of the toolset.

The decision for a scripting tools has had both advantages and disadvantages. On the plus side it allows the user to build end-to-end analysis work-flows, which combine data import, process analysis, and use of custom visualisations, data mining and statistical techniques. Furthermore, it makes it reasonably more easier for users to contribute with their own extensions.

On the downside, it means that the tool-set will not be accessible or attractive for *all* potential process miners. Yet, we do not claim the existence of *the perfect process mining tool*, let alone that we have created it. However, the provided toolset does fill a void in the spectrum of process analysis tools.

10.2.1.1 Student Trajectories

In the context of student trajectories in higher education, three different research questions were investigated. To which extent are students following the prescribed program, and where do they deviate from it? Secondly, how fast do students recover from failing a course, and how heavy is the burden of failed courses? And finally, which elements are related to the number of elective credits selected by students in a particular semester? For each of these questions, a process-oriented analysis was performed using bupaR, showing how it facilitates the use of statistical tests, custom visualisations and custom data preprocessing.

10.2.1.2 Train Reroutings

A second case study in the context of a railway infrastructure was performed. This case study proposed and illustrated a set of metrics and methods from a process analysis perspective which can be used as a guide for an exploratory analysis of train reroutings, using train describer data. It not only showed that the requirements concerning both design and functionality of the introduced tool-set are satisfied, but also that it is able to lead to precise and insightful results to optimise railway scheduling and dispatching.

10.2.2 Recommendations for Future Research

Based on the lessons learned we provide recommendations for future research, both with respect to the developed tool-set, as well as with respect to process analytics as a whole.

10.2.2.1 Toolset

Being designed as an extensible framework, recommendations for future work on `bupaR` mainly relate to the creation of new functionalities. Next to further extensions, challenges can be identified with regards to interoperability and performance.

Extensions
Of particular interest for practitioners, process discovery techniques and conformance checking should be considered, which implicitly requires additional support for process models.

Interoperability with PM4Py
The most promising and efficient source for extensions is to invest in the interoperability between `bupaR` and `PM4Py`. Whereas the former includes many functionalities for manipulating event data and describing and exploring patterns, the latter includes mostly functionalities geared towards process discovery, conformance checking and other advanced process mining techniques. As a result, the two are highly compatible. Currently, the first interfaces between the two are available on github, due to contributions of `bupaR`-users. In the future, more gains can be expected from this connection.

Statistical Modelling
One of the huge advantages of being situated in the R ecosystem is the availability of many statistical tools, which extend the functionalities from being mainly about describing and exploring processes, to also confirmatory analysis. First steps on this road are currently being taken to learn probabilities in the context of process models, in order to enhance the understanding of a process and to test different hypotheses about control-flow dependencies. More extensions with regard to statistical techniques can have a large impact on the maturity of process mining and the deployment of process mining results. This also relates back to the discussion of reproducible experimental design.

Database Interface
Other promising future work relates to the development of a database interface, which will allow to connect process analytics directly with a database. Not only will this impact the performance of the techniques, but it will also provide a means to increase the support for the data extraction phase of a process analysis project.

Performance
Next to performance improvements through a database interface, other gains can be obtained through translating parts of the tool-set from R to C++. With respect to extensions concerning discovery algorithms and conformance checking techniques, this might also mean that a native R/C++ implementation will have a higher performance than a link with PM4Py. However, even on the long-term both these extensions and improvement are promising to increase adoption of these process mining tools.

10.2.2.2 Challenges in Process Analytics

Note that the future work related to the tool-set discussed above has both a research and an implementation part—the balance between the two depending on the precise extension. In this last section, we would also like to discuss some challenges related to process analytics itself—i.e. unconnected to the tools used—which were identified based on the two case studies.

Process Mining Roadmaps
Data analysts who are new to process mining are confronted with an avalanche of terminology and techniques. Many techniques which have been developed are inspired by more theoretical problems, and not necessarily by research questions that exist in industry. We thereby not claim that all developed techniques cannot be used by practitioners in the field, but rather that it is challenging to find the right technique—or the right follow-up techniques—for practitioners who are not familiar with the scientific literature.

In order to solve this issue, we advocate for *roadmaps* or *templates* which allow practitioners to better decide upon the right technique or method to use, based on the questions or goal they have—whether it is related to performance, efficiency, resources, control-flow, or any combination of both. While some project methodologies, such as described in [52], exist, they often remain high-level and do not provide tangible strategies for analysts to tackle process mining problems.

The Curse of Granularity
While the curse of dimensionality is known, in process mining we can also think of a *curse of granularity* which refers to the different levels of detail in which we can look at processes. When our level of detail is too small, we will find that every process instance is unique. When it is too high, we loose too much information. Relatedly, we predominately try to analyse processes in an end-to-end manner, while—given the curse of granularity—we could opt to analyse some parts of the process at a very high level of detail. These parts should of course be selected based on the importance or the questions asked, which relate back to the importance of process mining roadmaps. Next to that, the relevance of aggregation techniques, such as those discussed in Sect. 7.5 cannot be underestimated, as well as tools to detect interesting aggregations from low-level granularity logs.

Process Mining as a Straitjacket

While we often refer to *process* mining and *event* data, it would be more correct to refer to process mining and process data. Indeed, process mining techniques place strong assumptions and perspectives on event data, consisting of cases, activities, resources, etc. These assumptions have some benefits since they create a uniform understanding of process data and make sure that all techniques are applicable as long as these assumptions are satisfied. However, at the same time, they also create a *straitjacket* in which certain types of analyses are not possible or harder to achieve. If we refer to *event data*, the process notion should not be implied. Not all events are generated by a clear process, and follow the same rules. For example, we can look at train describer events from a process perspective, stating that each train trip is a process instance, and each passing of a signal is an event. However, through that straitjacket, we risk missing a lot of other interesting events and dependencies. Furthermore, it is not straightforward to detect dependencies between different process instances, i.e. train trips, while these certainly have a massive impact on the operations of the railway infrastructure.

Of course, this does not mean that we cannot use a *process-oriented* view in these cases. In fact, in Chap. 8, there are multiple ways to look at, and aggregate, the event data as well, and the analyses—while process-oriented—aim to take into account the whole context and use less-conventional techniques, such as correlating event data. The recommendation is therefore to think about event data more broadly than just process data—a movement already occurring, as exemplified by process analysis research related to IoT—and to think outside of the box when analysing more generic event data, by both using process-oriented methods as well as other techniques, both proven and new.

Afterword

A not very scientific but rather entertaining experiment by Jordan Ellenberg, a mathematician of the University of Wisconsin and author of the book *How not to be wrong* [53], estimated how many readers reach the end of a book by looking at frequently quoted passages in Amazon Popular Highlights. Notwithstanding the fact that the conclusion of a book is often the most important component, it appeared that quotes from the beginning of books are mentioned considerably more often. While an estimated 98.5% of the readers finished *The Goldfinch*—a 2013 bestselling novel by Donna Tart, to be released as motion picture in the fall of 2019—only a mere 6.8% are estimated to have done so for the famous, oft-quoted seminal work *Thinking, fast and slow*, by the Nobel prize-wining Daniel Kahneman (and lifelong collaborator Amos Tversky)[1]. When comparing the contents of the latter work with that of this dissertation, it is not expected that many readers will reach this point—except perhaps for the conscientious jury member. So, for the happy few who did reach this point, allow me to add a few additional comments from a personal perspective.

As perfectionistic as I am in writing, it is little exaggerated that every word in this dissertation—from the major conclusive points all the way down to the least relevant footnote—was chosen with considerable care and thought.[2] The same goes for the epigraphs which precede the content of each chapter. They have not been added as a means to demonstrate any unusual literacy by extensive name dropping, but rather a tribute to—in my opinion—important writers, scientist and thinkers, who have each in their own way shaped who I am, and thereby this dissertation.

[1]Ellenberg named his estimate the *Hawking Index* (HI), after Stephen Hawking's *A Brief History of Time*—regarded as the most popular but unread book of all times. However, results show that, with an HI of 6.6%, Stephen Hawking's work is surpassed in literary desertion by Thomas Piketty's *Capital in the Twenty-First Century (HI: 2.4%). (Source: The Books many start but few finish. The Independent, 2014-07-08.)*

[2]I am obliged to admit that my obsession for word choice and structure does not always take into account spelling errors.

G. Janssenswillen: Unearthing the Real Process Behind the Event Data, LNBIP 412
https://doi.org/10.1007/978-3-030-70733-0

Each of the used quotes has been selected with care to fit the contents of the chapters they precede. Especially so are the words from detective-novel writer Arthur Conan Doyle—"Any truth is better than indefinite doubt". It epitomises where this thesis is looking for—the truth, a truthful and realistic idea of our processes. It is therefore no coincidence that the distinction between descriptive and confirmatory analysis in Chap. 5 is illustrated through analogy—the distinction between a detective and a judge. In our process mining endeavours, we should not only be detectives, gathering comprehensive lists of facts—not opinions—but we should also be a judge; being able to decide on the appropriate, justified actions, taking into accounts the facts and context.

Quality is everyone's responsibility. These are the words W.E. Deming, an American statistician who became know for the Plan-Do-Study-Act cycle—an achievement which in itself does not justice his legacy in engineering, psychology, management and epistemology. In line with his statement, qualitative data analysis and evidence-based decision making is not only the responsibility of the process miner or data scientist. It is the collective effort of data scientists, domain experts, knowledge workers, and, above all, it is facilitated by executive-level guidance and support. Without the appropriate culture, all efforts at data analysis are for nought.

Some processes are more complex than others. As such, some processes allow for more process behaviour than others. Often, we think of them as infinite. In Chap. 3 we calculated the number of distinct paths in process models. Basing ourselves upon some inevitable assumptions, we found that some models are more infinite than others. With more or less the same words, YA novel writer John Green implores us to keep on pushing boundaries. Through his fictional character Hazel, he continues:

> "I cannot tell you how grateful I am for our little infinity. You gave me forever within the numbered days, and I'm grateful."

It is Green's way of encouraging us to make possible the impossible. To learn to be unsatisfied when it counts, to fight the status quo, but also to *not* do things inefficiently because they were always done that way. It is this exact mindset that lead to the creation of bupaR, an project which not only showed me that change is possible, but also that academic work should not (always) be conducted in isolation from business needs. It showed me that academic work can have a direct and welcome impact on industry.

If I have to name three persons which have gone a long way to influence my thinking, they would be Nassim Nicholas Taleb, Amos Tversky and Daniel Kahneman. Taleb learned his readers that they should not be fooled by randomness, that the impossible—the black swan—is sometimes possible, and that the world we live in is vastly different from the world we think we live in.[3] This is not only true when talking about day-to-day transactions, our understanding of natural, political, or economical

[3] He also thought his readers to be wary of economist, a position in which he does not stand alone.

phenomena, but also when analysing processes. The by now legendary observation that processes when discovered from event data are significantly different from our prior believe about those processes is illustrative of that statement. Let it inspire us to think one step further, and not blindly trust these discovered models without accurate quality measurement.

That our view of the world is often distorted, has been expertly illustrated by the work which was produced by—in my opinion—the most important collaboration which ever has existed in social sciences, that of Tversky and Kahneman. Not only have they extensively shown us how distorted our views are, they have also learned us how difficult is it to change our faulty perceptions and theories. "Once you have accepted a theory, it is extraordinarily difficult to notice its flaw"—a quote by Kahneman—is probably how Chap. 5 of this thesis is best summarised. As irrational human beings, we are prone to what is called theory-induced blindness. The best illustration of which is why it took so long for the Copernican thinking about the universe to take over from Ptolemaic thinking. We fall prey to confirmation bias—only considering those parts of evidence which confirm our thinking, while we discard those that do not. Disbelieving is hard work. It is the reason that America is named after Amerigo Vespucci, and not after Christopher Columbus. It is the reason that until today, we are still struggling to quantify generalization as a fourth quality dimension.[4]

So sometimes, instead of trying to move forward, it is helpful to stop, contemplate, and discover other directions.

Whereas Kahneman, Tversky and Taleb have been influential in my thinking, Hadley Wickham has been influential in my doing. His impact on the popularity and success or R has by all means become immeasurable. Not only has he put his mark on the used tools, as the major founder of the *tidyverse*, his work and mindset also impacts responsible science and inclusion. He is not only he well-known proponent and advocate for reproducible and responsible data science and workflows; his inclusive and constructive stance has made, together with help of many others, the R community a place were people work together in harmony, with respect for each other, and together are able to achieve great successes. The importance of the tidyverse, as well as this accessible community have been paramount to the creation and success of *bupaR*.

The research and work of K. Anders Ericsson about deliberate practice has been mind-altering for me, being a inquisitive, life-long learner, as well as a teacher. In order to reach excellence in a certain field, discipline or task, it is not sufficient to keep on practising every day, doing the same tasks or work over and over. You have to be challenged. It is an idea I try to apply actively during my teaching. And it is surprising what people can achieve if they are challenged to achieve something.

[4]In once used the work title *Generalization: a case of theory-induced blindness* for a research paper. Eventually, me supervisor advised me to change it.

The final two epigraphs originated from two of my most cherished fiction writers—Becky Albertalli and Adam Silvera. More so than any non-fictional book can accomplish, their writings have changed me on a spiritual level and have been an inconceivable support. *History is all you left me* taught me the importance of forgiveness. Making things right before it's too late. *More happy than not* taught me how your happiness invariably depends on your environment, its acceptance and tolerance for the person you are. We should not only aim to be on the receiving side of acceptance, but especially on the rewarding side. Our attitude can create happiness for others, or destroy it altogether. *What if it's us* told me that love is most likely to occur when you are not looking for it. (So I stopped looking.) *They both die at the end* taught me to life each day to the fullest again. To celebrate the gift of life. To learn to enjoy every minute of it. Be happy now, and don't wait for something outside of yourself to make you happy in the future. Every minute should be savoured.

> Puzzles are sort of like life, because you can mess up and rebuild later. And you're likely smarter the next time around. (Adam Silvera)

For me, these words by Adam Silvera are a perfect wording of what growth means. Whether it is growth as a person, as a team, as a research discipline... Opening the conclusive chapter of this dissertation with these words is symbolic of the growth it has brought me, and which I tried to bring to my environment. Even if I only have contributed a single puzzle piece to the field or process mining, or perhaps just messed up some part of the puzzle, I hope that the future process minings while have an easier time to build their puzzle because of my work.

Becky Albertalli's words *there are so many different kinds of normal* reflect a central challenge in process mining: many things are unique, but that doesn't mean they are abnormal. Each student takes on the challenges of education in his or her own way. Trains can reach there destination in several ways. Where do we draw to line between normal and exceptional?

A key illustration of the fact that *average* does not exist is the image which was printed inside the cover of this dissertation. In shows an extract of a process map which was obtained from the data in Chap. 8. Each node resembles a unique set of courses a (group of) student(s) struggled with at a certain point. Each arrow represent a student getting closer to his goal. While the nodes—signifying groups of courses—where anonymised, you can still zoom in to look at the different flows between them. You will find that many of those were only used by a single student. Are all students abnormal? Certainly not. There are just many different kinds of normal. It poses a challenge not only for process or data scientists, but also for society. In an ever more individualistic world, where uniqueness is celebrated, we should not forget the things that unite us while they are still here. Friendship, family and love. Happiness, laughter and joy.

Which brings me to a final point of advise for future PhD students, aspiring scientists, or for anyone for whom it may concern. On some occasions, people have commented that my writing is clear and pleasant to read. On said occasions they have inevitable asked me the reason for this. While I do not want to confuse correlation with causation, one of the factors I have attributed to that finding has been my love for reading books. A passion which has influenced me in several ways, as was already clear from the comments so far.

Firstly, it has allowed me (and still continues to do so) to broaden my mind and to accept other views. While it is not evident, my advice to readers is to—at least once in a while—pick books with which thesis you do not agree, or on a topic you are not familiar with. It will allow you to appreciate others opinions, without the obligation to agree to them, which will help you to realise that not everyone thinks alike. And how to workaround those difference. Reading about new topics will subsequently allow you to appreciate new knowledge, which at a basic level can be relevant in your own context.

Secondly, just let's consider it *will* help you to become a better writer, and maybe a better communicator on the whole. Surely, reading a lot is not the holy grail you are looking for or which will work for anyone (remember there is not such thing as the average person), but effectively communicating your message—be it through text, data or speech—is one of the most crucial skills you need in this century. From my personal perspective, this is the most important thing I learned during my PhD research, and one where—let's be honest—I am still struggling with. But if you find yourself in a situations where your view and opinions are significantly different from your peers, where you think that everyone is falling victim to confirmation bias and theory-induced biased, then knowing the accept the opinions of others ánd knowing how to communicate your own, are two of the most important weapons you can have.

> "I am going to get a beer with some friends and stop working on this damn [dissertation]. Too few of you, Big Data tells me, are still reading." (Seth Stephens-Davidowitz)

Appendix A
Additional Figures and Tables Chapter 4

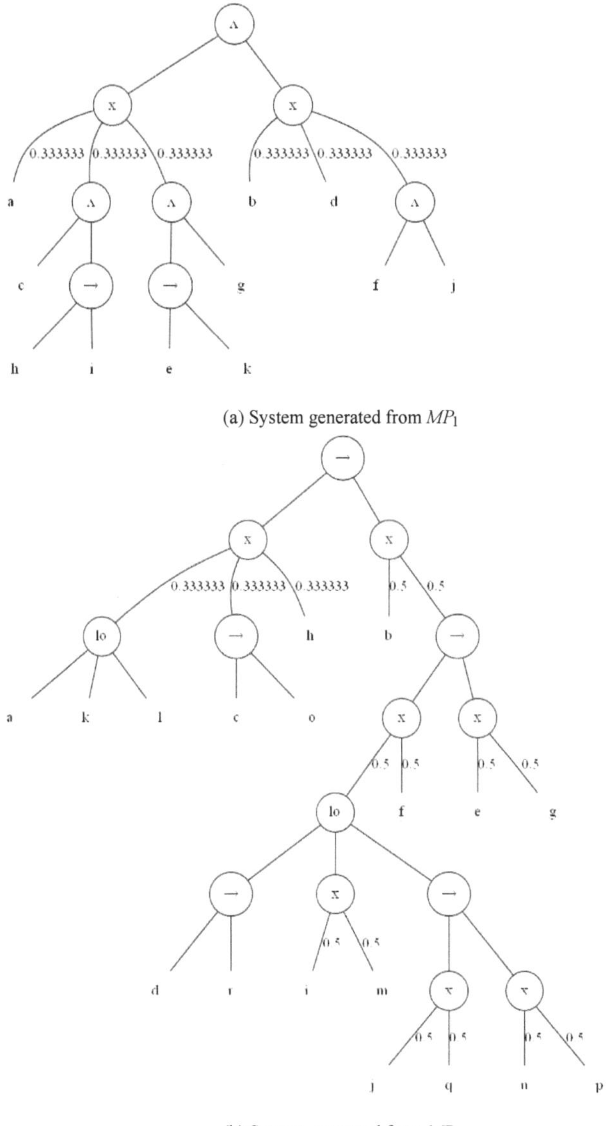

(a) System generated from MP_1

(b) System generated from MP_2

Fig. A.1 Systems used in Chap. 4.

G. Janssenswillen: Unearthing the Real Process Behind the Event Data, LNBIP 412
https://doi.org/10.1007/978-3-030-70733-0

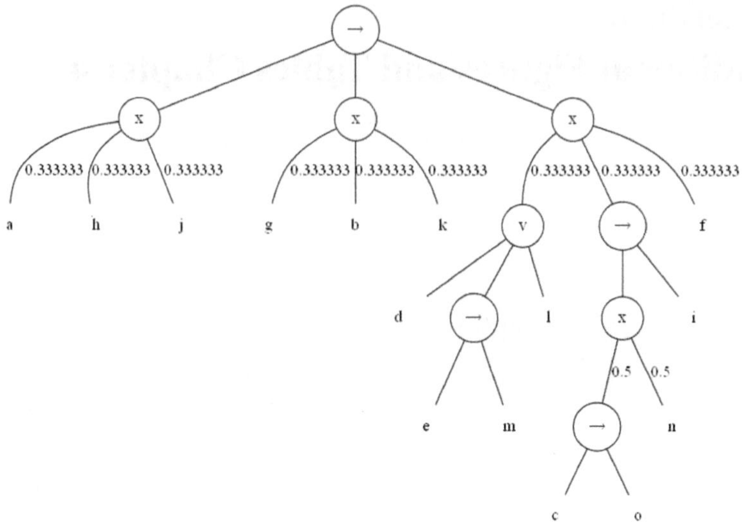

(c) System generated from MP_3

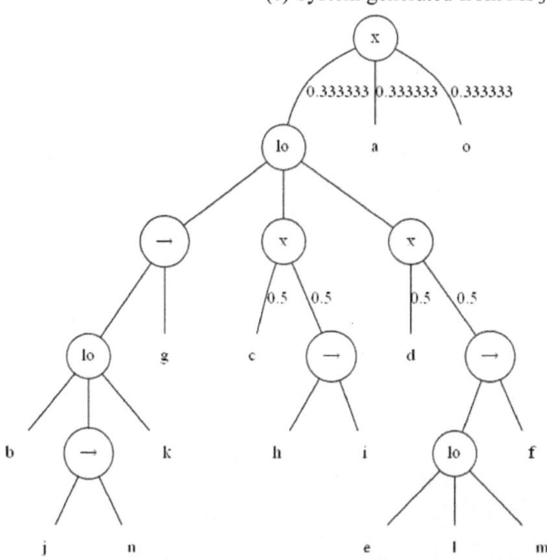

(d) System generated from MP_4

Fig. A.1 (continued)

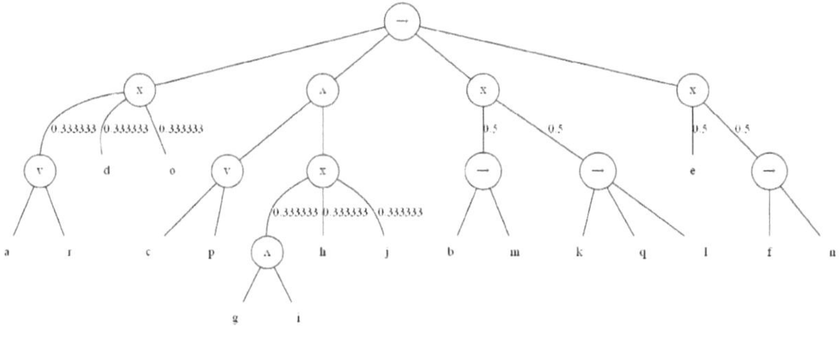

(e) System generated from MP_5

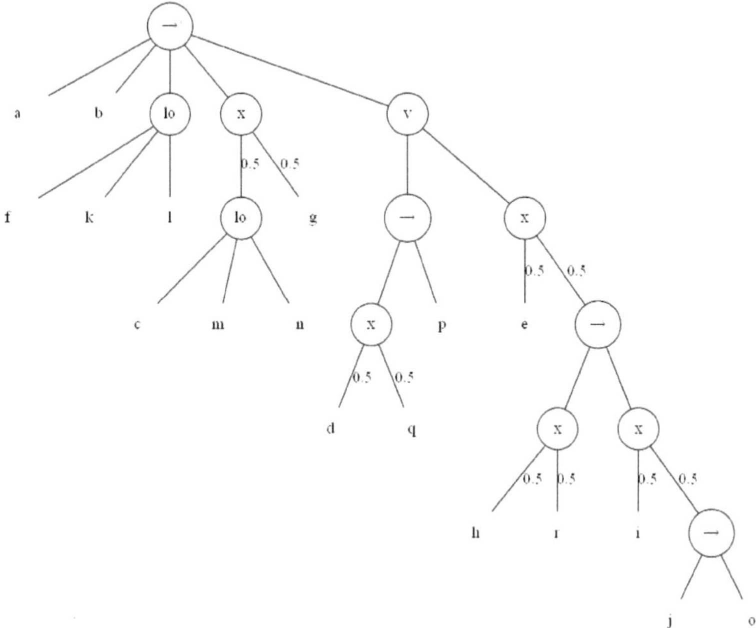

(f) System generated from MP_6

Fig. A.1 (continued)

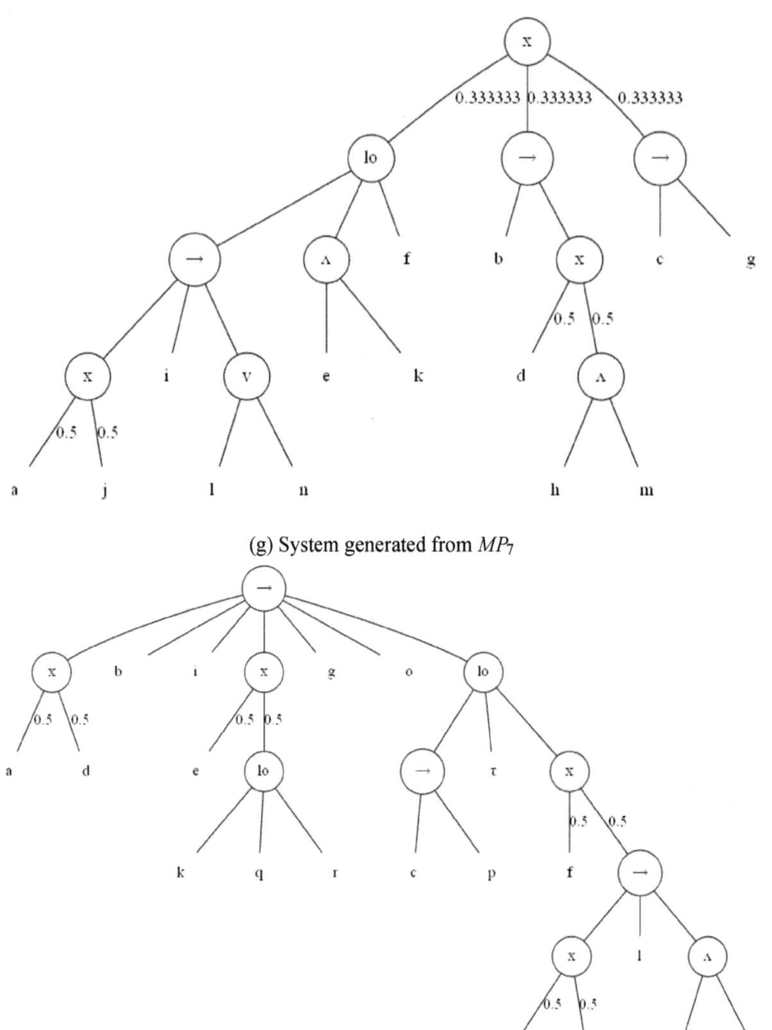

(g) System generated from MP_7

(h) System generated from MP_8

Fig. A.1 (continued)

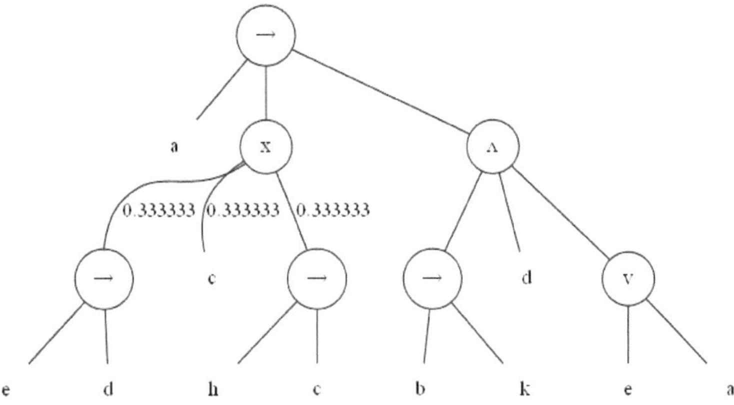

(i) System generated from MP_9

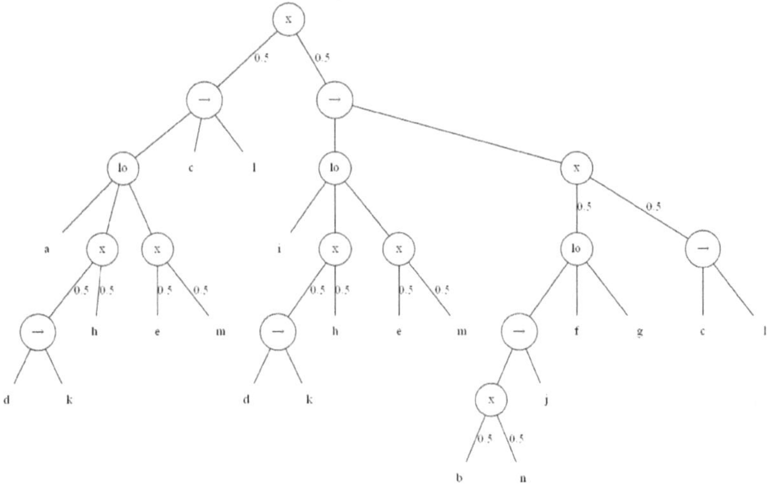

(j) System generated from MP_{10}

Fig. A.1 (continued)

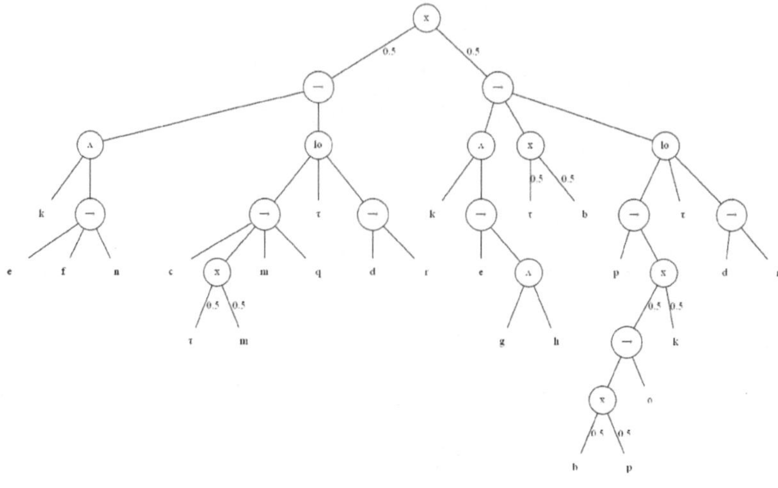

(k) System generated from MP_{11}

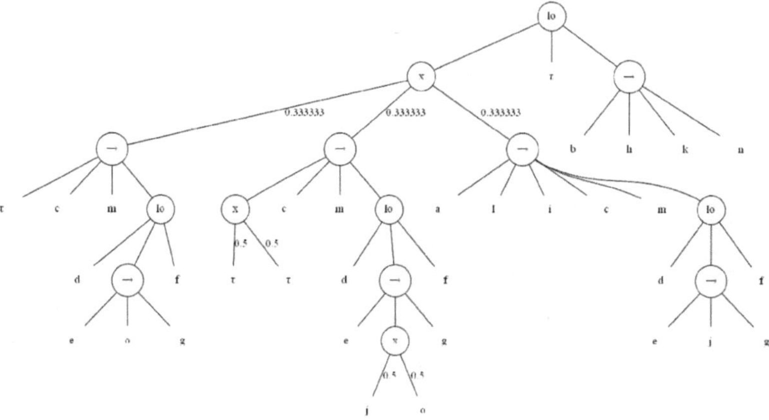

(l) System generated from MP_{12}

Fig. A.1 (continued)

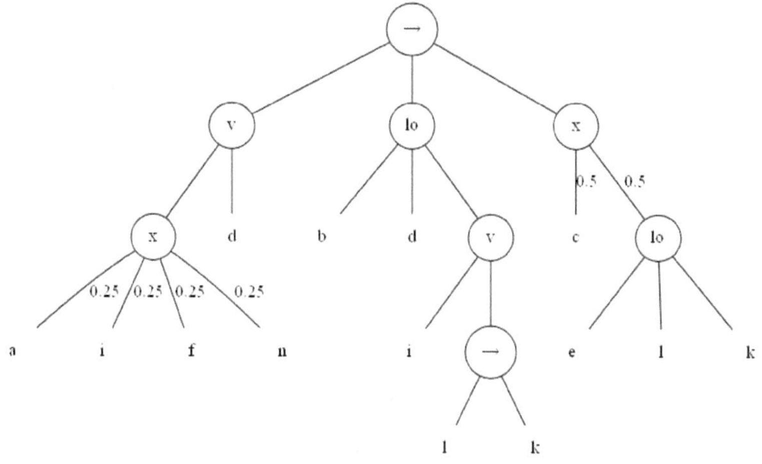

(m) System generated from MP_{13}

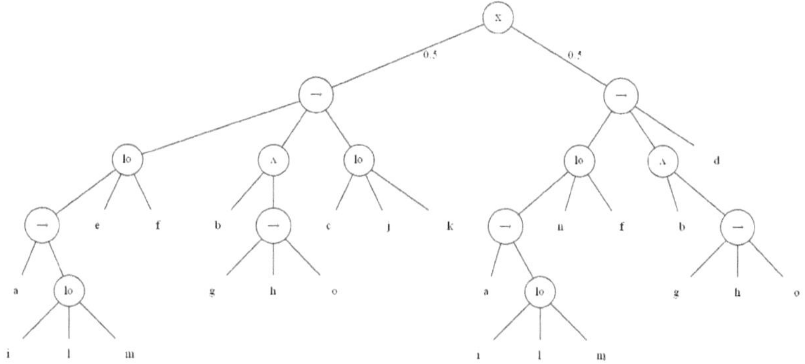

(n) System generated from MP_{14}

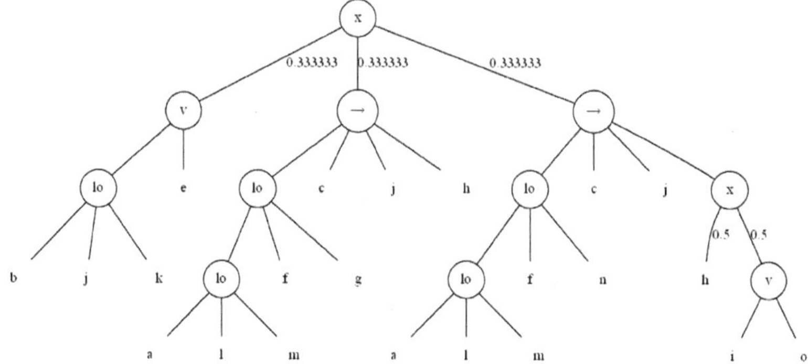

(o) System generated from MP_{15}

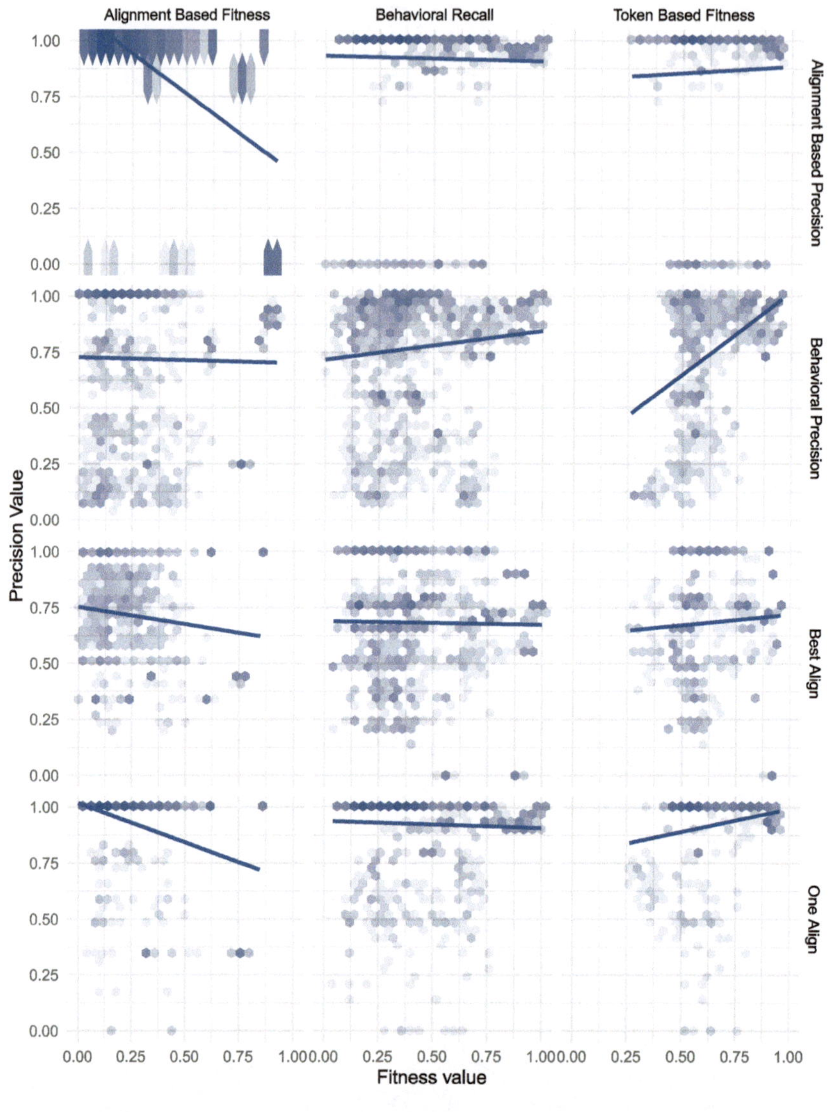

(a) Alpha Miner.

Fig. A.2 Detail of Fig. 4.14 showing each pair of fitness and precision measure for each discovery algorithm.

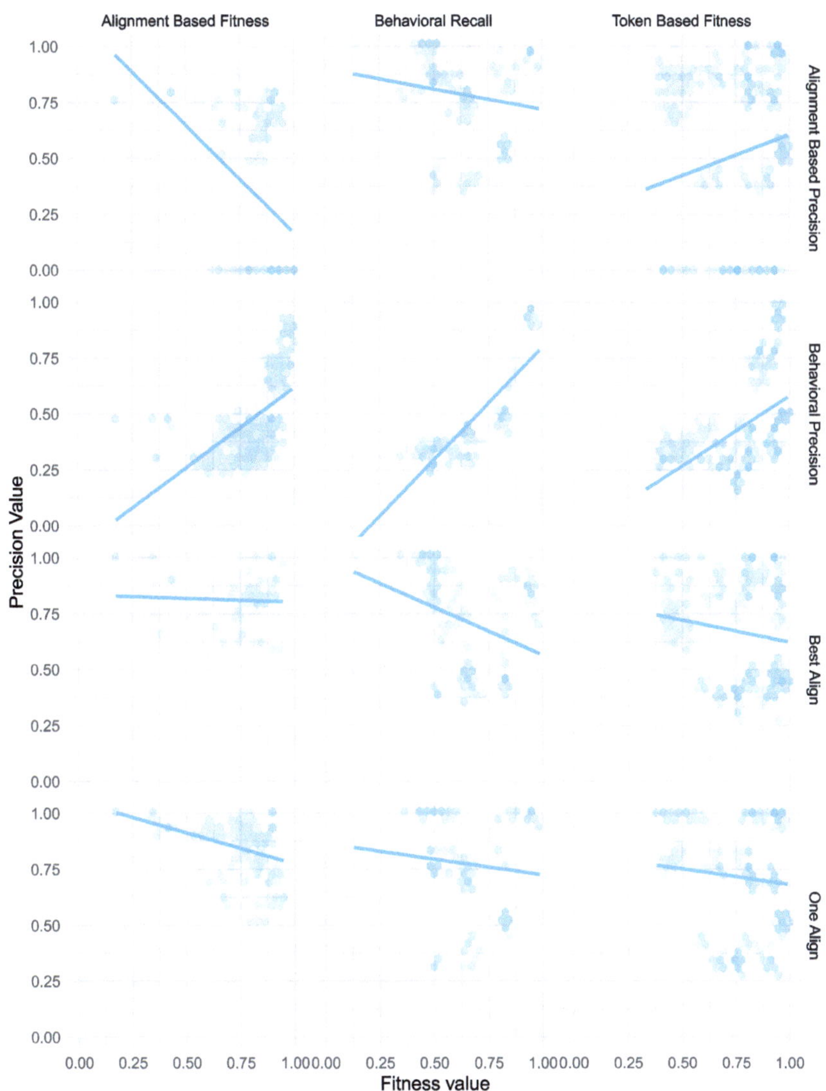

(b) Heuristics Miner.

Fig. A.2 (continued)

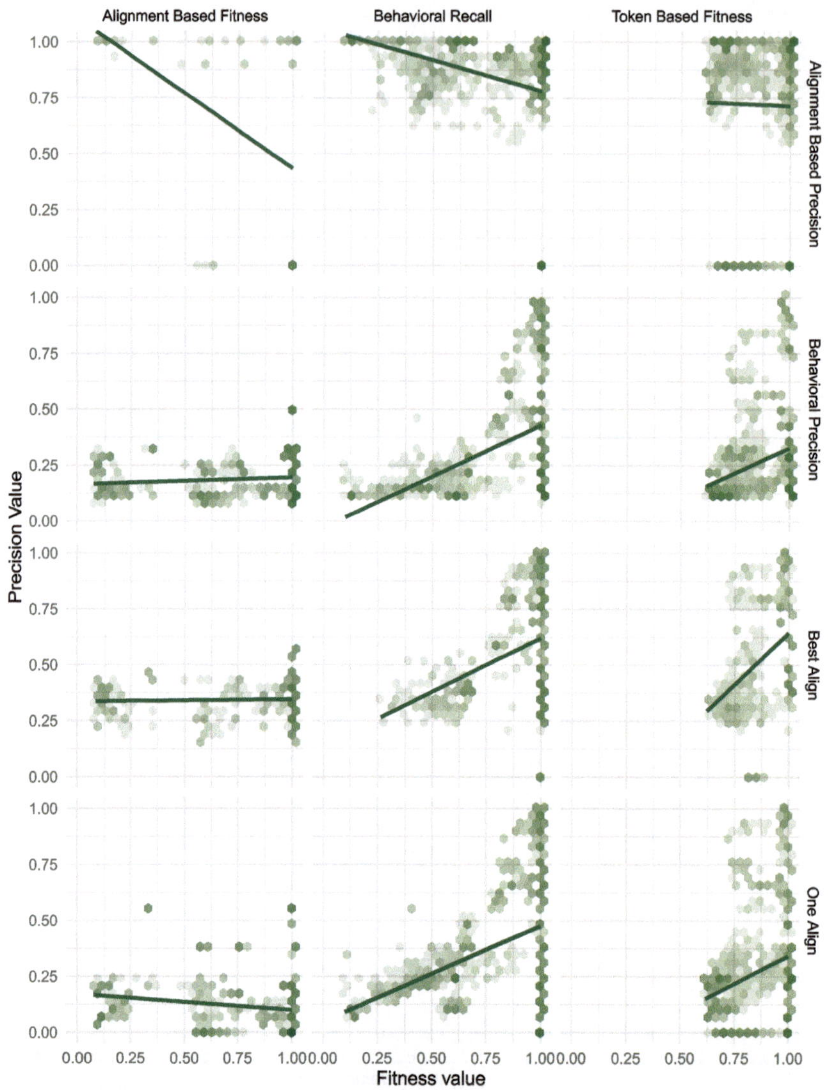

(c) ILP Miner.

Fig. A.2 (continued)

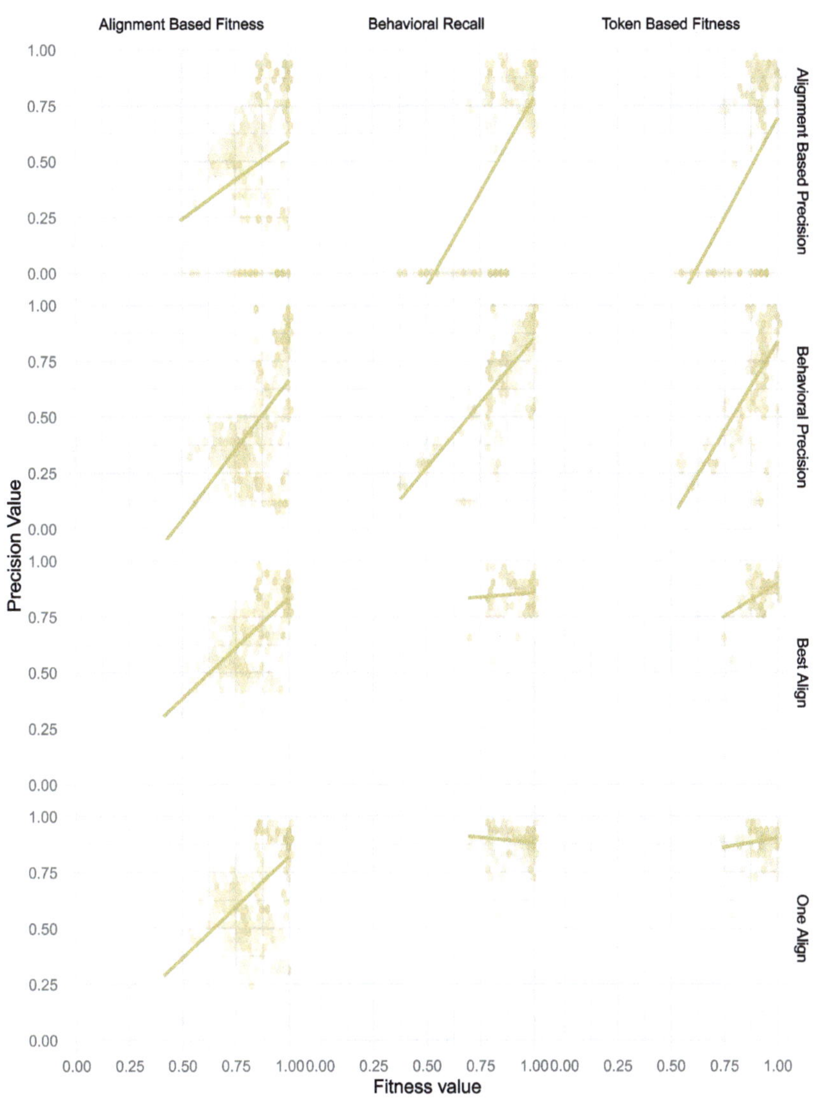

(d) Inductive Miner.

Fig. A.2 (continued)

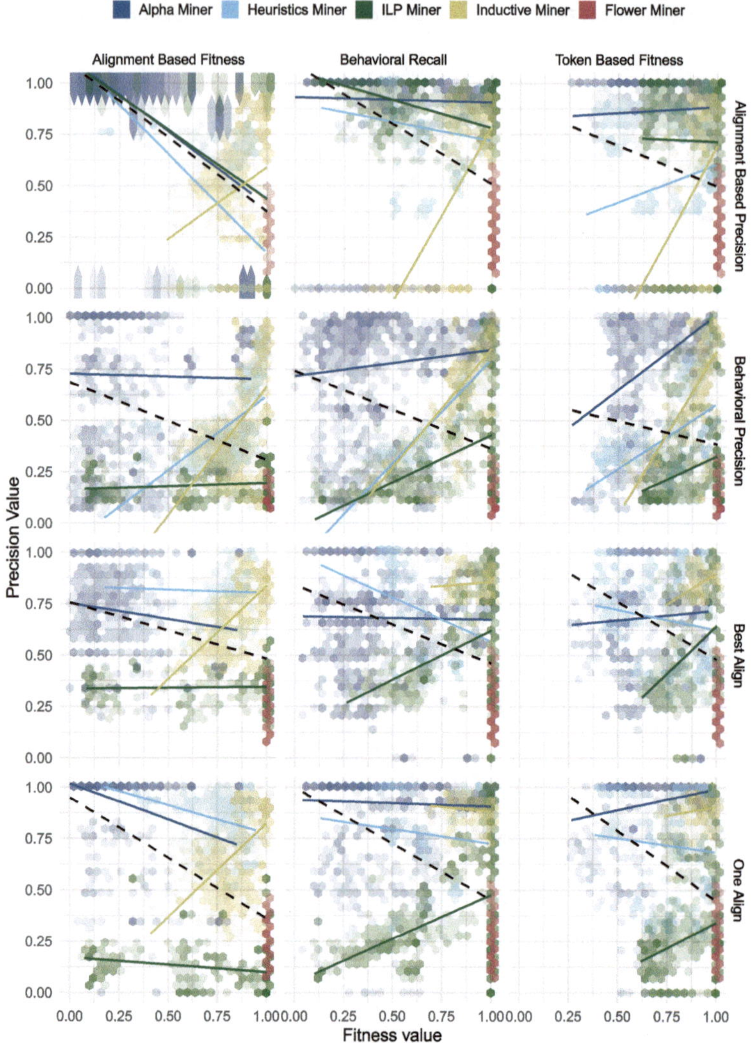
Alpha Miner
Heuristics Miner
ILP Miner
Inductive Miner
Flower Miner
Alignment Based Fitness
Behavioral Recall
Token Based Fitness
Alignment Based Precision
Behavioral Precision
Best Align
One Align
Precision Value
Fitness value
0.00
0.25
0.50
0.75
1.00

(e) All Miners.

Appendix B
Function Index bupaR packages

B.1 bupaR

Table B.1 Function index bupaR-package. Version 0.4.1 released on 2018-07-01.

Function	Description
activities()	Create table of activities with frequency information
activities_to_eventlog()	Create eventlog from list of activity instances with one ore more timestamp columns
activity_id()	Get activity classifier from eventlog
activity_instance_id()	Get activity instance classifier from eventlog
activity_labels()	Get vector of activity labels
act_collapse()	Collapse activity labels of a sub-process into a single activity
act_recode()	Recode activity labels
act_unite()	Unite activity labels
add_start_activity()	Add artificial start activities to eventlog
add_end_activity()	Add artificial end activities to eventlog
cases()	Create table of cases with descriptives
case_id()	Get case classifier from eventlog
case_labels()	Get vector of case labels
case_list()	Create table of cases
durations()	Create table with durations of cases
eventlog()	Create eventlog by mapping identifiers
ieventlog()	Create eventlog by mapping identifiers using interface
filter_attributes()	Generic filter function for eventlog
first_n()	Select first n activity instances of eventlog (first according to timestamp)

(continued)

G. Janssenswillen: Unearthing the Real Process Behind the Event Data, LNBIP 412
https://doi.org/10.1007/978-3-030-70733-0

Table B.1 (continued)

Function	Description
`group_by_activity()`	Group event log on activity identifier
`group_by_activity_instance()`	Group event log on activity instance identifier
`group_by_case()`	Group event log on case identifier
`group_by_resource()`	Group event log on resource identifier
`group_by_resource_activity()`	Group event log on resource and activity identifier
`last_n()`	Select last n activity instances (last according to timestamp)
`lifecycle_id()`	Get life cycle classifier from `eventlog`
`mapping()`	Get mapping of identifiers from `eventlog`
`n_activities()`	Count number of distinct activities in `eventlog`
`n_activity_instances()`	Count number of activity instances in `eventlog`
`n_cases()`	Count number of cases in `eventlog`
`n_events()`	Count number of events in `eventlog`
`n_resources()`	Count number of resources in `eventlog`
`n_traces()`	Count number of distinct traces in `eventlog`
`resources()`	Create table of resources with frequency information
`resource_id()`	Get resource classifier from `eventlog`
`resource_labels()`	Get vector of resource labels
`re_map()`	Apply `eventlog_mapping` to `eventlog` or data.frame to modify or create `eventlog`
`set_case_id()`	Set case identifier of `eventlog`
`set_activity_id()`	Set activity identifier of `eventlog`
`set_activity_instance_id()`	Set activity instance identifier of `eventlog`
`set_timestamp()`	Set timestamp identifier of `eventlog`
`set_resource_id()`	Set resource identifier of `eventlog`
`set_lifecycle_id()`	Set life-cycle identifier of `eventlog`
`simple_eventlog()`	Create `eventlog` by only setting case, activity and timestamp identifiers
`isimple_eventlog()`	Create `eventlog` by only setting case, activity and timestamp identifiers using interface
`slice_activities()`	Take a slice of activity instances (according to position)
`slice_events()`	Take a slice of events (according to position)
`timestamp()`	Get timestamp classifier from `eventlog`
`traces()`	Get table of traces with frequency information
`trace_list()`	Get table of traces
`ungroup_eventlog()`	Remove grouping from `eventlog`

B.2 edeaR

Table B.2 Function index edeaR-package. Version 0.8.1 released on 2018-07-02.

Function	Description
activity_frequency()	Metric: Activity Frequency
activity_presence()	Metric: Activity Presence
end_activities()	Metric: End activities
filter_activity()	Filter: Activity
ifilter_activity()	Filter: Activity (with interface)
filter_activity_frequency()	Filter: Activity frequency
ifilter_activity_frequency()	Filter: Activity frequency (with interface)
filter_activity_presence()	Filter: Activity presence
ifilter_activity_presence()	Filter: Activity presence (with interface)
filter_case()	Filter: Case
ifilter_case()	Filter: Case (with interface)
filter_endpoints()	Filter: Start and end activities
ifilter_endpoints()	Filter: Start and end activities (with interface)
filter_precedence()	Filter: Precedence relations
ifilter_precedence()	Filter: Precedence relations (with interface)
filter_processing_time()	Filter: Processing Time
ifilter_processing_time()	Filter: Processing Time (with interface)
filter_resource()	Filter: Resource
ifilter_resource()	Filter: Resource (with interface)
filter_resource_frequency()	Filter: Activity frequency
ifilter_resource_frequency()	Filter: Activity frequency (with interface)
filter_throughput_time()	Filter: Throughput Time
ifilter_throughput_time()	Filter: Throughput Time (with interface)
filter_time_period()	Filter: Time Period
ifilter_time_period()	Filter: Time Period (with interface)
filter_trace_frequency()	Filter: Trace frequency
ifilter_trace_frequency()	Filter: Trace frequency (with interface)
filter_trace_length()	Filter: Trace length percentile

(continued)

Table B.2 (continued)

Function	Description
ifilter_trace_length()	Filter: Trace length percentile (with interface)
filter_trim()	Filter: Trim cases
ifilter_trim()	Filter: Trim cases (with interface)
idle_time()	Metric: Idle Time
number_of_repetitions()	Metric: Number of repetitions
number_of_selfloops()	Metric: Number of self-loops in trace
number_of_traces()	Metric: Number of traces
processing_time()	Metric: Processing time
redo_repetitions_referral_matrix()	Referral matrix repetitions
redo_selfloops_referral_matrix()	Referral matrix self-loops
resource_frequency()	Metric: Resource frequency
resource_involvement()	Metric: Resource Involvement
resource_specialisation()	Metric: Resource Specialisation
resource_specialization()	Metric: Resource Specialisation
size_of_repetitions()	Metric: Size of repetitions
size_of_selfloops()	Metric: Size of self-loops
start_activities()	Metric: Start activities
throughput_time()	Metric: Throughput time of cases
trace_coverage()	Metric: Trace coverage
trace_length()	Metric: Trace length

B.3 evendataR

Table B.3 Function index eventdataR-package. Version 0.2.0 released on 2018-03-20.

Function	Description
patients	Patients eventlog
hospital	Hospital log
hospital_billing	Hospital billing log
sepsis	Sepsis cases - event log
traffic_fines	Road traffic fine management process log

B.4 xesreadR

Table B.4 Function index xesreadR-package. Version 0.2.2 released on 2017-12-04.

Function	Description
case_attributes_from_xes()	Read case attributes from XES file
eventlog_from_xes()	Create eventlog object from XES file
read_xes()	Create eventlog object from XES file
read_xes_cases()	Case attributes from Xes-file
write_xes()	Write XES file

B.5 processmapR

Table B.5 Function index processmapR-package. Version 0.3.2 released on 2018-07-03.

Function	Description
custom()	Custom map profile
dotted_chart()	Dotted chart
idotted_chart()	Interactive dotted chart
iplotly_dotted_chart()	Interactive plotly dotted chart
plotly_dotted_chart()	Plotly dotted chart
frequency()	Frequency map profile
performance()	Performance map profile
precedence_matrix()	Precendence Matrix
process_map()	Process map
resource_map()	Resource map
resource_matrix()	Resource matrix
trace_explorer()	Trace explorer

B.6 processmonitR

Table B.6 Function index processmonitR-package. Version 0.1.0 released on 2017-06-18.

Function	Description
activity_dashboard()	Activity dashboard
performance_dashboard()	Performance dashboard
resource_dashboard()	Resource dashboard
rework_dashboard()	Rework dashboard

B.7 petrinetR

Table B.7 Function index petrinetR-package. Version 0.2.0 released on 2018-07-03.

Function	Description
create_PN()	Create Petri Net
enabled()	Get enabled transitions
enabled_transition()	Check if transition is enabled
execute()	Execute transition
flows()	Get flows
is_place()	Check if element is place
is_transition()	Check if element is transition
marking()	Get marking
parse()	Parse trace
parsel()	Parse trace (logical)
part_of()	Check if node is part of Petri Net
places()	Get places
post_set()	Get post set of node
pre_set()	Get pre set of node
read_PN()	Read PNML
render_PN()	Render Petri Net
transitions()	Get transitions
tree_to_PN()	Convert tree to Petri Net
n_places()?	Get number of places
n_transitions()?	Get number of transitions
n_flows()	Get number of flows
n_nodes()?	Get number of nodes
nodes()?	Get nodes
rename_transitions()	Rename transitions
rename_places()	Rename places
add_places()?	Add places
add_transitions()	Add transitions
add_flows()	Add flows
visNetwork_from_PN()	VisNetwork from PN

B.8 ptR

Table B.8 Function index ptR-package. Version 0.1.0 released on 2016-04-24 (github).

Function	Description
choice_node	Calculate path dictionary of choice node
loop_node	Calculate path dictionary of loop node
number_of_paths	Calculate number of paths in process tree
or_node	Calculate path dictionary of or node
parallel_node	Calculate path dictionary of parallel node
path_dictionary	Calculate path dictionary of process tree
process_tree	Read process tree from Newick file
sequence_node	Calculate path dictionary of sequence node

B.9 discoveR

Table B.9 Function index discoveR-package. Version 0.0.1 released on 2018-07-12 (github).

Function	Description
alpha_miner	Discover Petri Net from eventlog using alpha miner

Appendix C
Scripts Chapter 8

Code Extract C.1 Code for Fig. 8.1.

```
# Prerequisites

'students': eventlog where each student (student_id) is a case and each course (course_id) an activity. other attributes are: semester, the semester that a course was taken; and result: TRUE if course was successfully finished, FALSE if student failed.

'major': a data.frame with information on the courses of the major: course_id: the courses belong to the major; scheduled_semester: the semester the course should be taken.

# Code

#compute the number of courses scheduled in each semester
courses_per_semester <- major %>% count(scheduled_semester)

students %>%
    # select only courses of the major
    inner_join(major, by = "course_id") %>%
    # consider only successful instances
    filter(result == TRUE) %>%
    # compute number of successful courses for each planned semester
    group_by(student_id, scheduled_semester) %>%
    mutate(n_passed = n()) %>%
    # add information on number of courses to pass
    inner_join(courses_per_semester, by = "scheduled_semester") %>%
    # compute whether semester was finished
    mutate(finished_semester = n_passed == n) %>%
    # create label for finished semester
    mutate(label = paste0("Finished Semester ", scheduled_semester)) %>%
    # Set activity id to newly created label, and save to output8.1
    set_activity_id(label) -> output8.1

output8.1 %>%
    # Draw process map
    process_map(type = frequency(value = "relative_case"))
```


G. Janssenswillen: Unearthing the Real Process Behind the Event Data, LNBIP 412
https://doi.org/10.1007/978-3-030-70733-0

Code Extract C.2 Code for Fig. 8.2.

```
# Prerequisites
output8.1: eventlog created in previous code extract

# Code
output8.1 %>%
    # set activity to finished_semester
    set_activity_id(finished_semester) %>%
    # draw trace explorer with all traces
    trace_explorer(coverage = 1)
```

Code Extract C.3 Code for Fig. 8.3.

```
# Prerequisites

'students': eventlog where each student (student_id) is a case and each course (course_id) an activity. other attributes are: semester, the semester that a course was taken; and result: TRUE if course was successfully finished, FALSE if student failed.

'major': a data.frame with information on the courses of the major: course_id: the courses belong to the major; scheduled_semester: the semester the course should be taken.

# Code

students %>%
    # select only courses of the major
    inner_join(major, by = "course_id") %>%
    # consider only successful instances
    filter(result == TRUE) %>%
    # consider only students that completed the major
    filter_trace_length(interval = c(10, 10)) %>%
    # compute number of completions per semester per course. Include scheduled semester for later use.
    count(semester, scheduled_semester, course_id) %>%
    # compute average completion semester per course
    group_by(course_id) %>%
    mutate(avg_completion = sum(semester*n)/sum(n)) %>%
    # draw ridge plot
    ggplot() +
    geom_density_rides(aes(x = semester, y = course_id, height = n), stat = "identity") +
    # draw vertical lines between years
    geom_vline(xintercept = seq(2.5, 12.5, by = 2), linetype = "dotted") +
    # add red lines to indicate scheduled semester
    geom_segment(aes(x = scheduled_semester - 0.5, xend = schededule_semester + 0.5, y = course_id, yend = course_id), size = 2, color = "red") +
    # add points to indicate average completion
    geom_point(aes(x = avg_completion, y = course_id), size = 3) +
    # create horizontal facts
    facet_grid(scheduled_semester ~ ., scales = "free", space = "free")
```

Code Extract C.4 Code for Fig. 8.4.

```
# Prerequisites

'students': eventlog where each student (student_id) is a case and each course (course_id) an activity. other attributes are: semester, the semester that a course was taken; and result: TRUE if course was successfully finished, FALSE if student failed.

'major': a data.frame with information on the courses of the major: course_id: the courses belong to the major; scheduled_semester: the semester the course should be taken.

# Code

Remove course Major 6.2

major <- filter(major, course_id != "[Major 6.2]")

#compute the number of courses scheduled in each semester
courses_per_semester <- major %>% count(scheduled_semester)

students %>%
    # select only courses of the major
    inner_join(major, by = "course_id") %>%
    # consider only successful instances
    filter(result == TRUE) %>%
    # compute number of successful courses for each planned semester
    group_by(student_id, scheduled_semester) %>%
    mutate(n_passed = n()) %>%
    # add information on number of courses to pass
    inner_join(courses_per_semester, by = "scheduled_semester") %>%
    # compute whether semester was finished
    mutate(finished_semester = n_passed == n) %>%
    # create label for finished semester
    mutate(label = paste0("Finished Semester ", scheduled_semester)) %>%
    # Set activity id to newly created label, and save to output8.1
    set_activity_id(label) -> output8.4

output8.4 %>%
    # Draw process map
    process_map(type = frequency(value = "relative_case"))
```

Code Extract C.5 Code for Fig. 8.5.

```
# Prerequisites
output8.4: eventlog created in previous code extract

# Code
output8.4 %>%
    # set activity to finished_semester
    set_activity_id(finished_semester) %>%
    # draw trace explorer with all traces
    trace_explorer(coverage = 1)
```

Code Extract C.6 Code for Table 8.2.

```
# Prerequisites
'students': eventlog where each student (student_id) is a case and each course (course_id) an activity. other attributes are: semester, the semester that a course was taken; and result: TRUE if course was successfully finished, FALSE if student failed; n_credits: the number of credits of a course; score: the score on a course.

'major': a data.frame with information on the courses of the major: course_id: the courses belong to the major; scheduled_semester: the semester the course should be taken.

# compute fit
students %>%
    # select only courses of the major
    inner_join(major, by = "course_id") %>%
    # consider only successful instances
    filter(result == TRUE) %>%
    # compute correlation for each student through nesting
    select(student_id, semester, scheduled_semester) %>%
    group_by(student_id) %>%
    nest(.key = data) %>%
    mutate(fit = map_dbl(data, cor)) -> fit

# compute score major
students %>%
    # select only courses of the major
    inner_join(major, by = "course_id") %>%
    # compute score for each student
    group_by(student_id) %>%
    summarize(score_major = sum(n_credits*score)/sum(n_credits)) -> score_major

# compute global score
students %>%
    # select courses not in major
    anti_join(major, by = "course_id") %>%
    # compute score for each student
    group_by(student_id) %>%
    summarize(score_global = sum(n_credits*score)/sum(n_credits)) -> score_global

# combine results
fit %>%
    inner_join(score_major, by = "student_id") %>%
    inner_join(score_global, by = "student_id") -> regression_data

# regression
lm(score_major ~ fit + score_global, data = regression_data)
```

Code Extract C.7 Code for Fig. 8.7.

```

# Prerequisites
'students': eventlog where each student (student_id) is a case and each course (course_id) an activity. other attributes are: semester, the semester that a course was taken; and result: TRUE if course was successfully finished, FALSE if student failed.
```

```
# Code


# function to check bag
# input: .bag a vector of course ids
# .new_id a string in the form of "course_id result"

check_bag <- function(.bag, .new_id) {
    #split course id from schore
    split <- str_split(.new_id, " ")[[1]]

    # if bag is empty and course is failed, the new bag is this course
    case_when(length(.bag) == 0 && split[2] == "FAIL" ~ split[1],
            # if bag contains course and course is passed, remove course from bag
            str_detect(.bag, split[1]) && split[2] == "PASS" ~ str_replace(str_remove(.bag, split[1]), "  ", " "),
            # if bag does not contain course and couse is failed, add course to bag
            !str_detect(.bag, split[1]) && split[2] == "FAIL" ~ str_c(.bag, split[1], sep = " "),
            # in all other cases, return original bag
            T ~ .bag) %>%
    return()
}

students %>%
    # combine course with result
    mutate(course_id_result = str_c(course_id, result, sep = " ")) %>%
    # group by student and sort data
    group_by(student_id) %>%
    arrange(sem, course_id) %>%
    # add bag info by accumulating the check_bag function over course_id_result
    mutate(bag = accumulate(course_id_result, check_bag)) %>%
    # select bag and semest
    arrange(student_id, sem) %>%
    # convert bag from vector to collapsed string
    mutate(bag = map(bag, ~str_trim(str_c(.x, collapse = " ")))) %>%
    # if bag is empty, indicate with ""
    mutate(bag = map_chr(bag, ~ifelse(length(.x) == 0, "", .x))) %>%
    # for each semester, select the final bag
    group_by(student_id, sem) %>%
    last_n(1) -> bags


# create log where each bag is a case
  eventlog %>%
    group_by(student_id) %>%
    arrange(semester) %>%
    # when bag is empty, a new one starts
    mutate(start_new = bag == "") %>%
    mutate(bag_id = paste(student_id, cumsum(start_new), "_") %>%
    set_case_id(bag_id) %>%
```

```
    set_activity(bag) -> bags_log


# figure 8.7a
bags_log %>%
    # compute number of bags (cases) per student
    group_by(student_id) %>%
    n_cases() %>%
    # draw bar plot
    ggplot(aes(n_cases)) +
    geom_bar()

# figure 8.7b
bags_log %>%
    # remove empty bags
    filter(bag != "") %>%
    # compute weight
    mutate(weight = length(str_split(bag, " ")) %>%
    # draw bar plot
    ggplot(aes(weight)) +
    geom_bar()

# figure 8.7c
bags_log %>%
    # remove empty bags
    filter(bag != "") %>%
     # compute weight
    mutate(weight = length(str_split(bag, " ")) %>%
    # compute average weight per bag
    group_by(bag_id) %>%
    summarize(avg_weight = mean(weight)) %>%
    # draw plot
    ggplot(aes("", avg_weight)) +
    geom_boxplot()

# figure 8.7d
bags_log %>%
    filter(bag != "") %>%
    # compute length of bags (trace length)
    trace_length(level = "case") %>%
    # draw bar plot
    ggplot(aes(trace_length)) +
    geom_bar()
```

Code Extract C.8 Code for Fig. 8.8.

```
# Prerequisites
'students': eventlog where each student (student_id) is a case and each course (course_id) an activity. other attributes are: semester, the semester that a course was taken; and result: TRUE if course was successfully finished, FALSE if student failed; n_credits: the number of credits of a course; score: the score on a course; type: type of course, mandatory/elective.

# Code
```

```
students %>%
    filter(type == "elective") %>%
    group_by(student_id, semester) %>%
    # compute number of elective credits
    summarize(n_elective_credits = sum(n_credits) %>%
    # draw boxplot
    ggplot(aes(semester, n_elective_credits) +
    geom_boxplot() +
    # add horizontal line
    geom_hline(yintercept = 10) +
    # add marker for average
    stat_summary(fun.y = mean, geom = "point", color = "red")
```

Code Extract C.9 Code for Fig. 8.9.

```
# Prerequisites
'students': eventlog where each student (student_id) is a case and each course (course_id) an activity. other attributes are: semester, the semester that a course was taken; and result: TRUE if course was successfully finished, FALSE if student failed; n_credits: the number of credits of a course; score: the score on a course; type: type of course, mandatory/elective.

# Code

# compute difficulty of courses
students %>%
  # compute number of tries per student
  group_by(course_id, student_id) %>%
  summarize(n = n()) %>%
  # compute average number of tries per course
  summarize(avg_n_tries = mean(n)) -> course_avg_tries


students %>%
  # compute avg score
  group_by(course_id) %>%
  summarize(avg_score = -mean(score, na.rm = T)) -> course_avg_score

course_avg_tries %>%
    full_join(course_avg_score) %>%
    # normalize
    mutate(avg_n_tries = (avg_n_tries - mean(avg_n_tries))/sd(avg_n_tries)) %>%
    mutate(avg_score = (avg_score - mean(avg_score))/sd(avg_score)) %>%
    mutate(difficulty = (avg_n_tries + avg_score)/2) -> course_difficulty


# compute difficulty of students semesters
students %>%
    inner_join(course_difficulty) %>%
    group_by(student_id, semester, type) %>%
    summarize(difficulty = mean(difficulty)) -> difficulty_semesters

# compute failrate and nr of credits
students %>%
```

```
    mutate(result = ifelse(result == TRUE, "PASS", "FAIL")) %>%
    # compute failrate
    group_by(student_id, semester, type, result) %>%
    summarize(n_credits = course_credits) %>%
    spread(result, credits, fill = 0) %>%
    mutate(total_credits = FAIL + PASS) %>%
    mutate(fail_rate = FAIL/total_credits) %>%
    select(-FAIL, -PASS) %>%
    # combine with difficulty
    inner_join(difficulty_semesters) -> correlation_data

correlation_data %>%
    # transform to long format
    gather(metric, value, fail_rate, total_credits, difficulty) %>%
    # create variable label of semester, type (elective/mandatory) and metric
    unite(variable, semester, type, metric) %>%
    # spread values
    spread(variable, value, fill = 0) %>%
    select(-student_id)
    # compute correlations
    cor() -> correlations

# draw plot

# tidy data
correlations %>%
    as.data.frame() %>%
    mutate(var_a = rownames(.)) %>%
    gather(var_b, cor_value, -var_a) %>%
    separate(var_a, c("semester_a","type_a","metric_a"), remove = F) %>%
    separate(var_b, c("semester_b","type_b","metric_b"), remove = F) %>%
    # select only correlations within semester or between successive semesters
    filter(semester_a == semester_b | semester_a == semester_b + 1) %>%
    # add variable for facets
    mutate(period = ifelse(semester_a == semester_b, "Current Semester", "Previous Semester")) %>%
    # prepare var_a for y-axis
    # remove semester indicator
    mutate(var_a = str_remove(var_a, "[0-9]*_")) %>%
    # remove elective credits from y-axis, unless from previous semster
    filter(!(str_detect(var_a, "elective") & period == "Current semester") %>%
    # clean labels for y-axis
    mutate(var_a = str_replace(var_a, "_"," ") %>% str_to_title() %>% str_replace("mandatory ","Normal") %>% str_replace("fail_rate","Credits % Failed")) %>%
    # change labels var_b for x-axis
    mutate(var_b = paste0("Number of elective credits in semester ", semester_b)) %>%
    # draw plot
    ggplot(aes(var_b, var_a)) +
    geom_tile(aes(fill = cor_value)) +
    geom_text(aes(label = round(cor_value, 2)), fontface = "bold", size = 5) %>%
    facet_grid(period~., scales = "free_y")
```

Appendix D
Scripts Chapter 9

Code Extract D.1 Code for Table 9.6.

```
# Prerequisites
'train_events': eventlog with cases defined by train_id and date, and signals (actual_signal_id) as activities

'planned_trajectories': table with train_id, date, and a list of all signals (planned_signal_id) planned. Planned trajectory id is a unique id for each planned trajectory.

# Code

# for rerouting severity

train_events %>%
    full_join(planned_trajectories, by = c("train_id","date")) %>%
    # add move description for insertions and deletions
    mutate(move = case_when(is.na(planned_signal_id) ~ "insertion",
                            is.na(actual_signal_id) ~ "deletion",
                            planned_signal_id == actual_signal_id ~ "synchr",
                            T ~ NA)) %>%
    filter(!is.na(move)) %>%
    group_by(train_id, date) %>%
    summarize(length_planned = sum(!is.na(planned_route)),
            length_actual = sum(!is.na(actual_route)),
            n_insertions = sum(move == "insertions"),
            n_deletions = sum(move == "deletion")) %>%
    mutate(train_severity = (n_insertions + n_deletions)/(length_planned + length_actual)) %>%
    summary()

# for rerouting diversity

train_events %>%
    full_join(planned_trajectories, by = c("train_id","date")) -> train_events


for (i in planned_trajectories$planned_trajectory_id) {

```


G. Janssenswillen: Unearthing the Real Process Behind the Event Data, LNBIP 412
https://doi.org/10.1007/978-3-030-70733-0

```
    train_events %>%
        filter(planned_trajectories == i) -> this_trajectory

    planned_trajectoies %>%
        filter(planned_trajectory_id == i) %>%
        nrows() -> length_planned_trajectory

    this_trajectory %>%
        process_map(render = F) -> map


    n_trains <- n_cases(this_trajectory)

    map %>%
        get_edge_df %>%
        nrows() -> e

    map %>%
        get_node_df -> nodes

    nrow(nodes) -> n

    nodes %>%
        filter(label = n_trains) %>%
        nrows() -> n_cut_vertices

    h_diversity = (e - n + 2)/length_planned_trajectory
    v_diversity = 1 - n_cut_vertices/length_planned_trajectory

    planned_trajectories$h_diversity[planned_trajectory_id == i] <- h_diversity
    planned_trajectories$v_diversity[planned_trajectory_id == i] <- v_diversity

}

planned_trajectories %>%
    summary
```

Code Extract D.2 Code for Fig. 9.9.

```
# Prerequisites
'severity': A data.frame with for each connection the rerouting severity, based on the previous
    ↪ code extract.

# Code

posthoc.kruskal.nemenyi.test(x = severity$value, y = severity$connection) -> test

test$p.value %>%
    # transform to long data.frame
    as.data.frame() %>%
    mutate(connection_a = row.names(.)) %>%
    gather(connection_b, pvalue,-connection_a) %>%
    # create label for significance
    mutate(sign = case_when(pvalue < 0.001 ~ 0.001,
```

```
                              pvalue < 0.01 < 0.01,
                              pvalue < 0.05 < 0.05,
                              T ~ "Not␣significant")) %>%
  # draw plot
  ggplot(aes(connection_a, connection_b)) +
  geom_tile(aes(fill = sign)) +
  scale_fill_discrete(values = c("Red","Orange","Green","Dark␣Green"))
```

References

1. IEEE Standard for eXtensible Event Stream (XES) for Achieving Interoperability in Event Logs and Event Streams. IEEE Std 1849–2016, pp. 1–50 (2016). https://doi.org/10.1109/IEEESTD.2016.7740858
2. van der Aalst, W.M.P.: The application of petri nets to workflow management. J. Circ. Syst. Comput. **8**(1), 21–66 (1998)
3. van der Aalst, W.M.P.: Process Mining: Discovery, Conformance and Enhancement of Business Processes. Springer, Heidelberg (2011). https://doi.org/10.1007/978-3-642-19345-3
4. van der Aalst, W.M.P.: Mediating between modeled and observed behavior: the quest for the "Right" process. In: IEEE Computing Society, pp. 31–43 (2013)
5. van der Aalst, W.M.P.: Relating process models and event logs: 21 conformance propositions. In: Algorithm and Theories for the Analysis of Event Data, pp. 56–74 (2018)
6. van der Aalst, W.M.P., Adriansyah, A., van Dongen, B.: Replaying history on process models for conformance checking and performance analysis. Wiley Interdisc. Rev. Data Min. Knowl. Discovery **2**(2), 182–192 (2012)
7. van der Aalst, W., et al.: Process Mining Manifesto. In: Daniel, F., Barkaoui, K., Dustdar, S. (eds.) BPM 2011. LNBIP, vol. 99, pp. 169–194. Springer, Heidelberg (2012). https://doi.org/10.1007/978-3-642-28108-2_19
8. van der Aalst, W.M.P., Bolt, A., van Zelst, S.J.: RapidProM: mine your processes and not just your data. arXiv:1703.03740 [cs] (2017)
9. van der Aalst, W.M.P., et al.: Business process mining: an industrial application. Inf. Syst. **32**(5), 713–732 (2007)
10. van der Aalst, W.M.P., Weijters, T., Maruster, L.: Workflow mining: discovering process models from event logs. IEEE Trans. Knowl. Data Eng. **16**(9), 1128–1142 (2004)
11. Adriansyah, A., Munoz-Gama, J., Carmona, J., van Dongen, B.F., van der Aalst, W.M.P.: Alignment Based Precision Checking. In: La Rosa, M., Soffer, P. (eds.) BPM 2012. LNBIP, vol. 132, pp. 137–149. Springer, Heidelberg (2013). https://doi.org/10.1007/978-3-642-36285-9_15
12. Adriansyah, A., Munoz-Gama, J., Carmona, J., van Dongen, B.F., van der Aalst, W.M.P.: Measuring precision of modeled behavior. Inf. Syst. e-Bus. Manage. 1–31 (2014). https://doi.org/10.1007/s10257-014-0234-7
13. Agrawal, R., Gunopulos, D., Leymann, F.: Mining process models from workflow logs. In: Schek, H.-J., Alonso, G., Saltor, F., Ramos, I. (eds.) EDBT 1998. LNCS, vol. 1377, pp. 467–483. Springer, Heidelberg (1998). https://doi.org/10.1007/BFb0101003
14. Augusto, A., Conforti, R., Dumas, M., La Rosa, M.: Split miner: discovering accurate and simple business process models from event logs. In: 2017 IEEE International Conference on Data Mining (ICDM), pp. 1–10. IEEE (2017)

G. Janssenswillen: Unearthing the Real Process Behind the Event Data, LNBIP 412
https://doi.org/10.1007/978-3-030-70733-0

15. Augusto, A., et al.: Automated discovery of process models from event logs: review and benchmark. IEEE Trans. Knowl. Data Eng. **31**(4), 686–705 (2018)
16. Bache, S.M., Wickham, H.: magrittr: A Forward-Pipe Operator for R (2014). https://CRAN.R-project.org/package=magrittr. R Package version 1.5
17. Baier, C., Katoen, J.P., et al.: Principles of Model Checking, vol. 26202649. MIT Press, Cambridge (2008)
18. Blizard, W.D.: The development of multiset theory. Mod. Logic **1**(4), 319–352 (1991)
19. Bolt, A., de Leoni, M., van der Aalst, W.M.P.: Scientific workflows for process mining: building blocks, scenarios, and implementation. Int. J. Softw. Tools Technol. Transf. **18**(6), 607–628 (2015). https://doi.org/10.1007/s10009-015-0399-5
20. Bose, R.J.C., van der Aalst, W.M.P.: Abstractions in process mining: a taxonomy of patterns. In: Business Process Management, pp. 159–175 (2009)
21. vanden Broucke, S.K.L.M.: Advances in process mining. Ph.D. thesis, Katholieke Universiteit Leuven, Leuven (2014)
22. vanden Broucke, S.K.L.M., De Weerdt, J., Vanthienen Jan, B., Baesens, B.: Determining process model precision and generalization with weighted artificial negative events. IEEE Trans. Knowl. Data Eng. **26**(8), 1877–1889 (2014)
23. vanden Broucke, S.K.L.M., De Weerdt, J., Vanthienen, J., Baesens, B.: A comprehensive benchmarking framework (CoBeFra) for conformance analysis between procedural process models and event logs in ProM. In: 2013 IEEE Symposium on Computational Intelligence and Data Mining (CIDM), pp. 254–261. IEEE (2013)
24. vanden Broucke, S.K.L.M., Delvaux, C., Freitas, J., Rogova, T., Vanthienen, J., Baesens, B.: Uncovering the Relationship Between Event Log Characteristics and Process Discovery Techniques. In: Lohmann, N., Song, M., Wohed, P. (eds.) BPM 2013. LNBIP, vol. 171, pp. 41–53. Springer, Cham (2014). https://doi.org/10.1007/978-3-319-06257-0_4
25. Bru, F., Claes, J.: The perceived quality of process discovery tools. arXiv preprint arXiv:1808.06475 (2018)
26. Buijs, J.C.A.M.: Flexible evolutionary algorithms for mining structured process models. Ph.D. thesis, Technische Universiteit Eindhoven, Eindhoven (2014)
27. Buijs, J.C.A.M., van Dongen, B.F., van der Aalst, W.M.P.: On the role of fitness, precision, generalization and simplicity in process discovery. In: Meersman, R., Panetto, H., Dillon, T., Rinderle-Ma, S., Dadam, P., Zhou, X., Pearson, S., Ferscha, A., Bergamaschi, S., Cruz, I.F. (eds.) OTM 2012. LNCS, vol. 7565, pp. 305–322. Springer, Heidelberg (2012). https://doi.org/10.1007/978-3-642-33606-5_19
28. Burattin, A., Sperduti, A.: PLG: a framework for the generation of business process models and their execution logs. In: zur Muehlen, M., Su, J. (eds.) BPM 2010. LNBIP, vol. 66, pp. 214–219. Springer, Heidelberg (2011). https://doi.org/10.1007/978-3-642-20511-8_20
29. Calvanese, D., Kalayci, T.E., Montali, M., Tinella, S.: Ontology-based data access for extracting event logs from legacy data: the onprom tool and methodology. In: International Conference on Business Information Systems, pp. 220–236 (2017)
30. Carey, M., Kwieciński, A.: Stochastic approximation to the effects of headways on knock-on delays of trains. Transp. Res. Part B Methodol. **28**(4), 251–267 (1994)
31. Chang, W., Cheng, J., Allaire, J., Xie, Y., McPherson, J.: shiny: Web Application Framework for R (2018). https://CRAN.R-project.org/package=shiny. R Package version 1.1.0
32. Chatti, M.A., Dyckhoff, A.L., Schroeder, U., Thüs, H.: A reference model for learning analytics. Int. J. Technol. Enhanced Learn. **4**(5–6), 318–331 (2012)
33. Cleveland, W.S.: LOWESS: a program for smoothing scatterplots by robust locally weighted regression. Am. Stat. **35**(1), 54 (1981)
34. Conte, C., Schöbel, A.: Identifying dependencies among delays. Ph.D. thesis, Niedersächsische Staats-und Universitätsbibliothek Göttingen, Germany (2008)
35. Cook, J.E., Wolf, A.L.: Automating process discovery through event-data analysis. In: 17th International Conference on Software Engineering, 1995. ICSE 1995, p. 73. IEEE (1995)
36. Cule, B., Goethals, B., Tassenoy, S., Verboven, S.: Mining train delays. In: Gama, J., Bradley, E., Hollmén, J. (eds.) IDA 2011. LNCS, vol. 7014, pp. 113–124. Springer, Heidelberg (2011). https://doi.org/10.1007/978-3-642-24800-9_13

37. Cureton, E.E., Mulaik, S.A.: The weighted varimax rotation and the promax rotation. Psychometrika **40**(2), 183–195 (1975)
38. Daamen, W., Goverde, R.M., Hansen, I.A.: Non-discriminatory automatic registration of knock-on train delays. Netw. Spat. Econ. **9**(1), 47–61 (2008)
39. D'Ariano, A.: Improving real-time train dispatching: models, algorithms and applications. Ph.D. thesis, Netherlands TRAIL Research School (2008)
40. Datta, A.: Automating the discovery of as-is business process models: probabilistic and algorithmic approaches. Inf. Syst. Res. **9**(3), 275–301 (1998)
41. Davenport, T.H.: Process Innovation: Reengineering Work Through Information Technology. Harvard Business Press (1993)
42. De Weerdt, J., De Backer, M., Vanthienen, J., Baesens, B.: A critical evaluation study of model-log metrics in process discovery. In: zur Muehlen, M., Su, J. (eds.) BPM 2010. LNBIP, vol. 66, pp. 158–169. Springer, Heidelberg (2011). https://doi.org/10.1007/978-3-642-20511-8_14
43. De Weerdt, J., De Backer, M., Vanthienen, J., Baesens, B.: A multi-dimensional quality assessment of state-of-the-art process discovery algorithms using real-life event logs. Inf. Syst. **37**(7), 654–676 (2012)
44. Statistical comparisons of classifiers over multiple data sets: Demšar. J. J. Mach. Learn. Res. **7**, 1–30 (2006)
45. Depaire, B.: Process model realism: measuring implicit realism. In: Fournier, F., Mendling, J. (eds.) BPM 2014. LNBIP, vol. 202, pp. 342–352. Springer, Cham (2015). https://doi.org/10.1007/978-3-319-15895-2_29
46. Desel, J., Reisig, W.: The concepts of Petri nets. Softw. Syst. Model. **14**(2), 669–683 (2014). https://doi.org/10.1007/s10270-014-0423-3
47. Devi, A.T.: An informative and comparative study of process mining tools. Int. J. Sci. Eng. Res. **8**(5), 8–10 (2006)
48. Dewilde, T.: Improving the robustness of a railway system in large and complex station areas. Ph.D. thesis, KULeuven (2014)
49. van Dongen, B., Carmona, J., Chatain, T., Taymouri, F.: Aligning modeled and observed behavior: a compromise between computation complexity and quality. In: Dubois, E., Pohl, K. (eds.) CAiSE 2017. LNCS, vol. 10253, pp. 94–109. Springer, Cham (2017). https://doi.org/10.1007/978-3-319-59536-8_7
50. van Dongen, B.F., Carmona, J., Chatain, T.: A unified approach for measuring precision and generalization based on anti-alignments. In: La Rosa, M., Loos, P., Pastor, O. (eds.) BPM 2016. LNCS, vol. 9850, pp. 39–56. Springer, Cham (2016). https://doi.org/10.1007/978-3-319-45348-4_3
51. Dumas, M., La Rosa, M., Mendling, J., Reijers, H.A.: Fundamentals of Business Process Management. Springer, Heidelberg (2013). https://doi.org/10.1007/978-3-662-56509-4
52. van Eck, M.L., Lu, X., Leemans, S.J.J., van der Aalst, W.M.P.: PM^2: a process mining project methodology. In: International Conference on Advanced Information Systems Engineering, pp. 297–313 (2015)
53. Ellenberg, J.: How Not to Be Wrong: The Power of Mathematical Thinking. Penguin (2015)
54. Erickson, B., Nosanchuk, T.: Understanding Ata. McGraw-Hill Education, Berkshire (1992)
55. Ferguson, R.: Learning analytics: drivers, developments and challenges. Int. J. Technol. Enhanced Learn. **4**(5/6), 304–317 (2012)
56. Flier, H., Gelashvili, R., Graffagnino, T., Nunkesser, M.: Mining railway delay dependencies in large-scale real-world delay data. In: Ahuja, R.K., Möhring, R.H., Zaroliagis, C.D. (eds.) Robust and Online Large-Scale Optimization. LNCS, vol. 5868, pp. 354–368. Springer, Heidelberg (2009). https://doi.org/10.1007/978-3-642-05465-5_15
57. Garcia-Banuelos, L., Dumas, M., La Rosa, M., De Weerdt, J., Ekanayake, C.C.: Controlled automated discovery of collections of business process models. Inf. Syst. **46**, 85–101 (2014)
58. Gelan, A., et al.: Affordances and limitations of learning analytics for computer-assisted language learning: a case study of the VITAL project. Comput. Assist. Lang. Learn. **31**(3), 294–319 (2018)

59. Gelman, A.: Exploratory data analysis for complex models. J. Comput. Graph. Stat. **13**(4), 755–779 (2004)
60. Goedertier, S., Martens, D., Vanthienen, J., Baesens, B.: Robust process discovery with artificial negative events. J. Mach. Learn. Res. **10**, 1305–1340 (2009)
61. Goldratt, E.M.: Theory of Constraints. North River Croton-on-Hudson (1990)
62. Goverde, R.M., Meng, L.: Advanced monitoring and management information of railway operations. J. Rail Transp. Plan. Manage. **1**(2), 69–79 (2011)
63. Greco, G., Guzzo, A., Ponieri, L., Sacca, D.: Discovering expressive process models by clustering log traces. IEEE Trans. Knowl. Data Eng. **18**(8), 1010–1027 (2006)
64. Günther, C.W.: Process mining in flexible environments. Ph.D. thesis, Technische Universiteit Eindhoven (2009)
65. Hair, J.F.: Black, Babin, Anderson: Multivariate Data Analysis. Pearson Education Limited, Harlow (2009)
66. Hammer, M., Champy, J.: Reengineering the Corporation: Manifesto for Business Revolution, A. Zondervan (2009)
67. Hand, D.J., Mannila, H., Smyth, P.: Principles of Data Mining (Adaptive Computation and Machine Learning). MIT Press, Cambridge (2001)
68. Higgins, A., Kozan, E.: Modeling train delays in urban networks. Transp. Sci. **32**(4), 346–357 (1998)
69. Hovdhaugen, E.: Do structured study programmes lead to lower rates of dropout and student transfer from university? Irish Educ. Stud. **30**(2), 237–251 (2011)
70. Iversen, G.R., Wildt, A.R., Norpoth, H., Norpoth, H.P.: Analysis of Variance. Sage (1987)
71. Jans, M., Soffer, P.: From relational database to event log: decisions with quality impact. In: Teniente, E., Weidlich, M. (eds.) BPM 2017. LNBIP, vol. 308, pp. 588–599. Springer, Cham (2018). https://doi.org/10.1007/978-3-319-74030-0_46
72. Jans, M.J., Soffer, P., Jouck, T.: Building a valuable event log for process mining: an experimental exploration of a guided process. Enterp. Inf. Syst. **1–30**, (2019). https://doi.org/10.1080/17517575.2019.1587788
73. Janssenswillen, G.: petrinetR: Building, Visualizing, Exporting and Replaying Petri Nets (2016). https://bupar.net. R Package version 0.1.0
74. Janssenswillen, G.: processmonitR: Building Process Monitoring Dashboards (2017). https://bupar.net. R Package version 0.1.0
75. Janssenswillen, G.: bupaR: Business Process Analytics in R (2018). https://bupar.net. R Package version 0.4.0
76. Janssenswillen, G.: eventdataR: Event Data Repository (2018). https://bupar.net. R Package version 0.2.0
77. Janssenswillen, G.: processcheckR: Rule-Based Conformance Checking of Business Process Event Data (2018). https://bupar.net. R Package version 0.1.0
78. Janssenswillen, G.: processmapR: Construct Process Maps Using Event Data (2018). https://bupar.net. R Package version 0.3.2
79. Janssenswillen, G., Depaire, B.: bupaR: Business Process Analysis in R. In: Business Process Managements, Demos (2017)
80. Janssenswillen, G., Depaire, B.: xesreadR: Read and Write XES Files (2017). R Package version 0.2.2
81. Janssenswillen, G., Depaire, B.: Towards confirmatory process discovery: making assertions about the underlying system. Bus. Inf. Syst. Eng. **61**(6), 1–16 (2018)
82. Janssenswillen, G., Depaire, B., Jouck, T.: Calculating the number of unique paths in a block-structured process model. In: Proceedings of the International Workshop on Algorithms & Theories for the Analysis of Event Data, vol. 2016, pp. 138–152 (2016)
83. Janssenswillen, G., Depaire, B., Swennen, M., Jans, M.J., Vanhoof, K.: bupaR: enabling reproducible business process analysis. Knowl. Based Syst. **163**, 927–930 (2019)
84. Janssenswillen, G., Depaire, B., Verboven, S.: Detecting train reroutings with process mining. EURO J. Transp. Logistics **7**(1), 1–24 (2017). https://doi.org/10.1007/s13676-017-0105-8

85. Janssenswillen, G., Donders, N., Jouck, T., Depaire, B.: A comparative study of existing quality measures for process discovery. Inf. Syst. **71**, 1–15 (2017)
86. Janssenswillen, G., Jouck, T., Creemers, M., Depaire, B.: Measuring the quality of models with respect to the underlying system: an empirical study. In: La Rosa, M., Loos, P., Pastor, O. (eds.) BPM 2016. LNCS, vol. 9850, pp. 73–89. Springer, Cham (2016). https://doi.org/10.1007/978-3-319-45348-4_5
87. Janssenswillen, G., Swennen, M.: edeaR: Exploratory and Descriptive Event-Based Data Analysis (2018). https://bupar.net. R Package version 0.8.0
88. Johannesson, P., Perjons, E.: An Introduction to Design Science. Springer, Cham (2014). https://doi.org/10.1007/978-3-319-10632-8
89. Johnson, D.B.: Finding all the elementary circuits of a directed graph. SIAM J. Comput. **4**(1), 77–84 (1975)
90. Jouck, T., Depaire, B.: Generating artificial data for empirical analysis of process discovery algorithms, Tech. rep. Hasselt University (2016)
91. Jouck, T., Depaire, B.: Generating artificial data for empirical analysis of control-flow discovery algorithms: a process tree and log generator. Bus. Inf. Syst. Eng. **61**, 1–18 (2018)
92. Kecman, P., Goverde, R.M.: Online data-driven adaptive prediction of train event times. IEEE Trans. Intell. Transp. Syst. **16**(1), 465–474 (2015)
93. Kecman, P., Goverde, R.M.P.: Predictive modelling of running and dwell times in railway traffic. Public Transp. **7**(3), 295–319 (2015). https://doi.org/10.1007/s12469-015-0106-7
94. Kerremans, M.: Market guide for process mining. Tech. rep, Gartner (2018)
95. Kruskal, W.H., Wallis, W.A.: Use of ranks in one-criterion variance analysis. J. Am. Stat. Assoc. **47**(260), 583–621 (1952)
96. Kunze, M., Luebbe, A., Weidlich, M., Weske, M.: Towards understanding process modeling – the case of the BPM academic initiative. In: Dijkman, R., Hofstetter, J., Koehler, J. (eds.) BPMN 2011. LNBIP, vol. 95, pp. 44–58. Springer, Heidelberg (2011). https://doi.org/10.1007/978-3-642-25160-3_4
97. Leemans, S.J.J., Fahland, D., van der Aalst, W.M.P.: Discovering block-structured process models from event logs - a constructive approach. In: Colom, J.-M., Desel, J. (eds.) PETRI NETS 2013. LNCS, vol. 7927, pp. 311–329. Springer, Heidelberg (2013). https://doi.org/10.1007/978-3-642-38697-8_17
98. Leemans, S.J.J., Fahland, D., van der Aalst, W.M.P.: Discovering block-structured process models from incomplete event logs. In: Ciardo, G., Kindler, E. (eds.) PETRI NETS 2014. LNCS, vol. 8489, pp. 91–110. Springer, Cham (2014). https://doi.org/10.1007/978-3-319-07734-5_6
99. de Leoni, M., Maggi, F.M., van der Aalst, W.M.P.: An alignment-based framework to check the conformance of declarative process models and to preprocess event-log data. Inf. Syst. **47**, 258–277 (2015)
100. Maldonado, J.J., Palta, R., Vázquez, J., Bermeo, J.L., Pérez-Sanagustín, M., Muñoz-Gama, J.: Exploring differences in how learners navigate in MOOCs based on self-regulated learning and learning styles: a process mining approach. In: Computing Conference (CLEI), 2016 XLII Latin American, pp. 1–12 (2016)
101. Mannhardt, F.: Sepsis Cases - Event Log (2016)
102. Mannhardt, F.: processanimateR: Process Map Animation (2018). R Package version 0.1.1
103. Maruster, L.: A machine learning approach to understand business processes. Ph.D. thesis, Technische Universiteit Eindhoven (2003)
104. McCabe, T.J.: A complexity measure. IEEE Trans. Software Eng. **2**(4), 308–320 (1976)
105. de Medeiros, A.K.A.: Genetic process mining. Ph.D. thesis, Technische Universiteit Eindhoven, Eindhoven (2006)
106. Mendling, J.: Detection and prediction of errors in EPC business process models. Ph.D. thesis, Wirtschaftsuniversität Wien Vienna (2007)
107. Mendling, J., Neumann, G., van der Aalst, W.: Understanding the occurrence of errors in process models based on metrics. In: Meersman, R., Tari, Z. (eds.) OTM 2007. LNCS, vol. 4803, pp. 113–130. Springer, Heidelberg (2007). https://doi.org/10.1007/978-3-540-76848-7_9

108. Mukala, P., Buijs, J.C., Leemans, M., van der Aalst, W.M.P.: Learning analytics on coursera event data: a process mining approach. In: Proceedings of the 5th International Symposium on Data-driven Process Discovery and Analysis, pp. 18–32 (2015)
109. Muñoz-Gama, J.: Conformance Checking and Diagnosis in Process Mining: Comparing Observed and Modeled Processes. LNBIP, vol. 270. Springer, Cham (2017). https://doi.org/10.1007/978-3-319-49451-7
110. Muñoz-Gama, J., Carmona, J.: A fresh look at precision in process conformance. In: Hull, R., Mendling, J., Tai, S. (eds.) BPM 2010. LNCS, vol. 6336, pp. 211–226. Springer, Heidelberg (2010). https://doi.org/10.1007/978-3-642-15618-2_16
111. Nemenyi, P.B.: Distribution-free multiple comparisons. Doctoral Dissertation, vol. 25, no. 2, p. 1233, Princeton University. Dissertation Abstracts International (1963)
112. Pesic, M., Schonenberg, H., van der Aalst, W.M.P.: Declare: full support for loosely-structured processes. In: 1th IEEE International Enterprise Distributed Object Computing Conference (EDOC 2007), p. 287 (2007)
113. Preacher, K.J., MacCallum, R.C.: Exploratory factor analysis in behavior genetics research: factor recovery with small sample sizes. Behav. Genet. **32**(2), 153–161 (2002)
114. Raichelson, L., Soffer, P., Verbeek, E.: Merging event logs: combining granularity levels for process flow analysis. Inf. Syst. **71**, 211–227 (2017)
115. Reißner, D., Conforti, R., Dumas, M., La Rosa, M., Armas-Cervantes, A.: Scalable conformance checking of business processes. In: Panetto, H., Debruyne, C., Gaaloul, W., Papazoglou, M., Paschke, A., Ardagna, C.A., Meersman, R. (eds.) OTM 2017. LNCS, vol. 10573, pp. 607–627. Springer, Cham (2017). https://doi.org/10.1007/978-3-319-69462-7_38
116. Rogge-Solti, A., Senderovich, A., Weidlich, M., Mendling, J., Gal, A.: In log and model we trust? A generalized conformance checking framework. In: La Rosa, M., Loos, P., Pastor, O. (eds.) BPM 2016. LNCS, vol. 9850, pp. 179–196. Springer, Cham (2016). https://doi.org/10.1007/978-3-319-45348-4_11
117. Rozinat, A., van der Aalst, W.M.P.: Conformance checking of processes based on monitoring real behavior. Inf. Syst. **33**(1), 64–95 (2008)
118. Rozinat, A., De Medeiros, A.K.A., Günther, C.W., Weijters, A.J.M.M., Van der Aalst, W.M.P.: Towards an evaluation framework for process mining algorithms. In: BPM Center Report BPM-07-06. BPM Center (2007)
119. Rummler, G.A.: The anatomy of performance. In: Handbook of Human Performance Technology: Principles, Practices, and Potential, pp. 986–1007 (2006)
120. Salazar-Fernandez, J.P., Sepúlveda, M., Muñoz-Gama, J.: Influence of student diversity on educational trajectories in engineering high-failure rate courses that lead to late dropout. In: IEEE EDUCON (2019)
121. Salazar-Fernandez, J.P., Sepúlveda, M., Muñoz-Gama, J., Janssenswillen, G.: Análisis de las trayectorias educacionales en cursus críticos, que llevan a egreso tardío en ingeriería civil en obras civiels, mediante minería de procesos. In: Congreso de la Sociedad Chilena de Educación en ingeniería (2018)
122. Sammouri, W.: Data mining of temporal sequences for the prediction of infrequent failure events: application on floating train data for predictive maintenance. Ph.D. thesis, Université Paris-Est (2014)
123. Senderovich, A., et al.: Conformance checking and performance improvement in scheduled processes: a queueing-network perspective. Inf. Syst. **62**, 185–206 (2016)
124. Singh, D., Ibrahim, A.M., Yohana, T., Singh, J.N.: Complementation in multiset theory. Int. Math. Forum **6**, 1877–1884 (2011)
125. Song, M., van der Aalst, W.M.P.: Supporting process mining by showing events at a glance. In: Proceedings of the 17th Annual Workshop on Information Technologies and Systems (WITS), pp. 139–145 (2007)
126. Song, M., van der Aalst, W.M.P.: Towards comprehensive support for organizational mining. Decis. Support Syst. **46**(1), 300–317 (2008)
127. Swennen, M., Janssenswillen, G., Jans, M.J., Depaire, B., Vanhoof, K.: Capturing process behavior with log-based process metrics. In: Proceedings of the 5th International Symposium on Data-driven Process Discovery and Analysis (SIMPDA), Vienna, pp. 141–144 (2015)

128. Swennen, M., et al.: Capturing resource behaviour from event logs. In: Proceedings of the 6th International Symposium on Data-driven Process Discovery and Analysis (SIMPDA), Graz (2016)
129. Tax, N., Lu, X., Sidorova, N., Fahland, D., van der Aalst, W.M.P.: The imprecisions of precision measures in process mining. Inf. Process. Lett. **135**, 1–8 (2018)
130. Törnquist, J.: Computer-based decision support for railway traffic scheduling and dispatching: a review of models and algorithms. In: 5th Workshop on Algorithmic Methods and Models for Optimization of Railways (ATMOS 2005). Schloss Dagstuhl-Leibniz-Zentrum für Informatik (2006)
131. Tukey, J.W.: Exploratory Data Analysis. Pearson (1977)
132. Tukey, J.W., Wilk, M.B.: Data analysis and statistics: an expository overview. In: Proceedings of the November 7–10, 1966, Fall Joint Computer Conference, pp. 695–709. ACM (1966)
133. Verbeek, H.M.W., Buijs, J.C.A.M., van Dongen, B.F., van der Aalst, W.M.P.: XES, XESame, and ProM 6. In: Soffer, P., Proper, E. (eds.) CAiSE Forum 2010. LNBIP, vol. 72, pp. 60–75. Springer, Heidelberg (2011). https://doi.org/10.1007/978-3-642-17722-4_5
134. Watson, A.H., McCabe, T.J., Wallace, D.R.: Structured Testing: A Testing Methodology Using the Cyclomatic Complexity Metric, vol. 500, no. 235, pp. 1–114. NIST Special Publication (1996)
135. Weber, P., Bordbar, B., Tino, P., Majeed, B.: A framework for comparing process mining algorithms. In: GCC Conference and Exhibition, pp. 625–628. IEEE (2011)
136. Weeda, V.A., Hofstra, K.S.: Performance analysis: improving the Dutch railway service. In: Eleventh International Conference on Computer System Design and Operation in the Railway and Other Transit Systems (COMPRAIL08) (2008)
137. Weidlich, M., Polyvyanyy, A., Desai, N., Mendling, J., Weske, M.: Process compliance analysis based on behavioural profiles. Inf. Syst. **36**(7), 1009–1025 (2011)
138. Weijters, A.J.M.M., van Der Aalst, W.M.P., De Medeiros, A.K.A.: Process mining with the heuristics miner-algorithm, Tech. rep. Technische Universiteit Eindhoven (2006)
139. van der Werf, J.M.E.M., van Dongen, B.F., Hurkens, C.A.J., Serebrenik, A.: Process discovery using integer linear programming. In: van Hee, K.M., Valk, R. (eds.) PETRI NETS 2008. LNCS, vol. 5062, pp. 368–387. Springer, Heidelberg (2008). https://doi.org/10.1007/978-3-540-68746-7_24
140. Wickham, H.: ggplot2: Elegant Graphics for Data Analysis. Springer, New York (2016). https://doi.org/10.1007/978-0-387-98141-3
141. Wickham, H.: tidyverse: Easily Install and Load the 'Tidyverse' (2017). https://CRAN.R-project.org/package=tidyverse. R Package version 1.2.1
142. Wickham, H.: stringr: Simple, Consistent Wrappers for Common String Operations (2018). R Package version 1.3.1
143. Wickham, H., François, R., Henry, L., Müller, K.: dplyr: A Grammar of Data Manipulation (2018). https://CRAN.R-project.org/package=dplyr. R Package version 0.7.5
144. Yang, H., van Dongen, B., ter Hofstede, A., Wynn, M., Wang, J.: Estimating completeness of event logs. BPM Center Report, 12-04-2012 (2012)
145. Yuan, J., Hansen, I.A.: Optimizing capacity utilization of stations by estimating knock-on train delays. Transp. Res. Part B Methodol. **41**(2), 202–217 (2007)